Patterns in Language and Linguistics

Topics in English Linguistics

Editors
Susan M. Fitzmaurice
Bernd Kortmann
Elizabeth Closs Traugott

Volume 104

Patterns in Language and Linguistics

New Perspectives on a Ubiquitous Concept

Edited by
Beatrix Busse
Ruth Möhlig-Falke

DE GRUYTER
MOUTON

ISBN 978-3-11-077686-7
e-ISBN (PDF) 978-3-11-059665-6
e-ISBN (EPUB) 978-3-11-059299-3

Bibliographic information published by the Deutsche Nationalbibliothek
The Deutsche Nationalbibliothek lists this publication in the Deutsche Nationalbibliografie;
detailed bibliographic data are available on the Internet at http://dnb.dnb.de.

© 2021 Walter de Gruyter GmbH, Berlin/Boston
This volume is text- and page-identical with the hardback published in 2019.
Printing and binding: CPI books GmbH, Leck

www.degruyter.com

Contents

List of tables and figures —— VII

List of contributors —— IX

Beatrix Busse and Ruth Möhlig-Falke
Patterns in linguistics: This volume, its aims and its contributions —— 1

Ruth Möhlig-Falke and Beatrix Busse
From term to concept and vice versa: Pattern(s) in language and linguistics —— 11

Michael Stubbs
How to do things with intertextual patterns: On Umberto Eco's *The Name of the Rose* —— 47

Ian Lancashire
Word-entry patterns in Early Modern English dictionaries —— 69

Tony McEnery and Vaclav Brezina
Collocations and colligations: Visualizing lexicogrammar —— 97

Elizabeth Closs Traugott
Constructional pattern-development in language change —— 125

Peter Petré
How constructions are born. The role of patterns in the constructionalization of *be going to* INF —— 157

Laura A. Michaelis
Constructions are patterns and so are fixed expressions —— 193

Barış Kabak
A dynamic equational approach to sound patterns in language change and second-language acquisition: The (un)stability of English dental fricatives illustrated —— 221

Martin Zettersten
Learning by predicting: How predictive processing informs language development —— 255

Index —— 289

List of tables and figures

Tables

Tab. 5.1: *knock* collocating with *of* in the BE06 corpus —— **109**
Tab. 5.2: Second-order collocates shared between *the* and *must* in the British English Brown family corpora —— **110**
Tab. 8.1: PSI types —— **204**
Tab. 9.1: Percent accuracy rates in target-like productions of English fricatives in different word positions —— **241**

Figures

Fig. 2.1: The "metonymic cycle" in the concept of *pattern* —— **26**
Fig. 5.1: Collocation network around 'I' in Trinity Lancaster Corpus —— **104**
Fig. 5.2: *knock* in the AmE06 corpus and the second-order collocates it shares with *and* —— **106**
Fig. 5.3: *knock* in the BE06 corpus and the second-order collocates it shares with *and* —— **107**
Fig. 5.4: *must* in the BE06 corpus and the second-order collocates it shares with *the* —— **111**
Fig. 5.5: *must* in the FLOB corpus and the second-order collocates it shares with *the* —— **112**
Fig. 5.6: *must* in the LOB corpus and the second-order collocates it shares with *the* —— **113**
Fig. 5.7: *must* in the BLOB corpus and the second-order collocates it shares with *the* —— **114**
Fig. 5.8: Immediate-right collocates of *help* as an infinitive in the BE06 corpus —— **116**
Fig. 5.9: Immediate-right collocates of *help* as an infinitive in the AmE06 corpus —— **116**
Fig. 5.10: Immediate-right collocates of VVI in the BE06 corpus —— **117**
Fig. 5.11: Immediate-right collocates of VVI in the AmE06 corpus —— **117**
Fig. 5.12: A colligation network based on VVI, showing shared R1 colligates with AT1 in British English —— **119**
Fig. 5.13: A colligation network based on VVI, showing shared R1 colligates with AT1 and IF in British English —— **120**
Fig. 7.1: Normalized frequency of 'BE *going to* INF' per million words —— **170**
Fig. 7.2: Topicalization assembly —— **172**
Fig. 7.3: Proportional frequency history of the topicalization assembly —— **175**
Fig. 7.4: Present-tense assertion assembly —— **176**
Fig. 7.5: Proportional frequency history of present-tense assertion assembly —— **179**
Fig. 7.6: Assembly with passive construction —— **180**
Fig. 7.7: Deprofiling of control and motion in assembly with passive construction —— **182**
Fig. 7.8: Combined deprofiling scores —— **184**
Fig. 8.1: The idiomaticity continuum —— **198**
Fig. 8.2: The listeme *cent* —— **209**
Fig. 8.3: Idiomatic listeme *red* —— **210**
Fig. 8.4: An ARC derivation —— **211**
Fig. 8.5: The Auxiliary-Initial construction —— **214**

Fig. 9.1: Rates for differential substitution of dental fricatives in the pilot production study —— 242
Fig. 10.1: Schematic representation of a simple recurrent network —— 273
Fig. 10.2: Illustration of the design of Saffran et al. (1996) —— 276

List of contributors

In alphabetic order

Vaclav Brezina
Department of Linguistics and English Language
County South, Lancaster University
Lancaster LA1 4YL
United Kingdom
v.brezina@lancaster.ac.uk

Beatrix Busse
English Department
Heidelberg University
Kettengasse 12
69117 Heidelberg
Germany
beatrix.busse@as.uni-heidelberg.de

Barış Kabak
English Linguistics
Würzburg University
Am Hubland
97074 Würzburg
Germany
baris.kabak@uni-wuerzburg.de

Ian Lancashire
Department of English
University of Toronto
St. George Campus
170 St. George Street
Toronto, Ontario, M5R 2M8
Canada
ian.lancashire@utoronto.ca

Tony McEnery
Department of Linguistics and English Language
County South, Lancaster University
Lancaster LA1 4YL
United Kingdom
a.mcenery@lancaster.ac.uk

Laura A. Michaelis
Department of Linguistics
295UCB, University of Colorado Boulder
CO 80309, USA
laura.michaelis@colorado.edu

Ruth Möhlig-Falke
English Department
Heidelberg University
Kettengasse 12
69117 Heidelberg
Germany
ruth.moehlig@as.uni-heidelberg.de

Peter Petré
Department of Linguistics
University of Antwerp
Prinsstraat 13
2000 Antwerpen
Belgium
peter.petre@uantwerpen.be

Michael Stubbs
Fachbereich II / Anglistik
Trier University
Universitätsring 15
54286 Trier
Germany
stubbs@uni-trier.de

Elizabeth Closs Traugott
Department of Linguistics
Stanford University
Margaret Jacks Hall, Building 460
Stanford CA 94305-2150
USA
traugott@stanford.edu

Martin Zettersten
Department of Psychology
University of Wisconsin-Madison
1202 West Johnson Street
Madison, WI 53706
USA
zettersten@wisc.edu

Beatrix Busse and Ruth Möhlig-Falke
Patterns in linguistics: This volume, its aims and its contributions

Pattern, both as a term and a concept in singular and plural use, is currently being hyped up, due to the prominence of artificial-intelligence discourse on algorithms and machine-learning, which are crucial for so-called pattern-detection, for instance, in big data and neural networks. In this volume, we want to critically reflect on the concept of *pattern* as it is used in different fields of *linguistics*, including corpus linguistics, sociolinguistics, historical/diachronic linguistics, construction grammar, discourse linguistics, psycholinguistics, language acquisition, phonology and second-language learning. Our aim is (i) to give an overview of the complex linguistic approaches to *pattern* as both a term and a concept; (ii) to outline and contest the analytical potential of *pattern*s for a variety of different linguistic data; and (iii) to stretch the limits of what may be considered "linguistic patterns", "communicative patterns" and "linguistically relevant patterns" by crossing the boundaries between contemporary linguistic approaches and other disciplines, such as literature studies, social studies, philosophy, and psychology.

Patterns, and the search for them, are fundamental for and ubiquitous in scientific research. At closer inspection of its respective conceptualizations, especially when comparing the natural sciences and the humanities, some interdisciplinary differences appear. On the one hand, in an existentialist approach to the "world", patterns may be taken to exist as ontological properties of natural phenomena that can be empirically detected by scientific means – an approach to patterns we have frequently discovered in the natural sciences; on the other hand, in a constructivist conceptualization – more often found in approaches from the humanities and social sciences – human beings and societies are considered the main agents in self-constructing the patterns by which the complexity of "the world" can be ordered and understood – i.e. patterns are considered to be epistemologically rather than ontologically "real" (see e.g. Dummett 1978; Kelso 1995; Searle 1995, 2014; Varela 1997; Latour 1999; Hacking 1999; Roepstorff 1999; Bartelborth 2007; Schmidt 2008; Keller 2008: 40–59; Gabriel 2014; Di Paolo et al. 2010).

Beatrix Busse, Heidelberg University, English Department, 69117 Heidelberg, Germany, beatrix.busse@as.uni-heidelberg.de
Ruth Möhlig-Falke, Heidelberg University, English Department, 69117 Heidelberg, Germany, ruth.moehlig@as.uni-heidelberg.de

https://doi.org/10.1515/9783110596656-001

In our view, both these conceptualizations work hand in hand. Our working definition of *pattern* is thus situated on a continuum between constructivism and existentialism and has an interdisciplinary scope. Patterns may be defined as
a) spatially and temporally determined complex configurations of features, of the same or of different modes, that are inherent in animate organisms as well as in inanimate objects, processes and situations;
b) having specific functions or effects in the "world";
c) being relational, i.e. they always relate to other entities;
d) being dynamic in space and time, i.e. they recur repeatedly and change in their formation, construction, and perception, and
e) being variable in their repeated recurrence, i.e. more concrete patterns may be variant tokens belonging to a more abstract type.

As properties of animate organisms, inanimate objects, processes and situations, patterns are consciously or subconsciously perceived (or learned) and can be scientifically investigated and measured. Measurability relates, for instance, to the frequency of recurrence of similar feature combinations (tokens) that are identified as belonging to a pattern (type). The role of token frequency for pattern recognition has been investigated from different angles, such as in the cognitive sciences, in cognitive and psycholinguistics (see e.g. Bybee and Hopper 2001; Tomasello 2003; Bybee 2007; Harley 2014: 181–183; see also Möhlig-Falke and Busse in this volume, section 4, and Petré and Zettersten in this volume). Once identified, patterns form our perception of our environment and influence us in our approach to the world as culturally mediated knowledge schemas (see e.g. Varela 1997; Tomasello 2000; Di Paolo et al. 2010). In short, *pattern* as a concept has both an ontological and an epistemological relevance and both sides of the same coin need to be considered.

This definition is based both on our investigation of the history of this term and concept (see Möhlig-Falke and Busse in this volume) as well as on our intensive analysis of studies on patterns in language and our own experience with analysing both historical and contemporary English language data (see e.g. Busse 2018, 2019, forthc.; Page, Busse and Nørgaard 2018; Möhlig-Falke 2012, 2017; Bech and Möhlig-Falke forthc.).

As in the sciences and academia in general, the concept of *pattern* at closer inspection shows a great range of variability in linguistics, too. The contributions to this volume take account of this variability by looking at patterns in language from a range of different linguistic perspectives, not only with respect to the levels of expression that are being focused on but also with regard to linguistic theory. Accordingly, they permeate between constructivism and empiricism in their various approaches to what constitutes *patterns* in language. They thus readily exemplify not only the range of applicability of the concept of *pattern* to language phenomena but also the "potential for controversy", or discussion, that is involved. Further, several of the contributions exemplify that the patterns that need to be recognized in linguistic analysis form "delicate networks" (Kabak, this volume) between language-internal and language-external factors, between language, "the world", and the mind – showing that patterns in language very often traverse the boundaries between the language system and the discourse context within which they are used.

Following this introductory chapter, **Ruth Möhlig-Falke** and **Beatrix Busse** (pp. 11–46) give a historical overview of the usage and development of the term and the concept of *pattern* in linguistic research, discussing different approaches and situating them in their respective linguistic traditions. This overview highlights that thinking about the language system and language usage as *patterned* has a longer history in linguistics than one might suspect, if one approaches it from the perspective of the concept of *pattern* rather than only from the perspective of terminological applications and their obvious similarities. It further shows that our different theories of language, its relation to "the world" and the mind, may have more in common than assumed. They constitute deeply ingrained patterns of thought which are sometimes worthy of being challenged in order to be able to stretch the limits of scientific research.

In his article, **Mike Stubbs** (pages 47–67) investigates patterns of intertextuality in Umberto Eco's *The Name of the Rose*. With this, his paper connects to the overall theme of this book in a dual way. On the one hand, Stubbs stresses that patterns, design and order constantly feature in the novel through character interaction, also in the way a false pattern leads to the truth. On the other hand, within a general kind of theoretical framework, Stubbs stresses that one prerequisite of intertextuality is the constant repetition of so-called semantic patterns across texts to which the reader can attribute a function. This type of pattern recognition and function-attribution has been discussed by literary critics but it has as yet not received much attention by linguists. Investigating the complex network of intertextual references on various levels in *The Name of the Rose* also by help of corpus linguistic methods, Stubbs finds that

> ... all language use is intertextual, since any text consists of a mosaic of lexicogrammatical patterns and typical collocations which have been frequently used by other speakers in the past. The central analytic method of studying a concordance has shown that routine phraseology in language use is much more extensive than previously realized, and that a text sounds idiomatic because of what has been said many times before. (Stubbs, this volume, page 60)

Investigating intertextuality from a linguistic perspective rather than a purely literary one and acknowledging that the understanding of the complex intertextual references expounded in a novel like *The Name of the Rose* may therefore renew the discussion about questions like where meaning is located, "... in the text or elsewhere?" (Stubbs, this volume, page 65), about the nature of semantic units, and the concept of reference.

The following two contributions both deal with words and the patterns they form, though from very different perspectives. As historical lexicographer, **Ian Lancashire** (pages 69–95) discusses how the idea of "the word" and "word meaning" exemplified in lexical and lexicographic works of the Tudor and Stuart periods differed from our modern conception:

> To some extent, nature, the world of things, has now lost some of the primacy it once enjoyed in dictionaries, but encyclopaedias emerged in the 18th century to describe things. What gave language a new sense of meaning was the individual mind that linked nouns and verbs to neural-networked ideas. A definition shift had given the mind the freedom to create systems of thought and define them in words rather than things. (Lancashire this volume, page 73).

In his article, Lancashire further shows how lexical patterns developed as lexicographic "meta-patterns" in the course of the Early to Late Modern English period. The lexical patterns that may be found by the historical lexicologist in early modern lexicographical works are demonstrated to have had a constitutive effect in establishing long-lasting ways of thinking about the object denoted by a word, i.e. patterns of usage forming patterns on the mind.

The contribution by **Tony McEnery** and **Vaclav Brezina** (pages 97–123) considers *word patterns* from the perspective of corpus linguistics by dealing with collocations and colligations, i.e. frequently recurring combinations of content words or content and function words. The authors critically reflect on the methodological caveats involved in the application of corpus linguistic tools for pattern recognition in lexicogrammar and describe a number of pragmatic trade-offs the corpus analyst usually has to decide on: "breadth against depth, choosing an available annotation scheme rather than one more closely aligning to their own theoretical position, focusing on frequent words and constructions rather than a broader range of features, accepting error in automated annotations or limiting investigations to expert verified datasets, etc." (McEnery and Brezina, this volume, page 101). The authors continue by exploring new ways of visualizing patterns of grammatical variation and change in large datasets by the help of collocation networks provided by #LancsBox program (Brezina, McEnery, and Wattam 2015). Collocation networks enable to see where words that do not necessarily collocate with one another have elements of lexicogrammar shared between them by virtue of having one or more joint collocates, thus assisting in the detection of larger patterns in the language data. The authors thus show that the methods by which patterns are identified in corpus linguistics need to be critically assessed and possibly improved, for, "[i]f we are to argue, on the one hand, that we are looking for multiply intersecting features in lexicogrammar while on the other hand we are limiting ourselves to looking for it by simply looking at pairwise associations through collocations, we clearly have an issue" (McEnery and Brezina, this volume, page 102).

Three contributions to this volume treat the question how the concept of *pattern* relates to that of *construction* and diachronic *constructionalization* (after Traugott and Trousdale 2013) in a construction grammar framework. In her article, **Elizabeth Traugott** (pages 125–155) discusses the various applications of the descriptive label *pattern* in different constructivist approaches and its divergent relationship to the theoretical notion of *construction*, the two being sometimes – but not always – used synonymously. By discussing several case studies of diachronic change in the history of English, she finds that

1) Not all patterns are constructions. This is because patterns are recurring sequences that have combinatoric potential, but are not necessarily conventionalized. While recurrent meaning is essential, it is relatively underspecified. By contrast, constructions are conventionalized form–meaning pairings.
2) However, all constructions are patterns, whether micro-constructions or schemas. This is because constructions originate in sedimented patterns.
3) Being tokens, constructs are not patterns, but clusters of replicated constructs may constitute transitional patterns that are among critical contexts for potential constructionalization. (Traugott, this volume, page 150)

Traugott thus demonstrates that a refined differentiation between *patterns* and *constructions* is particularly important when looking at processes of language change on different levels of generalization and abstraction.

In a similar vein, **Peter Petré** (pages 155–192) also focuses on the diachronic development of compositional patterns – which he calls *assemblies*, i.e. "recurrent configurations of existing constructions and their co-text/context, which do not (yet) have constructional status themselves" (Petré, this volume, page 159) – into new conventionalized constructions (see also Langacker 2009: 11). His main focus is on the role that frequency of assemblies plays in the neoanalysis of a new construction to help understand "the nature of gradualness and neoanalysis in language change" (Petré, this volume, page 161). He argues that *pattern* as a superordinate concept defined by the property of compositionality allows to see both assemblies and constructions as patterns, but of a different degree of abstractness, entrenchment and conventionalization, "hence the idea of 'patterns all the way down'" (Petré, this volume, page 162). He further demonstrates that a closer look at the assemblies leading to new constructions and their relative frequency allows to better understand processes of language change. As assemblies reaching a certain frequency threshold conventionalize, a new construction emerges.

Laura A. Michaelis's (pages 193–220) contribution is also constructivist but synchronic. Working in Sign-Based Construction Grammar (SBCG, e.g. Boas and Sag 2012), the central issue in her article is to work out in how far lexical and syntactic constructions (or *listemes* and *constructions*) are both patterns in the minds of speakers with combinatoric properties that may be productively applied. More precisely – taking the continuum of idiomaticity (Kay and Michaelis 2012) as starting point – she discusses the question whether it is indeed possible to call a word, a word class, or a fixed formula, which are considered to be *listemes* in SBCG, "patterns" on the basis of identifying their combinatoric properties. She concludes that they are indeed patterns, as

> [b]oth kinds of linguistic objects are modeled as feature structures that contain specifications for syntactic, semantic and contextual features: a listeme describes a feature structure that is a sign, while a construction describes a feature structure that contains a MTR [MOTHER] feature (whose value is a sign) and a DTRS [DAUGHTERS] feature (whose value is a list of signs). Words and constructs draw from one another: constructs realize word dependents, and words and word classes determine what signs cooccur in constructs. (Michaelis, this volume, page 217)

The last two articles in this collection share a language-developmental focus, though with different perspectives. **Barış Kabak's** contribution (pages 221–254) is concerned with patterns in phonology. He argues for a dynamic approach towards sound patterns, in which both phonetically and cognitively grounded developmental and processing principles are assumed to be the impetus behind variability in all facets and shapes of sound evolution. Accordingly, he sees sound patterns as epistemological entities which emerge from the entire sum of interacting variables (i.e. language-internal and language-external factors) that act upon ordinary sound structures (i.e. segments). Sound structures are discerned as sound patterns (i.e. dynamic images with a certain amount of frequency, probability, etc.) insofar as they modulate speech processing and trigger phonological change within and across life-spans. They should thus be viewed as unfixed ontological entities, which cannot be considered a priori as "stable" or "unstable". Focusing on the phonological category of dental fricatives in English, Kabak exemplifies in which ways this sound feature has formed dynamic patterns throughout the history of English, arguing that the development of the English dental fricatives was shaped by interconnected endogenous and exogenous forces. By drawing on evidence not only from historical linguistics but also from first- and second-language acquisition, he demonstrates how sound perception and production are influenced by similar principles both in language variation and change. Consequently, he argues that the distinction made between "natural" and "unnatural" causes of sound change (e.g. Blevins 2006) should be avoided.

Martin Zettersten's article (pages 255–288) considers patterns, pattern formation, and pattern perception, from the perspective of psycholinguistics. He demonstrates how the human faculty of learning in general, and learning of language in particular, is grounded in the mechanism of predictive processing. By reviewing research on infants' ability to track novel patterns and relating these statistical learning abilities to prediction-based explanations, he demonstrates how prediction-based models fit within current theoretical positions on language development and the mind, and discusses how predictive processes support language learning. The mechanism of prediction thus offers a unifying framework for understanding how infants succeed at language learning "by exploiting patterns in their language environment to develop expectations about upcoming auditory signals and the meanings they communicate" (Zettersten, this volume, page 279).

As could already be seen from the overview of the contributions to this volume, *pattern* as a term and a concept enjoys a certain prominence in contemporary linguistics, and especially in cognitive and usage-based, or corpus-linguistic approaches. For a long time, however, *pattern* was, if at all, used as a largely descriptive term and often lacked clear definition. The following article will provide an overview of the history of usage of the term as well as of the development of the concept of *pattern* in modern linguistics to work out similarities and differences in its various conceptualizations and linguistic applications.

References

Bartelborth, Thomas. 2007. *Erklären*. Berlin: Walter de Gruyter.
Bech, Kristin & Ruth Möhlig-Falke (eds.). forthc. *Grammar – discourse – context. Grammar and usage in language variation and change*. (Discourse Patterns). Berlin: de Gruyter Mouton.
Blevins, Juliette. 2006. New perspectives on English sound patterns: 'Natural' and 'unnatural' in evolutionary phonology. *Journal of English Linguistics* 34. 6–25.
Boas, Hans & Ivan A. Sag (eds.). *Sign-based construction grammar*. Stanford: CSLI Publications.
Busse, Beatrix. 2018. Current British English: A sociolinguistic perspective. In Vaclav Brezina, Robbie Love & Karin Aijmer (eds.), *Corpus approaches to contemporary British speech: Sociolinguistic studies of the Spoken BNC2014*, 16–26. London & New York: Routledge.

Busse, Beatrix. 2019. Patterns of discursive urban place-making in Brooklyn, New York. In Viola Wiegand & Michaela Mahlberg (eds.), *Corpus linguistics, context and culture*. Berlin: de Gruyter Mouton.

Busse, Beatrix. forthc. *Speech, writing and thought presentation in 19th-century narrative fiction*. (Oxford Studies in the History of English). Oxford: Oxford University Press.

Brezina, Vaclav, Tony McEnery & Stephen Wattam. 2015. Collocations in context: A new perspective on collocational networks. *International Journal of Corpus Linguistics* 20 (2). 139–173.

Bybee, Joan. 2007. *Frequency of use and the organization of language*. Oxford & New York: Oxford University Press.

Bybee, Joan & Paul Hopper. 2001. Introduction to frequency and the emergence of linguistic structure. In Joan Bybee & Paul Hopper (eds.), *Frequency and the emergence of linguistic structure*, 1–24. Amsterdam: John Benjamins.

Di Paolo, Ezekiel, Marieke Rohde & Hanne De Jaegher. 2010. Horizons for the enactive mind: Values, social interaction and play. In John Stewart, Olivier Gapenne & Ezequiel A. Di Paolo (eds.), *Enaction. Toward a new paradigm for cognitive science*, 33–87. Cambridge, MA: MIT Press.

Dummett, Michael. 1978. *Truth and other enigmas*. Cambridge, MA: Harvard University Press.

Gabriel, Markus. 2014. Existenz, realistisch gedacht. In Markus Gabriel (ed.), *Der Neue Realismus*. (Suhrkamp Taschenbuch Wissenschaft 2099), 171–199. Berlin: Suhrkamp.

Hacking, Ian. 1999. *The social construction of what?* Cambridge, MA: Harvard University Press.

Harley, Trevor A. 2014. *The psychology of language. From data to theory*. 4th edn. London & New York: Routledge.

Kay, Paul & Laura A. Michaelis. 2012. Constructional meaning and compositionality. In Claudia Maienborn, Klaus von Heusinger & Paul Portner (eds.), *Semantics: An international handbook of natural language meaning*. Vol. 3: 2271–2296. Berlin: de Gruyter.

Keller, Reiner. 2008. *Wissenssoziologische Diskursanalyse. Grundlagen eines Forschungsprogramms*. 2nd edn. Wiesbaden: VS Verlag für Sozialwissenschaften.

Kelso, J.A. Scott. 1995. *Dynamic patterns. The self-organization of brain and behavior*. Cambridge, MA: MIT Press.

Langacker, Ronald W. 2009. *Investigations in cognitive grammar*. Berlin: Walter de Gruyter.

Latour, Bruno. 1999. *Pandora's hope: Essays on the reality of science studies*. Cambridge, MA: Harvard University Press.

Möhlig-Falke, Ruth. 2012. *The Early English impersonal construction. An analysis of verbal and constructional meaning*. Oxford & New York: Oxford University Press.

Möhlig-Falke, Ruth. 2017. Contexts and conditions of grammatical change: The loss of the English impersonal construction in Middle English. In Tanja Rütten (ed.), *Anglistik* 28 (1): *The philologist's dilemma: Where context meets decontextualisation*, 87–110. Heidelberg: Winter.

Page, Ruth, Beatrix Busse & Nina Nørgaard (eds.). 2018. *Rethinking language text and context*. London: Routledge.

Roepstorff, Andreas. 1999. Deconstructing social constructionism: A review of *The social construction of what?* by Ian Hacking and of *Pandora's hope. Essays on the reality of science studies* by Bruno Latour. *FOLK: Journal of the Danish Ethnographic Society* 41. 139–154.

Schmidt, Jan C. 2008. *Instabilität in Natur und Wissenschaft. Eine Wissenschaftsphilosophie der nachmodernen Physik*. Berlin: Walter de Gruyter.

Searle, John. 1995. *The construction of social reality*. London: The Free Press.

Searle, John. 2014. Aussichten für einen neuen Realismus. In Markus Gabriel (ed.), *Der Neue Realismus*. (Suhrkamp Taschenbuch Wissenschaft 2099), 292–307. Berlin: Suhrkamp.
Tomasello, Michael. 2000. The item-based nature of children's early syntactic development. *Trends in Cognitive Sciences* 4 (4). 156–163.
Tomasello, Michael. 2003. *Constructing a language. A usage-based theory of language acquisition*. Cambridge, MA: Harvard University Press.
Traugott, Elizabeth Closs & Graeme Trousdale. 2013. *Constructionalization and constructional changes*. Oxford & New York: Oxford University Press.
Varela, Francisco J. 1997. Patterns of life: Intertwining identity and cognition. *Brain and Cognition* 34. 72–87.

Ruth Möhlig-Falke and Beatrix Busse
From term to concept and vice versa: Pattern(s) in language and linguistics

1 Introduction

The term *pattern* was not really used in the linguistics literature before Saussure, and even then, it remained a largely descriptive term until the later decades of the 20th century. Only with the advent of cognitive and usage-based, and corpus linguistics, the concept of pattern began to receive theoretical importance – however, often still lacking clear definition. Given the importance which patterns have for the formation of our capacities of learning and cognition and the way we see and approach the world, and given that language plays an important role in the way how we categorize and conceptualize experience (e.g. Tomasello 2000, 2003; Ellis and Frey 2009), we consider it a good idea to take a closer look at the concept of *pattern* in language and linguistics, how it has been used in the past, how it is used to-date, and potentially how it may be further explored in linguistics in the future. We aim to show why pattern has the potential for controversy with regard to its definition and application in different linguistic frameworks. One of these reasons may be found in the different theoretical groundings of linguistic approaches in constructivism and empiricism. Another may be said to lie in the semantics of the term itself, which is polysemous in meaning to begin with.

2 *Pattern* in historical perspective: On the diachronic development of a term and its applications

The lexeme *pattern* evokes an underlying concept with two different frames of reference (after Fillmore 1976, 1982; see also Ziem 2014). One is associated with

---

Ruth Möhlig-Falke, Heidelberg University, English Department, 69117 Heidelberg, Germany, ruth.moehlig@as.uni-heidelberg.de
Beatrix Busse, Heidelberg University, English Department, 69117 Heidelberg, Germany, beatrix.busse@as.uni-heidelberg.de

https://doi.org/10.1515/9783110596656-002

its first basic meaning, recorded in English since the 14th century, in which a *pattern* is understood as 'a model to be imitated' (OED s.v. *pattern* n. I).[1] The second frame of reference relates *pattern* to its second basic meaning, recorded in English since the late 16th century (OED s.v. *pattern* n. II), as 'a regular form or sequence of something (i.e. a sequence of decorative design, or of action or situation)'.[2] Both frames of reference include that some features are perceived as occurring more than once, i.e. repetitively. It may thus be concluded that the concept of *pattern* crucially involves 'a perceived repetition of some feature or features in combination'. However, in meaning I, the repetition occurs on different levels – i.e. an item 1 and an item 2 show a certain resemblance of features or feature combinations, with item 1 and 2 being in a hierarchical relationship in that item 1 is the more basic model from which item 2 is derived. In meaning II, the repetition of features or feature combinations occurs in or on the same level, i.e. there is no hierarchy involved but the features are combined in a row or sequence, as in a web or texture.

The existence of these two basic reference frames of *pattern* as a lexeme may lead to the fact that different understandings of the concept of *pattern* exist side by side in language as well as in linguistics and influence the choice of terminology. What is called a *pattern* in the different linguistic approaches – and what isn't called a *pattern* but nevertheless shows some conceptual relationship to it? Which different aspects of the concept of *pattern*, the hierarchical 'model' meaning or the non-hierarchical 'texture' meaning, give rise to its use in the different approaches to refer to language phenomena?

The differences in the understanding of *pattern* as a concept will be shown to be linked with the different foci evident in the study of language, i.e. whether the

---

1 The *Oxford English Dictionary* (OED) records the English word *pattern* (OED s.v. *pattern* n.) from 1324 onwards. The first record of *pattern* in Middle English cited by the OED has it with the meaning 'model, example, copy', referring to a workpiece shown by craftsmen as design model, from which similar pieces could then be made (OED s.v. *pattern* n. I.1a). From the early 15th century, *pattern* is recorded with the metaphorical meaning 'an example or model to be imitated; an example of particular excellence; a person who or thing which is worthy of copying; an exemplar; an archetype' (OED s.v. *pattern* n. I.2a). By metonymic extension from 1a, *pattern* may also be used for the item formed on the basis of a model workpiece from the 16th century onwards (OED s.v. *pattern* I.4).

2 This second basic meaning, which the OED records from 1581 onwards, is given as 'a decorative or artistic design, often repeated, esp. on a manufactured article such as a piece of china, a carpet, fabric, etc.; a style, type, or class of decoration, composition, or elaboration of form' (OED s.v. *pattern* n. II.9a). From this, the figurative meaning 'a regular and intelligible form or sequence discernible in certain actions or situations' develops in the late 19th century, such as in the phrase *pattern of behaviour* (OED s.v. *pattern* n. II.11a).

focus lies, for instance, on the investigation of our knowledge of language (e.g. mental grammar, cognitive schemas), or whether it lies on the investigation of variable language usage in its discourse contexts. Looking at *patterns in language and linguistics* from the point of view of the underlying concept may thus open up a wide array of linguistic and language-related phenomena which are, indeed, conceptually patterns, even if they may not always be termed as such.

3 The concept of *pattern* in modern linguistics

When does the term *pattern* show up in linguistic literature? Eclectic reading of the classics of (pre-)modern linguistics seems to suggest that *pattern* does not enter linguistic terminology before the early 20th century. Herder (1966 [1772]) and Humboldt (1994 [1820, 1822]), for instance, do not apply the term when writing about the uniqueness and formative characteristics of human language. The understanding of language being based on repetitive elements, may however, already be found, e.g.:

> What denotes a grammatical relation in a language, in such a way that it always recurs under the same circumstances, is a grammatical form for [that language]. In most of the developed languages, a conjunction of elements may still be perceived which is in no way differently combined than in the undeveloped languages; (Humboldt 1994 [1822]: 62, translation RMF)[3]

Throughout the course of the 19th century and the development of Historical-Comparative (Indo-European) Linguistics, the term does not seem to be much used either. Thus, while for instance Sievers (1885) writes about the phonology of Indo-European languages, *pattern* (or German *Muster*), such as with reference to sound patterns, does not occur as a term. The idea that language is formed on the basis of a combination of features is, however, found for instance in Sweet, who defines language as "the expression of ideas by means of speech-sounds combined into words. Words are combined into sentences, this combination answering to that of ideas into thoughts" (Sweet 1900: 6). Even if *pattern* does not occur as a term in linguistics for some time, the idea of language having recurring combinations

---

[3] The original German quote says: "Was in einer Sprache ein grammatisches Verhältnis charakteristisch (so, dass es im gleichen Fall immer wiederkehrt) bezeichnet, ist für sie grammatische Form. In den meisten der ausgebildetsten Sprachen lässt sich noch heute die Verknüpfung von Elementen erkennen, die nicht anders, als in den roheren verbunden sind" (Humboldt 1994 [1822]: 62).

of formal features, i.e. patterns, as its building blocks appears to have existed from the beginnings of philosophical reasoning about human language.

In order to approach the development of ideas of *patterns* in 20th-century language and linguistics, it is first useful to draw attention to the Saussurean distinction between *langue* as the abstract language system and *parole* as the concrete use of language in communication in the form of spoken utterances (Saussure 1967 [1915]: 27–32). Much of the difference in how *pattern* surfaces as a concept and as a descriptive term in different approaches to linguistics is due to the different foci placed on these two. Thus, for instance Chomskyan linguistics, i.e. generative and transformational approaches to the study of language, places the focus on the language system, more specifically on *linguistic competence* as the ideal speaker's knowledge of the linguistic system which is stored in his or her mind (Chomsky 1965: 4). The object of study is not *parole*, or *performance*, i.e. concrete language use in spoken utterances, but the underlying system of rules or principles (*mental grammar*) that enable speakers to produce an unlimited number of possible sentences. In contradistinction to this, several other strands of linguistics emphasize the importance of doing justice to *parole* or *performance* by investigating the range of variable language usage found in actual speaker-hearer interaction, such as is done in variational and sociolinguistics (e.g. Labov 1972, 1975; Trudgill 1978, 2011; Milroy 1987; Milroy and Milroy 1987; Milroy and Gordon 2003; Kortmann and Szmrecsanyi 2004; Kortmann and Wolk 2012; Eckert 2012, 2018; Pennycook and Otsuij 2015), anthropological and cultural linguistics (e.g. Palmer 1996; Duranti 1997; Enfield et al. 2014; Sharifian 2015), pragmatics and discourse linguistics (e.g. Leech 1983; Levinson 1983; Johnstone 2008; Van Dijk 2008, 2009; Flowerdew 2014), corpus linguistics (e.g. Leech 1991, 1992; Sinclair 1991, 2004; McEnery and Wilson 1996; Johansson and Oksefjell 1998), and usage-based linguistics (e.g. Bybee et al. 1994; Bybee 2010; Barlow and Kemmer 2000; Tomasello 2003; Hopper 2007; Mengden and Coussé 2014) – including cognitive linguistics (e.g. Lakoff 1987; Langacker 1987, [3]1991, 2000; Croft 1991, 2001; Croft and Cruse 2004) and construction grammar (e.g. Fillmore et al. 1988; Kay 1999; Goldberg 1995, 2006), the latter two combining the interest in patterns of usage in performance with the issue of speakers' knowledge of the system of language.

3.1 *Pattern* in relation to linguistic *system* and linguistic *structure*

Nowadays, *patterns* seem to be everywhere in language. In the early structuralist linguistics literature, however, it is hardly found. While Roy Harris's English translation of Ferdinand de Saussure's *Cours de Linguistique Générale* (1993

[1915]), uses the term *pattern* in the compound *sound pattern*, referring to the form component of the linguistic sign (Saussure 1993 [1915]: 67), the French original has the term *image acoustique* ('acoustic image') instead. Bally and Sechehay, who edited Saussure's lecture notes to publish them posthumously, add in an editorial note to this:

> Ce terme d'*image acoustique* paraîtrat peut-être trop étroit, puis-qu'à côté de la representation des sons d'un mot il y a aussi celle de son articulation, *l'image musculaire* de l'acte phonatoire. (Saussure 1967 [1915]: 98; emphasis ours)

which Harris (1993 [1915]) translates as

> Saussure's term '*sound pattern*' may appear too narrow. For in addition to the representation of what a word sounds like, the speaker must have a representation of how it is articulated, *the muscular pattern* of the act of phonation. (Saussure 1993 [1915]: 66, fn. 2; emphasis ours)

Here, *pattern* recurs in the compound *muscular pattern* in the English translation, referring to a sequence of muscle movements in articulating a specific sound combination that has to be known, or learned, by a speaker to be able to apply it. A *pattern* is thus associated with the articulatory learnability of language, but initially with reference to sound combinations that recur in speech. However, it needs to be noted that this is a much later usage of the term by the British linguist Roy Harris translating the French original. Saussure himself did not evoke the pattern-concept, which in French would probably rather have been denoted by the term *modèle*.[4]

Pattern with reference to the sound level is used by the American Structuralist linguist Bloomfield (1933: 135), who speaks of "structural pattern" with reference to syllable structure. Here, a *pattern* refers to a recurring configuration of sound combinations which on a more abstract level of analysis reveals an underlying more fixed structure. The idea of language consisting of structures implies a more stative conception than seems to be evident in the concept of *pattern*. *Structure* typically refers to a stable, or stative, framework formed by elements that have been "put together" as in a construct and which form the covert abstract basis for overt variation. This is in congruence with the general interest of traditional Structuralist Linguistics in finding out more about the system level of language, i.e. the conventionalized (and thus in a sense "stable") common core that is shared by all speakers of a language, i.e. *langue*, and that has to be "filtered

---

[4] We are grateful to Alexander Freihaut for information on possible equivalents to the English term *pattern* in French linguistics.

out" by the linguist in studying concrete linguistic data, i.e. *parole* (see Seuren 1998: 141–144). Hence, the European Structuralists Trubetzkoy (1969 [1939]), in his introduction to phonology, Jakobson and Halle (1960), and Hjelmslev (1968, 1974), do not apply the term *pattern* at all but rather speak of sound *structures* as their central theoretical concept. This idea is also evoked in Benveniste (1974 [1972]), who notes:

> From its basis upwards, from the sounds up to the most complex forms of expressions, language is *a systematic combination of components*. It consists of formal elements that are articulated in variable combinations by following certain structural principles. ... The structure of the linguistic system ... is uncovered bit by bit ..., acting on the observation that any language has a limited number of basic elements, but that these few elements by themselves may coalesce into a large number of combinations. (Benveniste 1974 [1972]: 31; translation RMF; emphasis ours)[5]

The language system (*langue*) is thus the collectivity of abstract structural principles which form the basis for systematically recurring combinations of variable elements (such as sounds or words), i.e. combinations of elements of linguistic expression that follow a certain order or sequence determined by the structural principles of the language. What needs to be noted, however, is that the "formal elements that are articulated in variable combinations" (see quote above) are reminiscent of the concept of *pattern* as defined in chapter 1 (see Busse and Möhlig-Falke, this volume, page 2). The fact that this concept does not surface in Structuralist Linguistics lies in their focus on uncovering the more stable underlying structures, in which the overt variable patterned combinations are simply the devices by which these structures may be accessed.

One of the first linguistic publications clearly focusing on language *patterns* is Hornby's *Guide to Patterns and Usage in English* (1954). This book explicitly addresses foreign or L2 learners of English "to provide help and guidance on problems of syntax and usage for advanced students of the English language" (Hornby 1954: v). The term *pattern* is used on all levels of language as descriptive and structuring concept (e.g. *verb patterns, noun patterns, adjective patterns*), without, however, defining what is understood by the term. The "patterns"

---

[5] The quote states in the German translation: "Von Grund auf, von den Lauten bis zu den komplexesten Ausdrucksformen, ist die Sprache eine *systematische Verküpfung von Teilen*. Sie besteht aus formalen, nach bestimmten Strukurprinzipien zu variablen Kombinationen artikulierten Elementen. ... [D]ie Struktur des linguistischen Systems ... [wird] nach und nach entschleiert ..., ausgehend von der Beobachtung, daß eine Sprache immer nur eine begrenzte Anzahl von Grundelementen besitzt, daß diese an sich wenigen Elemente jedoch eine große Anzahl von Kombinationen eingehen können" (Benveniste 1974 [1972]: 31, emphasis ours).

described by Hornby are similar to phrases, colligations or schematic constructions, e.g. Noun Pattern 1: Noun X *to*-infinitive (e.g. *in his anxiety to help*), Noun Pattern 3: Noun X *that*-clause (e.g. *the fact that you speak French well*; see Hornby 1954: 127). He thus applies the term *pattern* with reference to recurring combinations of language elements showing similar features, such as a postmodifying clause. Although the term of *pattern* is central in his description of English, it does not constitute a theoretical concept in need of further explanation or definition. Having a didactic aim, Hornby considers the patterns he describes as being recognizable on the "surface", i.e. in *parole*, and hence learnable by a non-native speaker of English. This already entails that the repeatedly occurring combinations of language elements on the surface level can be abstracted away from by identifying those features they have in common and on whose basis new sentences can be formed that follow the same pattern. However, Hornby himself does not assign any theoretical significance to this.[6]

Hockett's (1963 [1958]) *Course in Modern Linguistics* goes beyond this by having *pattern* as a theoretical concept as well as an esthetic guideline. Thus, in the phonology section he speaks of a *Principle of Neatness of Pattern*, which states that, if more than one option exists to decide which of several allophones should receive phoneme status, linguists should decide on the basis of the symmetry of the system (i.e. the "neatness of the phonological pattern", Hockett 1963 [1958]: 109). Patterns are no longer just a surface phenomenon but established as an abstraction of a combination of recurring features in the brain:

> ... but what [the child] does deduce or learn from these observations is abstracted from the speech and the situations, and established as a set of patterns, in the brain of the child, in the brain and the notebooks of the analyst. (Hockett 1963 [1958]: 137)

He identifies patterns on all levels, sound (phonemic) patterns, morphemic patterns, and syntactic patterns (Hockett 1963 [1958]: 142). *Pattern* equals *system* (*langue*) in Hockett's thinking: "[An utterance's] phonemic structure reflects some of the *phonemic pattern* or *system* of the language. Its grammatical structure reflects some of the *grammatical pattern* or *system* of the language" (Hockett 1963 [1958]: 142; emphasis in the original). Hockett thus seems to consider patterns to be hierarchical rather than being mere linear juxtapositions, and going from

---

[6] Hornby (1954) is often considered to be an important precursor of modern corpus linguistics, especially of Sinclair's strictly usage-based approach and the idiom principle, which entails that a language user in the process of language acquisition stores a large number of semi-preconstructed phrases that can then be used to produce new utterances (Sinclair 1991: 110–115; see section 3.3 below).

concrete to more and more abstract levels (Hockett 1963 [1958]: 157–158). His equation of *pattern* with the language system also becomes clear from the following quote, where he refers to mutual intelligibility among speakers of different varieties of one language:

> ... it makes sense to speak of an *overall pattern* for any set of idiolects which are in direct or indirect contact with each other and which contain a common core. The overall pattern includes everything that is in the repertory of any idiolect, productively and receptively. It includes, typically if not by definition, more than does any one idiolect, while any idiolect includes, typically if not by definition, more than does the common core. (Hockett 1963 [1958]: 336; emphasis in the original)

The "overall pattern" he refers to thus describes the common core of a language, i.e. the abstract combinations of features that recur in the idiolects of all of its speakers, but also the set of features that vary between them and make their speech different from each other on the surface. Thus, while *patterns* are merely a surface phenomenon which may be observed and noticed in concrete utterances for most of the traditional Structuralists, they are also part of the more abstract system level of language for Hockett (1963 [1958]). Hockett thus links the repetitive combinations of linguistic elements on the level of *parole* (*pattern* meaning II, see section 2) by a process of abstraction to a hierarchically superordinate – in terms of being cognitively more basic – underlying pattern on the level of *langue*, i.e. the system level (*pattern* meaning I, see section 2).

These different understandings of *patterns* and the way how they relate to the overall structure or composition of language can be found in different form in the various more recent approaches to and theories of language.

3.2 Patterns and mental grammar

Modern, let's call it "systemic" linguistics considers language patterns to exist as formal features of language, such as sounds and sound combinations, morphemes and morpheme combinations, words and word combinations, that recur in certain environments and circumstances on the level of *parole* and can be associated with a certain function. Patterns are thus phenomena of performance, or "E-language" (Chomsky 1986), i.e. the concrete linguistic output of speakers, which in turn forms the linguistic input language learners get in their experience of language. As Belletti and Rizzi (2002: 3–4) note with respect to generative linguistic theory,

> [k]nowing a language amounts to tacitly possessing a recursive generative procedure. When we speak[,] we freely select a structure generated by our recursive procedure and which accords with our communicative intentions; a particular selection in a specific discourse situation is a free act of parole in Saussure's sense, but the underlying procedure which specifies the possible 'regular patterns' is strictly rule-governed. (Belletti and Rizzi 2002: 3–4)

Hence, what is termed a "regular pattern" here is a surface phenomenon of *parole*, or E-language, whereas the underlying abstract concept is a *rule* as manifested in speakers' I-language, the system of mental grammar based on the innate principles of Universal Grammar (Chomsky 1986). As is well-known, Chomsky's focus of interest is in finding out more about the innate component of the human language faculty, i.e. the basic structural rules and principles which form speakers' mental grammar. As Chomsky does not assume that language is acquired solely on the basis of perceiving and generalizing across surface patterns of actual language usage, which would be found in E-language, patterns as such are of no further theoretical interest. This idea is also reflected, for instance, in Pinker (1994). For him, *patterns* are surface phenomena which are idiosyncratic and even at times "irregular" and "messy", whereas it is the *rule* which provides some structure and orderliness, which works on the system level and by which new utterances are productively formed, e.g.

> [o]ur ability to appreciate a pattern inside a word, while knowing that the pattern is not the product of some potent rule, is the inspiration for a whole genre of wordplay. ... Down at the level of word roots, we also find messy patterns in irregular plurals like *mouse–mice* ... [which are] ... mere fossils of [the Proto-Germanic/Indo-European morphological] rules. (Pinker 1994: 137–138)

The rules of grammar thus provide the abstract slots which may be filled by words (Pinker 1999: 1). This view of language is often referred to as a "slot-and-filler" model (see, e.g. Theakston et al. 2015: 1370). In such a model, it is the words that carry meaning, whereas the rules are devoid of meaning of their own but provide the structure without which the stringing together of words would be arbitrary and meaningless, such as is emphasized by Bickerton (1995):

> It should be appropriately deflating to human self-importance to discover that what crucially distinguishes us from other species is not something lofty and philosophical like "meaning," but something quite mechanical: the unconscious, mindless cranking out of formal syntactic patterns.
> But it is this mechanism that underlies all distinctively human behavior. "Only connect," said E. M. Forster in the epigraph to *Howards End*. Syntax only connects, but without its connections there would be very little for us to communicate. With it, we are able to talk about anything under the sun without attending to the means whereby we put our

sentences together. And the persons listening to us can understand everything we say without any assistance from linguistic or extralinguistic context or pragmatic knowledge or anything else – in stark contrast to the utterances of pidgin speakers[7], children under two, or trained apes, which may need massive doses of context to interpret. True language can be interpreted directly because syntax provides us with a host of structural clues that always suffice to tell us who did what, and with which, and to whom – clues that are provided automatically, indeed obligatorily, by the abstract structures that the syntactic mechanism produces. (Bickerton 1995: 39)

In the traditional generative linguistic paradigm, *patterns* as a performance-related phenomenon are accordingly of lesser relevance and the focus is instead placed on the system of rules that form competent speakers' innate linguistic knowledge (e.g. Chomsky 1957, 1986). But what makes the structural rules of language as described in the generative framework different from the abstract patterns identified by Hockett?

Jackendoff (1994: 12–14), provides a possible answer to the question of how *patterns* and *rules* are connected: Patterns may contain other, more abstract patterns within them, which are the "rules of language stored in memory. They [i.e. linguists] refer to the complete collection of rules as the *mental grammar* of the language, or *grammar* for short" (Jackendoff 1994: 14, emphasis in the original). The step from *patterns* to *rules* seems to lie in the transfer from cognition (as the perception and memorizing of an abstract pattern) to production (as the application of an abstract pattern for the production of a similar utterance based on that pattern). Jackendoff's conceptual approach, which attempts to fill the idea of an innate mental grammar, also called universal grammar (UG), with cognitive-semantic content, may thus be seen as a bridge between generative and nativist approaches to language on the one hand, and cognitive, functional, and usage-based approaches on the other, such as Langacker (1987, 1991, 2000, 2009), Fillmore (1976, 1982), or Tomasello (2000, 2003). What remains as a crucial difference between these two large "schools" of linguistic thought is the question whether UG is part of human beings' innate language capacity or whether it is formed on the basis of experience with discourse in the process of first-language

---

[7] Bickerton here reveals a view of pidgin languages which may be considered outdated today, namely the view that pidgin languages are simply a reduced form of "gibberish" of the original target language. Modern Pidgin and Creole Studies has shown that pidgin languages go through different developmental stages, beginning with a jargon stage – which may possibly be what Bickerton refers to here – but that once established in a speech community as stable pidgin languages follow their own set of rules and are fully functional as *lingua francas* that are typically used only in a reduced set of social interactions, such as in trading or in the work-place (see Mühlhäusler 1997: 128; Winford 2003: 268–273).

acquisition – i.e. what Hopper (1988) has called the *A Priori Grammar* as against the *Emergent Grammar Postulates* as two "competing ideologies", none of which can be ultimately proven to be true (Hopper 1988: 133).

3.3 Patterns in usage-based linguistics

In usage-based linguistics, the concept of *pattern* begins to achieve more than a descriptive value and gains theoretical relevance. This is mainly due to the fact that usage-based linguistics does not subscribe to the nativist point of view, which states that human language – in the form of UG – is innate. Rather, cognitive and usage-based theories of language acquisition, such as Ellis and Frey (2009) and Tomasello (2003), explain language acquisition as bottom-up and constructivist by being based on the perception, memorization and use of patterns with varying degrees of abstractness on all linguistic levels. Usage-based approaches emphasize the importance of the domain-general[8] human "pattern-finding skills" for the language-acquisition process:

> These skills ... include such things as:
> — the ability to form perceptual categories of "similar" objects and events ...;
> — the ability to form sensory-motor schemas from recurrent patterns of perception and action ...;
> — the ability to perform statistically based distributional analyses on various kinds of perceptual and behavioural sequences ...;
> — the ability to create analogies (structure mappings) across two or more complex wholes, based on the similar functional roles of some elements in these different wholes ...
> These skills are necessary for children to find patterns in the way adults use linguistic symbols across different utterances, and so to construct the grammatical (abstract) dimensions of human linguistic competence. (Tomasello 2003: 4)

The patterns found consist of specific combinations of linguistic symbols (sounds, words, morphemes, etc.) which recur in adult speech and can be identified by the child as having a particular communicative function.[9] In their

---

8 *Domain-general* means that the required cognitive skills do not only enable communication by language but also a range of other cultural skills and practices that children acquire routinely, such as tool use, pretend play, or rituals (Tomasello 2003: 4).
9 See Tomasello (2003: 30–31): "... once language acquisition begins in earnest[,] children use their pattern-finding skills on the functional (or meaning) side of things as well. That is, to learn the conventional use of a particular word the child not only must discern across instances that it is the same phonological form (the easiest, limiting case of pattern-finding) but also must see patterns in the way adults use a particular form communicatively across different usage events".

earliest form in language acquisition, these are "item-based schemas", or "item-based patterns" (Tomasello 2000), on the basis of which children gradually form more abstract categories and schemas.[10] Further, children do not just learn words in isolation, but they learn words in the context of what accompanies them:[11]

> Thus, for example, when children learn the word *give*, there is really no learning of the word apart from the participant roles that invariably accompany acts of giving: the giver, the thing given, and the person given to; in fact, we cannot even conceive of an act of giving in the absence of these participant roles. The same could be said of the words *out, from,* and *of,* which can only be learned as relationships between two other entities or locations.
> ... That is to say, children hear only concrete utterances, but they attempt to construct abstract linguistic constructions out of these, and this process has important implications for their cognitive development, especially with regard to the conceptualization of complex events, states of affairs, and their interrelations. (Tomasello 1999: 134–135)

Usage-based approaches do not see a difference in kind between *lexis* – as the set of signs a language has to refer to the more concrete categories, on the one hand – and *grammar* as the set of signs by which languages refer to more abstract categories (such as tense, modality, or agentivity), on the other. Further, it sees the relationship between performance and competence as a fluent transition of one into the other (e.g. Hopper 1988; Kemmer and Barlow 2000; Mengden and Coussé 2014).

---

10 Psycholinguistics also has the terms *chunk* and *chunking* (after Miller 1956), which refers to a small block of linguistic information that can be stored in short-term memory (Bußmann 2002: 138, s.v. *chunk(ing)*). *Chunks* are not specific for child language but denote building blocks that can be perceived in language and memorized by children and adults alike, and which may eventually form the basis from which patterns may be abstracted. According to Miller (1956), up to seven plus or minus two items can be stored in short-term memory. Recently, Green (2017) has revisited this hypothesis by drawing on the number of four (based on Cowan 2000) in a usage-based and corpus-linguistic approach investigating a variety of linguistic patterns such as phrasal verbs, idioms, n-grams, or the lengths of intonation units.

11 The same idea can be found in Fillmore's *frame semantics*; see, e.g. Fillmore (1976, 1982). It is also reflected in Sinclair's (1991) *idiom principle*: "The principle of idiom is that a language user has available to him or her a large number of semi-preconstructed phrases that constitute single choices, even though they might appear to be analysable into segments" (Sinclair 1991: 110). Under the idiom principle, grammar is considered to emerge for the language learner and user by abstracting away from these idioms – rather than being innate, as Chomskyan linguistics has it. See also, for instance, Partington et al. (2013: 25–42), and Hoey (2005), who claims that "every word is mentally primed for collocational use" (Hoey 2005: 8). As a word is acquired, it becomes "cumulatively loaded with the contexts and co-texts in which it is encountered and our knowledge of it includes the fact that it co-occurs with certain other words in certain kinds of context" (Hoey 2005: 8).

Even though cognitive and usage-based linguistics considers language acquisition to be based essentially on human pattern-finding skills and the formation of more abstract patterns on the basis of more concrete, item-based ones – this implying that language is essentially built of patterns of various degrees of abstractness – the *term* as such does not achieve theoretical status. This is to say, even though, for instance, Langacker (1987, 1991, 2000), Croft (2000), Croft and Cruse (2004), Goldberg (1995, 2006), Booij (2010), or recently Hunston and Su (2017), use *pattern* descriptively for recurring combinations of linguistic signs in concrete language usage, it is rather the *schema* or the *construction* which achieves theoretical importance for the abstract system level. Thus, for Langacker (2000), for instance, "[g]rammar resides in patterns of composition, which take the form of constructional schemas. Collectively, these patterns sanction the progressive assembly of expressions of any size and degree of symbolic complexity" (Langacker 2000: 20). These "constructional schemas" are patterns on a higher level of abstractness, the process of abstraction, "filtering out" those facets of individual expressions which do not recur.[12]

Recently, the issue about the relationship between the *construction*, the *pattern* and the (linguistic) *sign* has become relevant especially in construction-based approaches, this being reflected in three contributions to this volume (Traugott, Petré, and Michaelis, this volume).[13] As Goldberg (2006) states, "What makes a theory that allows constructions to exist a 'construction-based theory' is the idea that the network of constructions captures our grammatical knowledge of language *in toto*, i.e. *it's constructions all the way down*" (Goldberg 2006: 18, emphasis in the original). This entails the view that the way lexical knowledge is stored in the minds of speakers is not fundamentally different from grammatical knowledge but that words are also constructions:

---

12 See also de Smet's (2013) diachronic investigation of diffusional change in terms of *spreading patterns*, which is usage-based and constructivist. Even though *pattern* is used descriptively throughout the book, it is used for the phenomena on the level of *parole*, while *construction* – from very specific to highly abstract – is used for the theoretical concept on the system level. A similar usage of the two terms is found, for instance, in Möhlig-Falke (2012).
See also Nuyts (2008: 88) who uses *pattern* and *construction* more or less synonymously and contrasts these with a process-oriented approach to grammar and mind in Cognitive Linguistics.
13 See also Hunston and Su (2017: 4–5), who state in a recent article on *local grammars*, "[t]his article offers a way of integrating pattern and construction; it proposes, not that each pattern is a construction, but that each meaning–pattern combination is a construction".

> A constructionist grammar contains a set of interrelated constructions of various degrees of abstraction, from lexical idioms to general syntactic schemas and with default inheritance, based on the psychological operations of categorization and abstraction. (Booij 2010: 257).

On the basis of Goldberg (1995, 2006), Traugott and Trousdale (2013) develop a diachronic construction grammar. They define constructions as "conventional symbolic units" (Traugott and Trousdale 2013: 1). They are

> ... conventional in that they are shared among a group of speakers. They are symbolic in that they are signs, typically arbitrary associations of form and meaning. And they are units in that some aspect of the sign is idiosyncratic ... or so frequent ... that the sign is entrenched as a form–meaning pairing in the mind of the language user. (Traugott and Trousdale 2013: 1)

This means, just like words, constructions are form–meaning pairings that are stored in the minds of speakers.

Considering that usage-based approaches theoretically see no difference in kind between the more concrete and the more abstract categories of language, why is a different terminology needed with *patterns* on the concrete, descriptive level of the utterance (*parole*, performance) and *schemas* or *constructions* on the abstract and more theoretical level of linguistic knowledge in the minds of speakers (*langue*, competence)? The formation of schemas or constructions requires a process of abstraction, which is

> ... the emergence of a structure through reinforcement of the commonality inherent in multiple experiences. By its very nature, this abstractive process 'filters out' those facets of the individual experiences *which do not recur*. (Langacker 2000: 93; emphasis ours).

This means, if patterns are identified on the basis of the recurrence of the same or similar elements in combination, the abstraction process in schema formation entails that the variable elements, i.e. elements that differ, are filtered out so that only the abstract similarities remain and leave a fixed, or stable "structure" (cf. the notion of *structure* as used in Structuralist Linguistics, see section 3.1). The underlying cognitive mechanism behind this is analogical reasoning, i.e. the human capacity to compare new experiences with older ones and to see the similarities between them while "graciously ignoring the differences" (Fischer 2016; see also Fischer 2013: 517–520; Paul 1909, Tomasello 2003: 4, Hopper and Traugott 2003: 63–68).[14] Analogical reasoning as a domain-general cognitive process is crucial for pattern-finding and categorization in that it allows to identify

---

14 Kahnemann (2012) refers to this as "intuitive thinking" and "jumping to conclusions", i.e. fast thinking, as opposed to the slower logical reasoning.

similarities, i.e. features that recur between two or more items, to thus subsume them under one category and identify their similar functions in a sequence or combination.[15] The features that differ between two items but are ignored in the process of categorization give categories their fuzziness (Aarts et al. 2004: 5–9). Analogical reasoning also underlies the process of metonymization by which speakers identify meaning resemblances between two concepts, which enables them to subsume them under one category (e.g. Traugott and Dasher 2002).

The concept of *pattern* is also central to usage-based approaches on grammaticalization in situations of language contact and change (e.g. Hopper and Traugott 2003). Thus, pattern transfer in situations of language contact from a "model language" to a "replica language" (Weinreich 1963: 30–31) is at the core of Heine and Kuteva's (2005) framework of grammatical replication in that

> [s]peakers create a new use pattern or category in language R [i.e. the replica language] on the model of another language M [i.e. the model language], where the outcome of the process is not an exact copy of what exists in M but rather a new structure that is shaped, first, by what is available in R, second, by universal constraints on conceptualization, third, by what speakers of R conceive as being pragmatically most appropriate in the situation in which language contact takes place, and, fourth, by the length and intensity of contact and – accordingly – by the relative degree to which replication is grammaticalized. (Heine and Kuteva 2005: 7)[16]

Grammatical use patterns are understood as linguistic structures (such as clauses, phrases, or single forms) which are associated with specific grammatical meaning and which recur in linguistic discourse (Heine and Kuteva 2005: 41). They figure as primary units in the initial stage of grammatical replication and their use is optional, i.e. they are typically variants which are restricted in occurrence either to individual social layers of speakers, or to register or region (Heine and Kuteva 2005: 41).

While *pattern* seems to be favoured as a term for the more variable repetitive combinations and sequences of linguistic forms in concrete utterances, most cog-

---

15 Analogical reasoning as a cognitive mechanism is related to *analogy* as discussed in Langacker (2000: 144–145), who understands it as "referring to expressions being directly formed on the model of others, not as the basis of stored abstracted patterns".
16 As Heine and Kuteva (2005) state, "the prerequisite for grammaticalization is the use of existing forms or constructions in new contexts and, since new contexts tend to invite new semantic interpretations, also the emergence of new (grammatical) meanings" (Heine and Kuteva 2005: 15). The four parameters which Heine and Kuteva (2005) apply for grammaticalization are pragmatic *extension* in that novel grammatical meanings arise in new contexts, *desemanticization* or loss/generalization in meaning content, *decategorization* or loss in morphosyntactic properties, and *erosion* or loss in phonetic substance (Heine and Kuteva 2005).

nitive linguistic theories seem to see the need to terminologically distinguish these from the more stable combinations on the level of the system. If we look at *pattern* as a concept, however, comprising frame meaning I and II (see section 2), it is clear that both are conceptually *patterns*: They are two sides of the same coin, linked by analogical reasoning and metonymization. On the basis of their fixedness, *schemas*, *constructions* – as well as the *structures* and *rules* of Structuralist and Generative approaches – may be said to be *patterns* in the sense of frame meaning I, feeding the production of language. They are the abstract models stored in speakers' minds which can be applied in order to produce new utterances that follow this underlying pattern. The utterances accordingly become phenomena of performance and as such feed the perception and conceptualization of language on the part of the interpreter. Performance patterns are more unstable in that they typically incorporate a great deal of variation, for instance in terms of the variable lexical items used in them, intonation and word order differences, etc. They are *patterns* in the sense of meaning II, i.e. observable or perceivable linear sequences or combinations of linguistic elements of a certain kind that recur in different communicative situations with a similar function. *Pattern* as a concept, comprising frame meaning I and II, thus includes this metonymic chain, or rather cycle, from unstable and variable repetitive sequence on the perception side to the more fixed, stable abstracted model of the production side and back again, as illustrated in figure 2.1:

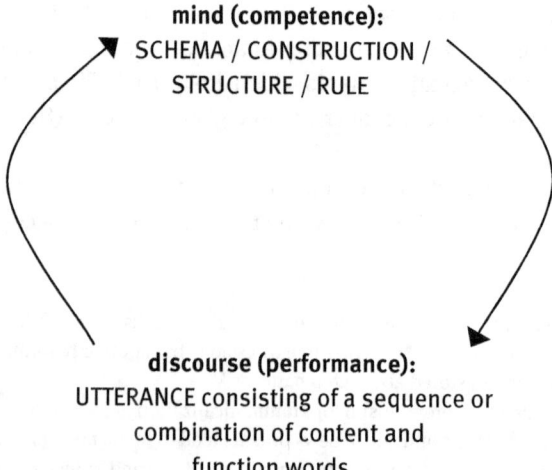

Fig. 2.1: The "metonymic cycle" in the concept of *pattern*

Identifying schemas, constructions, structures or rules to be in essence *patterns* does not mean that the terminological differentiation in the various linguistic approaches and theories is wrong or devoid. It is useful and needed for clarification sake when talking about language usage as against knowledge of language on the mind. However, it might also be useful to see the two sides of *patterns* as the building blocks on which our human perception and understanding, our conceptualization and categorization of the world rests, because one does not exist without the other. Patterns are everywhere, because we see them everywhere and because we need them in order to reduce the complexity around us to form categories of knowledge and enable communication about them.

3.4 Patterns in corpus linguistics and the issues of frequency and quantification

As a discipline, modern corpus linguistics has been developing since the 1960s and has come to dominate much of contemporary linguistic research. In corpus linguistics, the existence of patterns is typically taken for granted and the main objective is to find or identify them in (authentic) language data. Patterns are typically understood as *collocations, colligations,* and *collostructions* (e.g. Sinclair 1991; Hunston and Francis 2000; Stefanowitsch and Gries 2003; Gries and Stefanowitsch 2004; Brezina, McEnery, and Wattam 2015), i.e. frequent (or in a weaker sense, recurrent) cooccurrences of content words or content-and-function words in different contexts of language use found in digitized corpora, as outlined in the following quotation by Hunston and Francis (2000):

> The patterns of a word can be defined as all the words and structures which are regularly associated with the word and contribute to its meaning. A pattern can be identified if a combination of words occurs relatively frequently, if it is dependent on a particular word choice, and if there is a clear meaning associated with it. (Hunston and Francis 2000: 37)

Phraseologisms are similar to this, but here it is important that the cooccurring elements form a semantic unit (Gries 2008: 6). A phraseological pattern is thus[17]

> ... the co-occurrence of a form or a lemma of a lexical item and one or more additional elements of various kinds which functions as one semantic unit in a clause or sentence and

---

[17] Ebeling and Oksefjel-Ebeling (2013), however, also conclude that "at present there is no obvious way of automatically establishing what constitutes a semantic unit in text" (Ebeling and Oksefjel-Ebeling 2013: 63).

whose frequency of co-occurrence is larger than expected on the basis of chance. (Ebeling and Oksefjell-Ebeling 2013: 61)

Thus, the *patterns* in corpus linguistics are a performance-related phenomenon (see e.g. Hunston 2014: 115 and Traugott, this volume, page 128 fn. 6). Corpus linguistics has developed methodologies by which first and foremost linear *sequences* of words (content as well as function words) can be found in large digitized data-sets by the help of corpus software, which makes them available in the form of concordances; i.e. corpus linguistics is largely lexically based. *Patterns* as linear sequences of lexical items, or as combinations of lexical and grammatical items, observable in digitized texts of authentic spoken or written language data have achieved special significance in the debate about what is usually known as the *corpus-based* as against the *corpus-driven* approach. While a corpus-based approach is deductive in that it "avails itself of the corpus mainly to expound, test or exemplify theories and descriptions that were formulated before large corpora became available to inform language study" (Tognini-Bonelli 2001: 65), a corpus-driven approach is largely inductive, i.e. the investigation of language develops bottom-up from the text and "observation [of empirical corpus data] leads to hypothesis leads to generalisation leads to unification in theoretical statement" (Tognini-Bonelli 2001: 85). Rather than looking for certain prefabricated patterns in a text (such as would be done in a corpus-based approach), the corpus is searched for frequently recurring linear sequences of words, which thus emerge as *patterns* from the texts and discourses, i.e. from concrete and authentic (rather than made-up) language use (e.g. Sinclair 2004; Teubert 2010; see also McEnery and Brezina, this volume). This methodology in a way imitates how young children begin to identify and acquire the meaningful language patterns of their mother tongue in the flow of discourse around them. Thus, for instance, Hunston and Francis (2000) state in their Pattern Grammar approach, "… the priority given to pattern over structure represents a radical reinterpretation of grammar from the point of view of the learner rather than the academic" (Hunston and Francis 2000: 7). Going one step further, this approach may give new food for discussion to the question where linguistic meaning is located: in the minds of (competent) speakers, as generative and cognitive linguistic theories have it, or in discourse (e.g. Teubert 2010, 2013), taking account of the role which patterns (of various kinds) play in interpreting and establishing linguistic meaning (see also Stubbs, this volume).

The difference between the child in the process of first-language acquisition and the linguist attempting to analyse language in a strict corpus-driven approach is of course that the child has as yet no preformed patterns and structures on its mind – or at least in no way comparable to a trained linguist. The mere fact that linguists have an extended knowledge of linguistic structures, categories, and concepts, probably makes a purely inductive approach almost impossible. This is also one of the main points of critique that the corpus-driven approach has met with. Thus, Stubbs (2013) points out that the ability to find *order* (or patterns) in these sequences has to do with a certain theory which speakers have in their minds (see also Firth 1957; Leech 2000):

> The software cannot see patterns, but it can rip texts apart and shuffle the pieces into different formats, which allows humans to see patterns (though this still ignores the problem of what counts – intuitively – as the 'same' pattern). ... Some facts are best presented in tables, columns and statistics, and so on, but patterns (and their significance) depend on the point of view, interests and experience of the observer. You have to learn to see order in sequences. (Stubbs 2013: 22)

An issue about the concept of pattern that has been brought to the front by corpus linguistics is that of quantifying the frequencies of patterns in language data, relatively or absolutely, or based on statistical comparison. Especially in a corpus-driven approach, frequency of cooccurrence "[that] is larger than expected on the basis of chance" (Ebeling and Oksefjell-Ebeling 2013: 61) becomes the main criterion for selecting those sequences that are considered to be patterns (i.e. collocations, colligations, phraseologisms) worth of further investigation (e.g. Stubbs 2002; Hunston and Francis 2000; Sinclair 2004; Hoey 2005; Gries 2008; Ebeling and Oksefjell Ebeling 2013). Correspondingly, the focus is often placed on high-frequency phenomena, corpora tend to become larger and larger, and the analyses tend to rely heavily on statistical methods by simultaneously often neglecting the situational or communicative contexts of utterances. At the same time, such a procedure, which takes high frequency as the main criterion for selecting linguistic phenomena worth of further analysis, loses sight of low-frequency linguistic phenomena that may nevertheless be of interest.

With a different theoretical implication, pattern frequency also plays a role in psycholinguistics, cognitive and usage-based linguistics, especially with reference to first- and second-language acquisition but also to diachronic language change (see discussion in section 4 below; see also Zettersten, this volume). Recent approaches to corpus linguistics have thus started to fathom the common ground between frequency effects in corpus data and their potential implications for psycholinguistic and cognitive linguistic theory (e.g. Gries 2010; Gries and Divjak 2012; Rebuschat, Meurers, and McEnery 2017).

Another corpus-linguistic approach worth mentioning in the present context is known as the analysis of *register variation* (e.g. Biber 1988, 1995; Biber and Conrad 2001; Biber and Conrad 2009; Conrad 2015). Unlike social or regional varieties, which depend on the social or regional background of their speakers, *registers* are linguistic varieties defined by situational characteristics (Biber and Conrad 2001: 175; Nunan 2008: 58). The idea of register variation accounts for the fact that "any functional description of a linguistic feature will *not* be valid for the language as a whole" (Biber and Conrad 2001: 175), but that language in discourse shows certain complex patterns of use with one pattern being strong in one register but weak in another (Biber and Conrad 2001: 176). Patterns of register variation may consist of certain preferences for lexical and grammatical choices depending on

> ... the participants, their relationships, and their attitudes toward the communication; the setting, including factors such as the extent to which time and place are shared by the participants, and the level of formality; the channel of communication; the production and processing circumstances (e.g. amount of time available); the purpose of the communication; and the topic or subject matter. (Biber and Conrad 2001: 175).

The observation of the relevance of register variation has had important implications for (corpus) linguistics, as it makes clear that especially general and multipurpose corpora, which aim at being fully representative for a certain language or linguistic variety (synchronic or diachronic), need to include different situationally and functionally defined text categories to be able to account for the complexity of register variation.[18] It has also strong implications for pragmatics and discourse analysis, as well as for variational linguistics, as it shows that every speaker of a language may be able to apply variant patterns of usage depending on the requirements of the concrete communicative situation; i.e. it implies that linguistic analysis needs to account for the relationship between *language* and *communication*.

3.5 Patterns of communicative behaviour

The relationship between *language* and *communication* has been debated since the advent of generative linguistic theory. While generative linguistics have traditionally held up the view that language (in the sense of the abstract structural principles that are said to be part of the mental grammar of ideal native speakers and as such innate in all human beings, Chomsky 1965, 1986) is more or less independent of communication and can thus also be analysed without taking into

---

[18] Of lately, the idea of functionally defined lexicogrammatical patterns has been further developed in the concept of *local grammars* (e.g. Barnbrook 2002; Bednarek 2008; Hunston and Su 2017), which depend on the speech act function of the utterance, i.e. on the illocutionary act performed by the text producer.

consideration the communicative context in which real-world utterances are produced,[19] a range of linguistic approaches have developed since the 1930s that take on a different stance, considering language to be primarily a tool for communication (e.g. Bühler 1965 [1934]; Hymes 1964, 1968; Gumpertz 1968; Searle 1969; Dreitzel 1970; Labov 1972; Grice 1989; Everett 2013). Thus, for instance, Everett (2013) states,

> [... language is] in the first instance a tool for thinking and communicating and, though it is based in human psychology, it is crucially shaped from human cultures. It is a cultural tool as well as a cognitive tool.
> ... Language is a cobbled-together set of answers to different facets of the problems of communication and cooperation among humans. (Everett 2013: 19–20).

This view of language entails that the form of language is motivated, or even determined,[20] by the functions to which it is put in a given community of speakers (Everett 2013: 27). Thus, the differences between languages – or rather between the various forms and varieties of language that have developed world-wide – move into the focus of attention of linguistic analysis, as they may tell linguists (such as sociolinguists, pragmaticists, discourse analysts, text linguists, anthropological and cultural linguists) and ethnographers differences in the conceptualizations and categorizations of "the world", in social and cultural interaction as "patterns of communicative behavior" (Dreitzel 1970).[21]

The need to study such patterns of communicative behaviour in a previously unknown language unbiased by the categorizations already known from one's own first language and linguistic training was already noted by Whorf (2012 [1945]):

> In the reaction from conventional grammars of American languages based on classical models, there has been a tendency to restrict attention to the morphemes by which many grammatical forms are marked. This view loses sight of various word-classes that are not marked by morphemic tags but by types of patterning: e.g. by the systematic avoidance of certain morphemes, by lexical selection, by word order that is also CLASS-ORDER, in general

---

19 See, e.g. Bickerton (1995: 40): "Language is not (a means of) communication, but communication is just one use to which language can be put; other uses of language are: the enhancement of intelligence and the creation of our peculiar form of consciousness."
20 This view is known as *linguistic relativity*, or *linguistic determinism*, and typically associated with Edward Sapir and Benjamin Lee Whorf (see, e.g. Sapir 1929, Whorf 2012 [1956]).
21 Commonly in these approaches, the issue whether language is innate or not (or to put it in Everett's words, whether language is learned as a cultural tool or "grows" like a biological tool [Everett 2013: 28–29]) is answered against its being innate. For a summary of arguments against the nativity hypothesis, see e.g. Everett (2013: 29–45). See also Piatelli (2004 [1980]) for the famous debate between Noam Chomsky and Jean Piaget.

by association with definite linguistic configurations. (Whorf 2012 [1945]: 114, emphasis in the original).

That this claim is not always readily met with even up to today is reflected in Haspelmath (2015), who also argues for a "frame-work free grammatical theory", stating that as all languages have different structural patterns (or, to put it in cognitive linguistic terminology, have conventionalized their own unique set of conceptualizations of experiences of the world, see Sharifian 2015), the set of concepts needed for linguistic description and analysis must be constructed separately for each language – and maybe even separately for different historical stages of a language, as cultural patterns may undergo change (see e.g. Lancashire, this volume).

Acknowledging the primary communicative function of language means that language is understood as being dialogic between a sender and an addressee (see e.g. Bühler 1965 [1934]: 28; Bakhtin 1981 [1934–35]: 279–280; Halliday and Matthiesen 2004: 106–111). Patterns of communicative behaviour may thus be found where language is used in actual communication between a speaker and an addressee (an author and a reader, etc.), i.e. in performance. Linguistic subfields which study this kind of interaction from various perspectives are, for instance, functional linguistics (e.g. Halliday and Matthiesen 2004), variational and sociolinguistics (e.g. Labov 1975; Trudgill 2011; Milroy and Milroy 1987; Eckert 2018), anthropological and cultural linguistics (e.g. Palmer 1996; Duranti 1997; Enfield et al. 2014), pragmatics and discourse linguistics (e.g. Searle 1969; Leech 1983, 2014), text linguistics and stylistics (e.g. Halliday 2002 [1971]; Jeffries and McIntyre 2010; Burke 2014), but also conversation analysis, interactional and psycholinguistics (e.g. Sacks et al. 1974; Taylor and Cameron1987; Kress 2010; Maynard 2012; Sidnell and Stivers 2012; Couper-Kuhlen and Selting 2018).

The interwovenness of language and communication is described by Tomasello (2014) as having been there right from the start of the evolution of language in that early humanoids may have developed a pre-form of language by "mental combination" (Piaget 1952, quoted from Tomasello 2014: 67):

> [S]uccessive thoughts or intentions came to be integrated into a single utterance within a single intonation contour. With some minimal skills of categorization, individuals could form a schema comprising, for example, an iconic gesture for eating followed by indexical indication of anything edible either by oneself or by others.
> ... Combining symbolic and deictic vehicles is not the creation of new communicative intentions, primarily, but rather the parsing of existing ones into their component parts. This means that in combinations a single gesture is typically indicating only one aspect of a situation. ... This focus on function and the parsing of situations into components with different subfunctions are responsible for the hierarchical organization of human communication. (Tomasello 2014: 67)

Tomasello describes here how a message (meaning, intention) could possibly be expressed by a combination of symbolic and deictic gestures and utterances in a specific situation – exemplifying how more complex forms of language and linguistic interaction may have developed from basic forms of early humanoid communication involving symbolic, indexical (deictic) and iconic signs signaled as gesture, mimics, and sounds or sound combinations. The successful interpretation of such multimodal sign combinations requires a shared context, in this example the shared situational background of sitting together and eating.

The importance of context and the multimodal nature of communication for the interpretation of language meaning has been stressed long since, for instance in pragmatic research (e.g. Grice 1989; Halliday 1978, 2007 [1991]; van Dijk 2008, 2009; Flowerdew 2014; O'Halloran et al. 2014). But what is the nature of the *patterns* involved in this? Patterns of communicative behaviour may potentially be identified wherever linguistic forms of expression (sounds, words, phrases, sentences) are repeatedly combined with certain situational and otherwise contextual elements which are needed for interpreting their meaning or function. Thus, for instance for a declarative speech act like a wedding formula to be felicitous, it needs to be combined at least with (a) a speaker who has the socially assigned right or competence to utter it, i.e. a priest or marriage registrar, and (b) a couple sincerely willing to be married – the so-called felicity conditions of speech acts (Austin 1962; Searle 1969, 1979) – as extralinguistic components. Likewise, ritual language constitutes patterns of communicative behaviour, be these ritualized formulas such as *Once upon a time*, or longer formulaic expressions that are, for instance, part of religious ceremonies (Tavárez 2014). Being less ritualized and hence more variable or open in its linguistic expression, the polite request for the time by a stranger may, for instance, combine not only a meaningful selection of words (such as *time, please*, etc.) but also take the nature of the personal relationship between speaker and addressee into account, e.g. whether the person asked is the same age, younger or older, seems to be socially equal or not, seems to have the same regional, cultural or linguistic background or not, etc. This may influence the exact word choice and phrasing but also, for instance, intonation and accent, how closely the speaker may approach the person asked (body posture, body movement), what kind of smile is required (mimics), and if some accompanying gesture is considered necessary (e.g. tipping one's wrist to indicate a watch). That is, patterns of communicative behaviour – which every human being that is part of a community shows every day – involve a calibration of linguistic forms with contextual criteria pertaining to the interlocutors, the setting, mode and medium, and other possible signals that may be used in the communication (such as mimics, gestures, or body movement).

Patterns of communicative behaviour may also be found, for instance, where speakers use language (possibly in combination with multimodal indexical signs, see Busse 2019) to create places or establish their social identity, such as by using local, non-standard accent or dialect words in some situations and standard language in others (e.g. Eckert 2012; Paltridge 2015). It might further be said that the patterns of communicative behaviour determine the establishment of a linguistic norm, i.e. a *standard language*, in the first place. After all, it will usually be that specific combination of accent, words, phrases, and sentences developing into the norm and considered to be appropriate in certain social settings and situations that is favoured either by the majority of a community of speakers – or by those that are socially most dominant in a community (which need not be the majority group) by virtue of their social status and prestige – which would refer to what Eckert (2012) has described to be the first wave of variationist sociolinguistics.

Patterns of communicative behaviour are not really *linguistic patterns*, which as a term should probably be reserved for sequences or combinations of linguistic elements only (e.g. sounds, words, phrases, sentences), but they may be considered to be *linguistically relevant patterns*, as individual elements of the setting and situation of communicative interaction may influence the linguistic features as well, such as for instance, word choice, etc.

In more recent studies of the third wave of variationist sociolinguistic research (Eckert 2012) the indexical mutability of certain linguistic patterns on all levels of language has been highlighted to enregister social value (e.g. Busse 2018, 2019; Pennycook and Otsuji 2015). This echoes work in the area of stylistics and social styling where repetitive patterns are meaning-making and stylistic, trigger stylistic change both synchronically and diachronically and reflect and construe temporary positions of both speaker and addressee within a community of practice.

4 The properties of *patterns* in language and communication

From all that has been discussed so far, we may conclude that patterns are everywhere in language. Some of these patterns may count as *linguistic* patterns, whereas others are *linguistically relevant* patterns in combining language and communicative behaviour.

If language patterns are understood as repeatedly occurring combinations of language elements (e.g. sounds and sound combinations, content words, function words) in performance that may additionally recur in specific communicative settings and situations, *linguistic patterns* are more narrowly defined those that involve the combination of elements of linguistic expression only. Such linguistic patterns may achieve a certain degree of abstractness in that they reserve slots that stay stable (are perceived as similar) while others may be filled by variable elements. Thus, in English, for instance, [VERB + -*able*]_ADJ (as in *interpretable, observable, perceivable*), or SUBJECT_AGENT + VERB_GIVE + OBJECT_RECIPIENT + OBJECT_THEME (as in *I gave him a book* and *Peter gave Mary a kiss*), or [s p r V C(CC)] (e.g. *sprinkle, sprout, sprang*, but **sprminktl*) may possibly be said to constitute linguistic patterns in English in terms of showing a certain identifiable stable combination of abstract features, a structure or schema, that occurs repeatedly in this language.

This understanding of linguistic patterns yields different abstract *types* of expressions that may serve as "models to be imitated", i.e. patterns according to the conceptual frame I. In contrast to these, idioms, collocations, colligations, and phraseologisms as recurring combinations of individual words show lesser variability and are less abstract. They constitute linguistic patterns according to the conceptual frame II, i.e. "regular sequences" of word *tokens* (see section 2). Acknowledging their common "patternhood" implies accepting that they are just points on a continuum (see also, for instance, Michaelis's continuum of idiomaticity, this volume).

In contrast to the *linguistic patterns* of various kinds, *linguistically relevant patterns* may be perceived where linguistic elements are recurrently combined with non-linguistic signs and features pertaining to the interlocutors, the setting and situation, or the medium in which linguistic communication takes place. This would thus refer to what has been so far discussed as patterns of communicative behaviour, e.g. speech acts, choice of variety or register (such as using a standard form of language and more formal vocabulary in a job interview), multimodal communication, etc. On a metalinguistic level, patterns of cooccurrence of grammatical features shared by different varieties have been identified in variational linguistics, thus showing how, for instance, certain non-standard features have gained ground in various varieties of English (e.g. Chambers 2004; Kortmann and Szmrecsanyi 2004; Kortmann and Wolk 2012). Calling these patterns of communicative behaviour *linguistically relevant* suggests that the combination of linguistic and extralinguistic elements may have effects for the linguistic patterns proper, for instance in leading to systematic (i.e. not just idiosyncratic) language variation and language change, much along the lines of register variation discussed in section 3.4 (e.g. Biber 1988, 1995).

A common understanding seems to be that once a pattern has been perceived and identified in language use, it can be applied productively in concrete utterances. Within this context the question remains whether language patterns, i.e. linguistic and linguistically relevant ones, need to have a fixed meaning or communicative function? Are, for instance, the sound patterns that are typical and conventionalized in a given language – such as language-specific syllable structures or prosodic patterns – identified as having communicative import? Considering the fact that these are patterns that are analysed in phonology, which is concerned with phonemes as by definition meaningless, though meaning-differentiating, linguistic elements in a language, the spontaneous answer might be no. Sound patterns have no communicative function, hence, language patterns can exist without a meaning or communicative function. If we look at sound patterns in actual language use, i.e. in discourse, however, we may find that, though lacking semantic content or meaning in the narrow sense, language-specific sound patterns have a communicative function where, for instance, accent, tonality, and intonation are involved. Thus, potentially *all* language patterns are "meaningful" to us as speakers, because we perceive and identify them *in order to make sense* of what is going on around us. From early childhood on, human beings apply their unique pattern-finding skills *because* the identification of patterns helps us to understand our environment.

A property that is often discussed in the context of pattern formation is that of *frequency*. As noted before (see section 3.4), especially corpus-based approaches to language consider the frequency of a phraseological pattern "larger ... than expected on the basis of chance" (Ebeling and Oksefjel Ebeling 2013: 61) as the most important reason justifying further linguistic analysis. But frequency also plays a significant role in cognitive and constructivist linguistics as well as in psycholinguistic research (see Zettersten, this volume). By empirical research (such as language skill tests, e.g. with children) cognitive linguistics finds that frequency of occurrence of a recurrent item in the language input facilitates the establishment of an abstract pattern, i.e. its *entrenchment*,[22] in the minds of speakers and the formation of a routine of its perception and (re)production (e.g. Arnon 2010; Blumenthal-Dramé 2012: 4; Harley 2014: 181–183). Croft and Cruse (2004) differentiate between type and token frequency, stating that "... token-frequency determines the degree of entrenchment of a single word ... Type frequency determines the degree of entrenchment of a schema" (Croft and Cruse 2004: 309).

---

[22] See Tomasello (2003: 300): "Entrenchment simply refers to the fact that when an organism does something in the same way successfully enough times, that way of doing it becomes habitual and it is difficult for another way of doing that same thing to enter into the picture".

"Frequency of input" may thus influence the order of acquisition of a construction, though not as the only determining factor, factors like morphological complexity or semantic transparency also playing a role (Croft and Cruse 2004: 324–325). Looking at language change, frequency and entrenchment may be important factors in the loss of certain constructions (Croft and Cruse 2004: 310–311), or in the emergence of a new construction (see Bybee and Hopper 2001: 14–16; see also Traugott and Petré, this volume).

Bybee (2007: 9–15) discusses various frequency effects, differentiating between type and token frequency. Put simply, high token frequency may result in the conservation of structures that are increasingly irregular, i.e. no longer based on a productive pattern, in an increase of autonomy, or in morphophonological reduction. Type frequency may, for instance, lead to an increase in the productivity of a construction or in its semantic extension, depending on the properties of the types involved.

The strong relation between high frequency and productivity of a pattern, construction, or schema has also been discussed in Booij (2010: 88–93; see also Plag 1999: 24–34). Booji distinguishes between word-formation from an abstract schema that occurs with a high type and token frequency and word-formation processes from infrequent tokens on the basis of analogy, i.e. by identifying similarities between two entities and extending its observed pattern (see section 3.3).

All this shows that frequency in the input either of types or tokens and the process of pattern identification and formation are interlinked in language in complex ways. We would however like to stress that the identification of a pattern in the flow of discourse, on whatever level of expression and abstraction, probably requires a perceived similarity, i.e. a repetitive feature, between only two items, provided the repetitive feature receives a certain prominence or saliency in the communicative situation, for instance because it is perceived as particularly provocative or funny (which is sometimes the case with novel, "rule-breaking" and unexpected combinations resulting in *nonce* words). The cognitive mechanism of analogical reasoning does not require a recurring feature to be recurring particularly frequently. Thus, the effects of high type and token frequency should not blind us against linguistic phenomena of lower frequency (see also Traugott, Petré, and Zettersten, this volume).

However, it is clear that frequent recurrence of a given pattern facilitates its cognitive entrenchment and spread across a wider community of speakers, as well as its extension to new contexts (e.g. Heine and Kuteva 2005: 50), i.e. it is a driving force in processes of language change. High pattern frequency thus potentially plays a role in the degrees of conventionalization shown by linguistic expressions throughout a speech community and across registers, and in the establishment of linguistic norms. Again, it may however be argued that "the norm" is not necessarily what is used by the majority of speakers (see section 3.5). The history of the formation and development of Standard English between the 15th and 20th century, for instance, shows how the language usage of originally a small section of the English speech community came to be established as the norm that the majority learned and aspired to in order to be socially successful.

5 Conclusion

Coming back to Goldberg's (2006: 18) previously cited quote, we may modify it by concluding that it is – indeed – patterns all the way down (see also Petré, this volume, page 143). However, there is clearly more to language patterns than just observable linear sequences of words. Patterns are theoretical, or abstract, constructs which exist because we look for them (see also Stubbs 2013: 22 and section 3.4). They combine not only sequences of sounds, words, and morphemes into meaningful units, identified to belong to more abstract structures, but they also include non-linguistic signs, situationally, socially and culturally relevant features of communicative behaviour.

Our overview has aimed at highlighting that thinking about language and language usage as *patterned* has a longer history in linguistics as might be suspected, although the term as such does not appear to be significant in the linguistics literature before the second half of the 20th century and only begins to acquire more than a descriptive value in the course of the development of cognitive and usage-based linguistics on the one hand, and corpus linguistics on the other. The different understandings of what constitutes a pattern in the different theories and approaches – or whether patterns rather than, for instance, rules and structures, or schemas and constructions are at all of interest – in part goes back to the different frames of reference invoked in the concept of *pattern*: While *pattern* meaning I, the model reading, assumes a stable "structure" of features that are recognized as being similar between two or more items and hence repeatable, i.e. transferable to novel language items, *pattern* meaning II, the repetitive (linear) sequence or combination of items, is assumedly more variable and dynamic. Pattern as a term as well as a concept is in an area of conflict between these two interpretations, and the usual way out is terminological differentiation by usually labeling the "pattern as model" differently (e.g. *rule, structure, schema, construction*). However, especially usage-based theories of language acquisition show that both the "pattern as model" and "pattern as sequence" interpretation are two sides of the same coin (see figure 2.1 in section 3.3); none would exist without the other and both are the outcome of the highly developed human pattern-finding skills, which are possibly unique for their complexity in the animal kingdom. In this view, language in written and/or spoken *use* is "patterned verbal communication" in Hockett's (1963 [1958]) sense, and languages may show deviant "conventionalized verbal patterns of experience" (see e.g. Everett 2013; Sharifian 2015). Following Kretzschmar (2009, 2015), language usage, or as he says, speech, forms a *complex system* by following the principles of

> (1) continuing dynamic activity in the system, (2) random interaction of large numbers of components, (3) exchange of information with feedback, (4) reinforcement of behaviors, (5) emergence of stable patterns without central control. (Kretzschmar 2015: 11)

Maybe all this means stretching the concept of patterns in language and linguistics too far for being useful. We hope, however, that this discussion demonstrates which patterns we as linguists actually continuously apply. In this sense, our ways of *thinking about language* are also highly patterned. Our theories of language as well as about "the world" follow deeply ingrained patterns of thought that may, potentially, at times hinder us in seeing new aspects to a phenomenon. To take an example, the attitudes of thinking about non-standard forms of language usage have changed over the last 50 to 60 years, due to the developments in sociolinguistics, anthropological linguistics, and psycholinguistics. Maybe we do good in questioning our own assumptions about language once in a while, its relation to communication, and the theories and patterns on our minds that form the way how we perceive of and evaluate language usage, linguistic variation and change (see e.g. Kabak, this volume), or different linguistic theories.

Given the variety of ways in which patterns may be perceived and investigated in language as well as in linguistic communication, the contributions in this volume can only represent a very small selection of possible approaches and views. If, however, this volume helps in questioning and scrutinizing the patterns on our minds concerning how we think about language and how it functions – and maybe motivate some to go beyond old patterns and look for new, meaningful language patterns – we hope that we have reached the aim of widening our perspective on linguistics, on language and its relation to the world that it represents and creates.

References

Aarts, Bas, David Dension, Evelien Keizer & Gergana Popova (eds.). 2004. *Fuzzy grammar. A reader*. Oxford: Oxford University Press.

Arnon, Inbal. 2010. More than words: Frequency effects for multi-word phrases. *Journal of Memory and Language* 62 (1). 67–82.
Austin, John L. 1962. *How to do things with words*. Oxford: Clarendon.
Bakhtin, Mikhail M. 1981 [1934–35]. Discourse in the novel. In Michael Holquist (ed.), *The dialogic imagination. Four essays by M.M. Bakhtin*. [Translated by Caryl Emerson and Michael Holquist], 259–422. Austin, TX: University of Texas Press.
Barlow, Michael & Suzanne Kemmer (eds.). 2000. *Usage-based models of language*. Stanford: CSLI.
Barnbrook, Geoff. 2002. *Defining language: A local grammar of definition sentences*. Amsterdam: John Benjamins.
Bednarek, Monika. 2008. *Emotion talk across corpora*. Palgrave Macmillan.
Belletti, Adriana & Luigi Rizzi. 2002. Editors' introduction: Some concepts and issues in linguistic theory. In Adriana Belletti & Luigi Rizzi (eds.), *Noam Chomsky, on nature and language*, 1–44. Cambridge: Cambridge University Press.
Benveniste, Emile. 1974 [1972]. *Probleme der allgemeinen Sprachwissenschaft* (*Problèmes de linguistique générale*). [Translated by Wilhelm Bolle]. München: Paul List.
Biber, Doug. 1988. *Variation across speech and writing*. Cambridge: Cambridge University Press.
Biber, Doug. 1995. *Dimensions of register variation. A cross-linguistic comparison*. Cambridge: Cambridge University Press.
Biber, Doug & Susan Conrad. 2001. Register variation: A corpus approach. In Deborah Schiffrin, Deborah Tannen & Heidi E. Hamilton (eds.), *The handbook of discourse analysis*, 175–196. Oxford & Malden, MA: Blackwell.
Biber, Doug & Susan Conrad. 2009. *Register, genre, and style*. Cambridge: Cambridge University Press.
Bickerton, Derek. 1995. *Language and human behavior*. London: UCL Press.
Bloomfield, Leonard. 1933. *Language*. New York: Henry Holt and Co.
Blumenthal-Dramé, Alice. 2012. *Entrenchment in usage-based theories. What corpus data do and do not reveal about the mind*. Berlin: Mouton de Gruyter.
Booij, Geert. 2010. *Construction morphology*. Oxford & New York: Oxford University Press.
Brezina, Vaclav, Tony McEnery & Stephen Wattam. 2015. Collocations in context: A new perspective on collocation networks. *International Journal of Corpus Linguistics* 20 (2). 139–173.
Bühler, Karl. 1965 [1934]. *Sprachtheorie. Die Darstellungsfunktion der Sprache*. 2nd edn. Stuttgart: Gustav Fischer Verlag.
Burke, Michael. 2014. Introduction: Stylistics from classical rhetorics to cognitive neuroscience. In Michael Burke (ed.), *The Routledge handbook of stylistics*. 1–8. London & New York: Routledge.
Busse, Beatrix. 2018. Current British English: A sociolinguistic perspective. In Vaclav Brezina, Robbie Love & Karin Aijmer (eds.), *Corpus approaches to contemporary British speech: Sociolinguistic studies of the Spoken BNC2014*, 16–26. London & New York: Routledge.
Busse, Beatrix. 2019. Patterns of discursive urban place-making in Brooklyn, New York. In Viola Wiegand & Michaela Mahlberg (eds.), *Corpus linguistics, context and culture*, 11–21. Berlin: de Gruyter Mouton.
Bußmann, Hadumod (ed.). 2002. *Lexikon der Sprachwissenschaft*. 3rd edn. Stuttgart: Kröner.
Bybee, Joan L. 2007. *Frequency of use and the organization of language*. Oxford & New York: Oxford University Press.
Bybee, Joan L. 2010. *Language, usage and cognition*. Cambridge: Cambridge University Press.
Bybee, Joan L., Revere Perkins & William Pagliuca. 1994. *The evolution of grammar: Tense, aspect and modality in the languages of the world*. Chicago: University of Chicago Press.

Bybee, Joan L. & Paul Hopper. 2001. Introduction to frequency and the emergence of linguistic structure. In Joan Bybee & Paul Hopper (eds.), *Frequency and the emergence of linguistic structure*, 1–24. Amsterdam: Benjamins.

Chambers, Jack. 2004. Dynamic typology and vernacular universals. In Bernd Kortmann (ed.), *Dialectology meets typology*, 127–145. Berlin: Mouton de Gruyter.

Chomsky, Noam. 1957. *Syntactic structures*. The Hague: Mouton.

Chomsky, Noam. 1965. *Aspects of the theory of syntax*. Cambridge, MA: MIT Press.

Chomsky, Noam. 1986. *Knowledge of language. Its nature, origin and use*. Westport & London: Praeger.

Conrad, Susan. 2015. Register variation. In Doug Biber & Randi Reppen (eds.), *The Cambridge handbook of English corpus linguistics*, 309–329. Cambridge: Cambridge University Press.

Couper-Kuhlen, Elizabeth & Margret Selting. 2018. *Interactional linguistics. Studying language in social interaction*. Cambridge: Cambridge University Press.

Cowan, Nelson. 2000. The magical number 4 in short-term memory: A reconsideration of mental storage capacity. *Behavioral and Brain Sciences* 24. 87–185.

Croft, William. 1991. *Syntactic categories and grammatical relations. The cognitive organization of information*. Chicago: Chicago University Press.

Croft, William. 2001. *Radical construction grammar: Syntactic theory in typological perspective*. Oxford: Oxford University Press.

Croft, William & D. Alan Cruse. 2004. *Cognitive linguistics*. Cambridge: Cambridge University Press.

De Smet, Hendrik. 2013. *Spreading patterns: Diffusional change in the English system of complementation*. Oxford & New York: Oxford University Press.

Dreitzel, Hans Peter (ed.). 1970. *Patterns of communicative behavior*. London: Macmillan.

Duranti, Alessandro. 1997. *Linguistic anthropology*. Cambridge: Cambridge University Press.

Ebeling, Jarle & Signe Oksefjell Ebeling. 2013. *Patterns in contrast*. Amsterdam: John Benjamins.

Eckert, Penelope. 2012. Three waves of variation study: The emergence of meaning in the study of sociolinguistic variation. *Annual Review of Anthropology* 41. 87–100.

Eckert, Penelope. 2018. *Meaning and linguistic variation: The third wave in sociolinguistics*. Cambridge: Cambridge University Press.

Enfield, Nick J., Paul Kockelmann & Jack Sidnell (eds.). 2014. *The Cambridge handbook of linguistic anthropology*. Cambridge: Cambridge University Press.

Ellis, Nick C. & Eric Frey 2009. The psycholinguistic reality of collocation and semantic prosody (2): Affective priming. In Roberta Corrigan, Edith A. Moravcsik, Hamid Ouali & Kathleen Wheatley (eds.), *Formulaic language*. Vol. 2: *Acquisition, loss, psychological reality, and functional explanations*, 473–497. Amsterdam: John Benjamins.

Everett, Daniel. 2013. *Language. The cultural tool*. London: Profile Books.

Fillmore, J. Charles. 1976. Frame semantics and the nature of language. *Annals of the New York Academy of Sciences: Conference on the Origin and Development of Language and Speech* 280. 20–32.

Fillmore, J. Charles. 1982. Frame semantics. In Linguistic Society of Korea (ed.), *Linguistics in the Morning Calm*, 111–138. Seoul: Hanshin.

Fillmore, J. Charles, Paul Kay & Mary C. O'Connor. 1988. Regularity and idiomaticity in grammatical constructions: The case of *let alone*. *Language* 64 (3). 501–538.

Firth, John. 1957. *Papers in linguistics*. Oxford: Oxford University Press.

Fischer, Olga. 2013. An inquiry into unidirectionality as a foundational element of grammaticalization. On the role played by analogy and the synchronic grammar system in processes of language change. *Studies in Language* 37 (3). 515–533.

Fischer, Olga. 2016. Presidential address. ISLE-4. 4th Conference of the International Society for the Linguistics of English, Poznań, 18–21 September 2016.
Flowerdew, John, ed. 2014. *Discourse in context*. London & New York: Bloomsbury.
Goldberg, Adele E. 1995. *Constructions. A construction grammar approach to argument structure*. Chicago & London: The University of Chicago Press.
Goldberg, Adele E. 2006. *Constructions at work. The nature of generalization in language*. Oxford & New York: Oxford University Press.
Green, Clarence. 2017. Usage-based linguistics and the magic number four. *Cognitive Linguistics* 28 (2). 209–237.
Grice, Herbert P. 1989. *Studies in the way of words*. Cambridge, MA: Harvard University Press.
Gries, Stephan Th. 2008. Phraseology and linguistic theory: A brief survey. In Sylvaine Granger & Fanny Meunier (eds.), *Phraseology. An interdisciplinary perspective*, 3–25. Amsterdam: John Benjamins.
Gries, Stefan Th. 2010. Corpus linguistics and theoretical linguistics: a love–hate relationship? Not necessarily ... *International Journal of Corpus Linguistics* 15 (3). 327–343.
Gries, Stefan Th. & Anatol Stefanowitsch. 2004 Extending collostructional analysis: A corpus-based perspectives on 'alternations'. *International Journal of Corpus Linguistics* 9 (1). 97–129.
Gries, Stefan Th. & Dagmar Divjak (eds.). 2012. *Frequency effects in language learning and processing*. Berlin: de Gruyter Mouton.
Gumperz, John J. 1968. Types of linguistic communities. In Joshua H. Fishman (ed.), *Readings in the sociology of language*, 460–472. The Hague: Mouton.
Halliday, Michael A. K. 2002 [1971]. Linguistic function and literary style: an inquiry into the language of William Golding's *The Inheritors*. In Jonathan J. Webster (ed.), *Linguistic studies of text and discourse: Volume 2 in the collected works of M. A. K. Halliday*, 88–125. London: Continuum.
Halliday, Michael A. K. 1978. *Language as a social semiotic: The social interpretation of language and meaning*. London. Arnold.
Halliday, Michael A. K. 2007 [1991]. The notion of "context" in language education. In Jonathan J. Webster (ed.), *Language and education: Volume 9 in the collected works of M. A. K. Halliday*, 269–290. London: Continuum.
Halliday, Michael A. K. & Christian M. I. M. Matthiesen. 2004. *An introduction to functional grammar*. 3rd edn. London: Arnold.
Harley, Trevor A. 2014. *The psychology of language. From data to theory*. 4th edn. London & New York: Routledge.
Haspelmath, Martin. 2015. Framework-free grammatical theory. In Bernd Heine & Heiko Narrog (eds.), *The Oxford handbook of linguistic analysis*, 287–310. Oxford: Oxford University Press.
Heine, Bernd & Tania Kuteva. 2005. *Language contact and grammatical change*. Cambridge: Cambridge University Press.
Herder, Johann Gottfried. 1966 [1772]. *Abhandlung über den Ursprung der Sprache*. [Ed. by Hans Dietrich Irmscher]. Stuttgart: Reclam.
Hjelmslev, Louis. 1968. *Die Sprache: Eine Einführung*. Darmstadt: Wissenschaftliche Buchgesellschaft.
Hjelmslev, Louis. 1974. *Prolegomena zu einer Sprachtheorie*. München: Hueber.
Hockett, Charles F. 1963 [1958]. *A course in modern linguistics*. 6th edn. New York: Macmillan.
Hoey, Michael. 2005. *Lexical priming: A new theory of words and language*. London: Routledge.

Hopper, Paul. 1988. Emergent Grammar and the A Priori Grammar postulate. In Deborah Tannen (ed.), *Linguistics in context. Connecting observation and understanding. Lectures from the 1985 LSA/TESOL and NEH Institutes*, 117–134. Norwood, NJ: Ablex.

Hopper, Paul. 2007. Linguistics and micro-rhetoric: A twenty-first century encounter. *Journal of English Linguistics* 35 (3). 236–252.

Hopper, Paul & Elizabeth Traugott. 2003. *Grammaticalization*. 2nd edn. Cambridge: Cambridge University Press.

Hornby, Albert S. 1954. *A guide to patterns and usage in English*. London: Oxford University Press.

Humboldt, Wilhelm von. 1994 [1820]. Ueber das vergleichende Sprachstudium. In Jürgen Trabant (ed.), *Wilhelm von Humboldt: Über die Sprache, Reden vor der Akademie*, 11–32. Tübingen & Basel: Francke.

Humboldt, Wilhelm von. 1994 [1822]. Ueber das Entstehen der grammatischen Formen. In Jürgen Trabant (ed.), *Wilhelm von Humboldt: Über die Sprache, Reden vor der Akademie*, 52–81. Tübingen & Basel: Francke.

Hunston, Susan. 2014. Pattern grammar in context. In Thomas Herbst, Hans-Jörg Schmid & Susen Faulhaber (eds.), *Constructions, collocations, patterns*, 99–119. Berlin: De Gruyter Mouton.

Hunston, Susan & Gill Francis. 2000. *Pattern Grammar: A corpus-driven approach to the lexical grammar of English*. Amsterdam: John Benjamins.

Hunston, Susan & Hang Su. 2017. Patterns, constructions, and local grammar: A case study of 'evaluation'. *Applied Linguistics* amx046. 1–28. (https:// doi.org/10.1093/applin/amx046)

Hymes, Dell. 1964. Toward ethnographies of communication. *American Anthropologist* 66. 1–34.

Hymes, Dell H. 1968. The ethnography of speaking. In Joshua H. Fishman (ed.), *Readings in the sociology of language*, 99–138. The Hague: Mouton.

Jackendoff, Ray. 1994. *Patterns in the mind. Language and human nature*. New York: Basic Books.

Jakobson, Roman & Morris Halle. 1960. *Grundlagen der Sprache*. Berlin. Berlin: Akademie Verlag.

Jeffries, Lesley & Daniel McIntyre. 2010. *Stylistics*. Cambridge: Cambridge University Press.

Johansson, Stig & Signe Oksefjell (eds.). 1998. *Corpora and cross-linguistic research*. Amsterdam: Rodopi.

Johnstone, Barbara. 2008. *Discourse analysis*. 2nd edn. Malden, MA: Blackwell.

Kahnemann, Daniel. 2012. *Thinking, fast and slow*. London: Penguin Books.

Kay, Paul. 1999. Grammatical constructions and linguistic generalizations: The *What's X doing Y?* construction. *Language* 75 (1). 1–33.

Kemmer, Suzanne & Michael Barlow. 2000. Introduction: a usage-based conception of language. In Michael Barlow & Suzanne Kemmer (eds.), *Usage-based models of language*, vii–xxii. Stanford: CSLI.

Kortmann, Bernd & Benedikt Szmrecsanyi. 2004. Global synopsis: Morphological and syntactic variation in English. In Bernd Kortmann & Edgar W. Schneider (eds.), *A handbook of varieties of English. A multimedia reference tool*. Vol. 2: *Morphology and syntax*, 1142–1202. Berlin: de Gruyter Mouton.

Kortmann, Bernd & Christoph Wolk. 2012. Morphosyntactic variation in the anglophone world: A global perspective. In Bernd Kortmann & Kerstin Lunkenheimer (eds.), *The Mouton world atlas of variation in English*, 906–936. Berlin: de Gruyter Mouton.

Kress, Gunther. 2010. *Multimodality: A social semiotic approach to contemporary communication*. New York: Routledge.

Kretzschmar, William A. Jr. 2009. *The linguistics of speech*. Cambridge: Cambridge University Press.

Kretzschmar, William A. Jr. 2015. *Language and complex systems*. Cambridge: Cambridge University Press.
Labov, William. 1972. *Sociolinguistic patterns*. University of Pennsylvania Press.
Labov, William. 1975. *What is a linguistic fact?* Berlin: de Gruyter.
Lakoff, George. 1987. *Women, fire and dangerous things: What categories reveal about the mind*. Chicago: University of Chicago Press.
Langacker, Ronald W. 1987. *Foundations of Cognitive Grammar*. Vol. 1: *Theoretical prerequisites*. Stanford, CA: Stanford University Press.
Langacker, Ronald W. ³1991. *Foundations of Cognitive Grammar*. Vol. 2: *Descriptive applications*. Stanford, CA: Stanford University Press.
Langacker, Ronald W. 2000. *Grammar and conceptualization*. Berlin: Mouton de Gruyter.
Langacker, Ronald W. 2009. *Investigations in Cognitive Grammar*. Berlin: de Gruyter.
Leech, Geoffrey N. 1983. *Principles of pragmatics*. London: Longman.
Leech, Geoffrey N. 1991. The state of the art in corpus linguistics. In Karin Aijmer & Bengt Altenberg (eds.), *English corpus linguistics*, 8–29. London: Longman.
Leech, Geoffrey N. 1992. Corpora and theories of performance. In Jan Svartvik (ed.), *Directions in corpus linguistics*, 105–122. Berlin: Mouton de Gruyter.
Leech, Geoffrey N. 2000. Grammars of spoken English: New outcomes of corpus-oriented research. *Language Learning* 50. 675–724.
Leech, Geoffrey N. 2014. *The pragmatics of politeness*. Oxford & New York: Oxford University Press.
Levinson, Stephen C. 1983. *Pragmatics*. Cambridge: Cambridge University Press.
Maynard, Douglas W. 2012. Everyone and no one to turn to: Intellectual roots and contexts for conversation analysis. In Jack Sidnell & Tanya Stivers (eds.), *The handbook of conversation analysis*, 11–31. Oxford: Wiley-Blackwell.
McEnery, Tony & Andrew Wilson. 1996. *Corpus linguistics*. Edinburgh: Edinburgh University Press.
Mengden, Ferdinand von & Evie Coussé. 2014. Introduction. The role of change in usage-based conceptions of language. In Evie Coussé & Ferdinand von Mengden (eds.), *Usage-based approaches to language change*, 1–19. Berlin: de Gruyter Mouton.
Miller, George A. 1956. The magical number seven, plus or minus two: Some limits on our capacity for processing information. *Psychological Review* 63 (2). 81–97.
Milroy, Lesley. 1987. *Language and social networks*. New York: Blackwell.
Milroy, Lesley & James Milroy. 1987. *Authority in language. Investigating language prescription and standardisation*. London: Routledge and Kegan Paul.
Milroy, Lesley & Matthew Gordon. 2003. *Sociolinguistics: Method and interpretation*. Oxford & Malden, MA: Blackwell.
Möhlig-Falke, Ruth. 2012. *The early English impersonal construction. An analysis of verbal and constructional meaning*. Oxford: Oxford University Press.
Mühlhäusler, Peter. 1997. *Pidgin and creole linguistics*. 2nd edn. London: University of Westminster Press.
Nunan, David. 2008. Exploring genre and register in contemporary English. *English Today* 24 (2). 56–61.
Nuyts, Jan. 2008. Pattern versus process concepts of grammar and mind: A cognitive-functional perspective. *Linguistics (Jezikoslovlje)* 9 (2). 87–107.
OED: Simpson, John (ed.) 2000–. *The Oxford English dictionary*. 3rd edn. online. Oxford University Press. (http://www.oed.com/; last accessed 3 May 2019)

O'Halloran, Kay L., Sabine Tan & Marissa K. L. E. 2014. A multimodal approach to discourse, context and culture. In John Flowerdew (ed.), *Discourse in context*, 247–272. London & New York: Bloomsbury.
Palmer, Gary B. 1996. *Toward a theory of cultural linguistics*. Austin, TX: University of Texas Press.
Paltridge, Brian. 2015. Language, identity, and communities of practice. In Dwi Noverini Djenar, Ahmar Mahboob & Ken Cruickshank (eds.), *Language and identity across modes of communication*, 15–25. Berlin: de Gruyter Mouton.
Partington, Alan, Alison Duguid & Charlotte Taylor. 2013. *Patterns and meanings in discourse. Theory and practice in Corpus-Assisted Discourse Studies (CADS)*. Amsterdam: John Benjamins.
Paul, Hermann. 1909. *Prinzipien der Sprachgeschichte*. 4th edn. Halle: Niemeyer.
Pennycook, Alastair & Emi Otsuji. 2015. *Metrolingualism. Language in the city*. London & New York: Routledge.
Piattelli, Massimo, ed. 2004 [1980]. Language and learning: The debate between Jean Piaget and Noam Chomsky. In Barbara C. Lust & Claire Foley (eds.), *First language acquisition: The essential readings*, 64–97. Oxford: Blackwell.
Pinker, Steven. 1994. *The language instinct*. London: Penguin.
Pinker, Steven. 1999. *Words and rules*. London: Phoenix.
Plag, Ingo. 1999. *Morphological productivity. Structural constraints in English derivation*. Berlin: Mouton de Gruyter.
Rebuschat, Patrick E., Detmar Meurers & Tony McEnery. 2017. Language learning research at the intersection of experimental, computational and corpus-based approaches. *Language Learning* 67 (S1). 6–13.
Sacks, Harvey, Emanuel A. Schegloff & Gail Jefferson. 1974. A simplest systematics for the organisation of turn-taking in conversation. *Language* 50 (4). 696–735.
Sapir, Edward. 1929. The status of linguistics as a science. *Language* 5 (4). 207–214.
Saussure, Ferdinand de. 1967 [1915]. *Cours de linguistique générale*. [Edited by Charles Bally & Albert Sechehaye]. 3rd edn. Paris: Payot.
Saussure, Ferdinand de. 1993 [1915]. *Course in general linguistics*. [Edited by Charles Bally & Albert Sechehaye. Translated and annotated by Roy Harris]. 3rd edn. London: Duckworth.
Searle, John R. 1969. *Speech acts*. Cambridge: Cambridge University Press.
Searle, John R. 1979. *Expression and meaning: Studies in the theory of speech acts*. Cambridge: Cambridge University Press.
Searle, John. 1995. *The construction of social reality*. London: The Free Press.
Seuren, Pieter A.M. 1998. *Western linguistics. An historical introduction*. Oxford & Malden MA: Blackwell.
Sharifian, Farzad. 2015. Cultural linguistics. In Farzad Sharifian (ed.), *The Routledge handbook of language and culture*, 473–492. London: Routledge.
Sidnell, Jack & Tanya Stivers (eds.). 2013. *The handbook of conversation analysis*. Chichester: Wiley-Blackwell.
Sievers, Eduard. 1885. *Grundzüge der Lautphysiologie zur Einführung in das Studium der Lautlehre der indogermanischen Sprachen*. 3rd edn. Leipzig: Breitkopf & Härtel.
Sinclair, John. 1991. *Corpus, concordance, collocation*. Oxford: Oxford University Press.
Sinclair, John. 2004. *Trust the text. Language, corpus and discourse*. London & New York: Routledge.
Stefanowitsch, Anatol & Stephan Th. Gries. 2003. Collostructions: Investigating the interaction of words and constructions. *International Journal of Corpus Linguistics* 8 (2). 209–243.
Stubbs, Michael. 2002. Two quantitative methods of studying phraseology in English. *International Journal of Corpus Linguistics* 7. 215–244.

Stubbs, Michael. 2013. Sequence and order. The neo-Firthian tradition of corpus semantics. In Hilde Hasselgård, Jarle Ebeling & Signe Oksefjell Ebeling (eds.), *Corpus perspectives on patterns of lexis*, 13–34. Amsterdam: John Benjamins.

Sweet, Henry. 1900. *A new English grammar logical and historical*. Vol. I: *Introduction, phonology, and accidence*. Oxford: Clarendon.

Tavárez, David. 2014. Ritual language. In Nick J. Enfield, Paul Kockelmann & Jack Sidnell (eds.), *The Cambridge handbook of linguistic anthropology*, 516–536. Cambridge: Cambridge University Press.

Taylor, Talbot J. & Deborah Cameron. 1987. *Analysing conversation: Rules and units in the structure of talk*. Oxford: Pergamon.

Teubert, Wolfgang. 2010. *Meaning, discourse and society*. Cambridge: Cambridge University Press.

Teubert, Wolfgang. 2013. Die Wirklichkeit des Diskurses. In Dietrich Busse & Wolfgang Teubert (eds.), *Linguistische Diskursanalyse: Neue Perspektiven*, 55–146. Wiesbaden: Springer.

Theakston, Anna L., Paul Ibbotson, Daniel Freudenthal, Elena V. M. Lieven & Michael Tomasello. 2015. Productivity of noun slots in verb frames. *Cognitive Science* 39. 1369–1395.

Tomasello, Michael. 1999. *The cultural origins of human cognition*. Cambridge, MA: Harvard University Press.

Tomasello, Michael. 2000. The item-based nature of children's early syntactic development. *Trends in Cognitive Sciences* 4 (4). 156–163.

Tomasello, Michael. 2003. *Constructing a language. A usage-based theory of language acquisition*. Cambridge, MA: Harvard University Press.

Tomasello, Michael. 2014. *A natural history of human thinking*. Cambridge, MA: Harvard University Press.

Tognini-Bonelli, Elena. 2001. *Corpus linguistics at work*. Amsterdam: John Benjamins.

Traugott, Elizabeth Closs & Richard B. Dasher. 2002. *Regularity in semantic change*. Cambridge: Cambridge University Press.

Traugott, Elizabeth Closs & Graeme Trousdale. 2013. *Constructionalization and constructional Changes*. Oxford: Oxford University Press.

Trubetzkoy, Nikolai. 1969 [1939]. *Principles of Phonology*. Berkeley: University of California Press.

Trudgill, Peter (ed.). 1978. *Sociolinguistic patterns in British English*. London: Arnold.

Trudgill, Peter. 2011. *Sociolinguistic typology: Social determinants of linguistic complexity*. Oxford & New York: Oxford University Press.

Van Dijk, Teun A. 2008. *Discourse and context: A socio-cognitive approach*. Cambridge: Cambridge University Press.

Van Dijk, Teun A. 2009. *Society and discourse: How social contexts influence text and talk*. Cambridge: Cambridge University Press.

Weinreich, Uriel. 1963. *Languages in contact: Findings and problems*. 2nd edn. The Hague: Mouton.

Whorf, Benjamin Lee. 2012 [1945]. Grammatical categories. In John B. Carroll (ed.), *Language, thought, and reality: Selected writings of Benjamin Lee Whorf*, 113–130. Cambridge, MA: MIT Press.

Whorf, Benjamin Lee. 2012 [1956]. Science and linguistics. In John B. Carroll (ed.), *Language, thought, and reality: Selected writings of Benjamin Lee Whorf*, 212–214. Cambridge, MA: MIT Press.

Winford, Donald 2003. *An introduction to contact linguistics*. Oxford & Malden, MA: Blackwell.

Ziem, Alexander. 2014. *Frames of understanding in text and discourse: Theoretical foundations and descriptive applications*. Amsterdam: John Benjamins.

Michael Stubbs
How to do things with intertextual patterns: On Umberto Eco's *The Name of the Rose*

I like to listen to words, and then I think about them. (William of Baskerville)

Abstract: The unresolved debate about where the meaning of a text is located – in the text itself or in the mind of the reader – can be approached empirically by studying the relation between an individual text and its intertext. The basic idea of intertextuality is that a pattern in one text repeats a pattern in an earlier text, that readers recognize this repetition, and that this affects how they interpret the text. In terms of theory, this concept has changed how we see the relation between author, text and reader. The author's intention is less relevant than the reader's understanding of the text itself and of other related texts. The concept is widespread in literary and cultural studies, but has been largely neglected within linguistics. This is odd, first, because literary theorists regularly acknowledge the origins of the concept in Saussure's demonstration that all meaning is relational, and second, because corpus studies (especially concordance data) have shown that words mean what they do because of the patterns in which they have occurred in the past.

In terms of method, there is a severe problem of subjectivity. A repeated pattern such as a word-for-word quotation can be objectively identified. However, a "plot" is a very abstract pattern, which may be impossible to define formally. A decision as to whether two plots represent a meaningful parallel, or only a coincidental similarity, inevitably depends on individual interpretations. In both cases, since it is readers who must recognize both what is being repeated and why, it follows that this subjectivity limits the possibility of replicable analysis.

This article is a case study of Umberto Eco's *The Name of the Rose*. Since the novel provides a very diverse range of intertextual references, it can be used to test the concept of intertextuality itself. It can also be used to assess whether narrative fiction can express ideas in a way which is difficult or impossible in conventional academic prose: that is, whether a novel can contribute to theory. The novel was written in Italian and has been translated into over twenty languages. These translations are paraphrases (that is, intertextual variants) of each other. Since many points are independent of the language of the text, I mainly discuss its English

---

Michael Stubbs, Trier University, English Department, 54286 Trier, Germany, stubbs@uni-trier.de

https://doi.org/10.1515/9783110596656-003

translation. However, some meanings are generated by the English-language text, and may be absent or less evident in translations into other languages.

1 Preamble

It has long been debated how much of the meaning of a text is in the text itself, and how much is in the mind of the reader. An empirical approach to this question is to study the relation between an individual text and its intertext.[1]

I will discuss the concept of intertextuality by using examples from Umberto Eco's *The Name of the Rose* (henceforth *NR*, Eco 1983). The novel contains very many intertextual references, and also much literary, linguistic, philosophical and religious content. It was explicitly designed in this way (Eco 1984a), and therefore lends itself to discussing whether narrative fiction can express ideas which are difficult or even impossible to express in conventional academic prose. That is, can fiction contribute to theory?

The article has two specific connections to the overall theme of this book. In terms of the content of *NR*, throughout the whole novel the characters constantly debate about pattern, design and order, including a false pattern which leads to the truth. In terms of general theory, intertextuality involves the repetition of a semantic pattern across two or more texts, with the proviso that the reader recognizes the repetition and its purpose. This type of pattern recognition is much discussed by literary theorists, but largely neglected by linguists.

I begin by discussing my data and some essential concepts. I then discuss whether the concept of intertextuality meets standard empirical criteria of objectivity and falsifiability.

2 History, terminology, etc.

The concept of intertextuality is very widely used within literary and cultural studies (in December 2017 JSTOR indexed over 1,000 items with "intertext*" in the title). The term itself is usually attributed to Kristeva (1969). Allen (2000) provides a good overview and references to other important theorists, including Bakhtin, Barthes, Eco, Foucault, Genette, and Riffaterre.

---

[1] For critical comments on an earlier draft I am grateful to Gabi Keck, Jim Stansfield, Amanda Murphy (who wishes to reserve her position on several points) and two anonymous referees.

The concept is neglected within linguistics, though see Hüllen (1987) on *NR*, and publications by De Beaugrande (2000), Fairclough (1995), Lemke (2000) and Teubert (2010). This neglect is part and parcel of the neglect of textual study (including literary texts) which has plagued linguistics from the 1960s onwards, but is nevertheless odd. First, literary theorists regularly acknowledge Saussure's proposals for semiotics and his demonstrations that all meaning is relational and therefore ultimately circular. Second, corpus linguists have shown in detail that we know what expressions mean because of the way in which they have been used in the past. Since anything we say is always a reaction to things which have been said before, all texts are related diachronically to other texts. It is only if utterances can be related to other utterances that discourse becomes coherent and understandable. Any theory of text is therefore incomplete without a theory of intertext, but empirical corpus findings have hardly been used to relate the literary concept of intertextuality to textual data.

The main interest of the concept is how it sees the relation between author, text and reader. It plays down the role of the author in the meaning of what they write, because texts depend on other texts, and on what the reader recognizes, rather than on what the author may have intended. This is the point underlying Barthes' slogan "the death of the author" (Barthes 1977 [1967]). Since meanings differ across different readers, texts cannot be given a single stable interpretation.

A clear illustration that texts have different meanings for different readers is that *NR* has been reviewed from an extraordinarily wide range of points of view, in the popular press, as well as in specialist journals for anthropologists (Carroll 1984), historians (Burton Russell 1983), librarians (Garrett 1991), philosophers (Baxter 1989), and of course literary scholars (e.g. Cobley 1989). Academic readers who know Eco's books on semiotics, including the philosophy of C. S. Peirce, on popular culture, including detective stories, plus his literary and cultural parodies (e.g. Eco 1984b; Eco and Sebeok 1983) will read the novel with these other texts in mind.

At its simplest, intertextuality is repetition. A pattern in one text repeats a pattern from another text. More precisely, a unit of meaning in one text is a referring expression whose referent is a unit of meaning in another text. This already creates a problem of interpretation, since it is an axiom of corpus linguistics that meaning and co-text are related. So the units don't mean the same. In addition, since the referent is itself in a text, it can turn into a referring expression – and so on *ad infinitum*. This is part of what Peirce calls "infinite semiosis". This is also a favourite expression of Umberto Eco's (e.g. Eco 1992: 23).

Despite the apparent simplicity and plausibility of the concept – repetition of a semantic pattern – and despite hundreds of articles on the topic since the 1960s, there remain serious conceptual problems. "Intertextuality" is often a cover term for a wide range of relations, including allusion, imitation, implicit meaning, leitmotif, paraphrase, parody, pastiche, quotation and sub-text (not to mention plagiarism). The terms themselves are not important, however they indicate that intertextual references range from unproblematic examples, which are observable and objectively identifiable (e.g. explicit references and word-for-word quotations), via quotations which have been modified, to problematic examples which would be impossible to identify automatically in raw text (e.g. similar plots). A word-for-word quotation is objectively definable. But it is unclear how to establish whether two plots show significant parallels or only coincidental similarities. The most problematic cases might be allusions to shared knowledge, which would seem to be inherently subjective, and therefore of limited use for replicable analyses of observable textual data.

In what follows, quotations from *NR* and other books are in double quote marks, word-forms are in italics, and lemmas and word families are in upper case (e.g. the word family HERESY is realized by words such as *heresy* and *heretic*).

3 The data

NR was published in Italian in 1980. I will quote the English translation by William Weaver (unattributed page references are to Eco 1983). Most points are independent of the language of the text, but some do depend on the English-language translation, which inevitably generates meanings which were not intended by the author, and which may be less evident in versions in other languages. As Eco (1992: 74) says: "The text is there, and it produces its own effects".

In studying a concept, it is often productive to take an extreme example. *The Name of the Rose* by Umberto Eco is such a case: a 500-page best-selling postmodernist novel, which was deliberately designed to include a large number of intertextual references. The novel is an esoteric game, packed with so many elaborate allusions that no average reader could possibly recognize them all. Haft et al. (1987) have therefore published a "key" to the historical figures and events and translated all the non-English passages. *NR* shows that a theory of intertextuality has to account for a wide range of units, which rely on both specialized literary knowledge and also everyday cultural knowledge.

3.1 Plot and content

After a parodic Preface by an anonymous and pedantic narrator, an old German monk, Adso or Adson[2] of Melk tells of dramatic events which he witnessed as a naïve young novice. His first-person narrative takes place over seven days in 1327 in a Benedictine monastery in Italy. Adso and his teacher, an English Franciscan called William of Baskerville, arrive in the monastery shortly after a monk has died under suspicious circumstances. Other monks die in increasingly bizarre ways, and William investigates using his powers of observation, logic and textual interpretation (though the last method leads him partly astray). It becomes clear that the dead monks were all looking for a book, which is referred to in other books, but is hidden or lost, or was perhaps never written at all. Only the librarian and his assistant are allowed to enter the monastic library, which is constructed as a labyrinth, in order to hide books from those forbidden to read them. This whodunnit plot alternates with an account of religious politics: William has travelled to the monastery to mediate between the Franciscans and Pope John XXII.

These two plots are related. One concerns a search for Aristotle's book on comedy, which is considered heretical. The other concerns a debate about a biblical interpretation which is considered heretical. It is clear simply from raw frequencies of occurrence that "heresy" is a key semantic field. Members of the word family *heresy/ies*, *heretic/s/ical*, *heresiarch*, etc. occur over 200 times (see below).

The novel revolves around intellectual jokes and parody. First, it turns out that the book for which everyone is searching – a book about comedy – is itself one of the murder weapons. Second, *NR* is both a murder-mystery, and a parody of a detective story. William finds the villain and the book, but as a result of faulty reasoning, and his investigations have disastrous results: the book, the library and the whole monastery are destroyed. Despite the validity of the concept of the "intentional fallacy" (Wimsatt and Beardsley 1946), in cases of parody, the intention of the author is not in doubt. Parody depends on formal patterns in two texts, but also on a communicative relation between author and reader. The author must, by definition, intend the reader to recognize the parody, and if the reader does not recognize this intention, then the communication fails.

Several topics in *NR* are of immediate, but superficial, interest to linguists. The story takes place in a multilingual monastery, and involves signs and symbols, cryptography, handwriting analysis, syllogisms, and deduction, induction and abduction (à la Peirce). The elementary discussion of these ideas – in itself –

---

[2] Throughout the novel, he is referred to as "Adso". But on the first two pages of the Preface, he is given both names. "Adson" makes the similarity to "Watson" more obvious: see below.

hardly justifies serious interest in the novel. However, they suggest a more interesting question. Can literary fiction contribute to linguistic theory?

Is *NR* a poor novel, because the frequent discussion of semiotics detracts from the narrative? Or a good novel, but only superficial philosophy of language? From the point of view of the novel, the story-line is often interrupted by a crude narrative technique, as William explains, often to the naïve Adso, some semiotic principle. For example, with reference to the story in *Genesis* about Adam naming the animals, he formulates the principle that the meaning of words depends on social convention within communities of speakers (*NR*, page 353). From the point of view of the philosophy of language, this principle is likely to be news only to students who have not done an elementary linguistics course. So, does the novel fall between the two stools of narrative practice and semiotic theory? Or does this hybrid genre of literature as linguistic-cultural-philosophical theory demonstrate some things which cannot easily be expressed in conventional academic forms? (Agassi 1970, Baxter 1989, Dubnick 2002).

3.2 Quotations

I should first get some simple examples of intertextuality out of the way. Some intertextual relations between *NR* and other texts are straightforward, though even they illustrate the wide range of references which a theory has to account for. Even quotations depend on whether readers recognize the source and the function of the reference.

Example 1: Probably most readers – though perhaps even this could not be assumed nowadays – recognize the opening sentence of Adso's story (*NR*, page 11) as a Biblical quotation from John 1: 1: "In the beginning was the Word". Perhaps fewer recognize the origin of the phrase "you hypocrites, whited sepulchres" (*NR*, page 347). This is from Matthew 23: 27: "[H]ypocrites! ... ye are like unto whited sepulchres, which indeed appear beautiful outward, but are within full of dead men's bones". Alternatively, they might recognize the word *whited* as unusual, and therefore suspect that Eco is quoting something, even if they do not know what.

Example 2: William quotes Wittgenstein:

> The order that our mind imagines is ... like a ladder, built to attain something. But afterward you must throw the ladder away, because you discover that, even if it is useful, it was meaningless. Er muoz gelîchesame die leiter abewerfen, sô er an ir ufgestigen. (*NR*, page 492.)

This is a translation into Middle High German (Adso's native language) of "Er muss sozusagen die Leiter wegwerfen, nachdem er auf ihr hinaufgestiegen ist" (Wittgenstein 1921: 6.54). Ironically, Haft et al. (1987: 172) do not identify the source, and in addition give a nonsensical translation ("One must cast away, as it were, the ladder, so that he may begin to ascend it."), although the correct translation is given by what William himself has just said. Not everything in literary interpretation is purely subjective: some readings are simply wrong.

Example 3: William quotes the principle that "one should not multiply explanations and causes unless it is strictly necessary" (*NR*, page 91), but does not mention that it is conventionally named "Occam's Razor", after his teacher. This principle might be news to students who have not done an elementary course on scientific method. But this reveals a central problem with the concept of intertextuality. For me, the principle is obvious, because I have come across it frequently, with and without reference to Occam. But I have no memory of where I first encountered it. And then, to explain the phrase "Occam's Razor", we have to explain the joke that Occam uses his razor to shave Plato's beard: i.e. to eliminate unnecessary metaphysical concepts.

Example 4: Quotations may have no single source. In response to a clichéd complaint that learning has declined, William counters (*NR*, page 86) with: "We are dwarfs ... who stand on the shoulders of ... giants, and ... we sometimes manage to see farther on the horizon than they." This is usually attributed to Isaac Newton in the 1600s, but Eco (cited by Bondanella 1997: 16) attributes the quote to Bernard of Chartres in the 1100s.

These are just four examples out of many others which are identified in the commentaries on *NR* or by Eco himself (e.g. Eco 1992). However, listing them does not tell us anything about their literary functions. They may also illustrate cases where the meaning of the text depends on the language of the translation. I do not know how well these references survive outside Western European religious and philosophical traditions, and whether they would be recognized by readers of, say, Chinese or Japanese translations of *NR*.

3.3 Literary and cultural knowledge

NR frequently refers to three sets of texts: the final book of the New Testament (known as the *Book of Revelation* or the *Apocalypse of John*), stories by Jorge Luis Borges (e.g. 1972), and stories about Sherlock Holmes.

Set 1, *Revelation*. The most extensive parallelism is between the novel and the *Book of Revelation*. In seven days, seven monks are killed, in an almost symmetrical pattern.

1	(it turns out) is a suicide
2 and 3	(it turns out) are accidental / self-inflicted, due to handling a book
4	is murder with a blunt instrument
5 and 6	5 is similar to numbers 2 and 3; 6 is rather different
7	is a deliberate suicide, due to eating (*sic.*) the book.

In constructing the plot, Eco clearly started from the *Book of Revelation*, took individual words out of the seven prophecies (*hail, blood, water, sun/moon/stars, scorpion, fire/smoke* and *book/eat*), and made these words significant in the reports of the seven deaths. For example, the first death takes place on a night when snowflakes fell "almost like hail" (*NR*, page 32). The second dead body is found head down in a barrel of pigs' blood (*NR*, page 104). And so on to the seventh death, in which the villain commits suicide by eating the pages of the poisoned book (*NR*, page 480): "I took the little book and ate it up" (*Revelation* 10:10). These are not intertextual allusions – in fact they are not allusions at all, but explicit references to the biblical text, and the necessary quotations from *Revelation* are given in the novel.

Many of the monks believe that the deaths follow the seven prophecies of the seven angels with their seven trumpets. However, their belief depends on very selective over-interpretations of the biblical text, and demonstrates one of Eco's pet hates: the over-interpretation or "paranoid interpretation" of texts to find some hidden meaning (Eco 1992, Bondanella 1997: 129–147). Even William is deceived in this way. Some monks think the deaths follow the prophecies. William starts to think this too. He sees a pattern which relies on taking single words out of context and ignoring other words. The villain realizes that William thinks this and encourages this belief. But it's all over-interpretation. The biblical text has no secret message.

Ultimately, all the disasters in *NR* are due to the censorship and misinterpretation of texts: the deaths of seven monks, the torture by the Inquisition, the loss of the book, the burning of the library, the destruction of the whole monastery. Eco's ultimate joke is that all the death and devastation is due a faulty theory of text analysis: reading expectations into a text, rather than respecting what is there.

Set 2, Jorge Luis Borges. The villain in the novel is Jorge of Burgos, the blind ex-librarian. The name *Jorge of Burgos* refers most obviously to "Jorge Luis Borges", but not so much the person of the Argentinean author, as the cluster of similar themes in his stories: libraries, labyrinths, dreams, visions. One story, *Death and the Compass*, has a similar plot to Eco's novel. A detective thinks that the death of a rabbi and two following deaths follow a kabbalistic pattern taken from Jewish mystical writing.

At the level of the whodunnit plot, Jorge is to Moriarty as William is to Holmes. When Jorge and William finally confront each other, Adso realizes that they admire each other (*NR*, page 472), just as the deadly enemies Moriarty and Holmes admire each other's intelligence (see Conan Doyle's story *The Final Problem*).

Set 3, Sherlock Holmes. Most readers presumably recognize references throughout to Arthur Conan Doyle's stories about Sherlock Holmes. The name *William of Baskerville* alludes most obviously to the story *The Hound of the Baskervilles*. The name of William's assistant, *Adso* or *Adson* (see fn. 2), is similar to the name of Holmes' assistant *Watson*. Like Holmes, William is English, is tall and thin, has a prominent nose, and takes drugs. Adso, in his old age, writes down William's story, just as Watson writes down Sherlock Holmes' adventures many years after the events.

These three sets of intertextual references illustrate further points about the relations between a text, its intertext, and its readers. Since a detailed knowledge of *Revelation* can be assumed of only a small group of modern readers, Eco provides the necessary quotes in the novel itself. Even highly educated readers may not have read Borges. But familiarity with Sherlock Holmes is part of widespread cultural knowledge. General encyclopaedic knowledge is necessary to recognize the parody of a detective story. But specialized academic knowledge is necessary to recognize Eco's criticism of the kind of literary interpretation in which "the rights of interpreters have been overstressed" (Eco 1992: 23).

4 Unlimited intertextuality

Culler (1976) warns against the tendency to reduce intertextuality to a list of identifiable sources to which a text alludes. He argues rather that any text assumes everyday shared knowledge of an undefined discursive space. It is impossible to trace sources back unambiguously to other texts, because these other texts rely on codes, conventions and presuppositions which are lost. Eco's own version of this point (Eco 1992) is that words elicit "infinite series of connotations" and that there is always "unlimited semiosis" (à la Peirce).

But since intertextual references are potentially unlimited, the question arises: which earlier texts are relevant? Eco (1984a) cites *Der Zauberberg* by Thomas Mann as an influence on *NR*. It is a *Bildungsroman*, a story of a "simple young man" who spends seven years in a sanatorium in the Swiss mountains, where he holds many conversations about philosophical topics. If we allow this parallel, then why not other *Bildungsromane,* and other murder-mystery thrillers, some of which involve a serial killer in a closed community (isolated country house, boat at sea, etc.)? The Sherlock Holmes stories refer to Edgar Allan Poe's detective stories, which in turn inspired Borges (Bennett 1983; Kushigian 1983), whose *Death and the Compass* explicitly mentions Poe's detective Dupin. The opening incident in *NR*, in which William demonstrates his powers of inference by identifying the horse Brunellus (*NR*, pages 22–24), is not modelled on Sherlock Holmes, but on an incident in *Zadig* (Voltaire 1747), which Voltaire in turn had borrowed from Italian and French adaptations of medieval oriental tales (Bondanella 1997: 111).

And so on in "endless chains of causes and effects" (*NR*, page 30). Ultimately, every novel assumes familiarity with other novels, and *NR* contains archetypes and narrative universals which occur over and over again in world literature: the hero and searcher for knowledge (William), the villain and evil trickster (Jorge), the hunt/the search/the quest, and the world which ends in fire (Frye 1957, Wilson 1998: 248–249). This potentially infinite regress provides a fundamental problem for the concept of intertextuality.

5 Criteria for a theory

In order to decide whether the concept of intertextuality is worth pursuing, we need to formulate more precisely the problems which require a solution, and the criteria with which to judge acceptable solutions (here adapted from Chomsky 1957).

Observational adequacy would require a definitive list of the intertextual links in *NR*. However, a viable theory falls at this first hurdle. Comprehensive coverage of the data is impossible, since it would have to include allusions to individual authors (e.g. Wittgenstein), knowledge of genre conventions (e.g. detective stories), and shared cultural knowledge (e.g. about the Bible), sources which have themselves other sources, and so on *ad infinitum*.

Descriptive adequacy would require generalizations which hold for all texts and text-types: for example, a hierarchical classification of intertextual links from more to less general (e.g. universal archetypes, text-types, individual texts, literal quotations, etc.). But neither linguistic nor literary theory can provide a systematic classification of such units.

Explanatory adequacy would require at least a theory of the function of such links and the literary competence required by readers to recognize them. Given the current state of linguistic and literary theory, such a demand looks unrealistic.

5.1 Function

A theory of the literary function of the relations should explain which references are essential to a literary appreciation. For example, if readers do not recognize the frequent references to Sherlock Holmes, then they fail to recognize *NR* as a pastiche of a whodunnit and have missed an essential pattern in the novel. However, only real fans will recognize individual references, such as Holmes observing Watson's blackened finger (*A Scandal in Bohemia*, cf. *NR*, page 260) and discovering a powder which produces poisonous fumes when heated over a flame (*The Adventure of the Devil's Foot*, cf. *NR*, page 90; see also Carroll 1984). And although *The Hound of the Baskervilles* is probably the most famous story, not all readers will remember that it begins, somewhat like *NR*, with a character reading from a manuscript, "early eighteenth century, unless it is a forgery". But then, this is a literary device common to many stories.

Similarly, no individual references to Borges are essential to the structure of *NR*. They contribute to the novel's overall coherence by emphasizing themes and symbols, but if readers do not spot them all, they have lost nothing but the minor intellectual *frisson* of spotting them.

5.2 Reference

Intertextuality depends, by definition, on a theory of reference, and *NR* illustrates aspects of reference which are neglected in linguistic theory.

It is typically much easier to identify referring expressions than their referents. For example, the expression *William of Baskerville* is one sign. It alludes to the short novel *The Hound of the Baskervilles*, but its referent is not this single text, but a complex of indefinite extent: potentially all we know about Sherlock Holmes, whether from the stories by Conan Doyle or not. This takes us back immediately to the point that intertextual referents can turn into referring expressions and so on *ad infinitum*.

In a long discussion of the ontology of fictional characters, Eco (2001) argues that they are inten*s*ional semiotic objects (inten*s*ional with an "s"). That is, they have no material referent in the external world, but are defined by a bundle of semantic features. In the case of Sherlock Holmes, these features were originally in the canonical stories by Conan Doyle, but Sherlock Holmes long ago broke free from these original stories, wanders from text to text, and is now probably better known from his appearance in other stories, films and so on (such as the BBC television series *Sherlock*). Intertextual references do not always have unambiguous sources in particular books, but often undefined sources in everyday language use and therefore in general encyclopaedic knowledge.

Eco refers briefly to work by Searle (e.g. Searle 1995: 7–13; Searle 2010: 17–18) who develops a detailed analysis of the ambiguity of the opposition objective/subjective. This distinction has both an epistemic and an ontological sense:
- epistemically objective and subjective are predicates of judgements
- ontologically objective and subjective are predicates of entities.

Epistemology concerns knowledge. Compare two statements:

(1) *Sherlock Holmes lived at 221B Baker Street.*
(2) *Sherlock Holmes was a better detective than Hercule Poirot.*

(1) is epistemically objective and true. Its truth is not a mere personal opinion, but something we can be absolutely certain of. (It is conceivable – though unlikely – that someone might discover evidence to show that Bacon wrote *Hamlet*, but it is not reasonable to doubt that Hamlet kills Polonius.) (2) is epistemically subjective. It is a matter of personal opinion and judgement.

In contrast, ontology concerns modes of existence. Compare two noun phrases:

(3) *Baker Street in the Marylebone district of London.*
(4) *Sherlock Holmes' flat at 221B Baker Street.*

The referent of (3) is ontologically objective. It does not require to be experienced by someone in order to exist, and would continue to exist without any humans to experience it. The referent of (4) is ontologically subjective. It is a product of a human mind, created in texts, and exists only insofar as it is experienced by individual human subjects.

6 Patterns: schemas, frames, scripts, prototypes, etc.

In a famous article, Auden (1948) identifies the basic structures of the classic detective story, and shows incidentally how these are parodied in *NR*. As Auden says, "many detective stories begin with a death that appears to be suicide and is later discovered to have been murder". *NR* begins with a death that appears to be suicide, is suspected to be murder, but is then discovered to have been suicide.

We could try to state the essential default schema for "Sherlock Holmes": a very observant English detective, who recognizes the significance of clues which others miss. He has a naïve assistant, and takes drugs (but his pipe, hat and violin are non-essential features?). And it is relatively easy to state informally a prototypical script for a detective story. A detective investigates a crime (often a murder), by following clues, some of which are misleading. The crime is solved, the obvious suspects turn out to be innocent, and the villain turns out to be someone else.

Similarly, it is clear in general what is meant by a schema, in the sense of a cognitive framework which helps us to simplify, organize and interpret information, by giving priority to what is important and ignoring what is irrelevant. For example, the schema "gothic" consists of death-and-destruction clichés with diabolic monks, ghosts, subterranean passages, a sealed room, a cemetery and ossarium (all of which occur in *NR*). But it is doubtful if the concept can be made precise enough for automatic textual analysis. Intertextual reference sets no limits on the segments which it links or on how similar they have to be. This problem was well known to Saussure (1916 [1968]: 151), who pointed out that the concept of identity is entirely context-dependent. The train which leaves Paris for Geneva every evening at 8:45 might be the same train as far as the passengers are concerned, but not to an engineer who has to repair different combinations of locomotive and carriages.

This question of identity can be answered only if we can say something about the nature of units of meaning, and whether they are text segments and/or linguistic and cultural units. This, in turn, is one of the deepest problems in the philosophy of language, which has received precise answers in only very limited areas.

At the lexical level, a religious frame of reference may be triggered by choosing one out of a pair of otherwise synonymous words, such as *brethren* vs. *brothers*, *genuflection* vs. *kneel*, *defrock* (a priest) vs. *remove from office*, *mendicant* vs. *beggar*, *vestment* vs. *garment* or *robe*. Some phrases, such as *cenacle of virtue* and *thurible of sanctity* (*NR*, page 102), are certainly not frequent in everyday English. Readers might recognize many other words in *NR* as having religious uses, although they have little idea of the exact meaning. For example: *apostasy, calvary, cabalistic, canticle, chasuble, conclave, ecclesiastic, eucharist, hebdomadary, kyrie, intercession, liturgical, monstrance, prebend, schismatical, theophanic, transfiguration, trinity, versicle.* Quantitative methods can plot the uneven distribution of lexis in texts for lay people and texts for specialists, and can illustrate that readers can have only an incomplete idea of the meaning of words (and therefore of texts) especially in unfamiliar text-types.

At the phraseological level, concordance data has documented a particular concept of schema by showing that individual lemmas, along with the lexical and grammatical patterns in which they typically occur, trigger evaluative meanings. For example, the meaning of the verb LURK can be paraphrased as "to wait", with an added evaluative meaning of "sinister purpose" (cf. Stubbs 2001: 201–202, 211). It implies a narrative sequence: someone or something lies in wait somewhere (there is usually a place adverbial), often partly hidden, with some furtive intention of causing harm. It can be used of concrete situations or metaphorically, as in:

> "Like a pair of assassins, we *lurked* near the entrance, behind a column." (*NR*, page 456)
> "This is the pride that *lurked* and is still *lurking* within these walls." (*NR*, page 400)

Such phraseological examples show that all language use is intertextual, since any text consists of a mosaic of lexicogrammatical patterns and typical collocations which have been frequently used by other speakers in the past. The central analytic method of studying a concordance has shown that routine phraseology in language use is much more extensive than previously realized, and that a text sounds idiomatic because of what has been said many times before. It is therefore odd that intertextuality is so little discussed by corpus linguists (though see Teubert 2010).

7 Practice and theory in *The Name of the Rose*

There remains the question of whether fiction can contribute to theory.

First, what is implicit in *NR* must be made explicit. Since this question is largely answered by one of Eco's own textbooks (Eco 1984b), written at the same time as the novel, I can simply further illustrate three related semantic concepts which underlie the narrative practice in *NR*: encyclopaedia, labyrinth, and unlimited semiosis.

The labyrinth is symbolized by the library, which contains books on every known subject. Entries in an encyclopaedia can be represented only as a labyrinthine network, in which every point is connected to every other point. This results in "unlimited semiosis" (à la Peirce), since further details can always be added to any entry by following other links in the network. An argument familiar to linguists is that it is impossible to maintain a clear distinction between a dictionary and an encyclopaedia, since dictionary definitions always rely on users' real-world knowledge. Only very limited semantic information can be represented in purely logical form (e.g. All monks are male).

7.1 Keyword: Heresy

The dictionary/encyclopaedia problem can be illustrated with the example of the word family HERESY. As noted above, the simple frequency of its word-forms makes it a key semantic field: *NR* contains over 200 occurrences in total of *heresy, heresies, heretic, heretics, heretical* and *heresiarch*. Adso spends much of the novel listening to monks talking about heresy, and asking them to define it and explain it to him.

1) Their collocates give some information about their antonyms, hyponyms and evaluative meanings:
   - it must be distinguished from the *orthodox*
   - it exists in many forms, Bogomil, Donatist, Lombard, Oriental, etc.
   - it is dangerous, insidious, a crime, an evil, a viper
   - someone can be *accused* of it, *condemned to death* and *burned* for it
   - it is only the Church, *custodian of the truth*, which *identifies* it
   - heretics are different from heresiarchs and schismatics

2) But Adso also realizes that HERESY has no fixed meaning:
   - it may be an illusion (everyone is heretical, everyone is orthodox) (NR, page 203)
   - it may be imagined where it does not exist (*NR*, page 50).

Even a single speaker uses the word differently on different occasions. Meanings are created from moment to moment, depending on the immediate needs of the conversation. He says to William:

> When you were speaking with Ubertino, I had the impression you were trying to prove to him that all are the same, saints and *heretics*. But then, speaking with the abbot, you were doing your best to explain to him the difference between one *heretic* and another, and between the *heretical* and the orthodox. (*NR*, pages 196–197.)

3) It is a cliché that meaning depends on context. However, in judging whether a statement is heretical, the relevant context is not only the local context of utterance, but also other texts within a network of institutions, at a particular time and place, such as 14th-century Italy.
4) Classic speech act theory concerns everyday speech acts which anyone can perform, but largely ignores speech acts – such as accusations of heresy – which can be performed only by experts authorized by judicial institutions. Once Adso has concluded that "often inquisitors create heretics" (*NR*, page 50), he has realized that "heresy" cannot be separated from "authority" with-

in a large-scale theological framework. Both the whodunnit and the religious plots are about what authority defines as heretical interpretations of books. Heresy is seen as threatening "the very foundation of the church's *authority*" (*NR*, page 52). The Abbot believes that "it is *authority*" which decides how texts should be interpreted. Adso bemoans the fact that "correct interpretation can be established only on the *authority* of the fathers" (*NR*, page 248).

5) Heresy is a purely intertextual phenomenon. It does not refer to anything in the external world, but to interpretations of a text which, according to those in authority, are *mis*interpretations. One person accuses another of misinterpreting a text. The authority to make this accusation typically depends on a religious institution, which claims that it has the correct interpretation. This authority is – by definition – under dispute. The authenticity of the text may also be under dispute (perhaps, like Aristotle's book, it has never existed). It is not surprising that heresy requires "a monumental history" (*NR*, page 232) to document it, as different authorities and different interpretations are further glossed and explained.

These points, 1) to 5), all involve a model of meaning which is syntagmatic, pragmatic and global. The denotative core of the word family HERESY is greatly reduced. It has "meaning potential rather than meaning as such" (Hanks 2013: 66). The potential is realized as a result of its positions, locally in a discourse sequence, and globally in the intertext of an institution.

7.2 Dictionary definitions

Adso's problem can be illustrated by the definitions in any dictionary. *Chambers 21st Century Dictionary* and *Collins COBUILD Advanced Dictionary on CD-ROM* define HERESY respectively as:

> 1. An opinion or belief contrary to the authorized teaching of the religious community to which one ostensibly belongs. 2. An opinion opposed to the conventional or traditional belief; heterodoxy.

> 1. Heresy is a belief or action that most people think is wrong, because it disagrees with beliefs that are generally accepted. 2. Heresy is a belief or action which seriously disagrees with the principles of a particular religion.

Since these definitions depend on other definitions in the dictionary (e.g. the difference between "opinion" and "belief"), the whole dictionary is circular. They assume that the user understands what is meant by "religion", and why a religion might "authorize" beliefs: this could not be explained in a dictionary definition. In turn, since religion is a complex part of many cultures, there is no limit to the knowledge which might be included here, and of course whole encyclopaedias have been devoted to this topic alone. Even worse, both definitions assume that the user knows what "most people think" or what is involved in "conventional or traditional" beliefs (within their own culture?).

A structuralist definition of word meaning also fails. The word *heresy* cannot be defined by its lexical relations to other words in the language. One could try to start from its potential hypernyms (*crime*?), hyponyms (*Bogomil heresy*), antonyms (*orthodoxy*?), typical accompanying verbs (*accuse, condemn*), and so on, but even potential synonyms and antonyms are context-dependent (*heresy* and *orthodoxy*), which means that there is no clear starting point. On the contrary, heresy has to be defined with reference to a whole frame (sacred texts, competing interpretations, competing religious institutions, etc.).

The failure of the dictionary view of meaning and the necessity of the encyclopaedic approach to meaning has been formulated in different ways:

Cognitive linguists conclude that it is not possible to distinguish linguistic meaning from encyclopaedic knowledge, since meaning cannot be isolated from larger conceptual domains. *Monk* implies monastery which implies a religious order and so on (see e.g. Tomasello 1998; Croft and Cruse 2004).

Corpus linguists argue that individual words do not have stable meanings, but that meaning arises from their variable cooccurrence with other words. They argue that "the text is the only authority on the way words are used" (Sinclair 2004: 163) and that "the meaning is in the discourse" (Teubert 2010: passim).

Lexicographers cannot produce a dictionary which contains purely linguistic information. Definition is a speech act, which has to take into account what the addressee knows. You don't define HERESY in the same way for a child as for an adult, and if your addressee is five years old, you probably don't even try.

These three formulations all emphasize that meaning cannot be analysed independently of use.

7.3 Key semantic field: pattern, order, etc.

Again, raw frequency of occurrence shows the centrality of the semantic field of "order" and "pattern". It includes the lemmas ORDER (frequency c. 225), RULE (frequency c. 75), LAW (frequency c. 65), PLAN (frequency c. 30), ARRANGEMENT (frequency c. 30), CONTROL (frequency c. 25), DESIGN (frequency c. 12), HARMONY (frequency c. 12), PRINCIPLE (frequency c. 10), PATTERN (frequency c. 10), BALANCE (frequency c. 5), REGULATION (frequency c. 5), and SYMMETRY (frequency c. 4). An explicit theme in *NR* is the possibility of discovering order and pattern where previously only disorder and chaos could be seen. In terms of theology, the characters live at a time of belief in the "divine order" (*NR*, page 474). In terms of the whodunnit: William conceives "a false pattern" (*NR*, page 470) in investigating the deaths, which nevertheless puts him on the correct trail. He arrives at Jorge through "an apocalyptic pattern that seemed to underlie all the crimes, and yet it was accidental" (*NR*, page 492).

Both Williams (1976) and Foucault (1980) argue, in their different ways, that a rule of thumb for recognizing keywords is their extreme ambiguity across different institutional domains, such as religion, education, and the law. The lemma ORDER (over 200 occurrences) is ambiguous in English, as in "pattern or rational design" ("there is no order in the universe" *NR*, page 492), "correct arrangement" ("in what order are the books recorded in this list" *NR*, page 75), a "religious institution" ("the Benedictine order" *NR*, page 1), "command or instruction" ("the abbot ordered each monk to hurry" *NR*, page 454).

This is one place where the language of the translation affects the text. In German, for example, the different meanings are distinguished (respectively, *Ordnung, Reihenfolge, Orden, Befehl*) and the semantic field is differently organized.

The main symbol of (dis)order is the library. Before William can solve the crimes, he has to work out the idiosyncratic system which is used to classify the books and the library shelves. William asks how books can be found: "In what *order* are they listed?" (*NR*, page 75). The librarian Malachi answers:

> "The librarian must have a list of all books, carefully ordered by subjects and authors, and they must be classified on the shelves with numerical indications." ...
> "They are difficult to find, then," William observed.
> "It is enough for the librarian to know them by heart and know when each book came here. As for the other monks, they can rely on his memory."

In the library "the maximum of confusion [is] achieved with the maximum of order" (*NR*, page 217). In the end, it is the confusing organization of the library which makes it impossible to save it from destruction by fire.

A further explicit theme is whether the world is systematically ordered, such that it can be understood via rules (such as syllogisms, which relate linguistic propositions to each other) or rational hypotheses (which lead to objective truths about the external world), or whether this order is purely in the mind.

> "Then there is an order in the world!" I cried, triumphant.
> "Then there is a bit of order in this poor head of mine," William answered. (*NR*, page 208)

"I arrived at Jorge through an apocalyptic pattern that seemed to underlie all the crimes, and yet it was accidental. I arrived at Jorge seeking one criminal for all the crimes and we discovered that each crime was committed by a different person, or by no one. I arrived at Jorge pursuing the plan of a perverse and rational mind, and there was no plan. ... I behaved, stubbornly, pursuing a semblance of order, when I should have known well that there is no order in the universe."
"But in imagining an erroneous order you still found something. ..." (*NR*, page 492)

8 Fiction as theory?

So, what can this hybrid literature-as-theory novel do which a conventional academic article cannot do?

A weak answer is pedagogic. If the reader knows nothing about semiotics, deductive reasoning, and so on, then *NR* provides entertaining tasters of important ideas.

A stronger answer is that *NR* can make the reader experience intertextuality in a way which is not possible in a conventional academic account, since it is itself a collage of text fragments which often have no single source. One of its central topics, heresy, is itself an inherently intertextual phenomenon. However, these points have to be made explicit in commentaries on the novel.

Or perhaps the theoretical conclusions are entirely negative. *NR* demonstrates that the concept of intertextuality can be applied only to isolated textual examples, but cannot provide comprehensive coverage of a complete novel. There are no corresponding typologies of intertextual links and their functions or of the textual units involved. Since everything depends ultimately on readers' knowledge, the concept cannot be studied by strictly empirical methods, and therefore fails standards of objectivity and falsifiability.

If the concept of intertextuality cannot be empirically tested, then perhaps it should simply be abandoned. Nevertheless, it has implications for both a theory of reference and also a contextual theory of meaning. *NR* provides practical demonstrations of important linguistic concepts: the difference between encyclopaedic and specialized knowledge, the concept of a semiotic object, and therefore the idea that "the meaning is in the discourse" (Teubert 2010).

An idea is important if it relates to other important ideas in a natural way. Before we abandon the concept of intertextuality, we should note that it connects – logically – with a complex of ideas which have a long history but no entirely satisfactory treatment in linguistics: the location of meaning (in the text or elsewhere?), the nature of semantic units, and the concept of reference. Intellectual progress often comes from relating areas which were previously seen as distinct.

References

Agassi, Joseph. 1970. Philosophy as literature: The case of Borges. *Mind* 79 (314). 287–294.
Allen, Graham. 2000. *Intertextuality*. London: Routledge.
Auden, Wystan. H. 1948. The guilty vicarage. *Harper's Magazine*, May 1948 issue.
Barthes, Roland. 1977 [1967]. The death of the author. In *Image, Music, Text* [Edited/translated by Stephen Heath], 142–148. London: Fontana. [First published in English, *Aspen Magazine*, 5 (6), 1967].
Baxter, David G. 1989. Murder and mayhem in a medieval abbey: The philosophy of *The Name of the Rose*. *The Journal of Speculative Philosophy* 3 (3). 170–189.
Bennett, Maurice J. 1983. The detective fiction of Poe and Borges. *Comparative Literature*, 35 (3). 262–275.
Bondanella, Peter E. 1997. *Umberto Eco and the open text*. New York: Cambridge University Press.
Borges, Jorge L. 1972. *A universal history of infamy*. New York: Dutton.
Burton Russell, J. 1983. [Review of] *The Name of the Rose* by Umberto Eco. *The Public Historian* 5 (4). 101–103.
Carroll, Michael P. 1984. [Review of] *The Name of the Rose* by Umberto Eco. *American Anthropologist* 86 (2). 432–434.
Chomsky, Noam. 1957. *Syntactic structures*. The Hague: Mouton.
Cobley, Evelyn. 1989. Closure and infinite semiosis in Mann's *Doctor Faustus* and Eco's *The Name of the Rose*. *Comparative Literature Studies* 26 (4). 341–361.
Croft, William & Cruse, D. Alan. 2004. *Cognitive linguistics*. Cambridge: Cambridge University Press.
Culler, Jonathan D. 1976. Presupposition and intertextuality. *Modern Language Notes* 91 (6). 1380–1396.
De Beaugrande, Robert. 2000. Text linguistics at the millennium: Corpus data and the missing links. *Text* 20 (2). 153–195.
Dubnick, Heather. 2002. [Review of] *Literary Philosophers: Borges, Calvino, Eco* by Jorge J.E. Gracia et al. *Modern Language Notes* 117 (5). 1143–1148.
Eco, Umberto. 1983. *The Name of the Rose*. [Translated by William Weaver. Page references to Picador paperback]. San Diego: Harcourt Brace Jovanovich.
Eco, Umberto. 1984a. Postscript to *The Name of the Rose*. [Translated by William Weaver]. San Diego: Harcourt Brace Jovanovich.
Eco, Umberto. 1984b. *Semiotics and the philosophy of language*. Basingstoke: Macmillan.
Eco, Umberto. 1992. *Interpretation and overinterpretation*. [Edited by Stefan Collini]. Cambridge: Cambridge University Press.
Eco, Umberto. 2001. *Confessions of a young novelist*. Cambridge, MA: Harvard University Press.
Eco, Umberto & Thomas A. Sebeok (eds.), 1983. *The sign of three: Dupin, Holmes, Peirce*. Bloomington: Indiana University Press.
Fairclough, Norman. 1995. *Critical Discourse Analysis*. London: Routledge.
Foucault, Michel. 1980. *Power/knowledge. Selected interviews and other writings, 1972–1977*. [Edited by Colin Gordon]. Brighton: Harvester.
Frye, Northrop. 1957. *Anatomy of criticism*. Princeton, NJ: Princeton University Press.
Garrett, Jeffrey. 1991. Missing Eco: On reading *The Name of the Rose* as library criticism. *The Library Quarterly* 61 (4). 373–388.
Haft, Adele, Jane G. White & Robert J. White. 1987. *The key to The Name of the Rose*. Harrington Park, NJ: Ampersand Associates. [Also 1999, Ann Arbor: University of Michigan Press.]

Hanks. Patrick. 2013. *Lexical analysis: Norms and exploitations*. Cambridge, MA: MIT Press.
Hüllen, Werner. 1987. Semiotics narrated: Umberto Eco's *The Name of the Rose*. *Semiotica* 64 (1/2). 41–57.
Kristeva, Julia. 1969. *Semiotiké: Recherches pour une sémanalyse*. Paris: Seuil.
Kushigian, Julia A. 1983. The detective story genre in Poe and Borges. *Latin American Literary Review* 11 (22). 27–39.
Lemke, Jay L. 2000. Intertextuality and the project of text linguistics. *Text* 20 (2). 221–225.
Saussure, Ferdinand de. 1916. *Cours de linguistique générale*. [Edited by Charles Bally, Albert Sechehaye & Albert Riedlinger. Page references to the 1968 edn.] Paris: Payot.
Searle, John R. 1995. *The construction of social reality*. London: Allen Lane.
Searle, John R. 2010. *The making of the social world*. Oxford: Oxford University Press.
Sinclair, John. 2004. *Trust the text*. London: Routledge.
Stubbs, Michael. 2001. *Words and phrases*. Oxford: Blackwell.
Teubert, Wolfgang. 2010. *Meaning, discourse and society*. Cambridge: Cambridge University Press.
Tomasello, Michael. 1998. Cognitive linguistics. In William Bechtel & George Graham (eds.), *A companion to cognitive science*. 477–487. Malden, MA: Blackwell.
Voltaire [François-Marie Arouet] 1747(?). *Zadig ou la destinée*. Amsterdam [London?].
Williams, Raymond. 1976. *Keywords: A vocabulary of culture and society*. London: Fontana.
Wilson, Edward O. 1998. *Consilience. The unity of knowledge*. New York: Knopf.
Wimsatt, William K. & Monroe C. Beardsley. 1946. The intentional fallacy. *Sewanee Review* 54. 468–488.
Wittgenstein, Ludwig. 1921. *Logisch-Philosophische Abhandlung*. Leipzig: UNESMA.

Ian Lancashire
Word-entry patterns in Early Modern English dictionaries

Abstract: The subject of this essay is how the formal structures of dictionary word-entries create lexical patterns. Historically, simple glosses (a term paired with its translation or meaning) were the first lexicographical structures. Eventually, each of the two partner variables (a headword/lemma and its postlemmatic explanation) could become embedded subentries. In this way, word-entries acquired various kinds of other information, as about grammar, etymology, class, and pronunciation. The two parts of the pair, and the embedded pairs they could support, increased the complexity of word-entries. The early lexicographer's theory of language, and the history of dictionaries, influenced each of the headword/lemma and postlemmatic segments. The Early Modern era characterized the headword/lemma as a sign-post, a name, or a pointer to a postlemmatic element that described a thing. As Shakespeare says, "What's in a name? that which we call a rose / By any other name would smell as sweet". Modern times have since transformed the word-entry structure into a schema where the mind of its maker typically defines, in the postlemmatic element, the headword rather than the thing it denotes. When headwords are sourced in mental ideation, lexical patterns increase. Lexicographers' re-use of earlier dictionaries also ensures the repetition of earlier phrasal combinations. A little history of one lexical pattern used in the headword/lemma "labyrinth" from the early 15th century up to the *Oxford English Dictionary Online* today illustrates this collocational mechanism. Last, I suggest how discoveries in cognitive psychology and neuroscience have expanded the role of the mind in transforming the modern word-entry into a vehicle for representing what and how the mind knows.

1 Introduction

Crossword puzzles and Google searches today build on an ancient abstract lexical pattern, the word-entry, which appeared six millennia ago and grew rapidly once printing technology enabled dictionaries to become widely-available, affordable

---

Ian Lancashire, University of Toronto, Department of English, Toronto, Ontario, M5R 2M8, Canada, ian.lancashire@utoronto.ca

https://doi.org/10.1515/9783110596656-004

social commodities.[1] Word-entries are a form-to-function mapping such as a simple two-part gloss: a headword/lemma/lexeme, or a phrase, followed by a postlemmatic expression that complements, characterizes, or is named by the first part. It is one of the very oldest administrative inventions, found in the Middle Babylonian period (1595–1155 BCE) in Sumerian-Akkadian bilingual glossaries (Veldhuis 2014: 226) and based on thematic word lists of "professions, metal objects, foodstuffs, containers, domestic animals, fish, birds, and so on" that originated two millennia earlier (Veldhuis 2014: 7). Crossword puzzles, popularized by the mid-19th century, invite us to guess a headword/lemma from clues (which correspond to a postlemmatic segment). Another very powerful mutation of the half-supplied "word-entry" pattern is the Google query, in which search terms and search results (the hits) are the two parts. Google departs from the Mesopotamian original and the crossword puzzle by having a machine rather than a human mind guess either a missing headword/lemma or a postlemmatic part. In 1998, each day, Google processed about 10,000 queries, and by early 2018 that sum rose to about three and a half billion (*Internet Live Stats*). Unsurprisingly, Google would have subsumed the function of word-look-up completely had not it unloaded so many hits of such different types that they overloaded the postlemmatic segment.

2 Tudor and Stuart semantics

Understanding the growth of word-patterns in Tudor and Stuart lexical works begins with knowledge of the semantics of that period. It has one surprise. The Early Modern English, c. 1475–1755, defined things instead of words. William Lily and other grammarians taught, for two centuries, that the English noun was the name of a thing, and the English verb the name of an action. Names did not connote the things they signified but were labels for or pointers to those things. Only the thing signified by a word-entry headword could be defined for what we call meaning. The headword could be defined, but only as a sign-thing, which Ralph Lever (preferring English) in 1573 termed a "showsay". He also disliked Latin

---

[1] I wish to acknowledge with thanks the support of a grant from the Social Sciences and Humanities Research Council of Canada, as well as the University of Toronto Library for its hosting of *Lexicons of Early Modern English* and its provision of laboratory space for its development. This essay has benefited from the judicious comments of two anonymous reviewers and the editors: to them, my sincere thanks.

> *definitio.* corruptly called a definition: but for that it is a saying which telleth what a thing is, it may more aptly be called a saywhat. (*LEME* 129-41).[2]

Lever objected to importing Latinate vocabulary from classical rhetoric when simple English terms, albeit invented compounds, could be found instead. Thomas Blount in 1656 gives a reasonable account of classical definition.

> Definition (*definitio*) *est oratio explicans essentiam rei per genus & differentiam*; a declaring what a thing is by a Gender or something that is common to the thing declared, and to other things also, and by a difference onely agreeing to the thing explicated, and distinguishing it from all things else (*LEME* 478-2461).

To define a thing in classical rhetoric is to explain its genus (or type) and its differentia (or how it differs from other instances of the same type). John Harris's *Lexicon Technicum* (1704) is "a Dictionary not only of bare *Words* but *Things*" (a2r),[3] an astounding book with terms of art as headwords and little essays in the postlemmatic element about the things they signify. His word-entry for "flexor" takes the Early Modern understanding of thing-based definition to an extreme:

> FLEXOR *Carpi Radialis*, is a Muscle of the Wrist, which ariseth Tendinous from the Internal Exuberance of the *Os Humeri*, becoming Fleshy, adheres strictly to the *Pronator Radii Teres*, and in half its Oblique Progress to the *Carpus*, it becomes a flat Tendon which passeth over the Annular Ligament, and is inserted to the upper part of the *Os Metacarpi*, which sustains the Fore-finger: Its Names shews its Use. (Harris, sig. hhh2r).[4]

The first encyclopaedia, by Ephraim Chambers, recognizes lexical definition – what Harris eschews – in the title: *Cyclopaedia, or, an Universal Dictionary of Arts and Sciences: Containing the Definitions of the Terms, and Accounts of the Things Signify'd Thereby* (1728). The first lexicographer to allocate a word-entry to lexical definition (where the postlemmatic segment defines its headword) is Joseph Nicol Scott in his new edition of Nathan Bailey's etymological English dictionary in 1755. He cites the habits of mathematicians in doing so:

> TO DEF'INE, *verb. act.* [*definir*, Fr. and Sp. *definer*, It. And Lat.] 1. To declare or explain any thing by its qualities or circumstances.

---

[2] Word-entries in *LEME* texts are identified by the number of the text, followed by the number of the word-entry in it.
[3] To define "bare *Words*" is to describe them literally as objects.
[4] Compare the OED definition: "A muscle whose function it is to produce flexion in any part of the body." (OED s.v. *flexor*)

> DEFINITION [Fr. *diffenizione*, It. *difinicion*, Sp. of *definitio*, Lat.] 1. A short and plain description of a thing, with its nature and principal qualities.
> DEFINITION [with mathematicians] is an explanation of the terms or words used for explaining the thing treated of. (Bailey and Scott 1755)

Samuel Johnson in the same year still held to the old view:

> To DEFI'NE. v. a. [*definio*, Lat. *definir*, French.] 1. To give the definition; to explain a thing by its qualities and circumstances.
> DEFINI'TION. n. s. [*definitio*, Latin; *definition*, French.] 1. A short description of a thing by its properties. (Johnson 1755; *LEME* 1345-10283, 1345-10277)

The Early Modern English period also did not understand the word "meaning" as we do: It meant an agent's purpose, not a word-definition.[5]

In *Treatise of the Figures of Grammar and Rhetorike* (1555), Richard Sherry clearly explains the relationship of words and things as the early English Renaissance learned it from classical Greece and Rome. When words stick to their principal property, denoting, they yield only "the proper pith of any thyng ... briefly & perfectly" (Sherry 1555: sig. g4r). Definition gives the essential distinguishing features of a thing expressed by the postlemmatic part. Defining is a creature of the analytic mind. It avoids amplification, which dramatizes and appeals to the senses, in favour of succinctness. Words themselves lack substance – "More matter, with less art", as Gertrude requests of verbose Polonius in *Hamlet* – and, unconstrained by their signifieds, tend to lose touch with the world. From this skepticism comes Plato's view that poets lie, as well as Sir Philip Sidney's defence of poets as prophets, secondary creators of worlds never seen before.

To say that words only denoted and could not act as signifieds was to give the principal role in argument to the things they signified and made words "not parties to the matter, but [a property that] may be taken out, or quite left of" (Sherry 1555: sig. h1r). Yet, as the title of John Florio's Italian–English dictionary, *World of Wordes* (1598, 1611), shows, even the term "word" was thought a thing in itself and, as such, could be defined. It had spelling, a part of speech, and an inflection, for example. Florio explains the Italian "Verilóquio" as "an etimologie, a true exposition or meaning of a word or sentence" (Florio 1611: 595). Etymology became increasingly popular as knowledge grew about how English words were borrowed from Greek, Latin, Old and Middle English, Italian, Dutch, Spanish, and other tongues. A word-entry links words first, as denoter, to a thing

---

5 See Lancashire (2002). Logicians Wilson (1551: d7v) and Blundeville (1599: 53–54) explain how to define words (see also e.g. Anderson 1996; Waswo 1987; Howell 1946).

described in its immediate postlemmatic part, and then also historically to another thing that its ancestor etymon signified.[6] Derivation also grants words new status. In it, new words are built on other words: Derivation pairs members of a family of terms with a common radical or root form, or with an affixed particle. That group has associative power. For example, the root form "sweet" (an adjective) was parent to derivative terms like "unsweetened" (adjective), "sweetness" (noun), "sweeten" (verb), and "sweetly" (adverb).

Sherry contends that words can be valuably notated themselves. Explication amplifies a word's signification circumstantially by glossing or expounding it with a group of associated words. Sherry has in mind Erasmus's celebration of *copia* in writing (Erasmus 1963). Notation associates a word with other related words so as to enable the reader to "see" the signified thing. The powers of words in themselves heighten the reader's senses. To Shakespeare, Spenser, and Milton, words are more than signs standing for the alphabetic shapes they signify. They are signifiers with "strength and … power" of their own (Sherry 1555: sig. a3v). Giving words any such power, on the other hand, risks barbarisms (words that are badly imported from other languages) and solecisms (words incoherently combined).

Today the mind uses ideation to define a headword conceptually in the postlemmatic element. *Lexical definition* thus shifts meaning from the denoted thing to the connoting headword. To some extent, nature, the world of things, has now lost some of the primacy it once enjoyed in dictionaries, but encyclopaedias emerged in the 18th century to describe things. What gave language a new sense of meaning was the individual mind that linked nouns and verbs to neural-networked ideas. A definition shift had given the mind the freedom to create systems of thought and define them in words rather than things.

3 Early dictionaries

The Early Modern understanding of word-entries appears clearly in *Lexicons of Early Modern English* (*LEME* 2.0, 2019-), a Web database of 1.1 million word-entries from more than 250 dictionaries and glossaries that document the period from 1475 to 1755. It begins with two bilingual, late-medieval printed Latin/English dictionaries and closes with two very large monolingual lexicons by Samuel Johnson and his chief competitors, Nathan Bailey and Joseph Nicol Scott.

---

[6] Attempts to define the thing that a word as such was, outside Wilkins (1668), were infrequent. John Baret's *Aluearie* (1574), however, made letters of the alphabet into word-entry headwords.

Most lexical works until the end of the 16th century were bilingual, matching a word in one language with synonyms or corresponding terms in another language. Such word-entries, in both bilingual and monolingual hard-word dictionaries, translated one sign into another sign, and the thing they signified was implicit. The monolingual English glossaries and dictionaries that seeded the 17th century and dominated the 18th competed at first in finding novel, challenging "hard words" often criticized as barbarisms. These lexical texts constructed a word-entry whose postlemmatic element[7] supplied easier, more familiar terms. The monolingual word-entry then functioned like a bilingual one. Care in delineating senses for headwords took a back seat to amplification. Whether or not English vocabulary grew then the fastest of any period in the history of English (Nevalainen 1999), "masses of words were borrowed" from Latin and French (Nevalainen 2006: 39). From 1475 to 1625, as lexicographers drew from a greatly-expanded publishing industry and new subject fields, headwords in the OED increased from about 38,000 to about 97,000.[8]

Lexicographers had much to do with this increase. They treated English as two early modern languages, the mother tongue and a to-be-learned language of so-called hard words that came, largely, from Latin and French. The rapid intake of non-English vocabulary characterized English uniquely among European languages at this time. No national language academy controlled the influx of new words in England (Brede 1937), unlike in France and Italy. A need to translate continental books so as to transfer new knowledge to English (what was confessedly a minor European language), a desire for greater variety of synonyms for rhetorical argumentation, and a general embarrassment at the limited resources of the mother tongue were felt at court. Under Henry VII, a pair of Latin–English and English–Latin dictionaries were published in 1499–1500, the *Promptorium Parvulorum* and *Ortus Vocabulorum*. His son, Henry VIII, replaced them by acting as patron for Sir Thomas Elyot's Latin–English *Dictionary* (1538), heavily indebted to the then very new work by Ambrogio Calepino (Englished as Calepine), and for John Palsgrave's *Leclarcissement* (1530), an English–French grammar and vocabulary that overwhelmed two English and French glossaries that Caxton and

---

7 The term "postlemmatic" is standard today. It implies that the headword always takes the modern-spelling, uninflected form that lexicographers use today (nouns in the nominative singular, verbs in the infinitive, etc.), but that is certainly untrue of early modern lexicons.

8 These numbers can be directly generated from information in the OED online database in 2015 (I am grateful to James McCracken at OUP for doing so). Thousands of OED word entries, however, have only one illustrative quotation and so in effect are active in English by only one person for a short time. Words cannot be part of a language if only one person employs them once. Most of these singletons are new ("strange" or "hard" words).

his successor Wynkyn de Worde published. By 1600, English still had no major English monolingual dictionary, but the reign of James I went on to produce six English glossaries by Robert Cawdrey, John Bullokar, and Henry Cockeram that "translated" hard English words into easy English words. Others like Holyoake, Cotgrave, Minsheu, Florio, and Verstegan translated Latin, French, Spanish, Italian, and Dutch headwords into English. Only when John Minsheu's *Ductor in Linguas* came out in 1617 and 1625 did the English possess a full dictionary with over 21,000 English headwords and their synonyms in ten other languages. Word-pairing of foreign word and English translation, and of hard and easy English words, remained the period's dominant lexicographical meta-pattern in word-entries.

Dictionaries became well-known commodities for the first time in the Renaissance, and they popularized lexical patterns, which focused both on explications of the headword as a thing apart from the postlemmatic thing. More than 400 printed editions of dictionaries and other lexical reference works (such as concordances and books of proper and place names) have survived from the mid-1470s, when Caxton introduced printing to England, to 1623, when Henry Cockeram published the first substantial English monolingual dictionary.[9] These texts have more than two million word-entries. Students setting out on a grammar-school education bought an inexpensive English–Latin dictionary such as that by John Withals, and most who had anything to do with professions such as law, medicine, trade, the church, education, and court life acquired a sizable Latin–English dictionary by lexicographers such as Sir Thomas Elyot, Richard Howlet, Jean Véron, Thomas Cooper, John Baret, Thomas Thomas, John Rider, or Thomas Holyoake. Merchants and courtiers would have purchased bilingual lexicons serving modern European tongues, or a polyglot one such as the many editions flowing from Noel Barlement's early Tudor handbook.

For more than a century, one line of Latin–English dictionaries dominated in England.[10] Sir Thomas Elyot's *Dictionary* (1538), developed with the active patronage and library of Henry VIII, went through five editions until 1559. It spawned three lexicographical streams. Richard Howlet's English–Latin *Abecedarian* (1552) turned Elyot's English explanations into headwords. Jean Véron's

---

9 These numbers are calculated from information in the *English Short Title Catalogue* (http:/estc.bl.uk), Alston's bibliographies, Schäfer's analysis of hard-word glossaries, and *LEME*'s database of 1347 primary glossaries and dictionaries that served English from 1475 to 1755.
10 Starnes (1954) analysed the train of indebtedness of Latin dictionaries to one another over time, and Schäfer (1989) the similar way that hard-word glossaries built on one another, and on bilingual and polyglot dictionaries.

Dictionariolum Puerorum translated the French explanations in Robert Estienne's Latin dictionary into English as well as used Elyot's postlemmatic English explanations. Howlet and Véron were short-lived, but Elyot's assistant Thomas Cooper published several revised editions of Elyot's work after his death and produced his own *Thesaurus*, a further revision of Elyot's work, from 1565 to 1584. The heir to the Elyot-Cooper tradition proved to be University of Oxford printer Thomas Thomas (1587), whose dictionary inspired John Rider's imitation in 1589, which Francis Holyoake revised in 1606, the first in a series edited by his family for over half a century. This great river of recurring and variant Latin/English word-entries fed the smallish English monolingual hard-word dictionaries by Edmund Coote (1596-), Cawdrey (1604-), Bullokar (1616-), and Henry Cockeram (1623-). Coote benefited from Richard Mulcaster's list of about 8,000 English words suitable for including in an English dictionary (1582). Cawdrey took 87 percent of Coote's entries and was indebted to Thomas Thomas for 43 percent of his own. John Bullokar's *English Expositor* (1616), like Cawdrey's, took many word-entries from Thomas Thomas, and bulked up on others from Cawdrey himself. Bullokar also exploited a century's train of legal glossaries by John and William Rastell, and John Cowell's *The Interpreter* (1607), which had been largely burnt by order of Parliament and the crown for asserting too much of the divine right of the monarchy. Cawdrey then responded to Bullokar in 1617 by adopting some of his entries. The next hard-word dictionary, by Cockeram (1623), drew word-entries from Randle Cotgrave's French lexicon (1611) as well as from Bullokar and Cawdrey. This intensive reuse of word-entries by other lexicographers intensified the growth of lexical patterns.

4 Word-entry structures and lexical patterns

To recapitulate briefly, word-entry structures have two variables, a headword/lemma, and a postlemmatic element or gloss. The postlemmatic part could be either a word in another language or a term in English, in which event their relationship is one of exchangeability or equivalence. One of the pair translates, explicates, or notates the other. The postlemmatic part of early word-entries seldom introduced definitions of the things that the headword/lemma denoted. However, headwords were sometimes treated as if they themselves, as objects, denoted things. These structures are the crucible where lexical patterns – repeating lexical combinations that become idioms – are forged. Word-entry pairings of headwords and postlemmatic elements are preserved and passed on as phrases and collocations. To these patterns I now turn.

The headword and its partner sometimes include embedded glosses, as the 10th-century ABC-Glossary entry for Latin "Bibliotheca" shows. The thing signified by the Latin word *Bibliotheca* is explained in Latin as a *librorum repositio*. The postlemmatic element then gives two Old English translations, a sub-headword "bochord" (book-hoard) and its sub-postlemmatic partner "fodder".

> Bibliotheca .i. libro*rum* repositio. bochord. uel fodder.

This large word-entry has four names for the one and same thing.

The more English words there are in the postlemmatic, the more opportunities for lexical idioms. The first monolingual English dictionary, John Rastell's glossary for young law students (c. 1525), explains procedures or actions designed by the present king, Henry VIII, to benefit himself.

> ¶ Deodande ys whan any man by mysfortune ys slayne by an hors or by a cartte or by any othere thynge that mouythe than thys thyng that ys the cause of hys deth & which at the tyme of the mysfortune mouyth shalbe forfet to the kyng / & that is callyd deodande & that perteynyth to the kyngys almener for too dyspose in almys and in dedys of charyte. (Rastell c. 1525; Lancashire 2006; *LEME* 836-74)

Rastell's *dramatis personae*, "any man", a horse, a cart, a slain man, the king, and the almoner, belong to a realistic scene that imagines events taking place in present and future time (governed by "whan" rather than by "what", by "shalbe" instead of "is"). The notation is vivid in comparison to the OED definition of "deodand":

> A thing forfeited or to be given to God; *spec.* in *Eng. Law*, a personal chattel which, having been the immediate occasion of the death of a human being, was given to God as an expiatory offering, i.e. forfeited to the Crown to be applied to pious uses, e.g. to be distributed in alms.

The thousands of English–French entries for verbs in John Palsgrave's *Lesclaircissement* (1530) uniformly begin with a sentence uttered by "I" (Stein 1987, 1997: 135–136).

> I Sewe at meate/ Ie taste. prime co*niu*. & ie sers du tasteur, or ie prens lassaye. Sewe who wyll/ I wyll karue: Serue du rasteur, or preigne lessaye qui vouldra ie seruiray descuyer trenchant. (Palsgrave 1530; *LEME* 49-14709)

"I" belongs to the present and incorporates the living lexicographer in what he is explaining. He becomes an aspect of what his word-entries are about. The entry for "Bougre" in Claude Hollyband's French–English dictionary (1593) is vivid:

> Bougre, he that committed such a fact and sodomite villanie: a buggerer: burne them all. (Desainliens 1593; *LEME* 205-2464)

To present-day readers, both its inhumanity and the sudden break from lexical structure are shocking: something may warrant definition but it should burn no one at the stake. Word-entries in Tudor lexical works routinely give opinionated commentary that etches itself into memory.[11]

From 1475 to 1623, the earliest word-entry pairing was bilingual, a foreign word translated by an English word, or vice versa. Hard words need simple translations, and the English translation usually was not memorable enough to spark a pattern.

8th cent.	Fatum;	wyrd (Leiden Glossary)
11th cent.	Uermis	wyrm (London Vocabulary.)[12]
1499	Reyne.	Pluuia uie. fe. ge. pri. (*Promptorium*; *LEME* 26-7189)
1500	Imber bris.	*anglice* rayne / or a dewe or a showre. m.t. (*Ortus*; *LEME* 35-11648)
1547	Pryf a vydd dan dafod ki dafod ki	The gredy worme (Salesbury *LEME* 62-5335)
1550	Pioua,	rayne. (Wm. Thomas; *LEME* 70-5621)
1552	Rayne.	Imber. ris, Pluuia. æ, Aqua cœlestis, Pluuis aqua (R. Howlet; *LEME* 75-17437)
1556	The greedye woorme in the dogges tongue,	lytta, tæ. (J. Withals *LEME* 78-672)
1587	Imber, bris, m.g.	A smoking shoure of raine falling with force, and continuing long: rayne, water: euery waterie humour: sometime weeping, or aboundant teares. (Th. Thomas. *LEME* 179-16846)
1593	Pluye,	raine: f. (C. Hollyband. *LEME* 205-15224)
1611	Rain: m. as Raim;	A bough. *Rain de forests*. The purlues, or skirts, of forrests; the places that be next, or neere adioyning, vnto them. (R. Cotgrave; *LEME* 298-37191)

Frequently, the headword and its postlemmatic element break down into small groups of features. *Ortus Vocabulorum* (1500), Richard Howlet (1552), Thomas Thomas (1587), and Randle Cotgrave (1611) add to the postlemmatic element

---

[11] Charles C. Fries, the editor of the *Early Modern English Dictionary*, introduced the field of contemporary comments into the design of word-entries for his now-lapsed period lexicon (Bailey 1985) because early lexicographers appeared undisciplined in how they explicated and notated words.

[12] See Stein (1985) for an analysis of the structure of the Leiden Glossary and the London Vocabulary.

either synonyms or phrases descriptive of the things being named. Howlet fuses four translations in the postlemmatic element. Thomas adds a genitive inflection and a gender for the headword. Cotgrave's entry nests a second word-pair, for the phrase "Rain de forests", after the first lemma and its gloss. A lexical pattern can be seen in the repetition of "the gredy worme" and "The greedye woorme" in Salesbury and Withals.

Monolingual dictionary word-entries extended the bilingual word-entry by equating an easy word and a hard word (often drawn from a foreign language), and vice versa. Again, some entries notate a word by historicizing or dramatizing a word or a thing. For example, Bartholomew Traheron refers to healing those who spit up blood, and Barnabe Googe to Colonus's discovery of cannibals.

1526?	Abominable /	lothesome. (G. Hervet. *LEME* 45-5.)
1534	Hell:	it is called in Hebrue the valeye of Hennon. A place by Ierusalem / where they burnt their chyldren in fyer vnto the ydole Moloch / & is vsurped & taken now for a place where the wycked and vngodlye shalbe tormented both soule and bodye / after the generall iudgement. (Wm. Tyndale. *LEME* 692-2)
1543	Clymanum.	Clymenon is an herbe whyche hath a square stalke lyke a beane stalke, and leaues lyke plantayn. A iuyce is strayned out of the roote of it, whych is good for them that spitte bloode. (B. Traheron. *LEME* 58-95)
1561	Canibals	a monstrous kynde of people, feadynge onlye wyth mans flesh, lately discouered by Colonus the spaniarde. (B. Googe. *LEME* 96-34)
1575	Nemrod.	Heb. Arque. Tyrannus. Profugus. Transgressor: A cruell prince. (W. Patten; *LEME* 140-4197)
1596	imperiall	belonging to the crowne. (E. Coote. *LEME* 216-742)
1599	Tiráno, vide Tyráno,	a tyrant, a cruell imperious ruler. (J. Minsheu)
1604	pluuiatile,	raine (R. Cawdrey. *LEME* 276-1796)
1616	Tyrant.	A cruell Prince, One that ruleth vniustly. (J. Bullokar. *LEME* 323-3976)
1623	Aquation.	Abundance of raine. (H. Cockeram. *LEME* 343-406)
1623	a cruell Prince.	Tyrant. (H. Cockeram. *LEME* 343-5508)

Although glossing pairs continue, the post-lemmatic element displays items of notation: a synonym, an explanation of the main term, or a reference to another language. Tyndale mentions Hebrew as the foreign language from which "hell" was taken, and Googe associates "cannibal" with Spanish. Latin sources are common and so go unacknowledged for "abominable", "clymanum", and "imperiall", and Greek for Minsheu and Bullokar on "Tyrant". Robert Cawdrey models an English hard word, "pluuiatile", on the Latin equivalent of "raine". Henry

Cockeram anglicizes a Latin term as "Aquation" to obtain another hard word for an easy word. A lexical pattern visible here is the joking of "tyrant" and "a cruel prince" (Salesbury 1547, Patten 1575, Bullokar 1616, and Cockeram 1623).

Two variant pairs can be found embedded in bilingual or monolingual lemmata or postlemmatic elements: an etymology, and derivations that shared the root of the lemma. The following examples make the English word the headword, and the postlemmatic element the etymon or antecedent form, generally in parentheses or brackets. Minsheu lists multiple-language sources, and Bailey the Greek, but Latin again goes unstated in Blount.

11618 a Tirant.	B. tyran. T. tyrann. G. Tyran. I.H.P. Tiranno. L. (J. Minsheu, 1617)
Tyrannicide	(tyrannicidium) the murdering of a Tyrant, cruel Lord or Ruler. (Th. Blount, 1656. *LEME* 478-9997)
DACTYLOGY	[of δάχτυλος a finger, and λόμος law, Gr. speech] a conversing by signs made by the fingers. (Nathan Bailey, 1737. *LEME* 1349-5069)

Some lexicographers recognize lexical families of words that share an identical root. These are lexical patterns. John Rider exploits this for both Latin and English in his bilingual dictionary. "Imber" has seven related forms, most with their own nested pairs, and English two, "shower" and "showery", and "rainy".

1589	A great Shower of raine.	1 Imber, nimbus, m. A little shower. 1 Imbriculus Bringing showers. 1 Imbrifer, Nimbifer, ad. Showery, rainy, or ful of showers 1 Nimbosus, imbricosus, ad (J. Rider. *LEME* 186-5764)

Such etymologies and derivations led to the making of new vocabulary (Görlach 1991; Nevalainen 1999).

Proximity searches in *LEME* and OED, and lists of idiomatic phrases, can often identify lexical patterns. The collocation "woody" and "wild" emerges in that way.

c. 1480	fferus a um	anglice Wilde or Wode (*Medulla Grammatice*; *LEME* 537-5773)
1550	Seluaggio,	wilde, or wooddelike (William Thomas; *LEME*; 70-7058)
1571	Lieu forestier & sauvage,	a wooddye and wilde place (Hollyband; *LEME* 205-8919)
1587	Sylvester ...	Of wood or forest, ful of trees or wood, woody: also wild (Thomas Thomas; *LEME* 179-34408)

| 1755 | Wald ... | | a wood, a wild woody ground. (Scott; *LEME* 1346-69234) |

Alliteration binds these, but even the greatest of lexicographers loses focus occasionally and a jest becomes quotable and thus, retold, a lexical pattern. Samuel Johnson displays his wit when he explains "oats" as "A grain, which in England is generally given to horses, but in Scotland supports the people." The first sense in the OED pays tribute to Johnson in this way: "The grain of a hardy cereal plant ... used as a food for people and animals, esp. horses." Only in the second OED sense[13] does a factual explanation appear.

The initial mechanism for spreading new patterns was not only by conversation, letters, and language-play, but also by the practice of lexicographers in copying from previous dictionaries. The act was less theft than a need for the authentification of English vocabulary. If a postlemmatic translation included English synonyms, and they were copied, those paired combinations had some chance at a well-extended book-life. They could become a stock explanation that future lexicographers would be likely to re-use. Johnson, on the other hand, is very selective in copying headwords not up to the quality of the great Renaissance writers from whom he extracts illustrative quotations. He does not seize rafts of word-entries from previous lexicographers. Here is a table of headwords that begin "tom-" in the dictionaries by Benjamin Martin (1749), Johnson (1755), and Joseph Nicol Scott (1755):

MARTIN 1749	JOHNSON 1755	SCOTT 1755	MODERN SENSE	in OED?
Tomb	Tomb.	Tomb		
	To Tomb	To Tomb		
	Tombless	Tombless		
		Tombstone		
Tomboy	Tomboy	Tom-boy		
Tome	Tome	Tome		
Tomentitious, or Tomentous		Tomentitious, or Tomentous	[made of flocks of wool]	
Tomentum		Tomentum	[wool locks]	
Tometica		Tometica	[pore-opening medicines]	no
Tomice		Tomice	[art of carving in wood]	
		Tomici Dentes	[fore-teeth]	no
Tomin		Tomin	[weight]	

---

13 "The cereal which yields this grain, which may be any of several grasses of the genus Avena, but principally Avena sativa, having loose panicles of large pendulous two- or three-flowered spikelets and widely grown in cool temperate regions."

MARTIN	JOHNSON	SCOTT	MODERN SENSE	in OED?
Tomineso		Tomineso	[American humming bird]	no
Tomkin, or Tompion		Tomkin, or Tompion	[stopple of great gun]	
Tomotocia		Tomotocia	[caesarian operation]	no
	Tomtit	Tomtit	[titmouse]	
		Tom-t—d-man	[Tom Turd-man]	

Scott's seventeen word-entries use Martin's eleven headwords, and all but one of Johnson's slender half-dozen. (All three lexicographers missed "tomato" and "tomorrow.") Scott gives etymologies from French, Italian, Spanish, Latin, and Greek, Martin from French, Latin, and Greek, and Johnson only from French and Latin. Johnson also fashions word-entries with quotations of authors he approves of. Half of his illustrative quotations are from Shakespeare, who did not employ many hard words taken from Greek and Latin or non-literary terms from trade, medicine, and ornithology.

There may be some bias in Johnson's description of a tomboy as "a wild coarse girl". Martin says, neutrally, "girl that tumbles about like a boy" and, with a nice variation, Scott "a ramping, frolicksome rude girl". His use of "ramping" for a tomboy echoes several earlier word-entries:

1611	Trenou: f. A great raumpe, or **tomboy**.	Cotgrave
1677	A Ramp, or **ramping** Wench, une coureuse, une prostituée.	Guy Miège
1699	Tom-boy, a Ramp, or Tomrig.	B.E.
1702	A Ramp, or ramp-scuttle, a ramping girl.	John Kersey
1735	A RIG, a wanton ramping Girl	Benjamin Norton Defoe

Even today, as any browser will show, "ramping girl" is still an idiom.

5 Labyrinths

One example will have to illustrate how a lexical pattern can survive for five hundred years: the headword "labyrinth" and the postlemmatic phrase "tornynges and wendynges".[14]

The medieval period received the myth of the labyrinth with the story of Dedalus, its architect, Minos, its owner, and the Minotaur, its monster; and it

---

14 See Appendix. The headword "labyrinth" occurred to me at random.

entered England in the popular *Polychronicon* written in manuscript by John Trevisa in the late 14th century for Lord Thomas Berkeley and later translated by Randolph Higden into English. His account was first to describe the maze as including "tornynges and wendynges". When one of Berkeley's retinue translated Vegetius's *De Re Militari* into English in 1408 (Vegetius 1988: 116), he took both the story of the labyrinth and its "tornynges and wendingges" from Trevisa. However, it was William Caxton's publication of Higden's *Polychronicon* in 1482 that ensured the survival of this pairing (Trevisa 1865: 313). Its lexicographical history begins in Sir Thomas Elyot's *Dictionary* (1538) in word-entries for "laciniosis" and "Maeander", though not yet collocating with "labyrinth". Robert Burdet's poem *Dyalogue Defensyue for Women* uses "wyndynges and tournynges" with "labyrinth" in 1542, when the second edition of Elyot's *Dictionary* employs the phrase "entrynges, & issuinges out" instead for "labyrinth". Higden's "wyndynges" again appears in Elyot's entries for "Lacinosis" and "Maeander". Thomas Cooper, Elyot's assistant, kept Elyot's phrasing in "Labyrinthus" from re-editions of his lexicon from 1545 to 1559. In 1565, however, Cooper in the first of five editions of his own *Thesaurus* added a word-entry under "Error" that read "Indeprehensus & irremeabilis error Labyrinthi. Virgil. The windyng and tourning of the maaze that no man can perceiue and finde out agayne". The phrasing of Higden's *Polychronicon* in 1482 next found its way into a word-entry on "labyrinthus" in Thomas Thomas's Latin–English dictionary in 1587, which reworked all Cooper's material. Thomas's successful lexicon fully established the collocation of "labyrinth" and variants of the phrase "windings and turnings". Thereafter it appears in word-entries on "labyrinth" in five English monolingual hard-word dictionaries from Cawdrey (1604) to Coles (1676), and three later general English dictionaries by Kersey (1702), Defoe (1735), and Bailey (1737). Bilingual lexicons by both John Florio (Italian) and Randle Cotgrave (French) in 1611 use it. The phrase goes missing from Ephraim Chambers's *Cyclopaedia* (1728), Johnson's *Dictionary* (1755), and the Bailey-Scott *Dictionary* (1755), yet it did not die out, as Noah Webster's first entry (1806) shows.

The OED has twenty non-lexicographical quotations with the collocation "turnings" and "windings", two from 1582 to 1587, ten from 1600 to 1689, six from 1701 to 1785, and the last two in 1801 and 1879. Many but not most are associated explicitly with a labyrinth. The bulk are in the 17th century, as with the evidence for occurrences in dictionaries. Two additional OED quotations are from Nathan Bailey's lexicon in 1731, and Noah Webster's in 1828. The lexical pattern occurring first in *Polychronicon* even appears in definitions authored by OED lexicographers.[15] Lexicographical history hints at how literal lexical patterns like the collocation of "labyrinth" and "windings and turnings" developed. They found their way into explications of headwords or occasionally what resemble logical definitions of things. "Labyrinth", being a hard word borrowed from a Greek and Latin story, is more complex than most headwords because it invited expansive explanations of the structure itself. They refer to "labyrinth" in Elyot's sense as a house (a type) with entrances and exits (a difference), or in Thomas Thomas's sense as a maze (a type) with "windings and turnings" (a difference). These explanations are sentences that extend beyond single-word glosses.

6 The mind in the word-entry

Today, Google searches, which are generally user-entered headwords, produce results – computer-generated, profuse, and of often questionable relevance – that are far from the postlemmatic abstract lexical pattern of most historical word-entries. Some might object that associating a word-entry with a Google query at all makes little sense, but artificial intelligence technology will in time learn how to tame the sheer mass of hits. The Google "word-entry" at present resembles a guessing game where the human poses the problem (the headword) and a machine answers it. In contrast, the *Oxford English Dictionary Online* and the lexicographic encoding language of the *Text Encoding Initiative* (TEI) are recommended for their exactitude and power in controlling the abstract word-entry lexical pattern. At present, Google appears massively *laissez-faire*, and OED and TEI unforgivingly standardized. Yet all are computational imitations of lexical patterning done by human cognitive networks.

One of them, the unself-conscious default mode network (DMN) of a day-dreaming brain, releases a turbulent flow of memories not associated with some controlled activity. The discoverer of the default mode network, Marcus Raichle, explains that it supports "emotional processing ... self-referential mental activity ... and the recollection of prior experiences" (Raichle 2015: 440). Examples of several Early Modern word-entries described above find just such aberrant, unexpected intrusions into the postlemmatic element, as if the mind of the lexicographer had temporarily lost track of its problem and included matter of questionable relevance. Such a breakdown appears in some of Johnson's word-entries,

---

15 See OED, "mazy", adj. 1, and n.2.a: "Resembling or of the nature of a maze; full of windings and turnings; labyrinthine, convoluted" (and see also "maze", n.1, 4.2).

however brilliant they are in both style and wit. We would expect the lexicographer's mind to be engaged in an "attention-demanding, goal-directed" task (Raichle 2015: 434) that is the business of another brain network, sometimes termed the "cognitive control network" (CCN), which toggles on and off in keeping with the current inactive or active state of the DMN. Not so in Johnson, whose well-stocked quotations can distract him from the lexicographer's dispassionate vocabulary collection.

To what extent does neuroscience account for cognitive control in making word-entries? Typical word-entry lexical patterns owe much to the "magic" number of items which the mind's conscious or "working" memory (of both language and space) can transfer and store in long-term memory. Originally the number of items was thought to be seven, after early telephone numbers. Plentiful research now shows that it varies between two and four chunks, each of which may have up to four items (Cowan 2000). Clarence Green (2017) recently has described various linguistic patterns that observe this capacity limit, including "phrasal verbs, idioms, n-grams, the lengths of intonation units and some abstract grammatical properties of phrasal categories and clause structure" (Green 2017: 209). Elsewhere I speculate that the size of most repeating fixed phrases is consistent with this working-memory capacity,[16] and here I argue from *LEME* that a constrained word-entry comprising a paired headword and postlemmatic element, each including optional items, fits into the capacity of working memory. Pairs of words (such as an English word and its corresponding word in French) are little associational networks that leave conscious working memory and enter long-term memory through the hippocampus, somewhat as lexical pairs "enter" long-term storage in dictionaries as word-entries. The tightly reasoned cognitive control network (CCN) that underlies this abstract lexical pattern helps explain why the collocation of "labyrinth" and "windings and turnings" lasts so long.

Paired chunks are a powerful lexical meta-pattern that manifests in old bilingual glossaries and class word-lists. The toggling of two dominant brain networks (DMN and CCN) can help explain anomalies in the lemmatic element of Early Modern word-entries (such as Claude Desainliens's "burne them all"), and the maximum word-load of working memory can help explain the size of most word-entries. It is important to reach beyond our grasp, as Robert Browning says, to see how the structures of lexical patterns can be illuminated by an understanding of the organ that generates them. Eighteenth-century lexicographers took one step in doing so. They accepted that the goal of a word-entry, definition, focused on a

---

[16] Lancashire, *Forgetful Muses* (2010). That there are four enzymes in DNA may only be my personal DMN run amuck.

headword and how the mind defined it. Although the DMN does not often mind what it generates, the most important paradigm of modern linguistics builds on a theory of universal grammar focusing on brain function.

Appendix

15th cent. (Trevisa, *Polychronicon*)

Laborintus is an hous wonderliche i-buld wi*th* halkes and hernes, wi*th* **tornynges and wendynges** and wonderful weyes so dyuersliche and so wrynkyngliche i-wrog*ht*, *t*hat who *t*hat is wi*th* ynne *t*hat hous and wil out wende, [*t*hey he wende] wel faste oo wey and o*t*her, hiderward and *th*iderward, estward and westwarde, nor*th*ward and sou*t*hward, whider euere *t*hey drawe, [and] of [alle] *t*he weies chese *t*he faireste; *t*hey he trauaile neuere so sore, al is for nou*gh*t. For out goo*th* he neuere, but he haue a craft *t*hat nede*th* *t*herfore.

1408 (Vegetius' *De Re Militari*)

Minotaurus ... poetes seyn þat he is hid priueliche in þe ynnermeste party of þe vncouþe place of priuete, þe whiche is cleped þe **Laberynthe. This Laberinthe** is a place þat Dedalus made in þe yle of Crete, þe whiche place was so wondirfulliche ycast and ymade by craft þat, what man oþer beest entred þe ȝate and walked þereynne eny while, he schulde neuere fynde þe ȝate aȝen þat he cam in by, þere were in þat place so many wondirful **tornynges and wendingges**. And þerfore it was yclepid **laberinthus**, *quasi labens intus*.

1482 (Randulf Higden and John Trevisa, *Prolicionycion*. Westminster: William Caxton. Fol. lxxxxvi)

Laborintus is a maner buyldynge wonderly buyld / with daungerous walles· therin minotaurus was closed yf ony man went theder in withoute a clewe of threde it were ful hard to finde away oute they that opene the yats shold here drede ful thondryng Hugo capitulo labor Me gooth a downe as it were by a honderd grees or steppes ther be also in derknes wonder many dyuerse **wyndynges and tournyngys** / and suche foure be in this worlde of suche howses One in egypte another in Creta the thyrd in the ylande lempno and the fourth in ytalye and be soo made that vnn·the they maye be destroyed while the world dureth ¶ Hugo capitulo Cilleo

1500? (Informacon for pylgrymes vnto the holy londe. London: Wynkyn de Worde.)

Laborintus. and that is a merueylous place wythin forth. wroughte out of harde stone of the rocke. and the grete hylle aboue. A man maye goo wythin that place dyuers wayes. some waye .x. myles. and some waye more / & some waye lesse. And but yf a man be wel ware how he gooth in. he may so goo he shall not come out agayn there be soo many **tornynges** therin.

1538 (Sir Thomas Elyot, *Dictionary*)

Labyrinthus, a maase, or any buildyng made like a maase, out of the which it were hard to gette forthe.

Laciniosus, a, um, cutte in sondrye facions, **wyndyng and tournynge** dyuers wayes.

Maeander, a ryuer of the countray of Phrigia, whiche hathe many **tournynges and wyndynges**: and of that all crooked and subtyll tournynge wayes, meanes, and deuyses, be called *Meandri*. There is also of that name a mountayne in India.

1542 (Robert Burdet, *Dyalogue Defensyue for Women,* sig. c3r)

Meandre the flude, that maketh men to muse
And laboryous labyrynth, that Dedalus deuysed
Suche wyndynges and tournynges, neuer dyd vse
As women in temptacyon, for men haue contryued
All gyftes of nature, they inclyne to prouoke
Man vnto pleasure, and his reason to blynde.

1542 (Sir Thomas Elyot, *Bibliotheca*). Minor changes in 1545, 1552, 1559 editions.

Labyrinthus, a place conteynynge many romes in suche wise prepared, that who so euer was brought into it, moughte not issue out of it, withoute a guyde very perfect in it, or without a threde leading hym, wherof the botome or klewe shoulde be left at the entre. ... An other **Labyrinthus** was in Creta, made by Dedalus by the commandement of Minos for a prison, but it was moch lasse than the other. But by dyuers doores, **entrynges, & issuinges out**, it deceyued them, whiche came into it. Sir Thomas Elyot, *Bibliotheca*

MEANDER, a riuer in Phrigia, whiche by sundry **wyndynges**, at the laste falleth into a creeke, whiche diuideth Miletum and Priena in Grece.

Laciniosus, a, um, cut in sundry fashions, **windyng and turnyng** dyuers ways, iagged.

1565 (Thomas Cooper, *Thesaurus Linguae Romanae et Britannicae*). Minor changes in 1573, 1578, 1584 editions.

Indeprehensus & irremeabilis error **Labyrinthi**. Virgil. The **windyng and tourning** of the maaze that no man can perceiue and finde out agayne. (under "Error, erroris").

Flexuosus, pen. pro. Adiectiuum. **That is crooked, or hath many windinges or turninges**. vt, Flexusa vitis. Cato. That turneth in and out. Flexuosus corporum impulsus. Plin. Iter flexuosum. Cic. A crooked way with many **turninges**.

Mæander, A riuer of the country Phrygia. Erasmus sayeth of Lydia: which hath many **turnings and wyndynges**. And hereof all crooked and subtylle **tournyng** wayes, meanes and diuises be called *Mæandri*. There is also of that name a mountaine in India.

Labyrinthus, A place made in suche wyse, that who so euer came into it, could not issue out without a very perfecte guyde, or without a threede leadynge him, whereof the bottome or clew should be lefte at the entrée. ... An other *Labyrinthus* was in Creta, made by Dedalus, by the commaundement of Minos, for a pryson: but it was muche lesse then the other. But by **diuers doores, entringes, and issuyngs out**, it deceyued them, whiche came into it. The thirde was in Italy, by a towne called *Clusium*, made by kynge Porsena: and (as Plinie and Varro wryte) was of square stone, the sydes .30. foote broade. in heighte .50. foote. Into the whiche who so euer wente, without a clewe or bottome of thréede, coulde neuer retourne.

1587 (Thomas Thomas, *Dictionarium Linguae Latinae et Anglicanae*)

Error, oris, m.g. An errour, a false opinion, a taking of a falsehood for truth: a wandring, a mistaking, deceit, ignorance: a **winding or turning**: a turning out of the way.

Flexŭ&omacron;sus, a, um. That is crooked, or hath many **windings and turn**ings.

Mæander, vel Mæandrus, dri, m.g. A **turning or winding**: also in apparell wrought with the needle a **winding** in & out of the threeds, welts, or borders after the manner of a **Labyrinth**, Iun.

Lăbyrinthus, thi, m.g. s.b. Plin. A labrinth or place ful of **intricate windings and turnings**, made in such wise, that whosoeuer came into it, could not get out againe without a verie perfect guide, or without a threede directing him, the clew or bottome whereof should be left at the entree: also an oration or other thing very difficult and intricate.

1589 (John Rider, *Bibliotheca Scholastica*)

A **Labyrinth. 1 Labyrinthus**, m. **Of a Labyrinth. 1 labyrintheus**
A **winding** in and out of threds welts, or borders in apparell wrought with a needle after the manner of a **Labyrinth**. (under "To Winde", sig. mm4v)

1 Versio, versatio, versura, volutatio, f. volutatus, m. A **turning, or winding**. 1 Inflexio, flexio, tortio, f. flexus, anfractus. The **turning, or winding** of a river. 3 **Meander**, meandrus, m. A turning rounde, or about. ... 1 Reciprocatio, f. A **turning, or winding** of a water banke. ... 1 Trusatilis, ad. That hath many **turnings, and windings**. 1 Sinuosus, tortuosus, ad. That turneth, or whirleth rounde (under "To Turne")

1598 (John Florio, *A World of Words*)

Labirinto, Labirintho, a laberinth or place full of **intricate windings and turnings**, made in such wise that whosoeuer came into it coulde not get out againe without a perfect guide, or without a thred directing him, the clew or bottom whereof should be left at the entrie, wee call it a maze.

1604 (Robert Cawdrey, *A Table Alphabetical*)

laborinth, a place so full of **windings and turnings**, that a man cannot finde the way out of it:

1611 (Randle Cotgrave, *A Dictionary of the French and English Tongues*)

Labyrinthé: m. ée: f. Made as a **laborinth**, framed like a maze; intricated; full of vnknowne crookes, creeks, **turnings, windings**.

1611 (John Florio, *Queen Anna's New World of Words*)

Labirínto, Labiríntho, a Laberinth or Maze or place full of **intricate windings and turnings**, so made that whosoeuer came into it could not get out againe without a guide or a thrid directing him. It is also taken for any intricate, difficult or intangled thing.

1616 (John Bullokar, *An English Expositor*)

Labyrinth. An intricate building or place made with so many **turnings and windings**, that whosoeuer went into it, could neuer get out without a perfect guide, or a thred to direct him, the end of which threed must be tyed at the doore where he entreth.

1656 (Thomas Blount, *Glossographia or a Dictionary*)

Labyrinth (labyrinthus) a Maze or intricate building, or place made with so many **turnings, and windings**, entries and doors, that whoever went into it, could never get out, without a perfect guide, or a thread to direct him, the end of which thread must be tyed at the door where he enters. ... Labyrinth, also signifies metaphorically an intricate Oration or difficult matter.

1658 (Edward Phillips, *The New World of English Words*)

Labyrinth, (Greek) a Maze, or place made with so many **turnings and windings** that a man once entered in, cannot finde the way out, whereof the two most famous were, that built by Miris King of Egypt, and that which Dædalus built for Minos, King of Crete, it is also by Metaphor used for any kinde of intanglement, or intricate businesse.

1664 (Francis Gouldman, *A Copious Dictionary* [Latin-English])

Labyrinthus, thi ... A **labyrinth** or place full of intricate **windings and turnings**, made in such wise, that whosoever came into it could not go out again without a very perfect guide, or without a threed directing him, the clue or bottom whereof should be left at the entry. (Ll8v)

1668 (John Wilkins, *An Essay towards a Real Character and a Philosophical Language*)

Maze. [Extasie] Structure full of perplex Windings] Turnings Place full of perplex **Windings Turnings**]

1676 (Elisha Coles, *An English Dictionary*)

Labyrinth, a maze, made with so many **windings, and turnings** that one cannot easily get out, also any intricate business.

1684 (Steven Blankaart, *A Physical Dictionary*)

Labyrinthus is a Body full of **windings and turnings**, as may be seen in the inner part of the Ear, and in the outer surface of the Brain.

1702 (John Kersey the younger, *A New English Dictionary*)

A **Labyrinth**, or maze with so many **windings and turnings**, that one cannot get out, without a guide, or a clew of thread for direction.

1735 (Benjamin Norton Defoe, *A New English Dictionary*)

LABYRINTH, a Maze, a Place with many **Windings and Turnings**, so that a Man once entered cannot find his way out

1737 (Nathan Bailey, *Universal Etymological English Dictionary*)

DELIASTS, the persons appointed to perform the ceremonies of this festival, were certain citizens deputed to go on an embassy or rather pilgrimage to the temple of Apollo, at Delos. They were crown'd with Laurel, the whole deputation set out in 5 vessels, carrying with them all things necessary for the feast and sacrifices. After the sacrifice a number of young men and maids danc'd round the altar, a dance in which by their various motions and directions, they represented the **turnings and windings of the labyrinth**.

LABYRINTH of Egypt ... built by Psamniticus, on the bank of the river Nile, situate on the south of the Pyramids, and north of Arsinoe: It contained within the compass of one continued wall, 1000 houses, and 12 royal palaces, all covered with marble; and had only one entrance; but innumerable **turnings and returnings**, sometimes one over another; and all in a manner scarce to be found, but by such as were acquainted with them; the building being more under ground than above; the marble stones were laid with such art, that neither wood nor cement was used in any part of the fabrick; the chambers were so disposed, that the doors at their opening gave a report as terrible as a crack of thunder.

1755 (Samuel Johnson, *A Dictionary of the English Language*)

LA'BYRINTH. n. s. [labyrinthus, Latin.] A maze; a place formed with inextricable **windings**. ... My soul is on her journey; do not now Divert, or lead her back, to lose herself I' th' maze and **winding labyrinths** o' th' world. Denham.

1806 (Noah Webster, *A Compendious Dictionary of the English Language*)

Lab'yrinth, *n.* a maze, a place full of **windings**

References

Alston, Robin C. 1965-. *A bibliography of the English language from the invention of printing to the year 1800*. Leeds: Printed for the author.
Anderson, Judith. 1996. *Words that matter: Linguistic perception in Renaissance English*. Stanford, CA: Stanford University Press.
Anonymous. 1497. *Englysshe and Frensshe*. Westminster: Wynkyn de Worde. STC 24866.
Anonymous. 1500? *Informacon for Pylgrymes vnto the Holy Londe*. London: Wynkyn de Worde.

Anonymous. c. 1480. *Medulla Grammatice*. Magdalene College, Cambridge, Pepys Library MS 2002.
Bailey, Nathan. 1737. *Universal Etymological English Dictionary*. London: Nathan Bailey.
Bailey, Richard W. 1985. Charles C. Fries and the Early Modern English dictionary. In Nancy de Fries (ed.), *Toward an understanding of language: Charles Carpenter Fries in perspective*, 171–204. Amsterdam: John Benjamins.
Baret, John. 1574. *An Aluearie or Triple Dictionarie, in Englishe, Latin, and French*. London: Henry Denham.
Berlement, Noël van. 1576. *Colloques ou dialogues auec vn dictionaire en six langues*. Anvers: H. Heyndrickx.
Blankaart, Steven. 1684. *A Physical Dictionary*. London: J. Gellibrand.
Blount, Thomas. 1656. *Glossographia*. London: Thomas Newcomb for Humphrey Moseley and George Sawbridge.
Blundeville, Thomas. 1617. *The arte of logick*. London: William Stansby.
Brede, Alexander. 1937. The idea of an English language academy. *English Journal* 26 (7). 560–568.
Bullokar, John. 1616. *An English Expositor: Teaching the Interpretation of the Hardest Words in our Language*. London: John Legatt.
Burdet, Robert. 1542. *A Dyalogue Defensyue for Women / agaynst Malycyous Detractoures*. [London]: Robert Wyer, for Rycharde Banckes. STC 24601.
Cawdrey, Robert. 1604. *A Table Alphabeticall, Conteyning and Teaching the Understanding of Hard Usuall English Wordes, Borrowed from the Hebrew, Greeke, Latine, or French, & c.* London: E. Weaver.
Caxton, William. c. 1480. *Fransois et Engloys Frenssh and Englissh*. Westminster: William Caxton. STC 24865.
Chambers, Ephraim. 1728. *Cyclopaedia, or, an Universal Dictionary of Arts and Sciences: Containing the Definitions of the Terms, and Accounts of the Things Signify'd Thereby*. London: James and John Knapton, and others.
Cockeram, Henry. 1623. *English Dictionarie: or, an Interpreter of Hard English Words*. London: Eliot's Court Press for N. Butter.
Coles, Elisha. 1676. *An English Dictionary: Explaining The difficult Terms that are used in Divinity, Husbandry, Physick, Phylosophy, Law, Navigation, Mathematicks, and other Arts and Sciences*. London: Samuel Crouch. Wing C 5070.
Cooper, Thomas. 1565. *Thesaurus Linguae Romanae et Britannicae*. London: Thomae Bertheleti. STC 5686.
Coote, Edmund. 1997 [1596]. *The English Schoole-Maister*. [Edited by Ian Lancashire, Linda Hutjens, Brent Nelson, Robert Whalen & Tanya Wood]. Toronto: University of Toronto Library. (http://www.library.utoronto.ca/utel/ret/ coote/ret2.html) [Originally published: London: Widow Orwin for R. Jackson and R. Dexter.]
Cotgrave, Randle. 1611. *A Dictionarie of the French and English Tongues*. London: Adam Islip.
Cowan, Nelson. 2000. The magical number 4 in short-term memory: A reconsideration of mental storage capacity. *Behavioral and Brain Sciences* 24. 87–185.
Cowell, John. 1607. *The Interpreter: or Booke Containing the Signification of Words*. Cambridge: John Legate.
Defoe, Benjamin Norton. 1735. *A New English Dictionary*. Westminster: John Brindley, and others.
Desainliens, Claude. 1593. *A Dictionarie French and English*. London: Thomas Woodcock. STC 6737.
Early English Books Online, 1475–1700 (EEBO). 2003–2011. Ann Arbor: ProQuest. (http://eebo.chadwyck.com/home)
Elyot, Sir Thomas. 1538. *The Dictionary of Syr Thomas Eliot*. London: Thomas Berthelet.

Elyot, Sir Thomas. 1542. *Bibliotheca Eliotae Eliotis Librarie*. London: Thomas Berthelet.
Erasmus, Desiderius. 1963. *On Copia of Words and Ideas* (*De Utraque Verborem ac Rerum Copia*). [Translated by Donald B. King and H. David Rix]. Milwaukee, WI: Marquette University Press.
Florio, John. 1598. *A Worlde of Wordes, or, Most Copious, and Exact Dictionarie in Italian and English*. London: Arnold Hatfield for Edward Blount.
Florio, John. 1611. *Queen Anna's New World of Words*. London: Edward. Blount and William Barret.
Googe, Barnabe. 1561. *The Zodiake of Life*. London: Rafe Newbery. STC 19149.
Görlach, Manfred. 1991. *Introduction to Early Modern English*. Cambridge: Cambridge University Press.
Gotti, Maurizio. 1992. The development of a scientific language in the seventeenth century. In Carmela Nocera Avila, Nicola Pantaleo & D. Pezzini. Biblioteca della Ricerca (eds.), *Early Modern English: Trends, Forms and Texts*. (Cultura Straniera 49), 319–343. Fasano: Schena.
Gouldman, Francis. 1664. *A Copious Dictionary*. Wing 1443. London: John Field.
Green, Clarence. 2017. Usage-based linguistics and the magic number four. *Cognitive Linguistics* 28 (2). 209–237.
Harris, John. 1704. *Lexicon Technicum: or, an Universal English Dictionary of Arts and Sciences: Explaining not only The Terms of Art, but the Arts Themselves*. London: Daniel Brown and others.
H[arrison]., L[ucas]. 1571. *A Dictionarie French and English*. London: Henry Bynneman.
Hervet, Gentian, trans. 1526. *De Immensa Dei Misericordia*. London: Thomas Berthelet. STC 10474. [Erasmus]
Higden, Randulf & John Trevisa. 1482. *Prolicionycion* [sig. ¶5r]. Westminster: William Caxton. STC 13438.
Holyoake, Francis. 1606. *Riders Dictionarie Corrected and Avgmented*. London: Adam Islip. STC 21032.
Holyoake, Thomas. 1676–1677. *A Large Dictionary*. Wing H2535. London: G. Sawbridge and others.
Howell, A. C. 1946. *Res et verba*: Words and things. *English Literary History* 13. 131–142.
Howlet (Huloet), Richard. 1552. *Abcedarium Anglico Latinum*. Londini: Gulielmi Riddel.
Internet Live Stats. World Wide Web Consortium. (Viewed 28 January 2018. http://www.internetlivestats.com/google-search-statistics/)
Johnson, Samuel. 1979 [1755]. *A dictionary of the English language*. [Introduction by Robert W. Burchfield]. London: Times Books.
Kersey, John. 1702. *English Dictionary: Or, a Compleat: Collection Of the Most Proper and Significant Words, Commonly Used in the Language*. London: Henry Bonwicke and Robert Knaplock.
Lancashire, Ian. 2002. 'Dumb significants' and Early Modern English definition. In Jens Brockmeier, Min Wang & David R. Olson (eds.), *Literacy, narrative and culture*, 131–154. Richmond, Surrey: Curzon.
Lancashire, Ian. 2006. Law and Early Modern English lexicons. In Roderick McConchie, Heli Tissari & Olga Timofeeva (eds.), *HEL-LEX: New approaches in English historical lexis*, 8–23. Somerville, MA: Cascadilla Press.
Lancashire, Ian. 2010. *Forgetful muses: Reading the author in the text*. Toronto: University of Toronto Press.
Lancashire, Ian & Elisa Tersigni. 2013. Early Modern English vocabulary growth. In Andrew Hardie & Robbie Love (eds.), *Corpus linguistics 2013*, 156–159. Lancaster: UCREL.
Lever, Ralph. 1972 [1573]. *The Art of Reason*. Menston: Scolar.
Levins, Peter. 1867 [1570]. *Manipulus Vocabulorum: A Rhyming Dictionary of the English Language*. [Edited by Henry B. Wheatley]. (EETS O. S. 27). London: Early English Text Society.

Lexicons of Early Modern English. LEME 2.0. 2018–. LEME 1.0. 2006–. [Edited by Ian Lancashire]. Toronto: University of Toronto Library and University of Toronto Press. (URL: leme.library.utoronto.ca)

Martin, Benjamin. 1747. *Lingua Britannica Reformata: Or, A New English Dictionary.* London: J. Hodges and others, ESTC T025324.

Minsheu, John. 1617. *Ductor in Linguas.* London: John Browne. STC 17944.

Minsheu, John. 1625. *Minshaei emendatio, vel a mendis expurgatio, seu augmentatio sui ductoris in linguas, The guide into tongues.* London: John Haviland. STC 17945.

Mulcaster, Richard. 1582. *The First Part of the Elementarie.* London: Thomas Vautroullier.

Nevalainen, Terttu. 1999. Early Modern English lexis and semantics. In Roger Lass (ed.), *The Cambridge history of the English language.* Vol. 3: *1476–1776*, 332–458. Cambridge: Cambridge University Press.

Nevalainen, Terttu. 2006. *An introduction to Early Modern English.* Edinburgh: Edinburgh University Press.

Ortus Vocabulorum. 1500. Westminster: Wynkyn de Worde. STC 13829.

Palsgrave, John. 1530. *Lesclarcissement de la Langue Francoyse.* London: R. Pynson and J. Haukyns.

Phillips, Edward. 1969 [1658]. *The New World of English Words.* (English Linguistics 1500–1800, 321.) Menston: Scolar Press.

Pollard, Alfred W. & Gilbert R. Redgrave. 1976, 1986, 1991. *A short title catalogue of books printed in England, Scotland, & Ireland, and of English books printed abroad, 1475–1640.* [Edited by William A. Jackson, F. S. Ferguson & Katherine F. Pantzer]. 2nd edn. 2 vols. London: The Bibliographical Society.

Promptorium Parvulorum. 1499. London: Richard Pynson. STC 20434.

Raichle, Marcus E. 2015. The brain's default mode network. *Annual Review of Neuroscience* 38. 433–447.

Rider, John. 1589. *Bibliotheca Scholastica.* Oxford: Joseph Barnes.

Rastell, John. c. 1525. *Exposiciones Terminorum Legum Anglorum.* London: John Rastell. STC 20702.

Rastell, John & William Rastell. 1579. *An Exposition of Certaine Difficult and Obscure Words, and Termes of the Lawes of This Realme.* London: Richarde Tottell. STC 20706.5.

Salesbury, William. 1547. *A Dictionary in Englyshe and Welshe.* London: N. Hill for J. Waley. STC 21616.

Schäfer, Jürgen. 1989. *Early Modern English lexicography.* 2 vols. Oxford: Clarendon Press.

Scott, Joseph Nicol & Nathan Bailey. 1755. *A New Universal Etymological Dictionary.* London: T. Osborne and others. ESTC T148730.

Sherry, Richard. 1555. *A Treatise of the Figures of Grammer and Rhetorike.* London: Richard Tottel.

Sidney, Sir Philip. 1595. *The Defence of Poesie.* London: William Ponsonby.

Simpson, John, ed. 2000–. *The Oxford English Dictionary.* 3rd edn. online. Oxford University Press. (http://www.oed.com/)

Starnes, De Witt Talmage. 1954. *Renaissance dictionaries, English–Latin and Latin–English.* Austin, TX: University of Texas Press.

Stein, Gabriele. 1985. *The English dictionary before Cawdrey.* Tübingen: Niemeyer.

Stein, Gabriele. 1986. Definitions and first-person pronoun involvement in Thomas Elyot's dictionary. In Dieter Kastovsky & Aleksander Swedek (eds.), *Linguistics across historical and geographical boundaries*, 1465–1474. Berlin: Mouton de Gruyter.

Stein, Gabriele. 1987. Reference point and authorial involvement in John Palsgrave's *Esclarcissement de la langue francoyse*. In Wolfgang Lörscher & Rainer Schulze (eds.), *Perspectives on language and performance: Studies in linguistics, literary criticism and language teaching and learning to honour Werner Hüllen on the occasion of his sixtieth birthday*. (TüBL 317), 530–546. Tübingen: Gunter Narr.

Stein, Gabriele. 1997. *John Palsgrave as Renaissance linguist: A pioneer in vernacular language description*. Oxford: Clarendon Press.

Stein, Gabriele. 2014. *Sir Thomas Elyot as lexicographer*. Oxford: Oxford University Press.

Stein, Gabriele. 2017. *Word studies in the Renaissance*. Oxford: Oxford University Press.

Stein, Gabriele, Starnes, DeWitt T. & Gertrude E. Noyes. 1991. *The English dictionary from Cawdrey to Johnson: 1604–1755*. 2nd edition. Amsterdam: Benjamins.

Text Encoding Initiative. 2017. "9 Dictionaries." Guidelines for electronic text encoding and interchange. Version 3.2.0. (URL: http://www.tei-c.org/release/doc/tei-p5-doc/en/html/DI.html)

Thomas, Thomas. 1587. *Dictionarium Linguae Latinae et Anglicanae*. Cambridge: Richard Boyle.

Thomas, William. 1550. *Principal Rvles of the Italian Grammer*. London: T. Berthelet. STC 24020.

Traheron, Bartholomew. 1543. The interpretation of straunge wordes, vsed in the translation of Vigon. In *The most excellent workes of Chirurgerye*. London: Edward Whitchurch. Fols. zz1r-{*}3v. [{*}: unidentified Latin contraction]

Trevisa, John. 1865. *Polychronicon Ranulphi Higden Monachi Cestrensis; together with the English Translations of John Trevisa and of an Unknown Writer of the Fifteenth Century*. Vol. 1. [Edited by Churchill Babington]. London: Longman.

Tyndale, William. 1534. *The Newe Testament*. Antwerp: Marten Emperowr. STC 2826.

Vegetius. 1988. *The Earliest English Translation of Vegetius' De Re Militari*. [Edited by Geoffrey Lester]. Heidelberg: Winter (Oxford MS Bodl. Douce 291, fol. 59v).

Veldhuis, Niek. 2014. *History of the cuneiform lexical tradition*. Münster: Ugarit-Verlag.

Véron, Jean. 1552. *Dictionariolum Puerorum*. London: R. Wolfium. STC 10555.

Verstegan, Richard, 1605. *A Restitvtion of Decayed Intelligence*. Antwerp: Robert Bruney. STC 21361.

Waswo, Richard. 1987. *Language and meaning in the Renaissance*. Princeton: Princeton University.

Webster, Noah. 1970 [1806]. *A compendious dictionary of the English language*. Facsimile. New Haven: Crown.

Wilkins, John. 1668. *An Essay Towards a Real Character and a Philosophical Language*. London: Royal Society. Antwerp: Robert Bruney. STC.

Wilson, Thomas. 1551. *The rule of reason, conteinyng the arte of logique*. London: Richard Grafton.

Withals, John. 1553. *A Shorte Dictionarie for Yonge Begynners*. London: T. Berthelet.

Tony McEnery and Vaclav Brezina
Collocations and colligations: Visualizing lexicogrammar

Abstract: This chapter explores the use of #LancsBox to explore collocations and colligations in the framework of lexicogrammar. The chapter presents lexicogrammar and relates it to collocation and colligation, noting how those concepts are best viewed as part of a continuum rather than as discrete concepts. We then use #LancsBox to look at lexicogrammar from different perspectives. Beginning with an exploration of learner language, the chapter proceeds to explore lexicogrammar at the level of lexis, across varieties of English, through time, as mediated by morphosyntax and, finally, by the use of collocation networks. The results presented focus largely on visualizing lexicogrammar, yet the chapter also shows that modern corpus analysis tools are capable of allowing for a range of approaches to lexicogrammar that permit analysts to use a single package to look at lexicogrammar from a range of linguistically meaningful perspectives.

1 Introduction

The work carried out in this chapter is based on a simple observation: collocation statistics do not identify associations between words related to meaning alone. Collocation, as derived by statistical measurement, captures links assumed to exist between words by virtue of their cooccurrence in text. In this chapter, we use #LancsBox, a freely available software package developed at Lancaster University (Brezina, McEnery and Wattam, 2015), which, among other things, visualizes collocations and builds collocation networks. While collocation can cover the lexical and the syntactic, most often it is used to explore lexical relationships between words. In contrast, colligation according to Hoey (as reported in Hunston 2001: 15) is "the grammatical company a word keeps (or avoids keeping) either within its own groups or at a higher rank", the "grammatical functions that the word's group prefers" and the "place in the sequence that a word prefers". If we

---

Tony McEnery, Lancaster University, Department of Linguistics and English Language, Lancaster LA1 4YL, United Kingdom, a.mcenery@lancaster.ac.uk
Vaclav Brezina, Lancaster University, Department of Linguistics and English Language, Lancaster LA1 4YL, United Kingdom, v.brezina@lancaster.ac.uk

https://doi.org/10.1515/9783110596656-005

see collocation as an operation looking at how language is ordered by cooccurrence at the lexical level, colligation becomes its partner at the syntactic level. While it is possible to think of ways of beginning to exclude colligations from a set of collocates, for example by discarding function words in the list, this approach is always bound to be approximate because lexis and grammar operate on a continuum and cannot be easily separated. Function words can encode semantic and discourse relations. By the same token, content words when collocating may betoken a grammatical relationship – if an adjective collocates with a noun in English showing a strong preference to appear in a left-hand position, this is, in part, an encoding of a grammatical relationship. A meaning relationship may be present too, but the collocation is conditioned to a degree by the grammar of English – lexis and grammar are interacting to bear meaning. Similarly, function words can convey meaning – while *by* collocating to the left of *river* may be seen as primarily a colligation, indicating that *river* is often in a noun phrase governed by *by* which is acting as the head of a prepositional phrase, this grammatical relationship also bears a semantics of relative location (see Zwarts and Winter 1997, and Vasardani, Stirling and Winter 2017 for a fuller discussion of the semantics of locative prepositions).

Accordingly, while it is often convenient to think of collocations and colligations as discrete categories, they should more properly be viewed as two poles of a lexicogrammatical continuum, meaning that it is almost inevitable that, in searching for meaning through collocation, we will uncover grammatical information. Contrariwise, while looking at colligates it is most inevitable that we will encounter semantic relations. Such a continuum is well established as a concept. Halliday (1991: 31–32) says:

> I have always seen lexicogrammar as a unified phenomenon, a single level of 'wording', of which lexis is the 'most delicate' resolution ... the 'two' form a continuum: at one end are the very general choices, multiply intersecting, which can readily be closed to form a paradigm, such as 'polarity: positive/negative', 'mood: indicative (declarative/interrogative)/ imperative', 'transitivity: material/mental/relational', and these are best illuminated by being treated as grammar; while at the other end are choices which are highly specific but open-ended, with each term potentially entering into many term sets, e.g. *run* contrasting (i) with *walk*, (ii) with *hop*, *skip*, (iii) with *jog* etc., and these are best illuminated by being treated as lexis. Midway along the continuum are things like prepositions and modals which do not yield a strong preference to either form of treatment .... 'lexis' and 'grammar' are names of complementary perspectives. (Halliday 1991: 31–32)

This continuum is apparent in the exploration of every set of collocates. While the statistics of collocation are focused on lexis, because lexis is part of a continuum as described by Halliday, an exploration of the relationship between lexical items via collocation naturally opens up the "multiply intersecting" levels of linguistic choice and structure that Halliday writes of.

Corpora are well placed to explore such complex patterns in language – most corpus linguistic tools are oriented towards discovering patterns, whether this be, for example, patterns of word cooccurrence through collocation, more general patterning through wildcard or regular expression searches, or the use of dispersion measures to see how well a word or pattern distributes through a text or corpus collection. Corpus linguistics permits such searches but the degree to which the findings represent psychological reality is usually approached through triangulation, where corpus results may be compared with those of a psycholinguistic experiment, for example (see Baker and Egbert 2019). This chapter thus works within the corpus linguistics paradigm without assumptions of a specific theoretical framework such as cognitive grammar (e.g. Langacker 1987) or psychological theory (e.g. Ellis and Beattie 1986). However, a broader set of conclusions about the patterning which corpus analysis reveals would be desirable as a product of the work of a larger interdisciplinary group, approaching the findings here from a perspective of methodological pluralism.

In this chapter, we explore the possibility of using collocation networks, identified by the #LancsBox program (Brezina, McEnery, and Wattam, 2015), to visualize and systematically investigate grammatical change and patterns of grammatical difference. We first look at different approaches to lexicogrammar to contextualize our approach (section 2). After this, we explore how the collocation networks technique can help us to visualize both synchronic difference (section 3) and diachronic change (section 4). We then take the investigation of colligation one step further, focusing on more abstract patterns based on visualization of relationships between part-of-speech tags (section 5).

2 Different approaches to lexicogrammar

Before using collocation statistics to explore the lexicogrammatical continuum, however, we should pause and ask an important question – are there other ways of doing so? The answer is, undoubtedly, yes. The most obvious way in which this is done, synchronically, diachronically and cross-linguistically is through corpus annotation. Corpora which are morphosyntactically annotated and which have been parsed represent a very obvious and effective way to begin to explore lexicogrammar – in the annotations it is possible to see the multiply intersecting levels of analysis in the data. Reasonably reliable automated morphosyntactic annotation is available for an ever wider range of languages, and while automated parsing is not as reliable as morphosyntactic annotation, there are an increasing number of manually verified parsed corpora available, making the use of annotated corpora to explore lexicogrammar a possibility. For English and a growing range of languages, both contemporary[1] and historical[2] corpora may be explored in this way. With suitable visualization and search software, designed to work effectively on appropriately annotated corpus data, such as ICECUP (Nelson, Wallis and Aarts, 2002) which helps users to explore parsed corpora of spoken and written British English from the *International Corpus of English* (Greenbaum 1996), one can begin to navigate the lexicographic continuum.

However, there are some caveats that must be made at this point. Firstly, in historical linguistics, the volume of parsed data available tends to be small. If we consider the major parsed historical corpora available, and set aside the question of the interoperability of their parsing schemes, we might conclude that there is approximately 8 million words of parsed data available for English scattered through time that could be drawn from the 5.7 million word *Penn Parsed Corpora of Historical English* (Kroch et al. 2000, 2004, 2010) and the 2.1 million word *Parsed Corpus of Early English Correspondence* (Taylor et al. 2006). While undoubtedly of high value, the resources are not of sufficient scale to allow the investigation of anything but the most frequent patternings – a point made well by Davies (2012) who notes that we need to move beyond "the constraints of small one- to five-million word corpora" (Davies 2012: 122). Secondly, we need also to be mindful that even where data is available, as noted, combining different parsed datasets can be problematic as the schemes used to morphosyntactically analyse or parse the data may be compatible to varying degrees; as noted by Jenset and McGillivray (2017), "[i]n historical corpus research, as well as in corpus linguistics in general, there are several schemes for corpus annotation, and no prevailing one … [Those annotation] projects often originated within different theoretical frameworks to address specific needs and goals, and therefore use their own (and often peculiar) approaches to annotation" (Jenset and McGillivray 2017: 16). Finally, factors which may play an important role in lexicogrammar – such as register and genre – represent a significant problem. Where they are present in a corpus, they fragment the data available further, making the issue of data sparsity more acute. Where a corpus addresses this issue, such as the *Parsed Corpus of Early English Correspondence*, by focusing on a single genre/register, this increased depth is, of necessity, gained at the cost of breadth. This does not

---

[1] See Abeillé (2012) for examples of approaches to parsing in a wide range of languages.
[2] Jenset and McGillivray (2017) provide an excellent overview of current parsed historical corpora and annotation practices.

mean that such resources are of no value – far from it, they are highly valuable. What it does mean is that when using corpora to explore grammatical change the analyst is forever facing trade-offs: breadth against depth, choosing an available annotation scheme rather than one more closely aligning to their own theoretical position, focusing on frequent words and constructions rather than a broader range of features, accepting error in automated annotations or limiting investigations to expert verified datasets, etc. As ever, the spectrum of possibility in reacting to such trade-offs is broad. At one extreme analysts, faced with the choice of abandoning the exploration of a feature which cannot be explored sufficiently with the corpus resources available, may choose to set aside the corpus approach as their method and to continue their studies using other modes of scholarship. At another, an analyst may decide to become invested only in those research questions that the available human verified annotated corpus evidence can support. Given the choices to be made it is clearly an area where pragmatism rather than idealism should be the guide.

One way in which pragmatism may help is in using one end of the lexicogrammatical spectrum as a way into exploring it as a whole. By looking at word forms alone and seeking, by composing suitable search terms, to explore grammatical structures, for example, one may offset the need for parsed corpora somewhat. If viable, this approach also relieves a number of other problems. For example, the *Corpus of Historical American English* (COHA, Davies 2012) provides over 406 million words of data, in a range of genres, from the 1810s to the early 2000s. Data of this scale allow us to explore a much wider range of features on the lexicogrammatical continuum, in principle, but to do so we need to think, where looking at features above the word level, of how to access these features using a search composed of word forms only. Searching for word forms and using patternings and order restrictions as a guide can be a productive way forward. For example, as Xiao and McEnery (2005a) show, it is possible to use such searches to explore a wide range of grammatical features and use those as the basis of a genre analysis. Another example is from Ecay's (2015: 107) work looking at negative declaratives in the *Early English Books Online* collection.

Yet once again, the results are not ideal – such heuristic searching is prone to error. Assessing the degree of error can be time-consuming and mitigating the degree of error by cyclically refining the search term used can be time-consuming also. In the context of historical linguistics, the degree to which spelling variation may impact upon the results of any search must also be taken into account. One way of dealing with (historical) spelling variants is using spelling standardization software such as VARD (Baron and Rayson 2008) or MorphAdorner (Burns 2006). Standardization of spelling in corpus data helps us focus on lexicogrammatical patterns and processes rather than, often accidental, features of graphology. The approach that focuses on word forms (with different types of automatic and semi-automatic mitigation of effects of spelling variants and other variations in lexico-grammatical patterns) has its virtues in terms of opening up the large historical and contemporary text collections which are becoming available to the linguist interested in lexicogrammar. The pragmatic approach becomes yet more valuable when reliable morphosyntactic annotation is available – the search terms that can be fashioned from words and parts of speech are, of necessity, more helpful in allowing us to explore the lexicogrammatical continuum than words alone are. Nonetheless, issues such as errors and false positives still dog these essentially heuristic searches.

It is in this context that we have situated our approach to looking at the use of #LancsBox to explore the use of collocation to look at lexicogrammar. As with the approaches discussed so far, this could be carried out on plain text or on annotated texts, as an analysis later in this chapter will show. The key to taking the collocational approach is that (a) collocation is a well-established approach to exploring lexicogrammar which produces results which are formed by and reflective of the multiply intersecting features that form lexicogrammar; (b) the approach can be used on large, unannotated, text collections; (c) issues of variant spelling notwithstanding, the approach does not have the issues that trying to proceed by creating searches based on patterns which we think may be significant, has, i.e. it is systematic and replicable.

What traditional collocation technique lacks, however, is a visually appealing form and, more importantly, a way of swiftly expressing wider networks of connection in lexicogrammar. This point is a presentational one but has important methodological (analytical) implications. In a context where we are dealing with large volumes of text, this is something not to be overlooked because it allows us to efficiently analyse and summarize large datasets focusing on the most important connections in language, both meaning-related and grammatical. Thus, considering the way in which complex linguistic information is visualized in large corpora, the visual form is important as it may aid their production and analysis.[3] Secondly, it may also help with their interpretation. If we are to argue, on the one hand, that we are looking for multiply intersecting features in lexicogrammar while on the other hand we are limiting ourselves to looking for it by simply looking at pairwise associations through collocations, we clearly have an issue. This is where we argue collocation networks may come in – if

---

[3] See Burghardt (2018) for example, who discusses the role visualization may play in corpus annotation.

A links to B and B links to C, a collocation network can allow us to easily traverse that potential connection between A and C via B, illuminating the lexicographic continuum more effectively, or at least more swiftly, than we would be able to do if we simply relied on a list of pairwise relations alone. In doing so, we can adopt measures which are more, or less helpful. For example, while the links between A, B and C may be viewable using a measure such as Mutual Information, we need to appeal to a measure such as Delta P (Gries 2013) if we want to be able to develop networks which show directionality, as Mutual Information is a symmetrical measure whereas Delta P is not, allowing the direction of the relationship to be visualized directly rather than induced by further, manual, exploration.

It needs to be noted that although visualization has many benefits, in some cases, it can obscure smaller differences in the data; these can be expressed with more precision with specific numbers and/or tabular presentation of the collocation statistics. We need to bear in mind that visualization is a particular way of summarizing the data. As in all summaries, the details are downplayed for the main picture to emerge.

In order to explore such networks effectively, however, we need appropriate software. Although such analyses can be undertaken manually (see McEnery 2005), even when supported by concordance packages, such networks are very time-consuming to create. This is what led Brezina, McEnery and Wattam (2015) to produce the #LancsBox program to facilitate the construction and exploration of collocation networks. The program takes as input raw data in any format (txt, xml, docx, pdf, etc.), adds part-of-speech annotation and produces collocation networks on the fly without the need to precompute the statistics. Collocation networks, first explored in depth by Phillips (1985) and subsequently by others, including Williams (1998, 2002), McEnery (2005) and Baker (2005), look at how patterns of collocation and colligation around words interact with those of other words by drawing arcs between words, where one is a collocate of the other. By doing this, one is able to see where words which do not necessarily collocate with one another have elements of lexicogrammar shared between them by virtue of having one or more joint collocates.

Consider the graph in figure 5.1 below, produced using the #LancsBox program to explore the language of advanced learners of English over 25 years of age in the *Trinity Lancaster Corpus* (Gablasova et al. 2017). In the graph, beginning with *i*, the analyst has expanded the network to explore the first order, i.e. immediate, collocates of the word (*need, was, like, think, that, would, will, am, love, do, started*). Second-order collocates – collocates of collocates – of the first-order collocate *think* are also shown, in the lower right quadrant of the graph. Two of these are simply second-order collocates (*is, it's*). One collocate (*that*) that is a first-order collocate of *think* is also a first-order collocate of *i*, however. In the top third of the graph, the second-order collocates of *need* are shown (*to*, *a*) – one of these words, *to*, is shown to be a second-order collocate of four of the first-order collocates of *i* (*started*, *need*, *want*, *like*) while *a* is a first-order collocate of three first-order collocates of *i* (*was*, *need*, *have*). Note that the figure also shows the intensity of the link between words – the shorter the arrow, the stronger the effect being measured. In this case also, a directional collocation measure (Delta P, Gries 2013) is being used, so the graph is showing both the degree and the direction of collocation – so, for example, *i* collocates strongly with *think*, but *think* does not collocate strongly with *i*.

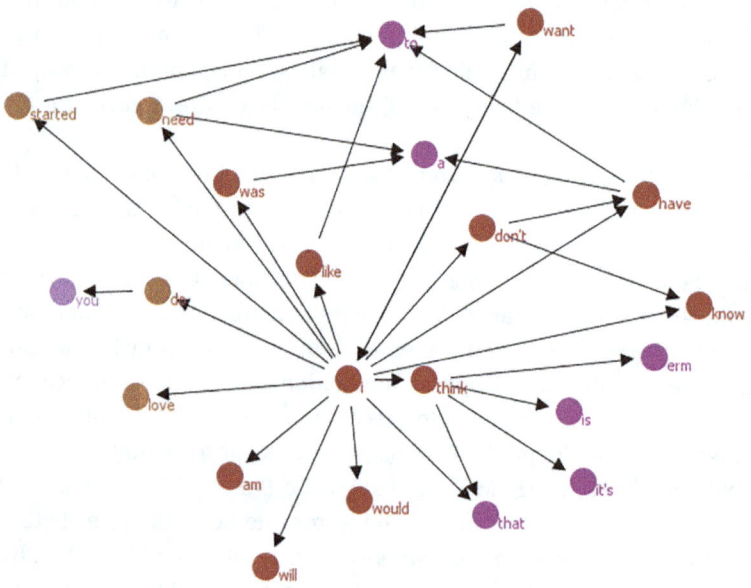

Fig. 5.1: Collocation network around 'I' in *Trinity Lancaster Corpus*

What is such a graph showing us? We would argue that this graph, for these speakers, is giving a rough sketch of the lexicogrammar of the word *i*. When we explore the concordances linked to these collocates, we can see that it has a strong preference for verbs (e.g. *need*, *was*, *like*, *think*, *love*). The second-order collocates show us something further about these verbs, however – four of them (*started*, *need*, *want*, *like*) have a preference for collocation with *to* – when we navigate back to the corpus we see that this is an infinitive marker and that the sequence I + VERB + TO INFINITIVAL CLAUSE is frequent in the corpus.[4] The graph is a useful gateway into making such an observation. While it could have been the case that, by working down the list of collocates of *I* we might finally have decided to follow up to see how the word interacted with words like *need* and starting from there we could have discovered the importance of this pattern, the graph allowed us to navigate through to the pattern with ease. As a result, the pattern became apparent swiftly.

We are also able to see that the participation of *need* in this pattern is only one of the choices that these speakers may make when navigating through the lexicographic continuum – I + VERB + IDEFINITIE ARTICLE is another pattern that *need* selects strongly, as measured by collocation. The words *was* and *have* are also strongly associated with that pattern in the graph. For both *a* and *to* we could, of course, have navigated on beyond the words in this graph to show third, fourth, fifth etc., order collocates of *i* if we had wished to do so. When judging the utility of these graphs, we begin with the mechanical – a graph produced by algorithm with parameters set by the analyst – and make sense through the manual: human experts traverse the graphs and engage in close reading and analysis of parts of the corpus that the graphs link to in order to understand and account for the connections that the graph is showing. Hence the graphs themselves, and the software that produces them, aids and guides a process of human expert interpretation rather than replaces it. However, the graphs clearly have the capacity to take data manipulated by other software packages which may add additional layers of analysis to the graph, as will be shown shortly.

3 *Knock* in British and American English

The example shown in figure 5.1 was provided in part to show the output of the #LancsBox software, but also to provide an example which demonstrated how an analyst could use the software to undertake a machine guided exploration of lexicogrammar. What that exploration shows, however, is clearly conditioned by the data that is loaded into the software. In figure 5.1 we were able to explore, relatively rapidly, a number of patterns emanating from the word *I*. However, what we found was relevant to high-proficiency speakers, over 25, of English as a

---

4 Note that what we are finding here are patterns analogous to those used in Pattern Grammar (Francis and Hunston 2000), hence the notation used. Using collocation to develop pattern grammars is another use of #LancsBox that is worthy of exploration.

second language. One way of summing this up is to say that the corpus data itself determines and limits the scope of the claims we are able to make based upon it. Yet a different way of looking at this is to say that, given the right data, we can make the observation that we need to, assuming it is amenable to corpus-based observation. So, for example, we can look at the stability of lexicogrammar across varieties of English – in figures 5.2 and 5.3 below we show two graphs, focused upon the wordform *knock* in American and British English, respectively.[5] The data used for the graphs are comparable – the AmE06 corpus and the BE06 corpus, both constructed using the Brown sampling frame and both collected from data produced synchronously (Baker 2011; Potts and Baker 2012).

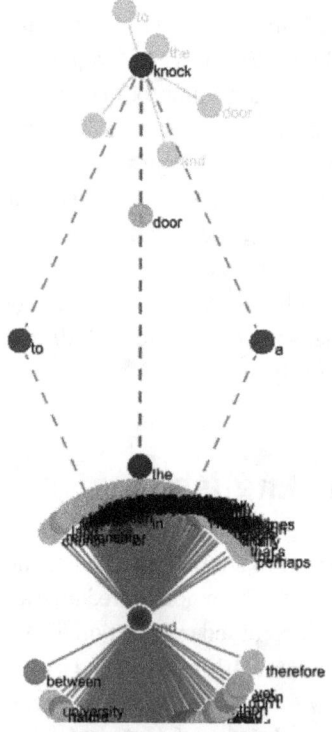

Fig. 5.2: *knock* in the AmE06 corpus and the second-order collocates it shares with *and*

---

5 The collocates were calculated using Delta P, with a window of +/- 5 around from the node word and a minimum cooccurrence threshold of 5.

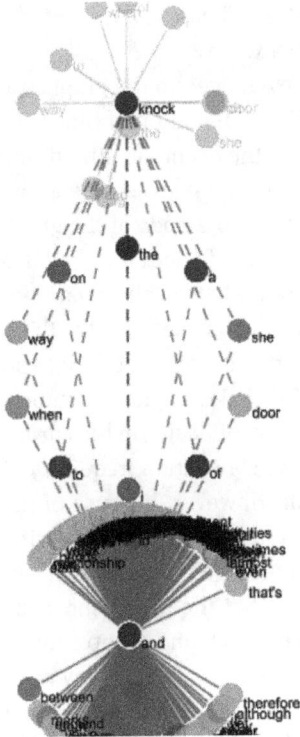

Fig. 5.3: *knock* in the BE06 corpus and the second-order collocates it shares with *and*

The two graphs, at a glance, show that the lexicogrammatical choices surrounding *knock* are similar at the first-order level – but at the second-order level there are two important observations to make. The first is that when we view the second-order collocates *knock* shares with *and*, #LancsBox also shows us the first-order collocates of *and*. This makes a difference immediately apparent – the complexity of the first-order collocates of *and* and those of *knock* are very different.

We can see, at a glance, that *knock* is relatively sparsely connected by comparison to *and* which is surrounded by a dense cloud of collocates. In short, the lexicogrammatical complexity of *and* is much greater than that of *knock*. The second point relates to the second-order collocates themselves – British English (*a, and, door, i, of, on, she, the, to, way, when*) has a larger number of these than American English (*and, at, door, the, to*), suggesting that, in the choices made in the lexicogrammatical continuum, there is a wider range of choices made in traversing between *knock* and *and* in British English than there is in American English. American English presents fewer second-order colligates (*a, and, the, to*) and collocates (*door*) than British English has second-order colligates (*a, and, of, on, the, to, when*) and collocates (*door, I, she, way*) for *knock*.

The choices which American English makes, as evidenced in the graph, are broadly a subset of those made in British English. The explanation of those differences needs to be developed from a close reading of the examples supporting the graph. #LancsBox very helpfully allows one to navigate between the graph and supporting concordances by simply right-clicking on the node of the graph you are interested in. For *way* as a second-order collocate of *knock* and *and* this quickly demonstrates that what appears to be a difference between two varieties is, in fact, a by-product of the lexicogrammatical choices of one author – the BE06 corpus includes the sentences "But whatever it was now, it was something, and she wished he would talk to her about it, the way— Knock, knock, knock, knock, knock". This example distorts the graph – *way* only ever collocates in the corpus with the word *knock* in this example. It also boosts the collocation frequency of *she*, which otherwise would not appear in the graph. However, because of the repetition of *knock*, this example alone generates 5 examples of *knock* collocating with *way* which, in this case, is sufficient to generate an effect size of sufficient magnitude to be graphed. This does not mean to say that the graph shows us nothing – what it does instead is to remind us that individual and group choices are another dimension along which the lexicogrammatical continuum may vary. This is a highly idiosyncratic choice that this author has made and they made it for stylistic effect. It is an artefact of individual and stylistic pressures on lexicogrammar. However, we have no compelling evidence to say that it is a feature of one variety of English or another.

By contrast, consider the second-order collocate *of* which shows another reason why we need to carefully examine the data behind our graphs. When we look at the examples producing a link between *knock* and *of* and *knock* and *and*, we notice that, within the span chosen, they are in complementary distribution – if *knock* collocates with *of*, *and* does not appear within that span of collocation. The two are rightly linked at a second order through *knock* and an exploration of the two links (*knock* with *of* and *knock* with *and*) reveals the nature of that connection – one of avoidance, as shown by table 5.1 below, which shows the examples of *knock* collocating with *of* in the corpus where *and* is absent from the span (+/- 5) shown:

Tab. 5.1: *knock* collocating with *of* in the BE06 corpus

5 left	Node	5 right
part of the building, they	knock.	Here they're likely to find
a poorly mixed sampler). To	knock	the bitrate of its flagship
helping of righteous indignation, I	knock	back yet another glass of
told her to take the Pill and	knock	her cycle out of sync
a man of few words. I did"	knock,'	she lied, but I guess

4 *Must* in British English: Diachronic perspective

The examples so far have focused on synchronic contrast – what of the diachronic? The graphs can also, given suitable data, allow analysts to explore diachronic change. In figures 5.4, 5.5, 5.6 and 5.7 below we show the same variety of English, British English, varying across four points in time, using the comparable BLOB, LOB, FLOB and BE06 corpora (see Leech 2014 for an overview of the Brown family of corpora). The focus of the investigation is *must*.[6]

The most striking feature of this graph is that in the most recent sample point, 2006, *must* is heavily denuded of both first- and second-order collocates. This is undoubtedly because of the reduced frequency of *must* as reported by others (Leech 2004; Leech et al. 2009; Baker 2017) but it also, as a consequence, implies a simplification of the lexicogrammar around *must* – the patterns being generated around the word are simplifying. For example, if we look at the question of the relation of pronouns to *must* shared in second-order collocation with *the*, they have changed over time. Table 5.2 below shows the second-order collocates shared between *must* and *the*:

---

[6] The collocates were calculated using Delta P, with a window of +/- 5 around from the node word and a minimum cooccurrence threshold of 50 to avoid over-population of the graph.

Tab. 5.2: Second-order collocates shared between *the* and *must* in the British English Brown family corpora

	i	you	she	he	her	his	we	they
BE06	X	X		X			X	
FLOB		X		X			X	X
LOB		X	X	X	X	X		
BLOB		X	X	X		X		

Some obvious patterns leap out of table 5.2 – the shift from what appear to be predominantly singular, third-person references in the early data towards plural and first-person usages in the present day is the most obvious. This shift in usage betokens a shift in the pragmatics of the usage of the word *must* as may be shown through lexicogrammar. Consider the pattern *we+must+*VERB*+the* – this occurs 14 times in the BLOB corpus. By using a strong modal with a plural first-person pronoun as a subject, the writer is forcing their viewpoint on the reader – the writer thinks that all "must", perforce the reader is implied in the "we". This is a very strong imposition on the reader. By contrast, the deletion of this pattern in present-day English, as the deletion of the second-order collocate *we* from the *must/the* relationship suggests, means that this imposition has not only been removed, but, by the inclusion of the first-person pronoun *i* instead in the pattern of second collocations in this relationship, the imposition of a shared point of view has been replaced with a statement of the writer's point of view – and with that the pattern *i+must+*VERB*+the* has become rarer, with only two examples in the BE06.[7]

---

[7] We will not discuss the second-person pronouns here as the discussion at this point in the paper does not include part-of-speech tagged data that would be necessary to use to explore this point.

Collocations and colligations: Visualizing lexicogrammar — 111

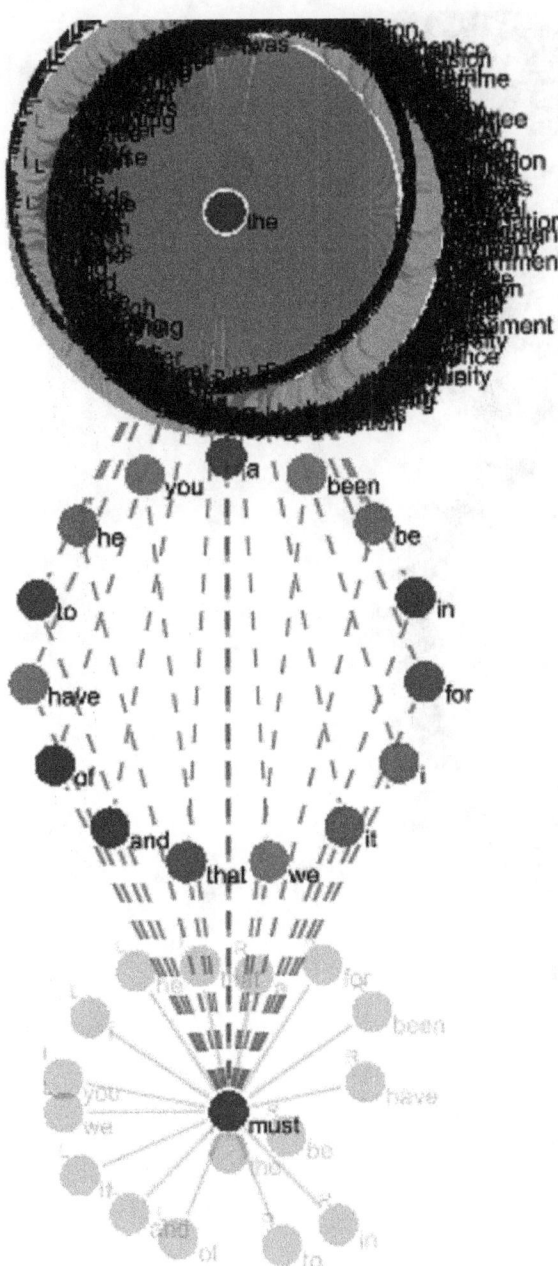

Fig. 5.4: *must* in the BE06 corpus and the second-order collocates it shares with *the*

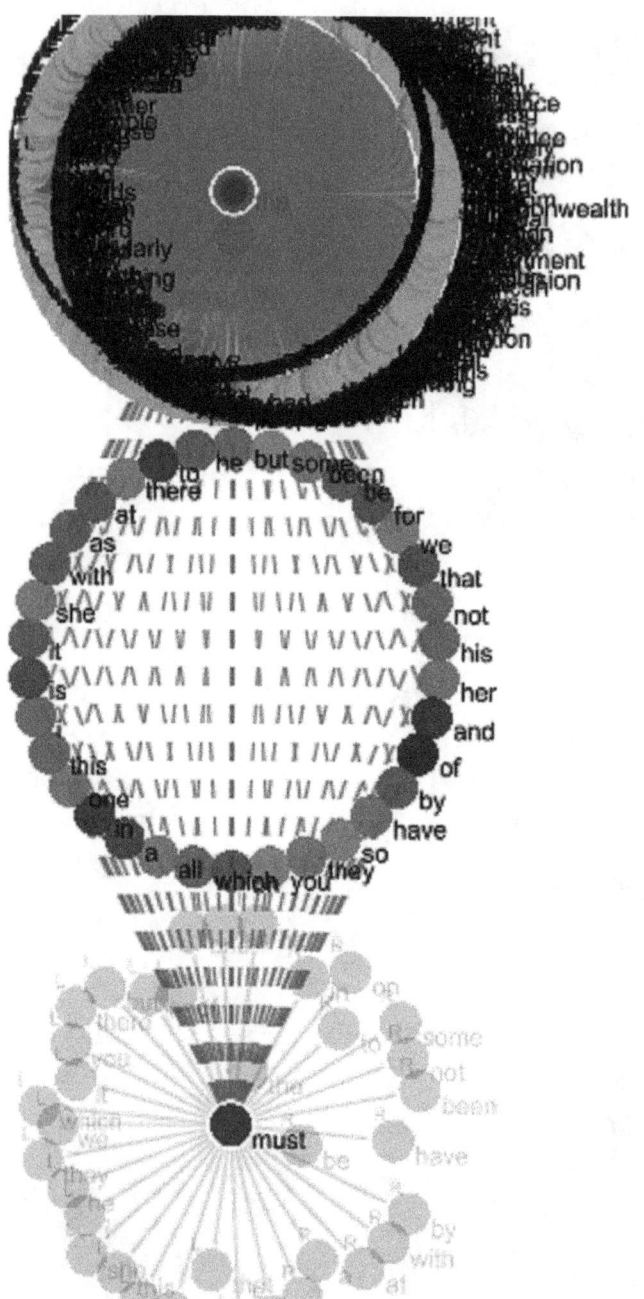

Fig. 5.5: *must* in the FLOB corpus and the second-order collocates it shares with *the*

Collocations and colligations: Visualizing lexicogrammar — **113**

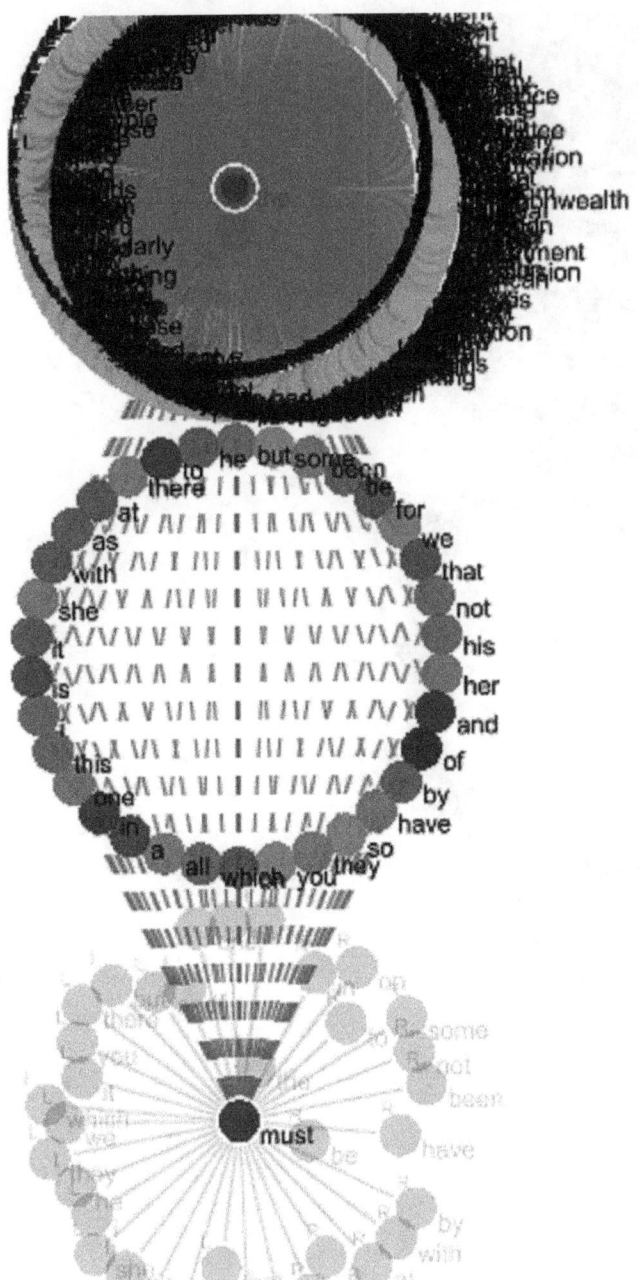

Fig. 5.6: *must* in the LOB corpus and the second-order collocates it shares with *the*

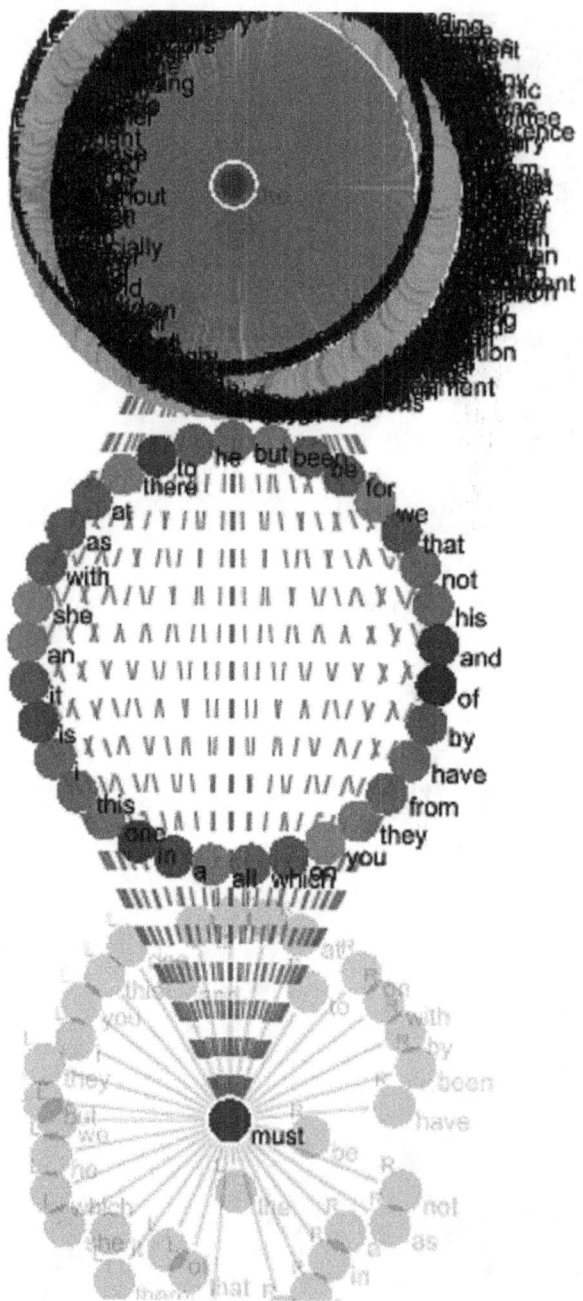

Fig. 5.7: *must* in the BLOB corpus and the second-order collocates it shares with *the*

5 Higher-level abstraction: POS-based graphs

These examples serve to briefly illustrate how #LancsBox can be used to start to explore corpora through time. We will conclude the paper by exploring how abstractions away from the wordform may help us, especially, though not only, in terms of dealing with the issue of graph over-population. So far in the chapter we have used frequency cut-offs to mitigate the issue of graph overpopulation, i.e. we have set a minimum threshold below which we will not consider a word to be a collocate. However, for closed-class items, as shown in the figures so far, they associate with so many words that the first-order association they produce, even with reasonably high thresholds as set in figures 5.4–5.7, very dense graphs that are hard to read in printed form.

As noted earlier in the chapter, it may be that other programs could modify the data read by #LancsBox before it is loaded in to allow for the data to be explored yet more swiftly for some research questions. A good example of this is part-of-speech tagged data. In figures 5.8 and 5.9 we demonstrate how this may be done. It is an exploration of whether we can visualize a difference between British and American English, the greater preference for British English to take the *to*-infinitive clause marker following a bare infinitive in constructions such as "help to get the shopping". The two corpora used in this study are part-of-speech tagged using the CLAWS part-of-speech tagger (Garside, Leech and Sampson 1988) as reported by Baker (2009) and Potts and Baker (2012). In what follows, we look at the wordform *help* in British English in the first graph and the same word in American English in the second.[8] In these graphs, considering that we wanted to focus on a dependency branching right from *help*, we limited the span to +1, looking immediately to the right of the word.

In these graphs we see the right collocates of *help* in two varieties of English – as a cursory inspection of the graphs shows, this set of words are better described as colligates. As predicted by previous scholarship (Xiao and McEnery 2005b), *to* as an infinitive marker links with *help* in British English, but not American English. One needs to be mindful that the threshold used in calculating the collocation statistic may mask a low frequency of usage in American English – this is not the case. Even if we set the threshold to 1 for American English, we simply discover that there are no examples in the corpus of the infinitive *help*

---

[8] The collocates were calculated using Delta P, with a window of + 1 around from the node word and a minimum co-occurrence threshold of 10 to avoid over-population of the graph.

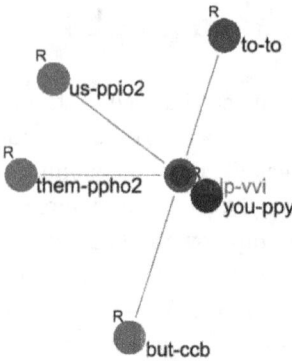

Fig. 5.8: Immediate-right collocates of *help* as an infinitive in the BE06 corpus

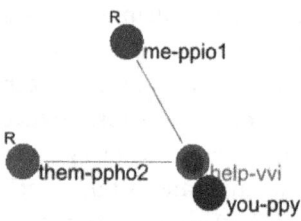

Fig. 5.9: Immediate-right collocates of *help* as an infinitive in the AmE06 corpus

followed by the infinitive marker *to*. Yet British English has 16 such examples. So, the graph successfully visualizes a very real lexicogrammatical difference for the word *help* between the two varieties. Yet this is just for one word – may the distinction hold more generally, i.e. that the class of infinitives, as opposed to a specific infinitive, in British English can take a following infinitival clause beginning with the *to*-infinitive marker where American English has infinitival clauses in that position but always drops the *to*-infinitive marker? By looking at the part-of-speech tags alone and building graphs from them, we can explore this. Figures 5.10 and 5.11 show, for British and American English respectively, the parts of speech colligating in the R1 position[9] with the part-of-speech for infinitive form of the lexical verb[10] (VVI in the CLAWS mnemonics[11]).

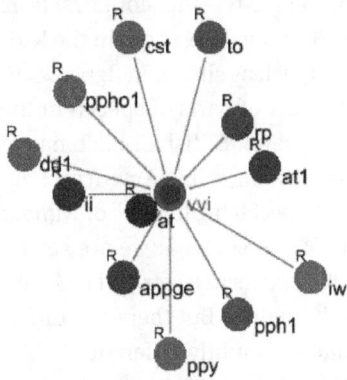

Fig. 5.10: Immediate-right collocates of *VVI* in the BE06 corpus

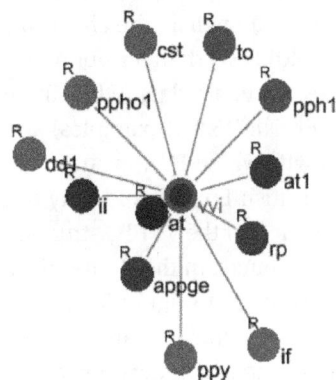

Fig. 5.11: Immediate-right collocates of *VVI* in the AmE06 corpus

---

9 R1 position refers to the first position on the right after the search term (node).
10 The collocates were calculated using Delta P, with a window of + 5 around from the node word and a minimum cooccurrence threshold of 350 – a high threshold is used because there is a small, finite set of POS tags and the token count for each is high.
11 For the full set of CLAWS part-of-speech tags see http://ucrel.lancs.ac.uk/claws7tags. html.

Before we comment on the relationship between the infinitive form and the infinitive marker in each variety, the graphs show us something very quickly – the range of parts of speech strongly associating with the R1 slot following an infinitive in British English is the same as in American English – the slot attracts 12 parts of speech in both. Yet there is also evidence of some differences in the lexicogrammar – the R1 slot in American and British English as shown in figures 5.10 and 5.11 appears to be the same, but while the number of parts of speech in the graphs is the same, there is an odd one out in each graph. British English has IF (part-of-speech tag for *for* as a preposition) in this position, while American English does not, and American English has IW (part-of-speech tag for *with* or *without* as a preposition) while British English does not. Of course, what we are seeing here is a difference in degree. Below the threshold IF occurs in R1 for VVI in American English and IW occurs in R1 for VVI in British English. But there is a difference in degree in the association – the lexicogrammar is subtly different.

But what of the VVI and its relationship to TO (part-of-speech tag for *to* as the infinitive marker)? As can be seen in figures 5.10 and 5.11, both British and American English, at the high threshold chosen for these graphs, select TO in the R1 position of VVI. However, the collocation statistic is our first piece of evidence to use to look for a difference – and there is one. For British English, the effect size of the collocation between VVI and TO is higher (at 0.013487) than it is for American English (at 0.011092). This is reflected in the raw frequency data. While there is little difference in the frequency of TO between British (15,992 examples) and American (15,583 examples) English, the frequency with which TO appears in the R1 slot for VVI is different, occurring 701 times in British English and only 635 times in American English. There is a stronger preference for the VVI TO structure in British than American English, which is shown, of course, in the shorter lines between the two parts-of-speech in figure 5.10 in contrast to figure 5.11. Once again, the graphs allow us to visualize a difference in lexicogrammar and the concordance allows us to navigate swiftly to the underlying data to understand better what we see in the graph.

Before leaving this approach to the use of #LancsBox, however, it is worth considering what this type of approach to corpus data means when applied to collocation networks. Navigating collocation networks, and in essence exploring colligation networks with data like this, opens up the prospect of looking at grammatical similarities. Consider the graph in figure 5.12 below. In this graph, we revisit the graph showing the R1 colligates of VVI in present-day British English, as shown in figure 5.10. However, here we have expanded the AT1 node – this is now showing us which R1 colligates of VVI also have AT1 as R1 colligates. In this case there is only one part-of-speech tag which matches this description, PPY (2nd person personal pronoun). This is interesting because, in essence, it gives us a way of visualizing and exploring the affinities, in terms of patterns of association, between different parts of speech, giving us another means of exploring the lexicogrammatical continuum.

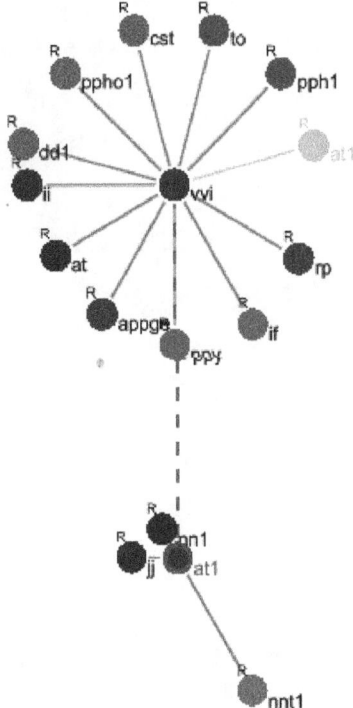

Fig. 5.12: A colligation network based on VVI, showing shared R1 colligates with AT1 in British English

Of course, as we expand other nodes this view of the continuum becomes more detailed. In figure 5.13 below, the node IF is expanded as well as AT1. This shows us which parts of speech attach to the R1 position of all three parts of speech, allowing us to see at a glance similarities and dissimilarities. This shows us some affinities at a glance – an adjective (JJ) may immediately postmodify PPY, AT, or IF in this network, but not VVI. APPGE may be an immediate complementation of VVI or IF in the network, but not AT1. NP1 will immediately follow IF, but not VVI or AT1 in the network. The explanation and exploitation of observations like this, which may be either absolute or by degree, depending on what further exploration shows, is the stuff, of course, of which grammars are made. Yet the concept of colligation networks allows us to begin to freely traverse some of these grammatical dependencies and view potential grammatical constraints.

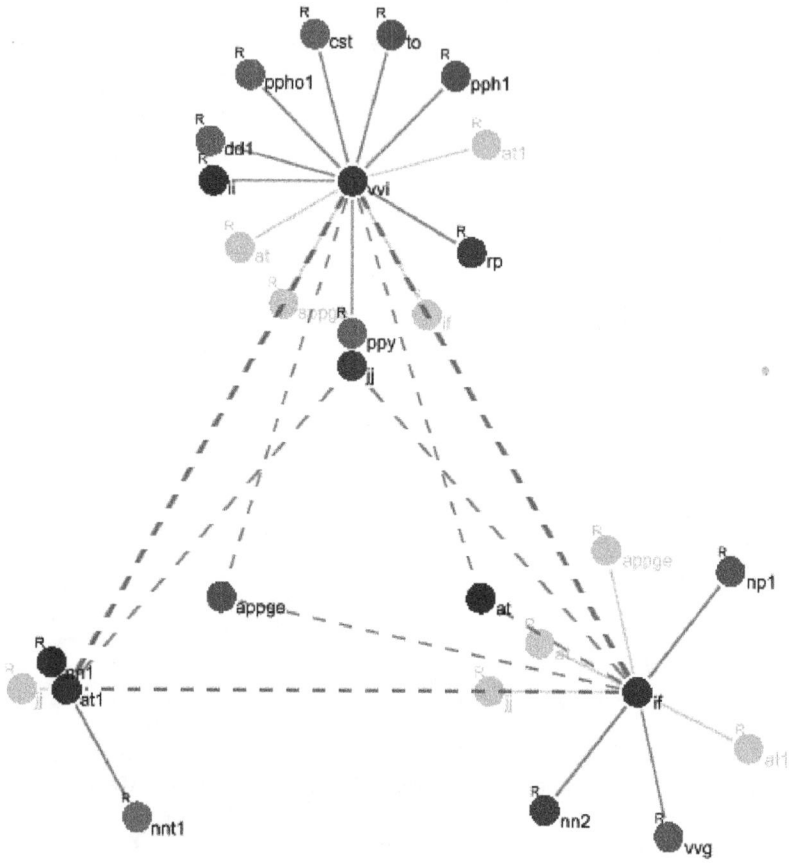

Fig. 5.13: A colligation network based on VVI, showing shared R1 colligates with AT1 and IF in British English

6 Conclusion

This chapter has focused principally on ways of seeing – the methodological aspect of visualization of the collocational and colligational relationships in language; the observations made in this chapter have largely been made by other linguists already. The aim of this chapter was to show that, by approaching an analysis of corpus texts using #LancsBox, we can, in one package, swiftly explore a range of interconnected lexicogrammatical relationships in a corpus using the visualization of collocational and colligational relationships via graphs which demonstrate the connections between words and/or part-of-speech categories in a corpus.

Of course, using one method and one package always leads to limitations in studies. Similarly, while we have focused here on one method, collocation networks, to emphasize the affordances of a visual analysis, tabular analyses should also be considered as they present data in a more precise numerical format. Indeed, such analyses (also provided by #LancsBox) were used throughout this chapter when we reported precise figures in the text. Yet, all studies are about choices and all choices entail positives and negatives. As noted at the start of the chapter, we are showing here what visualization may help us to achieve, but we are doing this simply to highlight its uses; as with all tools and methods, it is best employed in a context where the full range of tools and methods appropriate for the research question in hand are deployed.

Nonetheless, by using the concept of collocation networks, and by extending that to colligation networks, we have shown how the program can allow one to swiftly navigate a range of dependencies within the lexicogrammatical continuum, while providing the opportunity to move swiftly back to supporting examples in order to better understand the nature of the relationships the graphs embody. While much that has been presented in this chapter can, and has, been explored using different tools in the past, #LancsBox provides an environment within which multiple tools can be used at once, linked through to what we would argue is the powerful visual and theoretical tool of the network graph. Through that we "see" lexicogrammar and by navigating the graph and examining supporting data, we can rapidly gain a view of the "multiply intersecting" levels of linguistic choice and structure in our corpora and gain insights into diachronic and synchronic "forces" which shape that system and manifest themselves as systematic differences at one point in time or through time.

References

Abeillé, Anne (ed.) 2012. *Treebanks: Building and using parsed corpora*. New York: Springer.
Baker, Paul. 2005. *Public discourses of gay men*. New York: Routledge.
Baker, Paul. 2009. The BE06 corpus of British English and recent language change. *International Journal of Corpus Linguistics* 14 (3). 312–337.

Baker, Paul. 2011. Times may change but we'll always have money: a corpus driven examination of vocabulary change in four diachronic corpora. *Journal of English Linguistics* 4 (1). 65–88.

Baker, Paul. 2017. *American and British English. Divided by a common language?* Cambridge: Cambridge University Press.

Baker, Paul, & Jesse Egbert (eds.) 2019. *Triangulating corpus linguistics with other linguistic research methods.* New York: Routledge.

Baron, Alistair & Paul Rayson. 2008. VARD 2: A tool for dealing with spelling variation in historical corpora. *Proceedings of the Postgraduate Conference in Corpus Linguistics, Aston University, Birmingham, UK, 22 May 2008.* (Available at http://acorn.aston.ac.uk/conf_proceedings.html)

Brezina, Vaclav, Tony McEnery & Stephen Wattam. 2015. Collocations in context: A new perspective on collocational networks. *International Journal of Corpus Linguistics* 20 (2). 139–173.

Burghardt, Manuel. 2018. Visualization as a key factor for the usability of linguistic annotation tools. In Noah Bubenhofer & Marc Kupietz (eds.), *Visualisierung Sprachlicher Daten*, 315–330. Heidelberg: Heidelberg University Publishing.

Burns, Philip R. 2006. MorphAdorner: Morphological adorner for English text. (Available at http://morphadorner.northwestern.edu/morphadorner/; accessed 31/1/ 2019).

Davies, Mark. 2012. Expanding horizons in historical linguistics with the 400-million-word *Corpus of Historical American English*. *Corpora* 7 (2). 121–157.

Ecay, Aaron W. 2015. A multi-step analysis of the evolution of English *do*-support. PhD thesis, University of Pennsylvania. (Available at https://repository.upenn.edu/edissertations/1049/)

Ellis, Andrew W. & Geoffrey Beattie. 1986. *The psychology of language and communication.* Hove: Psychology Press.

Francis, Gill & Susan Hunston. 2000. *Pattern Grammar: A corpus-driven approach to the lexical grammar of English.* Amsterdam: John Benjamins.

Gablasova, Dana, Vaclav Brezina, Tony McEnery & Elaine Boyd. 2017. Epistemic stance in spoken L2 English: The effect of task and speaker style. *Applied Linguistics* 38 (5). 613–637.

Garside, Roger, Geoffrey Sampson & Geoffrey Leech (eds.). 1988. *The computational analysis of English.* London: Longman.

Greenbaum, Sidney. 1996. *Comparing English worldwide: The International Corpus of English.* Oxford: Clarendon.

Gries, Stefan Th. 2013. 50-something years of work on collocations: What is or should be next… *International Journal of Corpus Linguistics* 18 (1). 137–166.

Halliday, Michael A. K. 1991. Corpus studies and probabilistic grammar. In Karin Aijmer & Bengt Altenberg (eds.), *English corpus linguistics: Studies in honour of Jan Svartvik.* 30–43. Harlow: Longman.

Hunston, Susan. 2001. Colligation, lexis, pattern, and text. In Mike Scott & Geoff Thompson (eds.), *Pattern of text: In honour of Michael Hoey.* 13–33. Amsterdam: John Benjamins.

Jenset, Gard B. & Barbara McGillivray. 2017. *Quantitative historical linguistics: A corpus framework.* Oxford: Oxford University Press.

Kroch, Anthony & Ann Taylor. 2000. *Penn-Helsinki Parsed Corpus of Middle English.* 2nd edn. (Available at http://www.ling.upenn.edu/hist-corpora/)

Kroch, Anthony, Beatrice Santorini & Lauren Delfs. 2004. *Penn-Helsinki Parsed Corpus of Early Modern English*, CD-ROM, 1st edition.

Kroch, Anthony, Beatrice Santorini & Ariel Diertani. 2010. *Penn-Helsinki Parsed Corpus of Modern British English*, CD-ROM, 1st edition.

Langacker, Ronald W. 1987. *Foundations of Cognitive Grammar*. Vol. 1: *Theoretical prerequisites*. Stanford, CA: Stanford University Press.

Leech, Geoffrey. 2004. Recent grammatical change in English: Data, description, theory. In Karin Aijmer & Bengt Altenberg (eds.), *Advances in corpus linguistics: Papers from the 23rd International Conference on English Language Research on Computerised Corpora (ICAME 23)*, 61–81. Amsterdam: Rodopi.

Leech, Geoffrey, Marianne Hundt, Christian Mair & Nicholas Smith. 2009. *Change in contemporary English: A grammatical study*. Cambridge: Cambridge University Press.

Leech, Geoffrey. 2014. Growth and decline: How grammar has been changing in recent English. In Nikolaos Lavidas, Thomaï Alexiou & Areti Maria Sougari (eds.), *Major trends in theoretical and applied linguistics*. Volume 1: 47–66. London: Versita.

McEnery, Tony. 2005. *Swearing in English*. London: Routledge.

Nelson, Gerald, Sean Wallis & Bas Aarts. 2002. *Exploring natural language: Working with the British component of the International Corpus of English*. Amsterdam: John Benjamins.

Phillips, Martin. 1985. *Aspects of text structure: An investigation of the lexical organisation of text*. Amsterdam: North-Holland.

Potts, Amanda & Paul Baker. 2012. Does semantic tagging identify cultural change in British and American English? *International Journal of Corpus Linguistics* 17 (3). 295–324.

Taylor, Ann, Arja Nurmi & Terttu Nevalainen. 2006. *The Parsed Corpus of Early English Correspondence*. Oxford Text Archive (Available at http://ota.ox.ac.uk/desc/2510).

Vasardani, Maria, Lesley Stirling & Stephan Winter. 2017. The preposition *at* from a spatial language, cognition and information systems perspective. *Semantics and Pragmatics* 10 (Early access online at http://semprag.org/article/view/sp.10.3)

Williams, Geoffrey. 1998. Collocational networks: Interlocking patterns of lexis in a corpus of plant biology research articles. *International Journal of Corpus Linguistics* 3 (1). 151–171.

Williams, Geoffrey. 2002. In search of representativity in specialised corpora: Categorisation through collocation. *International Journal of Corpus Linguistics* 7 (1). 43–64.

Xiao, Richard & Tony McEnery. 2005a. Two approaches to genre analysis: Three genres in modern American English. *Journal of English Linguistics* 33 (1). 62–82.

Xiao, Richard & Tony McEnery. 2005b. *Help* or *help to*: What do corpora have to say? *English Studies* 86 (2). 161–187.

Zwarts, Joost & Yoats Winter. 1997. A semantic characterization of locative PPs. In Aaron Lawson (ed.), *Proceedings of the 7th Semantics and Linguistic Theory Conference*, 294–311. Stanford, CA: Stanford University.

Elizabeth Closs Traugott
Constructional pattern-development in language change

Abstract: Patterns of form and meaning pairings are an important topic in synchronic work on construction grammar, cf. discussion of syntactic patterns (Michaelis 2006) and morphological word-formation patterns (Booij 2010). From a historical perspective, the question arises how patterns come into being (Bybee 2010; Traugott and Trousdale 2013). I explore such questions as: What is the relationship between patterns and schemas, generalization, and regularity? How can we identify and distinguish in historical data the rise of (i) a new micro-constructional pattern such as *all but* 'nearly' within the extant schema of downtoners (de Smet 2012), (ii) a new schema such as contrastive adversative utterance-final discourse markers like *then, though, but* (Haselow 2012), and (iii) a new word-formation pattern such as N-*licious* (e.g. *beautilicious, fontalicious*)? What is the evidence for origins in speech, writing, or advertising (see Biber and Gray 2012)? What role do analogy and paradigmatization play in the rise of new patterns? How and why are patterns reorganized over time? Data are drawn mainly from electronic corpora for the history of English, including CLEMET 3.0, COCA, and COHA.

1 Introduction

The concept of "linguistic pattern" is important and widely used in construction grammar, but its meaning and its relation to "construction", understood as a form–meaning pairing, is not always consistent. Depending on the author, or the particular variety of construction grammar espoused, "pattern" may be conceptualized as related to but not equivalent to construction, or even synonymous with "construction".[1]

---

[1] Many thanks to Laura Michaelis, Peter Petré and an anonymous reviewer for helpful and thought-provoking suggestions. Many thanks too to Nikolas Gisborne and especially to Graeme Trousdale for constructive comments on, and lively discussion of, an earlier draft of this paper.

Elizabeth Closs Traugott, Stanford University, Department of Linguistics, Stanford CA 94305-2150, USA, traugott@stanford.edu

For example, using "pattern" to distinguish construction grammar from other types of grammar, Michaelis (2006: 73) points out that in projection-based models of sentence meaning such as Jackendoff (1997), "sentences have meaning but sentence patterns do not", because in such models, concepts are expressed exclusively by words, not combinations of words. One contribution of construction grammar in Michaelis's view (2006: 78) is that "a semantic licensor may be a skeletal syntactic pattern (e.g. an argument-structure construction) rather than a word". Outlining key concepts in construction grammar, Michaelis (2006) refers to "sentence pattern" (page 73), "patterns of word combination" (page 74), "phrasal pattern" (page 74), "presentational pattern" (page 81), among other patterns. In considering how children learn patterns, Casenhiser and Goldberg (2005) refer to "phrasal patterns and meanings" and how they are correlated. In these works, the term "pattern" refers primarily to combinatorial potentials.

The term is also used to refer to constructions. In a much-cited overview of her *Constructions at Work*, Goldberg says:

> Any linguistic pattern is recognized as a construction as long as some aspect of its form or function is not strictly predictable from its component parts or from other constructions recognized to exist. In addition, patterns are stored as constructions even if they are fully predictable as long as they occur with sufficient frequency. (Goldberg 2006: 5)

This implies that some patterns are not constructions. On the other hand, pattern and construction may be used synonymously. In his paper on the basic methods of collostructional analysis, Stefanowitsch (2014: 219) introduces examples of the *into*-causative (e.g. *I talked Peter into giving me those earrings*) as a "pattern" and refers back to the examples as "this construction". Similarly, the following quotation suggests that pattern and construction may be synonymous:[2]

> The trademark characteristic of Construction Grammar as originally developed consists in the insight that language is a repertoire of more or less complex patterns – CONSTRUCTIONS – that integrate form and meaning in conventionalized and in some aspects non-compositional ways. ... A grammar in this view consists of intricate networks of overlapping and complementary patterns that serve as 'blueprints' for encoding and decoding linguistic expressions of all types. (Fried n.d.)

---

[2] However, elsewhere Fried (2009) makes it clear that from a developmental perspective, especially that of language change, pattern and construction may initially not be correlated and therefore cannot be equivalent.

Adopting the Sign-Based Construction Grammar model (see e.g. Boas and Sag 2012) Michaelis (this volume) defines constructions as configurations and patterns as combinatorial. On this view "constructions are patterns".

In the present paper, I assume that "pattern" is not synonymous with "construction", and focus on the question of how patterns and constructions come into being. In particular I am concerned with the relationship between pattern and constructionalization, the development in language use of a new conventionalized form$_{new}$–meaning$_{new}$ pairing out of previously non-aligned material (Traugott and Trousdale 2013: 22). The new construction may be a micro-construction, a substantive micro-schema or a more abstract schema, and it may be procedural ("grammatical") or contentful ("lexical"), or a combination of both.[3] "Procedural" expressions signal linguistic relations and act as instructions or "linguistic road-signs" (Hansen 1998: 199). They are on the "grammatical" end of the lexical–grammatical pole. A "micro-construction" is a low-level substantive-type construction such as *after all* in its discourse-marker use, a micro-schema is a low-level type construction that has a substantive part and one or more open slots, e.g. *all but X, what is X doing Y?* Higher level schemas consist of abstract slots (e.g. ditransitive SUBJ V OBJ1 OBJ2 such as *I gave her a book*); how many higher-level schemas are posited depends on the level of systemic generalization that the researcher is interested in (e.g. ditransitives are a subset of transitives).

Discussing the relationship between grammaticalization and procedural constructionalization, Fried (2013: 424) characterizes the latter as "a process that leads to (1) the emergence of a new grammatical pattern (construction) out of previously independent material or (2) a reorganization of an existing construction".[4] In Fried (2009) the emerging "patterns" are interpreted as transitional replicated discourse and syntactic collocations prior to the development of new constructions. I build on the idea of "emerging patterns" and propose that a pattern is a replicated sequence that is associated with a recurring (but underspecified) meaning and that has combinatoric potential.[5] While "combinatoric" is usually understood to refer to phrases and sequential arrays such as ditransitive SUBJ V OBJ1 OBJ2 (see e.g. Goldberg 2013), it can also refer to "phonetic sequences"

---

3 An example of the latter is the association with iterative, hence aspectually conceived, actions of a subschema of the *way*-construction that developed in the early 19th century (cf. *shot my way home* discussed in Traugott and Trousdale 2013: 87).
4 Again, note the apparent synonymity between "pattern" and "construction".
5 This means that "patterns" are subsets of both "critical contexts" (Diewald 2002; Diewald and Smirnova 2010) and "constructional changes" prior to constructionalization (Traugott and Trousdale 2013: 26–28; Petré this volume), but are not equivalent to them. For "critical contexts", see section 2.2 below.

(Bybee 2010: 25), therefore monomorphemic constructions can be said to be combinatoric. A "pattern" may or may not be a "unit" or a "construction" in the sense of a conventionalized form–meaning pairing.[6] There is therefore an asymmetric relationship between pattern and construction. Not all patterns are constructions, but all constructions, whether micro- or macro-schemas, are patterns.

To make the discussion concrete, I briefly investigate the rise of three different kinds of constructions in English, two of them procedural and one contentful: (i) *all but X* 'everything except X', later 'nearly X' (De Smet 2012), (ii) *X after all* 'despite expectations regarding X' (Traugott 2018), and (iii) the recent adjective word-formation pattern *X-licious* (e.g. *beautilicious*) (Lehrer 2007).

Given my examples, I am not concerned in this paper with the kinds of assemblies that are the focus of Petré's paper (this volume). However, the overall objective – the investigation of how patterns and new constructions come into being – is similar. So is the distinction between pattern and construction and the use of Goldberg's broad definition of constructions.

The structure of the paper is as follows. As background for the case studies, section 2 touches on some basic issues in historical work. Section 3 outlines the rise of both exceptive *all but X* and downtoning *all but X*, section 4 the development of the clause-final retrospective contrastive discourse marker use of *after all*, and section 5 the rise of the word-formation pattern *X-licious*. Section 6 concludes.

2 Some issues in historical work

Several topics have long been debated in historical linguistics. Among those of particular relevance to this paper are: how should change be defined: is it innovation or conventionalization of innovations? (section 2.1), what is the role of context in change? (section 2.2), what is the role of analogy? (section 2.3), what is the role of emergence? (section 2.4), is historical data "bad data" as Labov (1994) suggested? (section 2.5). Space allows only a few key pointers in response to these questions.

---

6 It may be useful to mention that "pattern grammar" as outlined in Hunston (2014) distinguishes patterns from constructions in the following way: patterns involve lexical collocations, constructions need not (e.g. auxiliary inversion); patterns "are about output only" (Hunston 2014: 115), not about mental representations. In the proposal put forward in the present paper, patterns may initially be syntactic sequences, and may come to be associated with mental representations.

2.1 What is change?

For some researchers, change is equated with innovations that arise in the mind/brain of an individual child, given some kind of innate language ability (e.g. Lightfoot 2003: 495). Others argue that, in actual language use by children and older speakers, new combinations arise constantly. Most of these innovations are unintended (Keller 1994) and ephemeral. Most are not replicated, and do not count as changes; some are resisted. For a "change" to have occurred there must be evidence of transmission of innovations to others, in other words, of conventionalization in a community of language users (see e.g. Weinreich et al. 1968; Milroy 1992; De Smet 2013). The type of construction grammar espoused here, drawing on Goldberg (2006), is usage-based, therefore pattern-development is conceptualized in a usage-based model of change. New patterns come to be entrenched not only in individual minds ("innovations")[7] but come to be shared and entrenched within a community of speakers ("changes") (see Traugott and Trousdale 2013). In keeping with this distinction, I distinguish between (i) the innovation of a construct (token) in an individual[8] and (ii) constructionalization, the conventionalization of a construction in a community. The conventionalized construction is subject to variation (Fischer and Nikiforidou 2015).

2.2 The role of context

It has long been recognized that change occurs only in context. Writing about grammaticalization, Bybee et al. (1994: 297) say: "Everything that happens to the meaning of a gram happens because of the contexts in which it is used".[9] Here "contexts" are understood as linguistic contexts. Much the same can be said about changes in contentful expressions, but in this case the contexts tend to be more broadly cultural and less narrowly linguistic, as exemplified by the development of idioms such as *X is the new Y* (Traugott and Trousdale 2014).

Heine (2002) and Diewald (2002) theorize contexts for the onset of grammaticalization. Diewald and Smirnova (2010) link contexts for grammaticalization to

---

[7] I adopt Blumenthal-Dramé's (2012) working definition of entrenchment as "the strength or autonomy of representation of a form–meaning pairing at a given level of abstraction in the cognitive system" (Blumenthal-Dramé 2012: 4).
[8] The term "construct" is used differently in different models of construction grammar. Here it refers to an attested use. It is not necessarily licensed by a construction (as discussed below, historically, the use of constructs precedes the development of a construction).
[9] A "gram" is a minimal grammatical item (Bybee et al. 1994: 2).

contexts for constructionalization, mainly procedural, but also contentful. According to Diewald and Smirnova (2010: 113), initially there are slight, "untypical" shifts in the use of existing constructions. In these new contexts conversational implicatures may be replicated. At a second "stage", these contexts may become cognitively more complex, and serve a "critical context". Critical contexts typically involve ambiguities that are both pragmatic and structural and are logically necessary (but not sufficient) conditions for later developments. New constructions arise in critical contexts "that cannot be reduced to a combination of known constructions without losing information" (Diewald and Smirnova 2010: 114). Diewald and Smirnova associate this stage with Fillmore et al.'s (1988) notion of "extragrammatical idioms" that have structures that "are not made intelligible by knowledge of the familiar rules of the grammar and how these rules are most generally applied" (Fillmore et al. 1988: 505). However, Fillmore et al.'s model of grammar privileges discreteness and inflexible synchrony, and I will suggest below that at least some critical contexts, being replicated, may be thought of as "transitional patterns" (Fried 2009) on the margins of the system. Critical contexts may be local or systemic (Diewald and Smirnova 2010: 117). Systemic changes are general ongoing changes in the language at the time (Fischer 2007), for example a shift in word order, or expansion of a particular construction type, such as expansion of clefts, projectors, and other focusing elements in English (Los and Komen 2013). At a later, third stage, called "isolating contexts", the new constructions are consolidated and may ultimately "only partially resemble other existing constructions and show a unique form–meaning correspondence" (Diewald and Smirnova 2010: 114). A final, fourth stage involves paradigmatization, which I here interpret as alignment with other constructions in an extant schema.

2.3 The role of analogy

Until recently, analogy has not played a central role in much work on morphosyntactic change, as it was felt to be too amorphous a concept. It was explicitly problematized in work on grammaticalization. For example, Lehmann (2004) refers to "pure grammaticalization without analogy" (Lehmann 2004: 161). In the last decade, however, analogy has taken center stage in research on change (e.g. Fischer 2007, De Smet 2013), especially under the influence of work on frequency and usage-based models of change (see Bybee 2010). If, as De Smet (2013) proposes, "language users are tireless at inferring regularities from usage" (De Smet 2013: 8), analogy will necessarily be a crucial factor in the development of new expressions. Traugott and Trousdale (2013: 38) suggest distinguishing between "analogical thinking", a ubiquitous matching process that is a potential motivation and enabling factor and "analogization", the mechanism leading to specific changes. De Smet (2013: 64–71) further distinguishes, in cases of analogization, between what he calls semantic and formal analogy and paradigmatic analogy. Semantic analogization is "a mechanism of analogical extension" (De Smet 2013: 65) on the basis of semantic similarity between syntagmatically related source and target environments (De Smet 2013: 69). Both semantic and formal analogization have a syntagmatic relationship to the model and are semasiological. On the other hand, paradigmatic analogization involves extension to an existing set of alternatives and is based on "a semantic, formal, and/or distributional relation of similarity" (De Smet 2013: 69), in other words, it operates on an onomasiological dimension. In what follows, semantic and formal analogy are understood typically to result in changes to individual, substantive constructions, and paradigmatic analogy to changes in the variables within a (sub)schema.

2.4 The role of emergence

A usage-based account of change is dynamic and assumes gradualness (microsteps) and continua. Structure is viewed as emerging "from the repeated application of underlying processes" (Bybee 2010: 2). Two views of emergence are currently debated. One, known as the "emergentist view", is that grammatical structure is provisional and epiphenomenal to conversation; "categories don't exist in advance of the communicative settings" (Hopper 2011: 26). The other, articulated in Auer and Pfänder (2011: 18), is that both categorized linguistic knowledge and emergence in use are needed to account for variation and change – without a shared stock of expectations, speakers would not be able to recognize variation, nor could they be recognized as improvizing. The concept of "pattern development" requires the second view of emergence: Patterns and shared constructions, even though flexible and subject to change, are recognizable and contribute to language norms.

2.5 Kinds of data

Labov (1994: 11) famously said that historical linguistics is "the art of making the best use of bad data" (see also earlier, Labov 1966: 100). It is true that historical data have until recently been attested in writing only and have survived by chance rather than design. Sometimes data is extremely thin. However, historians of English are fortunate in having a rich data base of texts for testing hypotheses about change. These include not only texts such as royal proclamations, scientific reports and philosophical works that reflect and, in some cases, have given rise to primarily written traditions, but also diaries, dramas, trials, and represented conversation in fiction that give us considerable insight into interactional language use (Jucker et al. 1999; Culpeper and Kytö 2010).

Historical methodologies vary from qualitative to highly sophisticated quantitative work on electronic corpora when the data are sufficiently frequent to warrant it, or a combination of both (for overviews of qualitative methodology see Traugott 2016a, and of quantitative methodology see Hilpert and Gries 2016, Stefanowitsch 2014). The methodology in this paper is qualitative, and examples were drawn manually from a variety of data bases because the data are of insufficient frequency to allow for meaningful quantitative analysis.

3 Patterns in the rise of an approximating degree modifier: *all but X*

3.1 Background

In Present-day English (PDE) there is an approximating degree modifier microschema *all but X* meaning 'nearly X' as in (1):[10,11]

(1) a. *Poor Andy. He's **all but** ignored as our waiter brings George a free drink.* (2015 *ABC* [COCA])
 b. *Timber cutting took off after that, only to shrink and **all but** disappear in the 1990s.* (2015 *New York Times* [COCA])

Like *almost* and *nearly,* as a downtoner *all but* is a procedural item cueing that the speaker assigns a polar and a scalar component to the head X (where X is a verb or adjective). Furthermore, the speaker assesses that X is close to but not the highest outcome on the scale to which it has been assigned, see e.g. Amaral (2010) for characterization of *almost* (*almost missed the train* entails 'came close to missing, but actually did not miss the train') in contrast to *barely* (*barely missed the train* entails 'came close to catching the train but actually missed it'). *All but*

---

10 I am grateful to Laura Michaelis for help in clarifying discussion in this section.
11 By convention, downtoner *all but* is spelled as a phrase, despite its monomorphemic, "chunked" status (see also *after all*, discussed in the next section).

X in the sense 'almost X' can be partially characterized as a form–meaning pairing such as in (2):[12]

(2) Downtoner *all but* micro-schema
[[all but] V/Adj$_i$] ⇔ [SEM$_i$ is construed as a possible extreme state of affairs that is not completely attained]

There is also another micro-schema with similar, but less fixed, form and with exceptive meaning as in:

(3) *As a result,* **all but** *the sickest would choose to cancel their insurance, experts predicted.*

Exceptive *but* requires a prior indefinite such as *all, everyone, no-one, any time*, and can be postposed, as in (4) (Quirk et al. 1985: 708). It also requires a nominal complement:

(4) ***Everyone but me*** *was tired ~* ***Everyone*** *was tired* ***but me***.

Exceptive *but* is in a class with *except (for), excepting, apart from*, etc. (Quirk et al. 1985: 707). Because exceptive *but*, unlike the other members of this class, must be preceded by an indefinite, its status as a preposition in PDE has been called into question. Huddleston et al. (2002: 1312) and OED construe it as either a preposition or a coordinator. However, in earlier English it was a preposition (see section 3.2 below). The present-day micro-schema can be represented as in (5):

(5) Exceptive prepositional *all but* micro-schema
[all [but NP$_i$]] ⇔ [every member of a set X$_{NP}$ except SEM$_i$]

3.2 The history of downtoner *all but X*

Historically, (5) is the source of (2). *But* itself originated as *butan* 'outside'.[13] Nevalainen (1991: 125) hypothesizes that the exceptive prepositional use of *butan*

---
12 The notation is adapted from Booij (2010), where the skeletal constructional notation is [F] ⇔ [M] and meanings in [M] are indexed to forms in [F].
13 Approximate periods of English are: Old English c. 660–1150; Middle English c. 1150–1500; Early Modern English c. 1500–1700; Late Modern English c. 1700–1970; Present Day English 1970-present.

developed in an Old English expression that became fixed as *ealle buton anum* 'all except one', as in (6a), where *ealle* 'all' quantifies a set of elephants. This fixed expression is a "critical context" usage. The pattern coexisted with more typical, less fixed ones, as illustrated by (6b), where *ealle* introduces a set ('living things') from which one ('fish') is excluded:

(6) a. *þara   horsa   fela   forwurdon ge   þa*
that-GEN.PL hors-GEN.PL many died   and that-PL

*elpendas   **ealle**   **butan**   **anum***
elephant-PL all-PL   except   one-SG.DAT

'many of those horses died and all the elephants except one'
(c. 880 *Orosius* [DOE *butan* II.c.1.b])

b. *ac is seo lyft þe **ealle** lichamlice þing   on   lybbað*
but is that air that all-PL   bodily   thing-PL in   live

***butan** fixum   **anum**   þe   on flodum lybbað*
except fish-PL.DAT alone-PL.DAT that in oceans   live

'but it is the air that all physical things live in, except only fish, that live in the oceans'
(c. 1000 ÆLS, *Christmas* B1.3.14 [DOE *butan* II.c.1])

Nevalainen finds that initially the favoured context for exceptive *butan* was negative (either semantically negative contexts such as *forwurdon* 'died' in (6a) above or overtly negative polarity *ne* as in (7)).

(7) *gelyfað to soþan þæt nan   oþer   god nys*
believe in truth that NEG-one other god NEG-is

butan** Criste   **anum
except Christ-DAT alone-SG.DAT

'truly believe that there is no other god but God alone'
(c. 1000 ÆLS, *Chrysanthus* B1.3.33 [DOEC])

The exceptive meaning appears to result from use of the preposition *butan* 'outside' with a non-locational complement, especially in the context of quantifiers like *ealle* 'all' (6) and *nan* 'not-one' (7). Here there was an implicature of abstract 'except, outside the set of X' rather than physical 'outside the space'. Most of the examples in DOE and DOEC with *ealle butan anum* or similar ones like *ealle + butan + X* as in (6b), where X is a NP and not a numeral, appear in later Old English texts from around 1000. It seems reasonable to hypothesize that constructs with the syntactic sequence *ealle/nan + butan + X* with the exceptive implicature had come to be replicated sufficiently frequently during the 10th century that a pattern had developed. This pattern was conventionalized by the early 11th century, that is, a new micro-schema had been constructionalized and had become available to several speakers.

Ealle/nan buton X were not in a paradigmatic relation to other exceptives in Old English since there were none at this time, and therefore no larger schema can be hypothesized. However, in Middle English, other exceptive prepositions were borrowed from French, e.g. *save*, and later *except*. By 1600 speakers had a choice among exceptive prepositions, and a fully schematic, paradigmatic pattern had developed. As is typical of schemas, the meaning was roughly the same (exclusional) as was the form (preposition), but distributional constraints differed with individual members of the schema: *all but* and *except* both tended to be used in negative contexts, but *save* was not; although *all* could collocate with *except* and *save*, it appears with them far less frequently than with *but*.

In a paper discussing actualization, the extension to new environments of what I call a "neoanalysed" phrase,[14] De Smet (2012: 608) shows that actualization occurs gradually and almost imperceptibly ("sneakily").[15] Among his examples of actualization is downtoner *all but*. He hypothesizes that the context in which the downtoner meaning 'nearly' arose out of exceptive *all but* was "a pragmatic implicature that if something is 'everything but not X', it is 'nearly X'" (De Smet 2012: 611). De Smet says that, according to his data, the original quantifier + preposition *all but* was neoanalysed as a downtoner in the 19th century, as evidenced by its use with adjectives (*all but complete* 'almost complete') and verbs (*we all but apprehend*). This was a second construtionalization. The new microschema was aligned with and used as a member of the extant downtoner set that

---

14 The term "neoanalysis" (Andersen 2001: 213, fn.3) is preferred over "reanalysis", since a child or second-language learner cannot "re"-analyse a structure unknown to them.
15 See also Petré 's comments (this volume: section 5) on slight differences in clusters of local changes leading to "rather gradual development of more schematic syntactic and semantic characteristics".

included *almost, nearly*. The downtoner set was a subschema of the larger degree modifier schema, which at the time included not only these but also boosters such as *greatly, very*.

Especially in negative contexts, *all* is subject to cognitive processing leading to downward monotonicity, the licensing of inferences from supersets to subsets. Being exceptive, *but* is semantically negative. *All but* as a collocation was therefore a natural context in which *all* could come to mean 'not all'. That downward monotonicity in this context is not deterministic is evidenced by the fact that the downtoning use is not attested until relatively late and that *all but* was and still is used in the sense 'everything except' with NP and numeral heads (*all but Jim came, all but three left*).

From a constructional perspective, the hypothesized implicature from *all* in the context of *but X* was a critical context for the second constructionalization. To the extent that hearers interpreted the downtoning implicature, there was mismatch between the meaning and the form since *all* no longer meant 'everything', and *but* no longer meant 'except'. There is evidence prior to the 19th century that some individuals "resolved" the mismatch by neoanalysing exceptive prepositional phrase *all but X* as a degree modifier phrase, specifically a downtoner (note the collocation with the adjective *well* in (8)). Such examples are scattered and can be considered to be innovative precursors.

(8) Mr. Thorne ... dressed my Ancle, pronouncing it to be now **all but** well.
(1795 Woodforde, *Diary* 11 Apr. (1929) IV. 189 [OED *all*: Phrases P23])

A "pattern" had not yet developed. However, the appearance in COHA of the 1820s of a cluster of examples with degree modifier syntax and meaning suggests pattern development. This cluster arose in rather restrictive semantic contexts: those in which *all but* precedes Adj (N) and where the adjective is bounded (Paradis 2001) either inherently (see *impossible* in (9a)), or morphologically (*lowest* in (9b)). Additional unbounded collocates in the 1820s in COHA include *lost, desolated, divine, unanimous, absolutely certain, omnipotent*.

(9) a. Yet retraction then will be **all but impossible**. (1820 Green, *Discourses* [COHA])
   b. reading [became] a cheap amusement; accordingly the class of readers, before confined to a few, ... increased gradually to an almost unlimited extent, and comprehended **all but the very lowest ranks** in society. (1820 North American Review [COHA])

By hypothesis this pattern was repeated sufficiently frequently with the implicature 'nearly X' for speakers to start using *all but* with adjectives that are unbounded as well as those that are bounded, as evidenced by the appearance in the 1860s of examples with *ready*, as in (10).[16]

(10) *It was not so easy to be laughed at as he had imagined. He was **all but ready** to turn about and leave the room.* (1866 Coffin, *Winning his Way* [COHA])

De Smet (2012) shows that by the 1870s the pattern *all but X* where X is (a) an adjective used predicatively or as a modifier or (b) a verb used in the passive or past is robustly attested in COHA. Constructionalization of *all but X* as a degree modifier appears to have occurred since we find evidence of the association of new form (syntax: degree modifier, licensing use with Adjective and Verb heads: monomorphemic *all but*) with new meaning ('nearly'). Specifically, the exceptive micro-construction in (5) was neoanalysed as the downtoner micro-schema in (2). Exclusion of an entity had been reinterpreted as exclusion of an extreme state of affairs in the context of adjectives and verbs.

The prior existence of a general downtoner subschema and of unbounded modifiers was probably the most salient critical context for the change, which was based in paradigmatic analogization. However, the specific downtoner *almost* (< *ealle mæst* 'most(ly) all') may also have activated analogical thinking and allowed for formal and semantic analogization. Note the parallel, coordinated clauses with *almost* and *all but* in (9b). Ziegeler (2016: 10) cites (11) as an early example of the downtoner use of *almost* and notes the negative semantic prosody of the context:[17]

(11) *And I dowed the cony bytwene his eeris that **almost** I benamme his lyf from hym.* 'And I struck the rabbit between his ears so that I almost took his life from him'. (1481 Caxton, *Reynard the Fox*)

However, *all but* can have been only partially modeled on *almost* since its distribution is very different. *All but* is still understood as exceptive when used in environments such as NP and numeral, while *almost* is not restricted in this way (compare *almost 100 giraffes died* (+> not as many as 100 died) with *all but 100*

---

16 *Ready* appears with the degree modifier *very*, a diagnostic for non-bounded status (Paradis 2001), 9 times in the 1820s in COHA.
17 See Stubbs (1996) on negative semantic prosody, the collocation of attitudinally negative expressions, in this case *dowed* and *benamme*.

giraffes died (+> every giraffe died except for 100). This is a good example of De Smet's distinction mentioned in section 2.3 between semantic and distributional similarity. The semantics are similar, but the distribution very different.

3.3 Summary

In sum, evidence of patterns with the form *all but X* that can be considered to be relevant to the emergence of the degree modifier micro-schema can be found in:
(i) the relative fixing of the sequence *ealle butan anum* 'every X but one' in the late 10th century, enabling the rise of an exceptive micro-schema with the form [Indefinite *but* N],
(ii) the use of *all but* before unbounded adjectives and verbs in the early 19th century,
(iii) the probable analogical matching of *all but X* with *almost X*.

The two constructionalizations in question, first of exceptive [all [but X]] and then of downtoner [[all but] X], requires slight nuancing of Fried's (2009) observation that because "meaning/functions ... cannot be determined outside of specific constructions, we have to take constructions as the domain of change" (Fried 2009: 289). The domain of change may be higher-level schemas as well as specific micro-schemas and micro-constructions. In the case of exceptive *ealle butan X* the domain in question was the higher-level prepositional phrase schema, which was largely restricted to spatial, directional, and temporal expressions. By hypothesis, use of *ealle butan X* as an exceptive rather than spatial expression was adopted as a new pattern which led to the development of a micro-schema (and later of an exceptive schema, when *save*, etc. were borrowed). On the other hand, the invited inferences from *all but X* to 'nearly, almost' developed within the domain of the specific exceptive micro-schema, and in the 19th century a new downtoning degree modifying micro-schema came to be aligned to the preexisting degree modifier macro-schema.

4 Patterns in the rise of a clause-final retrospective contrastive discourse marker schema: *after all*

4.1 Background

A set of "linking adverbials" (Biber et al. 1999: 891), "adverbial connectors" (Lenker 2010), "retrospective contrastive adverbials" (Haselow 2012a), or "final particles" (Haselow 2012b), has recently received extensive attention, some historical (Lenker 2010; Haselow 2012a; Traugott 2016b), some synchronic (Barth-Weingarten and Couper-Kuhlen 2002; Haselow 2012b, 2016). The members of this set that are most frequently mentioned are *actually, then, though*. They are metatextual discourse markers, the subset of pragmatic markers that is used to manage a communicative event, and signal Speaker's view of the type of textual linking engaged in (see Fraser 2009). The function of many clause-final metatextual markers is to "link the unit of talk they accompany to an aspect of the preceding discourse unit and ... to signal that the unit of talk is a reactive turn within a dialogic sequence and thus motivated by prior talk" (Haselow 2016: 93). An example is (12):

(12) B: *but does he not like write for himself*
 A: *internally driven I meant*
   no he is not no (..)
 B: *yeah yeah (..)*
 A: *uh (..) I don't know* **though**
   uh uhm he's uhm working on his language (.)
 (ICE-GB s1a-015 [Haselow 2012b: 189])

Here A backs down from her implied statement 'no, he is not driven' and uses *though* "as a rhetorical device to mitigate the disagreement between two assertions produced by the same speaker" (Haselow 2012b: 189). The retrospective contrastive adverbials expressing relations of cause, contrast and concession "force a re-processing or even reinterpretation of the preceding assertions" (Lenker 2010: 198).

Haselow (2016) argues that expressions that appear in clause-final position in English, which he calls "final field", are elements of a macro-grammar that allows speakers to manipulate sequences of linguistic units in the production of text (Haselow 2016: 81), in this case responding to prior talk (Haselow 2016: 83). There are several types of element that may appear clause-finally. Morphosyntactically they are varied in origin. Functionally they are mostly "used to fine-tune epistemic stance" (epistemic adverbs like *of course*, comment clauses like *I think*), to facilitate involvement of the hearer (tag questions like *isn't it?*, *can you?*), to refer to shared knowledge (general extenders like *and stuff*), to comment on the adequacy or appropriateness of expression (*if* clauses like *if I may say so*) and to modify illocutionary force (retrospective contrastive adverbials like *then*, *after all*, which I call discourse markers) (Haselow 2016: 88).

The classes of pragmatic markers mentioned in the preceding paragraph have appeared incrementally in the history of English (Traugott 2016b). Particularly striking is that the retrospective contrastive adverbials/discourse markers are attested late. Lenker (2010) finds that in English clause-final *however* (see (13) below) and *though* appear only around the 1700s, and concludes that "in the past centuries and, in particular, the last decades, English has ... established a new slot for the placement of adverbial connectors, the sentence-final position" (Lenker 2010: 213).

(13) Dorinda: O, Madam, had I but a Sword to help the brave Man?
    Bountiful: *There's three or four hanging up in the Hall: but they won't draw. I'll go fetch one **however**.*
          (1707 Farquhar, *The Beaux Stratagem* [HC ceplay3b; Lenker 2010: 196; Traugott 2016b: 42])

Haselow (2012a) suggests that use of clause-final *then* may have its origins as early as Middle English in conditional discourses bracketed by *if–then*, such as (14), where *then* is clause-final, anaphoric, and expresses "summation or the inferred result or consequence of some state of affairs expressed in a preceding proposition" (Haselow 2012a: 164):

(14) | For | ***if*** | we | be | clene | in | levyng |
| --- | --- | --- | --- | --- | --- | --- |
| for | if | we | be | clean | in | living |

Oure	bodis	are	Goddis	tempyll	**þan**
our	bodies	are	God's	temple	then

In	the	whilke	he	will	make	his	dewllyng.
in	the	which	he	will	make	his	dwelling

'For if we are clean in living our bodies are the temple of God then in which he will make his dwelling'. (c. 1480 *The Baptism* [YP 182. 36; Haselow 2012a: 164; Traugott 2016b: 41])

However, although the syntactic template is a plausible context for the development of retrospective contrastive uses of *then*, there is no contrastive implicature in (14). Haselow (2012: 168) further notes that in Shakespeare's plays final inferential *then* appears primarily in paratactic response uses such as:

(15) Mistress Ford: ... *There is no hiding you in the house.*
 Falstaff: *I'll go out* **then**.
 (c. 1597 Shakespeare, *Merry Wives of Windsor* IV.ii.64 [Haselow 2012a: 168])

Here there is a conditional implicature ('if there is no hiding me in the house'), but still no contrastive meaning. (15) appears to be a likely partial critical context for the rise of contemporary uses such as:[18]

(16) A: *I haven't the faintest idea what you're talking about*
 B: *well you have to listen to the tape* **then**
 (Haselow 2012b: 190 [ICE-GB s1a-085])

It was in the context of the development of such clause-final adverbial markers that concessive, retrospective contrastive *after all* arose.

4.2 The history of the retrospective contrastive discourse marker *after all*

After all meaning 'following everything, at the end' had been available as a temporal phrase clause-initially, -medially and -finally from the early 17th century on. Later in the 17th century an inferential 'in the end' meaning is attested in all three positions (Lewis 2000). Examples of inferential *after all* 'in the end' introducing a change of heart appear to be precursors of the concessive retrospective contrastive adverbial use of *after all*, even though they typically occur clause-initially, e.g. (17):

---

18 When clause-final *then* became constructionalized as a concessive adversative remains to be determined.

(17) *at last he falls foul by his Cit upon Le Strange,*[19] *whom he calls Dog in a doublet or worse, but* **after all** *he ends in a panagyrick of his wisedome.*
(1680 E. P., *Dialogue between Crackbrain and Tom* [CED: D4HOEP; Traugott 2018: 35])

Clause-final *after all* with concessive contrastive meaning appears first in the early 18th century, as in (18):[20]

(18) a. *Why, if she should be innocent, if she should be wronged* **after all**? *I don't know what to think.*
(1700 Congreve, *Way of the World* V.v [Traugott 2018: 36])
b. *Lettice: But let me think a little. If my Mother shou'd be Alive,* **after all**. *Ay marry, that wou'd fright me worse than seeing twenty Ghosts, for she'll force me to marry Ned Ploughshare.*
(1730–1 Lillo, *Silvia* [CLMET 3.0_1_14])

In (18a) *after all* anaphorically indexes the speaker's prior accusations/suspicions and implicates a novel contrasting viewpoint ('despite what I thought/said before'). In (18b) Lettice has just had a dream that her deceased mother was alive. *After all* anaphorically indexes her presupposition that her mother is dead ('despite what (I thought) I knew'). Note both examples in (18) involve the conditional *if*. They are punctuated as "insubordinates": stand-alone clauses with subordinate syntax (e.g. Evans 2007; Traugott 2017). Whether or not this is the authors' original punctuation or the editor's, the examples show that, unlike clause-final concessive *then*, concessive *after all* appears in monologic discourses that counter the prior text or thought of the same speaker.

By the 19th century *after all* appears more frequently but still mainly in monologic texts. Example (19a) suggests that it was well entrenched because it is followed by the question tag *is it?* and is no longer in a conditional context (however, the author gives detailed contextual information). Likewise, there is no conditional in (19b):

(19) a. *'Oh! Ah!' he continued, rubbing his eyes, and beginning to distinguish between the reality, and the image that appeared to have been haunting his dreaming fancy: 'Why, Captain, it is only you* **after all**, *is it? Well, well,*

---

19 Reference is made to a satire *Citt and Bumpkin*, and to its author, Sir Robert L'Estrange (thanks to Peter Petré for elucidating this reference).
20 Clause-initial, justificational *after all* was not established until the mid-19th century.

now!' Why, who did you suppose it was, Darrow, I should like to know?' 'O, no matter, now, – I was in the middle of a cursed dream, and thought a different character had waited on me to do a little business in his line.' (1839 Thompson, *Green Mountain Boys* [COHA])
b. *the deceased was taken to the Bell and Anchor just before twelve o'clock and to the dead-house after the doctor had seen him – it turned out that he was not dead **after all** – I do not know how long he lay in the dead-house before he was taken to the hospital.* (1874 Trial of Alli [OBC t18741123-42])

By hypothesis, use of clause-final position for the specific inferential adverbial *then* with possible concessive implicatures became established during the 17th century, especially in second pair-parts. By the early 18th century *however* also appears to have become available in this position with retrospective contrastive meaning. *After all* came to be constructionalized in clause-final position in the early 18th century, primarily in monologic discourse. While a few specific individual clause-final retrospective contrastive adverbials appear to have been conventionalized around 1700, in the 18th century there is substantial evidence only of a pattern, not yet of a clause-final contrastive adversative schema. This is because, although the data attests to scattered replication of form (final position) and meaning (signaling some kind of counter-expectation), the distribution is different (dialogic for *then* and *however*, monologic for *after all*). Above all, the examples are insufficiently frequent for the researcher to infer that it was entrenched.

As more instances of concessive *after all* and contrastive *however* appear, evidence accumulates for conventionalization of individual, substantive micro-schemas. The later use of other micro-schemas in the same position with similar counter-expectational function suggests that a more abstract pattern, or subschema of discourse markers was conventionalized in the 19th century.[21] Recently this clause-final contrastive discourse marker slot has been used to license not only adverbials but also the coordinator *but* (see Mulder and Thompson 2008; Mulder et al. 2009; Hancil 2018 on the use of clause-final *but* in different varieties of English). It is a subschema of the larger set of pragmatic markers that are favoured in English in clause-final position. Haselow characterizes this larger set

---

21 De Smet (2013) points out that a construction type may be sanctioned as long as it corresponds to some uses of the type "without necessarily being fully consistent with the … type's entire range of uses" (De Smet 2013: 5). In the case under discussion, *after all* has justificational as well as concessive/retrospective contrastive uses (*She's the president after all*; *after all, she's the president*), which are shared with *of course* (Lewis 2000), but not with *however* or *then*.

as representing "sedimented patterns of expanding a unit of talk beyond a potential completion point" (Haselow 2016: 78).

4.3 Summary

Two kinds of pattern that contributed to the development of a clause-final retrospective contrastive schema have been mentioned in this section. Both are systemic:
(i) the expansion throughout the history of English of sets of pragmatic markers available in clause-final position,
(ii) the cumulative use of various adverbials with causal, conditional, and concessive implicatures in clause-final position leading to the development of a retrospective contrastive adverbial schema in the 19th century.

In the case of *after all*, a temporal construction meaning 'at the end' preexisted the development of an inferential 'in the end' meaning. So did pragmatic markers with inferential metatextual meaning (e.g. *now*). Furthermore, there were pragmatic markers that could be used in clause-final position (e.g. *I mean, isn't it, and all*). But use of a pragmatic marker in clause-final position as a concessive retrospective contrastive discourse marker to my knowledge had no precedent before 1700. Use of the specific concessive retrospective contrastive adverbials *after all* and *however* in clause-final position appears to have been accepted in the course of the 18th century as a new pattern on which a schema was later built.

The neoanalysis of the clause-final configurational prepositional phrase *after all* as a non-configurational metatextual discourse marker and the establishment of a productive non-configurational schema with wide scope syntactically and semantically calls into question the restriction of patterns to configurational expressions such as Michaelis (this volume) proposes. The data suggests there is a continuum between configurational and non-configurational patterns.

The two case studies presented in sections 3 and 4 show that pattern is not a matter of form only – a quantifier preceding a prepositional phrase does not entail approximative meaning, final position does not entail counter-expectational meaning, as evidenced by question tags (*has(n't) it?*), general extenders (*and everything*), etc. The development of a micro-schema such as degree modifier *all but X* or of a micro-construction such as the univerbated discourse marker *after all* is the outcome of sedimentation at the substantive level of a recurrent pattern of a form sequence with a relatively underspecified meaning. The development of new (sub)schemas such as the exceptive and contrastive adversative subschemas is the hypothesized outcome of abstraction away from particular examples as language users recruit additional members to a particular pattern. The result is a generalized and conventionalized abstract schema with a more defined meaning.[22]

5 Patterns in the rise of a word-formation schema: X-*licious*

I turn now to a case study involving the rise of lexical material, specifically word-formation.

5.1 Word formation as a constructional schema

In his monograph on word-formation, Booij (2010) develops a theory of "pattern-based morphology". The patterns are constructional schemas that are the basis of productive innovations. Among them are "word formation patterns ... abstractions over sets of related words" (Booji 2010: 3).

Historically there is evidence of word-formation micro-schemas developing gradually, as for example patterns with the forms X-*dom*, X-*hood* in later Old English and Middle English, which emerged from patterns of compounding (see e.g. Trips 2009; Traugott and Trousdale 2013: Chapter 4; Hüning and Booij 2014; Heine et al. 2016). However, once a word formation micro-schema has been established, instantiations of it can be coined instantaneously. For example, the micro-schema X-*dom* 'in the realm/regime of X', developed over several centuries, and, like most schemas, has undergone modifications. Whereas adjectives were available in X as well as nouns in earlier English (e.g. *freedom*), X is now limited to nouns. And whereas it was used with neutral pragmatics (e.g. *kingdom*), since c. 1800 it has been used with mocking, slightly pejorative pragmatics as in *slobdom, trampdom* (Marchand 1960: 206) and more recently *Blairdom, Obamadom, Trumpdom*. However, throughout its history it has licensed on-the-spot coining of new instances.

---

[22] The extent to which schematic meaning may be underspecified in a construction is a problem that cannot be addressed here.

5.2 The rise of X-*licious*

X-*dom* and X-*hood* have histories several hundred years long. A word-formation micro-schema that emerged rather recently, especially in ads and titles of events or books, is X-*licious*. Lehrer (2007) cites:

(20) -*Licious* < *delicious*: *applicious*; *bubblicious* (from a bubble gum ad); *piglicious* (item on a menu at a restaurant called Hog Heaven); *gobblicious* (a cat food flavor from Meow Mix ®); *berry-licious* (on a fresh strawberry package); *Hoge Day-licious* (an exhibit by artist Hoge Day). (Lehrer 2007: 122)

Most, probably all, of these examples have to do with food, which strongly suggests that -*licious* is derived from *delicious* (not, for example, from *malicious*). *Hoge Day-licious* is probably meant to evoke food since in his artist's statement online Hoge Day says: "There is a loop, from art to commercial design to public consumption and back, within which my work floats. I take part in this food chain as an end-user."[23]

Peter Petré (p.c.) points out that X-*licious* is somewhat older than Lehrer suggests, and provides the following pun on 'so delicious':

(21) *There are beautiful warm soda springs in Colorado, and people who go bathing in them at once exclaim: 'Oh! but this is* **soda-licious***!'* (1878 *N.Y. Observer & Chron.* 3 Jan. 8/4)

While Petré's early examples all pertain to food, some more recent ones are less semantically restricted, e.g. *groovalicious* (2002). Other examples I have found appear in book titles, e.g. *Beautylicious* in the title of a 2003 book by J. M. Reynes, *Beautylicious! The Black Girl's Guide to the Fabulous Life*, and *Thug-a-licious* in the title of a 2006 book by Noire, *Thug-a-licious: An Urban Erotic Tale* (both in COCA). X-*licious* is also found in trade names such as: *Carbolicious* low-carb muffins (the 'best tasting diet product ever'), and *Beautilicious* earings,[24] *Fontalicious* for a business designing 'From "fun and futuristic fonts to pop culture vector sets"',[25] *Winterlicious*, and *Summerlicious*, a culinary celebration in Canada from 2013 on.[26] An anonymous reviewer suggested in addition *scrumpalicious/*

---

23 http://hogeday.com/Statement.htm (accessed June 22 2016).
24 These examples are from amazon.com (accessed June 21 2016).
25 http://www.fontalicious.com (accessed June 21 2016).
26 From http://corpus.byu.edu/now/ (accessed June 22 2016).

scrumpilicious.²⁷ These expressions evoke not only "tasty" (or, in the case of *beautilicious earrings*, 'in good taste') but also 'sexy'. 'Erotic' appears in the subtitle of *Thug-a-licious*. *Urban Dictionary* provides the following definitions:

(22) *scrumpilicious*:
1: To describe delicious scraps or leftovers.
2: To describe how sexually attractive a person of an opposite sex is in a positive sense.

(23) *beautilicious*:²⁸
1. A girl that is both good to look at and good to eat.
2. A particularly tasty foodstuff.
3. Synonymous with any other word that means fantastic/awesome/ace etc.

All examples evaluate the base positively. Most have a noun as base, but *gobblicious* shows that verbs related to food consumption may be licensed as well. A schematic construction of the type in (24) can be posited, assuming that the base is usually a noun (N):²⁹

(24) X-*licious* micro-schema
 [[X]$_{Ni}$ [licious]] ⇔ [sexy, tasty SEM$_i$]

This particular kind of word-formation is a partial attributive blend (Mattiello 2013: 120, 123) consisting of a full lexical item + a reduced form of *delicious*. Blends are usually considered to be "extra-grammatical" because they do not fit regular morphosyntactic patterns.

The micro-schema in (24) is "productive" in Barðdal's (2008:1) sense of being "extensible" or able "to attract new or existing lexical items". It suggests a positive answer to Kay's (2013: 46) question "whether ... patterns of coining may grow into constructions", but it is neither type nor token frequent. To date there appear to be only two construction types, *beautilicious,* and *scrumpilicious*, which are

---

27 Entries for both appear in *Urban Dictionary*: http://www.urbandictionary.com/define.php?term=scrumpalicious, http://www.urbandictionary.com/define.php?term=scrumpilicious (both accessed June 6th 2017).
28 Accessed June 21st 2016. *Beautylicious* is possibly meant to evoke *Bootylicious*, a song in Destiny's Child's album *Survivor* (2001), where *booty* is slang for 'bottom' (thanks to Graeme Trousdale for this suggestion).
29 -*licious* is usually used after a vowel or a weak syllable like -*er*, -*le*, but the variant -*alicious* is preferred after a consonant (see *Thug-a-licious*). These are "allostructions" (Cappelle 2006).

used frequently enough and in enough different contexts to be listed in *Urban Dictionary*. Other examples appear to be unique trade names, innovations with specific referents, but not (yet) used in other contexts. The productivity appears to be limited to conscious word-formation, but it is possible that it will spread from ads and trade names to less conscious genres.

5.3 Summary

Potentials for "pattern" in the development of the *X-licious* micro-schema are:
(i) the coining of nonce words in *-licious* leading to the development of a pattern,
(ii) the development of the subschema itself.

In the case of X-*licious*, blending word-formation patterns for adjective formation preexisted the formation of (24) such as *scandicalous* (< *scandalous* + *ridiculous*; Mattiello 2013: 122). Other word-formations that might have been relevant are *X-ly* (a non-productive use 'recurring every X' as in *summerly, winterly* (Marchand 1960: 267), *X-ous* (e.g. *glamorous, glorious, scrumptious*) (Marchand 1960: 275). *-Ly* and *-ous* have N as their base and phonologically match one of the syllables in *-licious*. Despite its lack of a clearly patterned source and the limits on productive new constructions, speakers can process X-*licious* and coin new expressions based on it, so the schema is a marginal part of our knowledge of language. From a usage-based construction grammar point of view that embraces gradience and a range of construction types (e.g. Goldberg 2006), it is not "extra-grammatical".[30]

6 Conclusion

My aim in this paper has been to establish "the mutual relationship between any small-scale ... transitions and the larger patterns they occur in, thus keeping in

---

30 According to Kay (2013), X-*licious* would probably be considered to be an extra-grammatical "pattern of coinage" and not a "true construction" (Kay 2013). Kay draws on Fillmore (1997) where a sharp distinction is made between constructions (existing resources and patterns which are productive) and "patterns of coining". The latter are considered non-productive, non-compositional patterns which have to be learned, e.g. [ADJ as NP] ⊵ ['very ADJ'], exemplified by *easy as pie* 'very easy'. This is consistent with the SBCG model espoused in Michaelis (this volume).

focus the gradient nature of linguistic change" as Fried (2009: 262) recommends, while focusing on the notion of "pattern".

Each case study has illustrated use of constructs that are initially one-offs (innovations). They are replicated in "untypical" contexts that enable the subsequent development of a relevant construction. Since they occur only sporadically, they are by hypothesis originally not recognized as "the appropriate way to say something in a particular community" (Bybee 2010: 45), and at this stage are not entrenched within a broader community of language-users. If they are replicated sufficiently, some of these constructs can be considered to occur in what Fried (2009: 276) calls a "transitional pattern" with the potential of being conventionalized. Such transitional patterns are not integrated into the system of constructions. They are "critical" contexts, accumulations of token constructs that may come to be "packaged together in cognition so that the sequence can be accessed as a single unit", i.e. "chunked" (Bybee 2010: 7). Such packaging may be motivated by analogical thinking. The form–meaning chunks may become entrenched in the individual as constructions. If these innovated chunks or units are taken up and stored by other speakers, constructionalization has occurred. This is a historical reframing of the quotation from Goldberg (2006) cited at the beginning of section 1. The three case studies suggest that analogical thinking is a prerequisite to pattern-formation. However, analogization, which is the development of a new construction or micro-schema based on an exemplar model, cannot occur absent a model. It did not occur in the first constructionalization of the three case studies.

Specific findings are that:
(a) Exceptive [*all* [*but X*]] is attested occasionally in DOEC prior to the year 1000 in the string *ealle butan anum* 'all but one', a transitional pattern. After 1000 it is attested repeatedly, suggesting that it was conventionalized in the 11th century as an exclusive micro-schema [*Indefinite* [*but X*]]. While prepositional phrase constructions were well established, no specifically exceptive phrase pre-existed the emergence of *(all) but X*, and therefore no exceptive schema pre-existed. However, after it had been constructionalized, other exceptive micro-constructions were borrowed (e.g. *except, save*), which led to the rise of an exceptive subschema.
(b) Downtoning degree modifier [[*all but*] *X*] is attested sporadically at the end of the 18th century, a transitional pattern. It was constructionalized in the 19th century and came to be used as a member of the extant downtoning degree modifier subschema. In this case a construction (the exceptive) pre-existed, as did the subschema to which it was attracted.

(c) In the mid-18th century inferential *after all* 'in the end' came to be replicated in clause-final position with retrospective contrastive meaning. Although clause-final position was already the site for use of several construction-types by the 18th century, there was no class of retrospective contrastive adverbials that was used in this position. Use in clause-final position in the early 18th century of the micro-constructions *after all, however* and possibly *then* appears to have led to the development of a clause-final retrospective contrastive adverbial schema in the 19th century.

(d) In the case of N-*licious*, the use of a number of neologisms like *beautilicious* led to a word-formation micro-schema at the turn of the 21st century, largely in the restricted genres of ads and book titles.

In each case a new abstract subschema developed that now serves as a template licensing new members (a paradigm). It should be noted in passing that schemas not only license new members, they can also lose them. For example, *one* was used in Middle English as an exclusive focusing construction, along with *only*; *one* ceased to be used in the 16th century (Nevalainen 1991: 124).

From the case studies we may conclude that there is an asymmetric relationship between patterns and constructions:

1) Not all patterns are constructions. This is because patterns are recurring sequences that have combinatoric potential, but are not necessarily conventionalized. While recurrent meaning is essential, it is relatively underspecified. By contrast, constructions are conventionalized form–meaning pairings.
2) However, all constructions are patterns, whether micro-constructions or schemas. This is because constructions originate in sedimented patterns.
3) Being tokens, constructs are not patterns, but clusters of replicated constructs may constitute transitional patterns that are among critical contexts for potential constructionalization.

In the literature on construction grammar, the term "pattern" has usually been used to refer to several key aspects of constructional thought: sets, schemas, frames, and pairings of form and meaning. Exemplars and models to which analogization is possible have been equally foundational in constructional work on acquisition, language processing, and language change. I have zeroed in on patterns associated with micro-schemas, constructions and constructs in change, and suggest that these different levels of generalization be specified whenever possible and appropriate. These refinements are not meant to replace more syntactic pattern specification such as "phrasal pattern" (Michaelis 2006), or larger scale "design patterns" such as are suggested in Steels (2012). Rather, they are meant to complement them and to provide insights into pattern development over time in terms both of individual micro-schemas and of the larger sets of which they are members.

References

Amaral, Patrícia. 2010. Entailment, assertion, and textual coherence: The case of *almost* and *barely*. *Linguistics* 48 (3). 525–545.
Andersen, Henning. 2001. Actualization and the (uni)directionality. In Henning Andersen (ed.), *Actualization: Linguistic change in progress*, 225–248. Amsterdam: John Benjamins.
Auer, Peter & Stefan Pfänder. 2011. Constructions: Emergent or emerging? In Peter Auer & Stefan Pfänder (eds.), *Constructions: Emerging and emergent*, 1–21. Berlin: De Gruyter Mouton.
Barth-Weingarten, Dagmar & Elizabeth Couper-Kuhlen. 2002. On the development of final *though*: A case of grammaticalization? In Ilse Wischer & Gabriele Diewald (eds.), *New reflections on grammaticalization*, 345–361. Amsterdam: John Benjamins.
Barðdal, Jóhanna. 2008. *Productivity: Evidence from case and argument structure in Icelandic.* Amsterdam: John Benjamins.
Biber, Douglas, Stig Johansson, Geoffrey Leech, Susan Conrad & Edward Finegan. 1999. *Longman grammar of spoken and written English.* Harlow, Essex: Pearson Education.
Biber, Douglas & Bethany Gray. 2012. The competing demands of popularization vs. economy: Written language in the age of mass literacy. In Terttu Nevalainen & Elizabeth Traugott (eds.), *The Oxford handbook of the history of English*, 314–328. Oxford/New York: Oxford University Press.
Blumenthal-Dramé, Alice. 2012. *Entrenchment in usage-based theories. What corpus data do and do not reveal about the mind.* Berlin: Mouton de Gruyter.
Boas, Hans C. & Ivan A. Sag (eds.). 2012. *Sign-based construction grammar.* Stanford, CA: CSLI Publications.
Booij, Geert. 2010. *Construction morphology.* Oxford: Oxford University Press.
Bybee, Joan L. 2010. *Language, usage and cognition.* Cambridge: Cambridge University Press.
Bybee, Joan, Revere Perkins & William Pagliuca. 1994. *The evolution of grammar: Tense, aspect, and modality in the languages of the world.* Chicago: University of Chicago Press.
Cappelle, Bert. 2006. Particle placement and the case for 'allostructions. In Doris Schönefeld (ed.), *Constructions all over: Case studies and theoretical implications*, special issue of *Constructions*. http://www.blogs.uni-osnabrueck.de/ constructions/files/2014/06/2006-SI-Cappelle22-80-1-PB.pdf
Casenhiser, Devin & Adele E. Goldberg. 2005. Fast mapping between a phrasal form and meaning. *Developmental Science* 8. 500–508. (DOI: 10.1111/j.1467).
CLMET3.0. = *The Corpus of Late Modern English Texts*, 1710–1920, version 3.0 compiled by Hendrik De Smet, Hans-Jürgen Diller & Jukka Tyrkkö, Leuven University. (https://perswww.kuleuven.be/~u0044428/clmet3_0.htm).
COCA = *The Corpus of Contemporary American English.* 1990–2015. Compiled by Mark Davies. Brigham Young University. (http://corpus.byu.edu/coca/).

Culpeper, Jonathan and Merja Kytö. 2010. *Early Modern English dialogues: Spoken interaction as writing*. Cambridge: Cambridge University Press.

De Smet, Hendrik. 2012. The course of actualization. *Language* 88 (3). 601–633.

De Smet, Hendrik. 2013. *Spreading patterns: Diffusional change in the English system of complementation*. Oxford: Oxford University Press.

Diewald, Gabriele. 2002. A model for relevant types of contexts in grammaticalization. In Ilse Wischer & Gabriele Diewald (eds.), *New reflections on grammaticalization*, 103–120. Amsterdam: John Benjamins.

Diewald, Gabriele & Elena Smirnova. 2010. *Evidentiality in German: Linguistic realization and regularities in grammaticalization*. Berlin: De Gruyter Mouton.

DOE = *Dictionary of Old English: A to G Online*. 2007. Angus Cameron, Ashley Crandell Amos, Antonette diPaolo Healey et al. (eds.). Toronto: Dictionary of Old English Project.

DOEC = *Dictionary of Old English Corpus Online*. 2007. Angus Cameron, Ashley Crandell Amos, Antonette diPaolo Healey et al. (eds.). Toronto: Dictionary of Old English Project.

Evans, Nicholas. 2007. Insubordination and its uses. In Irina Nikolaeva (ed.), *Finiteness: Theoretical and empirical foundations*, 366–431. Oxford: Oxford University Press.

Fillmore, Charles J. 1997. *Construction grammar lecture notes*. (http://www.icsi.berkeley.edu/~kay/bcg/lec02.html).

Fillmore, Charles J., Paul Kay & Mary Catherine O'Connor. 1988. Regularity and idiomaticity in grammatical constructions. *Language* 64 (3). 501–538.

Fischer, Kerstin & Kiki Nikiforidou (eds.). 2015. *On the interaction of constructions with register and genre*. Special issue of *Constructions and Frames* 7 (2).

Fischer, Olga. 2007. *Morphosyntactic change: Functional and formal perspectives*. Oxford: Oxford University Press.

Fraser, Bruce. 2009. Topic orientation markers. *Journal of Pragmatics* 41 (5). 892–898.

Fried, Mirjam. 2009. Construction grammar as a tool for diachronic analysis. *Constructions and Frames* 1 (2). 262–291.

Fried, Mirjam. n.d. *Construction grammar*. Amsterdam: John Benjamins. (http://www.constructiongrammar.org).

Fried, Mirjam. 2013. Principles of constructional change. In Hoffmann and Trousdale (eds.), *The Oxford handbook of construction grammar*, 419–437. Oxford/New York: Oxford University Press.

Goldberg, Adele E. 2006. *Constructions at work: The nature of generalization in language*. Oxford: Oxford University Press.

Goldberg, Adele E. 2013. Constructionist approaches. In Thomas Hoffmann & Graeme Trousdale (eds.), *The Oxford handbook of construction grammar*, 15–31. Oxford/New York: Oxford University Press.

Hancil, Sylvie. 2018. Transcategoriality and right periphery. *Cognitive Linguistic Studies* 5(1). 61–76.

Hansen, Maj-Britt Mosegaard. 1998. *The function of discourse particles. A study with special reference to spoken Standard French*. Amsterdam: John Benjamins.

Haselow, Alexander. 2012a. Discourse organization and the rise of final *then* in the history of English. In Irén Hegedüs & Alexandra Fodor (eds.), *English historical linguistics 2010. Selected papers from the sixteenth International Conference on English Historical Linguistics (ICEHL 16), Pécs, 23–27 August 2010*, 153–175. Amsterdam: John Benjamins.

Haselow, Alexander. 2012b. Subjectivity, intersubjectivity and the negotiation of common ground in spoken discourse: Final particles in English. *Language & Communication* 32 (3). 182–204.

Haselow, Alexander. 2016. A processual view on grammar: Macrogrammar and the final field in spoken syntax. *Language Sciences* 54. 77–101.

Heine, Bernd. 2002. On the role of context in grammaticalization. In Ilse Wischer & Gabriele Diewald (eds.), *New reflections on grammaticalization*, 83–101. Amsterdam: John Benjamins.

Heine, Bernd, Heiko Narrog & Haiping Long. 2016. Constructional change vs. grammaticalization: From compounding to derivation. *Studies in Language* 40 (1). 137–175.

Herbst, Thomas, Hans-Jörg Schmid & Susen Faulhaber (eds.). 2014. *Constructions, collocations, patterns*. Berlin: De Gruyter Mouton.

Hilpert, Martin & Stefan Th. Gries. 2016. Quantitative approaches to diachronic corpus linguistics. In Päivi Pahta & Merja Kytö (eds.), *The Cambridge handbook of English historical linguistics*, 36–53. Cambridge: Cambridge University Press.

Hoffmann, Thomas & Graeme Trousdale (eds.) *The Oxford handbook of construction grammar*. Oxford/New York: Oxford University Press.

Hopper, Paul J. 2011. Emergent grammar and temporality in interactional linguistics. In Peter Auer & Stefan Pfänder (eds.), *Constructions: Emerging and emergent*, 22–44. Berlin: De Gruyter Mouton.

Huddleston, Rodney, John Payne & Peter Peterson. 2002. Coordination and supplementation. In Rodney Huddleston & Geoffrey Pullum. *The Cambridge grammar of the English language*. 1273–1362. Cambridge: Cambridge University Press.

Hunston, Susan. 2014. Pattern grammar in context. In Thomas Herbst, Hans-Jörg Schmid & Susen Faulhaber (eds.), *Constructions, collocations, patterns*, 99–119. Berlin: De Gruyter Mouton.

Hüning, Matthias & Geert Booij. 2014. From compounding to derivation: The rise of derivational affixes through constructionalization. *Folia Linguistica* 48 (2). 579–604; special issue on *Refining Grammaticalization*, ed. by Ferdinand von Mengden and Horst Simon.

ICE-GB = *International Corpus of English-Great Britain*. http://ice-corpora.net/ice/ index.htm.

Jackendoff, Ray. 1997. *The architecture of the language faculty*. Cambridge, MA: MIT Press.

Jucker, Andreas H., Gerd Fritz & Franz Lebsanft (eds.) 1999. *Historical dialogue analysis*. Amsterdam: John Benjamins.

Kay, Paul. 2013. The limits of (construction) grammar. In Thomas Hoffmann & Graeme Trousdale (eds.), *The Oxford handbook of construction grammar*, 32–48. Oxford/New York: Oxford University Press.

Keller, Rudi. 1994. *On language change: The invisible hand in language*. Translated by Brigitte Nerlich. London: Routledge (first published in German, 1990).

Labov, William. 1966. Some principles of linguistic methodology. *Language in Society* 1. 97–120.

Labov, William. 1994. *Principles of linguistic change: Internal factors*. Oxford: Blackwell.

Lehmann, Christian. 2004. Theory and method in grammaticalization. In Gabriele Diewald (ed.), *Grammatikalisierung*. Special issue of *Zeitschrift für Germanistische Linguistik 32*. 152–187 (available at http://www.christian lehmann.eu/ling/index.html under Schriftenverzeichnis, year 2004).

Lehrer, Adrienne. 2007. Blendalicious. In Judith Munat (ed.), *Lexical creativity, texts and contexts*, 115–133. Amsterdam: John Benjamins.

Lenker, Ursula. 2010. *Argument and rhetoric. Adverbial connectors in the history of English*. Berlin: De Gruyter Mouton.

Lewis, Diana M. 2000. *Some emergent discourse connectives in English: Grammaticalization via rhetorical patterns*. Oxford: University of Oxford Ph.D. dissertation.

Lightfoot, David. 2003. Grammaticalisation: Cause or effect? In Raymond Hickey (ed.), *Motives for language change*, 99–123. Cambridge: Cambridge University Press.
Los, Bettelou & Erwin Komen. 2012. Clefts as resolution strategies after the loss of a multifunctional first position. In Terttu Nevalainen & Elizabeth Closs Traugott (eds.), *The Oxford handbook of the history of English*, 884–898. New York: Oxford University Press.
Marchand, Hans. 1960. *The categories and types of present-day English word formation. A synchronic-diachronic approach.* Wiesbaden: Harrassowitz.
Mattiello, Elisa. 2013. *Extra-grammatical morphology in English – abbreviations, blends, reduplicatives and related phenomena.* Berlin: De Gruyter Mouton.
Michaelis, Laura A. 2006. Construction grammar. In Keith Brown (chief ed.), *Encyclopedia of language and linguistics*. Vol. 3: 73–84. 2nd edn. Oxford: Elsevier.
Michaelis, Laura A. This volume. Constructions are patterns and so are fixed expressions.
Milroy, James. 1992. *Linguistic variation and change: On the historical sociolinguistics of English.* Oxford: Blackwell.
Mulder, Jean & Sandra A. Thompson. 2008. The grammaticalization of *but* as a final particle in conversation. In Ritva Laury (ed.), *Crosslinguistic studies of clause combining: The multifunctionality of conjunctions*, 179–204. Amsterdam: John Benjamins.
Mulder, Jean, Sandra A. Thompson & Cara Penry Williams. 2009. Final *but* in Australian English. In Pam Peters, Peter Collins & Adam Smith (eds.), *Comparative studies in Australian and New Zealand English*, 339–359. Amsterdam: John Benjamins.
Nevalainen, Terttu. 1991. BUT, ONLY, JUST: Focusing on adverbial change in Modern English 1500–1900. Helsinki: Société Néophilologique.
NOW = *News on the Web*, 2010-present. Compiled by Mark Davies. http://corpus.byu.edu/now/.
OBC = Huber, Magnus, Magnus Nissel, Patrick Maiwald & Bianca Widlitzki. 2012. *The Old Bailey Corpus. Spoken English in the 18th and 19th centuries.* University of Giessen. (www.uni-giessen.de/oldbaileycorpus).
OED = *Oxford English Dictionary*. (http://www.oed.com/).
Pahta, Päivi & Merja Kytö (eds.). 2016. *The Cambridge handbook of English historical linguistics.* Cambridge: Cambridge University Press.
Paradis, Carita. 2001. Adjectives and boundedness. *Cognitive Linguistics* 12 (1). 47–65.
Petré, Peter. This volume. How constructions are born. The role of patterns in the constructionalization of *be going to* INF.
Quirk, Randolph, Sidney Greenbaum, Geoffrey Leech & Jan Svartvik. 1985. *A comprehensive grammar of the English language.* London: Longman.
Steels, Luc (ed.). 2012. *Design patterns in fluid construction grammar.* Amsterdam: John Benjamins.
Stefanowitsch, Anatol. 2014. Collostructional analysis: A case study of the English *into*-causative. In Thomas Herbst Hans-Jörg Schmid & Susen Faulhaber (eds.), *Constructions, collocations, patterns*. 217–238. Berlin: De Gruyter Mouton.
Stubbs, Michael. 1996. *Text and corpus linguistics.* Oxford: Blackwell.
Traugott, Elizabeth Closs. 2016a. Identifying micro-changes in a particular linguistic change-type: The case of subjectification. In Päivi Pahta & Merja Kytö (eds.), *The Cambridge handbook of English historical linguistics*, 376–389. Cambridge: Cambridge University Press.
Traugott, Elizabeth Closs. 2016b. On the rise of types of clause final pragmatic markers in English. *Journal of Historical Pragmatics* 17 (1). 29–62.
Traugott, Elizabeth Closs. 2017. 'Insubordination' in the light of the uniformitarian principle. In Thomas Hoffmann & Alexander Bergs (eds.), Special issue on *Cognitive approaches to the history of English. English Language and Linguistics* 21 (2). 289–310.

Traugott, Elizabeth Closs. 2018. Modeling language change with constructional networks. In Salvador Pons Bordería & Óscar Loureda Lemos (eds.), *Beyond grammaticalization and discourse markers: New issues in the study of language change,* 17–50. Leiden: Brill.
Traugott, Elizabeth Closs & Graeme Trousdale. 2013. *Constructionalization and constructional changes.* Oxford: Oxford University Press.
Traugott, Elizabeth Closs & Graeme Trousdale. 2014. Contentful constructionalization. *Journal of Historical Linguistics* 4 (2). 256–283.
Trips, Carola. 2009. *Lexical semantics and diachronic morphology: The development of* -hood, -dom *and* -ship *in the history of English.* Tübingen: Max Niemeyer Verlag.
Urban Dictionary (http://www.urbandictionary.com/).
Weinreich, Uriel, William Labov & Marvin Herzog. 1968. Empirical foundations for a theory of language change. In Winfred P. Lehmann & Yakov Malkiel (eds.), *Directions for historical linguistics*, 95–189. Austin: University of Texas Press.
Wischer, Ilse & Gabriele Diewald (eds.) 2002. *New reflections on grammaticalization.* Amsterdam: John Benjamins.
YP = *The York Plays.* 1982. Richard Beadle (ed.). London: Arnold.
Ziegeler, Debra. 2016. Intersubjectivity and the diachronic development of counterfactual *almost. Journal of Historical Pragmatics* 17 (1). 1–25.

Peter Petré
How constructions are born. The role of patterns in the constructionalization of *be going to* INF

Abstract: This paper addresses the question if and why constructions, conventionalized form–meaning pairings, should have a privileged status among patterns in modelling our knowledge of a language. Constructionist approaches regard constructions as the basic unit of our language knowledge. They range from words to schematic patterns such as the ditransitive (*he gave Mary a book*). Construction grammar also recognizes the existence of connections based on similarity or repeated cooccurrence between forms alone or meanings alone. The emphasis on constructions, however, runs the risk of relegating them to second place. The strict division between constructions and connections between constructions also potentially obliterates the importance of an in-between category such as compositional combinations of constructions, which I refer to as assemblies. While these connectivity patterns have also been captured under the category of constructions broadly defined, I will argue for a separation of non-compositional form–meaning pairings from the dynamics of compositional connectivity patterns, particularly focusing on the role frequency shifts in assemblies play in a constructionalization process.

1 Introduction

In construction grammar, semantic or formal similarities are treated as (horizontal or vertical) links between constructions rather than constructions in their own right.[1] This is why Traugott and Trousdale (2013) restrict the definition of

---

[1] The research reported on in this paper was funded by the Special Research Fund (BOF) from the Flemish Government, and is part of the project *Mind-Bending Grammars*, funded by the ERC Horizon 2020 programme (Project ID 639008; https://www.uantwerpen.be/mind-bending-grammars/). Both institutions are hereby gratefully acknowledged. I also would like to thank Elizabeth Traugott, Laura Michaelis, and an anonymous reviewer for their generous comments, from which I have much benefited when preparing the final text.

Peter Petré, University of Antwerp, Department of Linguistics, 2000 Antwerp, Belgium, peter.petre@uantwerpen.be

https://doi.org/10.1515/9783110596656-007

constructionalization to the emergence of a new form–meaning pairing. Since such a process logically implies an abrupt leap from an old symbolic interpretation to a new one, they see neoanalysis (using the term coined by Andersen 2001) as the primary mechanism of change. Other scholars, such as Fischer (2007) have argued that analogy, i.e. similarity with existing material, is the primary force in the emergence of (grammatical) constructions. In this vein, De Smet (2012) argues that the actualization of a new construction proceeds gradually, and emphasizes that an item's use can be subject to multiple, potentially conflicting generalizations. These generalizations take as their input any kind of similarity between instances, not just form–meaning pairings. De Smet's argumentation suggests that there is no hard distinction between constructional change and constructionalization. Constructionalization is the cumulative result of unobtrusive shifts. There is no point at which the original form–meaning node is replaced by a new one wholesale, because each time there is an extensive period in which either the old form or the old meaning is shared between the conventionalized and the innovative uses.

This paper fleshes out the theoretical ramifications of these different viewpoints. To this end I will carry out a high-resolution form-function analysis of the constructionalization of the string "BE *going to* INF" into [BE *going to* INF]. This constructionalization comprises the early development from a motion verb plus purposive adjunct towards a future auxiliary with infinitival complement. As such it can be said to constitute the first 'episode' of a longer grammaticalization process (cf. Petré and Van de Velde 2018 for this term). I distinguish constructionalization from grammaticalization here. We might still, with Traugott and Trousdale (2013: 25), call this first constructionalization "grammatical constructionalization", in that a more grammatical function emerges. Grammaticalization however, particularly in its later stages, also includes other types of change such as increase in schematicity and productivity, or phonetic reduction, which are not or only weakly in evidence at this earliest stage. According to Traugott (2015: 6) the actualization of the hypothetical new construction [BE *going to* INF] culminates in the early 18th century with raising structures like *there is going to be such a calm among us* (1725), whose lack of an independent subject for *be going* clearly reveal its auxiliary status. This is more than half a century after instances that do no longer refer to motion had become common, and metalinguistic comments appeared that indicate that *be going to* was established as an auxiliary of the imminent future. Assuming that the later appearance of raising is not simply an accidental gap in the data, this raises the question whether the new construction had already emerged at this earlier point, but did not yet entail any formal changes. And if this is indeed the case, is it possible to detect when exactly the new construction came into being, in the absence of clear formal clues? And what is the status of utterances that are similar to the new construction before this point in time?

The main goal of this paper is to identify the timing and nature of the different stages of the constructionalization of [BE *going to* INF]. Specifically, I will tackle the gradualness problem by zooming in onto the nature of the changes that occur in the run-up to constructionalization. The locus of these early changes cannot be the construction itself, as this did not yet exist. However, they are also not random. Rather, the run-up phase reveals certain patterns that systematically background (or DEPROFILE) certain lexical aspects of the string "BE *going to* INF", such as motion or control. These patterns pave the way for the constructional status of [BE *going to* INF]. I will refer to them as ASSEMBLIES, recurrent configurations of existing constructions and their co-text/context, which do not (yet) have constructional status themselves. Evidence is also provided that a complex constructionalization process may feed on more than one such assembly simultaneously.

The nature of assemblies, their development, and their interaction with constructions, will be examined in four sections. Section 2 discusses the status of constructions in two major constructionist approaches, that by Goldberg (2006), and that by Traugott and Trousdale (2013), followed by the formulation of an alternative with an independent status for assemblies. Section 3 zooms in on the nature of these assemblies, and how frequency shifts in them may lead to change. This section also outlines the corpus used and the data retrieval procedure. In a fourth section, three assemblies that are particularly salient in the usage of [BE *going to* INF] are analysed in detail. Finally, section 5 discusses to what extent the notions of assembly and similarity between assemblies may help to understand how the emergence of a new construction is prepared by means of gradual strengthening of similarity clusters.

2 The status of patterns and constructions in construction grammar

2.1 Frequency and the status of constructions

Despite the confessed usage-basedness of construction grammar, the potential roles that frequency can play are arguably still not properly understood. In this section I discuss the view on frequency in one major synchronic theory of construction grammar, that of Goldberg (2006), and one major diachronic one, that of Traugott and Trousdale (2013). I will argue that each of them underplays the distinctively dynamic nature of entrenched compositional patterns in language, which is at play in the run-up to the process of constructionalization, and important in a proper understanding of language change.

In the synchronic theory of Goldberg (2006) frequency is used as a secondary criterion for identifying constructions. Any conventional form–meaning pairing (stored in memory) is considered a construction (cf. Langacker 1987). This includes the narrower definition (Goldberg 1995: 5) in which either the form and/or the meaning/function is not predictable from its component parts. Take for instance the expression *I am going to reply to her email*. In isolation, *I am going* means 'I am in motion (towards X)'. *To reply to her email* can be interpreted as a fragment expressing purpose (as in *I will turn on my computer to reply to her email*). However, when combined, the meaning of the first component part changes. The idea of motion is no longer inherently present. Constructionist theory assumes that language users have stored the complex string as a separate, non-compositional construction of the type [[X_{SUBJ} BE *going to* Y_{INF}][X intends to do Y]]. In addition, compositional strings are also considered to be "stored as constructions even if they are fully predictable, as long as they occur with sufficient frequency" (Goldberg 2006: 5). Goldberg's inclusion of compositional strings into the constructicon is motivated by her assumption that "it's constructions all the way down". Constructions, in her view, are *the* basic unit of linguistic knowledge. Usage-based linguistics and psycholinguistics have provided ample evidence that linguistic patterns are also stored if they are sufficiently frequent. Because they are stored units, and because all stored form–meaning units are considered constructions, frequent compositional patterns are also constructions.

The diachronic theory advocated by Traugott and Trousdale (2013) is a diachronic extension of this synchronic view. In addition, they draw attention to the intrinsic difficulty of the concept of frequency to work with in actual analyses of change. They argue that the notion of "sufficient" frequency cannot be operationalized (Traugott and Trousdale 2013: 11). In their words, "establishing what level of frequency is sufficient for pattern storage and entrenchment is problematic" (Traugott and Trousdale 2013: 5), because the necessary frequency for entrenchment is "gradual and relative, not categorical or universal" (Clark and Trousdale 2009: 38).

While both synchronic and diachronic theories share the qualitative delineation of constructions as "conventionalized form–meaning pairings" (in essence an extension of the symbol beyond the word unit), they are both struggling with the role of frequency in the constructicon. Both views acknowledge the importance of frequency, but neither tries to operationalize it. Traugott and Trousdale (2013) support their assumption that the role of frequency in constructionalization cannot be operationalized by referring to research on the gradual propagation of phonetic variants (Clark and Trousdale 2009). However, this research takes a variationist perspective where frequency is considered as a relative proportion in an onomasiological space. It also takes an aggregate perspective, whereas the effect of frequency is arguably primarily located in how individuals process frequency data. If we want to come closer to the operationalization of entrenchment thresholds in the process of constructionalization, we should operationalize frequency not (only) from a variationist perspective. The variationist perspective assumes that there already is a construction, and measures its entrenchment in terms of its share in the onomasiological space. The emergence of a construction is better measured by a more fine-grained quantitative analysis of the contexts in which the pre-construction material occurs. This paper provides a way of operationalizing such a quantitative analysis.

The inclusive definition of Goldberg (2006) arguably does not give enough weight to the difference between non-compositional constructions and entrenched patterns. One obvious cognitive difference lies on the perception side. A language learner has to learn a non-compositional construction *as is* in order to use it properly. However, it may suffice to store only the component parts in the second case. Separate storage may still facilitate production, and is expected to occur spontaneously with higher entrenchment (Schmid 2016: 9), but it is neither logically required nor necessarily expected from the start.

Insistence on terminological differentiation should not merely serve categorical fastidiousness. The main point I will argue for is that viewing frequent patterns as something in their own right helps understanding the nature of gradualness and neoanalysis in language change. From a diachronic point of view, it is an open question, to be investigated empirically, whether the effect of frequency shifts of compositional patterns is limited to entrenchment and separate storage. Alternatively, frequency shifts may play a decisive role in the emergence of new form–meaning pairings, that is, constructionalization in the sense of Traugott and Trousdale (2013). Traugott and Trousdale discuss frequency mainly as an effect following constructionalization, related to the idea of grammaticalization as reduction (see their footnote 24, page 35). The primary mechanism of change is neoanalysis, the new interpretation of a construction as something else. Even though ample room is left for the role of analogy and gradualness, such a view still treats constructionalization as the eventual outcome of a consecutive series of discrete changes in either form or meaning. What matters are the steps in this process. The role of frequency is not denied and is implied in the mechanism of pattern matching or analogization (the systematic copying of structure; see Traugott and Trousdale 2013: 38), but even then each instance of analogization would be neoanalysis, and increased frequency of analogized exemplars would merely be entrenchment of the new analysis, and hence, again, an effect rather than a cause. Quantitative research into the emergence of constructions in language acquisition (e.g. Tomasello 1992, Tomasello 2000, Israel 2002) however has shown that more abstract generalizations typically emerge out of a combination of local (exemplar) clusters after these have gathered a critical mass. The role of frequency growth has been explored in more detail in recent quantitative work (e.g. De Smet 2016), but in this work it is still assumed that one step naturally leads to the next (by being semantically or formally minimally disruptive), relegating frequency to a kind of subsidiary position. This model may seem sufficient when simple lineages of consecutive changes are involved (which are the majority of cases studied). However, cases of multiple lineages arguably reveal that frequency has a more fundamental role to play (see e.g. Petré and Van de Velde 2018). In such cases it may well be the frequency balance itself that determines the way in which eventually a novel construction crystalizes.

2.2 An alternative view: Patterns all the way down

I will now turn to the difference between an assembly and a (Goldbergian) construction. Both can be seen as types of patterns, among other types, hence the idea of "patterns all the way down". I will return to the more general view on patterns and the central role of connections between them in the concluding discussion. For a detailed complementary discussion of patterns (and pre-patterns) versus constructions I refer to Traugott (this volume). Her account – even if not quantitatively conceived – shares much in spirit with my own.

The term assembly is inspired by Langacker (2009: 10–15). While Langacker refers to an assembly as a construction, from a construction grammar perspective an assembly is a meaningful compositional configuration of constructions and/or recurrent co-texts rather than a proper construction. Langacker's notion encompasses any kind of combination of constructions (his "symbolic structures"). Assemblies are not unlike the concept of idiomatic chunks, referred to for example as "reusable fragments" (Thompson 2002: 141) or "prefabs" (Erman and Warren 2000). The concept is also reminiscent of Torres-Cacoullos and Walker's "niches" (2009). They observe how functionally similar constructions typically stake out distributional "niches" that make them distinct from each other and more or less complementary. They do not, however, discuss the possibility of niche-like distributions in a context where competition is lacking. To some extent assemblies are equivalent to co-text (plus context). However, co-text is typically evoked when a construction is already there, and its context is examined. But the string

"BE *going to* INF" is not yet a construction. Co-text is also non-committal when it comes to structure. Underlyingly the recurrence of co-texts implies structure, i.e. the instantiation of other constructions. A lexicalist alternative to this idea, which approaches structure in phrasal patterns partly in terms of lexical dependencies, is provided in Michaelis's chapter in this volume. Traugott and Trousdale speak of a "constellation of constructions" specifically with regard to the case of "*be going to* INF" (Traugott and Trousdale 2013: 223). An assembly is just that – though I will argue that the relevant assemblies are even more complex than what is already combined in "*be going to* INF".

Assemblies are not unlike the exemplar clusters that occur at the pre-construction stage in first-language acquisition, but differ from these in that they are built up from already existing component parts of the grammar. If they reach a critical mass, they may be stored separately. Once they are at this stage, they do no longer involve a truly creative act on the part of the language user. Before they may be viewed as associative clusters between constructions/co-textual elements, which vary in strength. The assumption of variable associative strength arguably provides a more promising route to the operationalization of entrenchment, than simply counting occurrences. Under this assumption separate storage is the result of strengthening of associations between the component parts of the assembly beyond a certain threshold. What needs to be accounted for, then, is how associative shifts in different assemblies may conspire and lead to constructionalization. Frequency is of particular importance when multiple shifts feed into each other at various times in the development. Each frequency shift is related to a lineage underlying the resulting construction (Croft 2000: 32). The dynamics is reminiscent of what has been described as multiple source constructions (De Smet, Ghesquière and Van de Velde 2015), with two addenda: (i) The multiple sources are all instances of the sequence "BE *going to* INF" themselves, a possibility that is not discussed very often in the literature (except for Petré 2012). (ii) The multiple sources need not be constructions themselves.

Reasons for the growth in the frequency of an assembly may be pragmatic or system-related. An obvious system-related reason in the case of [*be going to* INF] is the increase of the progressive construction independently from the verb *go* (Petré 2016a). A plausible pragmatic motivation is sheer novelty. Specifically, it may be assumed that there is a reverse correlation between "noticeability" and frequency. When an assembly still has a rather low frequency, it may stand out among competing and otherwise equivalent expressions, simply because it is less entrenched. This, in turn, may lead to the assembly being used more often. The role of noticeability in grammaticalization has been discussed in detail by Detges and Waltereit (2002), who refer to it as expressivity, or Haspelmath (1999), who refers to it as extravagance, and also specifically with regard to the data presented here (Petré 2016b, 2017). The increased frequency of assemblies may also have some specific semantic effects. In early literature on grammaticalization, one such effect was called "bleaching", i.e. the loss of semantic content. However, scholars such as Sweetser (1988: 392) and Heine, Claudi and Hünnemeyer (1991) have pointed out that what occurs in the early stages of grammaticalization is rather a redistribution or shift of meaning. Hopper and Traugott (2003: 94–95) adopt this view and illustrate it with future [BE *going to* Inf], pointing out that the loss of motion in the construction is compensated by the gain of new meaning, that of intention or future prediction. I will argue that bleaching, as a gradual process, occurs even at these early stages, but is then better understood as what Langacker calls "deprofiling", i.e. the process whereby a certain semantic aspect of an assembly receives less prominence than when all component parts conveyed their semantics to the fullest extent. Deprofiling in itself does not constitute a semantic change in the strict sense.[2] Occasionally, however, these frequency effects lead to a more qualitative change. At this point a new construction may be said to emerge.

2.3 Methodology

When frequency shifts also lead to functional shifts, strengthening of associations potentially goes beyond mere frequency increase. Various diachronic construction grammarians, such as Hilpert (e.g. 2008) have focussed on frequency shifts as indices of functional change. Bottom-up operationalizations of the effects and cognitive representation of associative strengths to language change may be achieved by the implementation of connectionist models of language (cf. pioneering work by Tabor 1994 or Bates and Elman 1993; recent advocates in McClelland 2015; Manning 2015). Very recently, connectionist or related methods are also finding their way into historical linguistics, taking into account co-text and context in a richer way than traditional collocational analysis (e.g. Perek and Hilpert 2017, which makes use of refined vector space models; Petré and Budts forthc., which implements neural network representations). Yet such methods are typically data-hungry, and tend to focus on post-constructionalization constructional change. They are generally less suitable to look into the emergence of a construction. To better assess the role of frequency in functional shifts within

---

2 My view here is in line with Disney (2009a), who offers a cognitive perspective on the grammaticalization of [BE *going to* INF] from the related point of view of domain-shifting.

and across assemblies in the process of constructionalization I propose a more fine-grained method combining qualitative and quantitative research. This operationalization involves a scoring system of various functions associated with various assemblies, where functions that are conducive to grammatical constructionalization are interpreted in terms of the degree to which they deprofile original semantic features. Degree of deprofiling is measured by means of a ternary system. Wherever original semantic features are not particularly backgrounded in the assembly's interpretation, a score of 0 is assigned. Wherever some deprofiling is involved a score of 1 is assigned. Cases where a certain semantic feature is lost receive a score of 2.

To test for trends in the frequency of higher deprofiling in assemblies, and their significance, I make use of two non-parametric statistical tests (using the R package, R Core Team 2013), meaning that it is not assumed that the data reflect a single global mathematical function (of change). The first is Kendall's tau-b correlation test, which is a robust and widely used test for trend analysis (see e.g. Agresti 2010: 196). The second is loess regression, a method of locally weighted regression, which calculates a polynomial function for each data point (here a second-degree polynomial), based on a local subset of all data points (Cleveland et al. 1992, Cleveland and Loader 1996). A more detailed explanation of what these tests imply is provided when they are first applied in the analysis section.

3 Assemblies as multiple sources in grammatical constructionalization

3.1 Hypothesis

The specific hypothesis that will be tested is that simultaneous frequency growth of assemblies may lead to their interconnection and eventually to the emergence of a new construction. A second hypothesis is that the appearance of raising is the result of further strengthening of associations, and as such may appear considerably later than first constructionalization. The hypothetical scenario is as follows. Assemblies combine a set of constructions. In the current case, we are dealing with recurrent combinations of [[BE V*ing*][ongoing involved activity]], [[GO]['go'] and [[*to* Vinf (NP$_{OBJ}$)][Purpose]] + one other construction. If the set of constructions that is combined is partly shared between these assemblies – as in the current case – they share multiple links, which may, under certain conditions, result in a more global association between the assemblies. Some assemblies may catch on in the speech community and grow in frequency. It is furthermore assumed that these increases are initially largely independent from each other. However, when their parallel development reaches a critical level, the assemblies will become interconnected. At this point, the language user may make a more abstract generalization, which captures all instances of all assemblies under a single cognitive schema. Such a generalization, then, constitutes a new form–meaning pairing, i.e. a new construction (in this case [[BE *going to* VInf][imminent future]]). Frequency in this scenario is not merely a symptom or effect of routinization, but instead functions as a dynamic catalyst enabling the emergence of a new association and, hence, construction.

3.2 Assembling [BE *going to* INF]

In the following discussion of the pre-1700 development I draw freely on the literature while specifically zooming in on the earliest stages, in which [BE *going to* INF] has arguably not yet crystallized as a construction and where the notion of assembly will turn out to be most relevant. The literature on [BE *going to* INF] is extensive, with, within the past ten years, work by Hilpert (2008), Disney (2009b), Torres-Cacoullos and Walker (2009), Nesselhauf (2010), Garrett (2012), Traugott (2012, 2015), Traugott and Trousdale (2013), Budts and Petré (2016), Petré (2016b) and Petré and Van de Velde (2018).

The source of [BE *going to* INF] was a fully compositional combination of a progressive construction, expressing ongoing activity, the lexical construction [GO] expressing physical motion, plus a purposive non-finite clause. The combination may be represented in construction grammar formalization in (1), with double arrows dividing the form and the function of the constructions involved (see e.g. Traugott and Trousdale 2013). An early attestation is (2).

(1) [[BE V*ing*] ↔ [ongoing activity]] +
 [[GO] ↔ ['go']] +
 [[*to* INF] ↔ [intended activity]]

(2) *You thinke I* **am going** *to market* **to buy rost meat**, *do ye not?*
 (Robert Wilson, 1592)

At this stage the assembly is not yet a construction, and remains fully compositional. Both form and semantics of the assembly can be predicted on the basis of the component constructions. Additional evidence that the assembly is compositional is found in the simple observation that combinations with one construction less are perfectly adequate and commonly attested. This is obvious for a sentence such as (3), which lacks the purposive adjunct, but in the 17ᵗʰ century, it is also possible to leave out the progressive construction while retaining the purposive, as in (4).

(3)   Well, well, *I **am going*** now to the Market, and thy head shall pay for it. (J.H., 1650)
(4)   Neighbour, this cow is much like mine. It is very true (quoth he) and therefore *I **go to sell*** her, because our wiues contend about them euery night, not knowing which to take. (Richard Carew?, 1607)

A proper [BE *going to* INF]-construction emerges when the assembly acquired holistic semantic and formal properties of its own. Formally, BE *going* acquired the characteristics of an auxiliary, and the purposive adjunct (*to buy some chocolate* in (5)) was neoanalysed as the complement of this auxiliary, as in (6).

(5)   [*I am going*] [*to buy some chocolate*] >
(6)   [*I am going to buy some chocolate*]

Semantically, futurity was semanticized and became the primary meaning of the construction, resulting, among other things, in its expansion to situations where motion is no longer at stake.

The new construction [BE *going to* INF] remained restricted to imminent or "relative" future (Traugott 2015: 67), as well as to intentional actions until somewhere in the 18ᵗʰ century (Budts and Petré 2016). Metalinguistic evidence suggests that it became a conventional means of expressing such futures between 1620–1640. A *terminus a quo* is provided by some comments first published in 1616 on a biblical passage that makes use of the Hebrew equivalent of *be going* combined with *to die*.[3] The presence of an elaborate comment, which tries to link the passage to motion, where a non-motion reading is the more natural one, reveals a certain uneasiness with the futurate use of [*be going to* INF]. A *terminus ad quem* is provided in 1646 by a reference in a Latin school grammar, where it is said that "*going to*, is the signe of the Participle of the future … I am … going to read" (cf. Petré and Van de Velde 2018 for a detailed overview of the evidence).

---

[3] This is the passage by Ainsworth that is referred to by Traugott and Trousdale (2013: 221) as an indication of conventionalization, and dated 1639 by them. This date is not that of the first edition, however. Petré and Van de Velde (2018) also argue that the passage points to the lack of conventionalization of *be going* INF instead.

According to Traugott (2015: 69), the new analysis is formally actualized when sentences appear of the type in (7), where *go* no longer has a subject of its own, but instead appears with dummy *there* and is notionally catered for by the subject of the infinitive. Together with the semantic loss of motion this may be taken as formal evidence that [BE *going to*] is now conceived of as an auxiliary. The earliest attestation of this type found by Traugott dates from 1725 (Traugott 2015: 69). In the corpus used for the current analysis, an instance in an English work from 1701 occurs (for another early instance from New England, 1693, see Petré and Van de Velde 2018).

(7) ... *told him* **there was going to be** *an Inquisition made in some Accounts* (Anonymous. 1701)[4]

The main challenge, now, is to determine which steps had to occur in the two centuries stretching out between the first attestations of "BE *going to* INF" (in the late 15th century), and the structural actualization of the new analysis by the end of the 17th century.

Two cautionary remarks are in place before trying to analyse this transitional period. First, one has to be careful not to project the new construction too far back in time in a classic case of *Hineininterpretierung*. It has been argued, for instance by Garrett (2012), that the neoanalysis takes place early in the 17th century, with the occurrence of instances where motion is lacking. Garrett (2012: 69) gives (8), dating from 1611, as the earliest example.

(8) *The Gentleman tooke the dog in shagge-haire to be some Watch-man in a rugge gowne; and swore hee would hang mee vp at the next doore with my lanthorne in my hand, that passengers might see their way as they went without rubbing against Gentlemens shinnes. So, for want of a Cord, hee tooke his owne garters off; and as he* **was going to make a nooze**, *I watch'd my time and ranne away.* (1611)

In itself it is likely enough that the anonymous *Gentleman* tries to convert his garters into a device for hanging someone on the spot. However, the writer may well have had in mind for the gentleman to walk to this *next doore* mentioned in the

---

4 EEBO, whose copy is undated on the cover, gives 1680 as the date and the Earl of Rochester as the author, but these metadata are inaccurate. The text consists of an inscription in honour of the Earl by an unknown author, followed by short biographical material. The date of writing, 1701, is printed in the body of the text as a signature to this inscription.

previous sentence, to attach his garters there as a noose – many doors at the time had a sign or emblem above them that was ideally suited for hanging someone. In general, one has to be very careful in assigning a label like "no motion", in order to avoid anachronistic interpretations fed by the current situation.

Second, while there are some early instances where one would indeed have a hard time arguing that motion is still there, one has to be careful about what kind of evidence this presents. Specifically, looking at the aggregate behaviour of the speech community may be misleading in this respect, because the earliest examples may be realized by an unrepresentative minority of progressive language users. As Hilpert (2018) points out, practitioners of Construction Grammar more often than not carry out analyses on aggregate data while making use of a theory that is framed as a psychologically plausible model of how linguistic knowledge is stored in individual minds. Such a misalignment of theory and practice is far from ideal (see also Fonteyn 2017 for some thoughts on the aggregate-individual-mismatch). However, the more one returns to the period where innovation begins, the less likely one will have sufficient data to do such an individual analysis. This is why I will focus on aggregate data. Individual analyses on prolific authors is possible from roughly the 1630s onward, and yields results that are compatible with and complementary to those presented here (Petré 2016b; Petré and Van de Velde 2018).

With these two caveats in mind, let us turn again to the question: what happened in the run-up to the appearance of sentences such as (7)? First, it appears that "BE *going to* INF" as a string (so remaining agnostic about its status of assembly or construction), after a stable though marginal existence in the 16th century, exhibits an ever stronger increase in the 17th century, as is shown in figure 7.1 below (adopted from Petré 2016b).

Importantly, this increase was not random. Specific assemblies featuring "BE *going to* INF" were more successful than others. I will focus on three such assemblies: (i) combinations of "BE *going to* INF" with a topicalized object (e.g. *the death I am going to seeke* [1636]); (ii) combinations with present-tense assertions (*He's going to kill me!* [1699]); (iii) combinations with the passive construction (*He was going to be Marry'd to a Whore* [1688]). Each of these, it will be argued, has contributed significantly to the emergence of an auxiliary construction [BE *going to* INF]. Specifically, in each of them a certain semantic aspect of the original, non-grammaticalized assembly, is susceptible to being backgrounded or "deprofiled". Deprofiling here is not to be understood as a conventionalized property of a construction, as in Goldberg (1995: 57). Rather it involves the loss of a profiled aspect of a construction, and is similar to Langacker's notion of profile shift

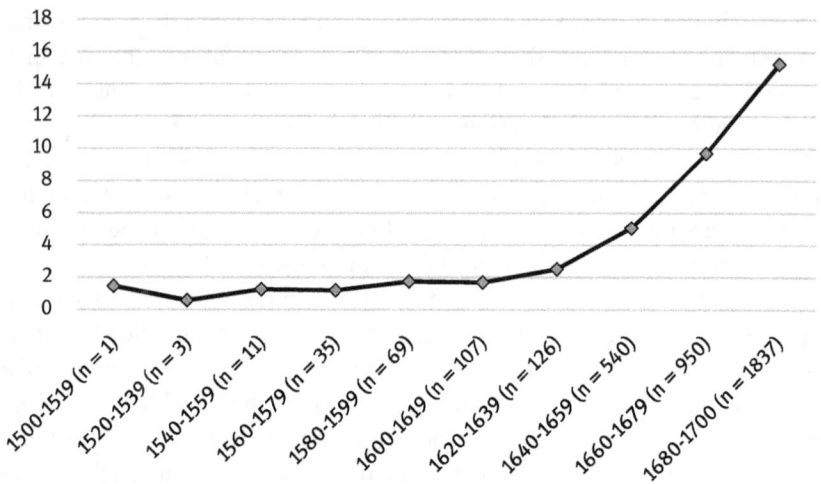

Fig. 7.1: Normalized frequency of "BE *going to* INF" per million words

(Langacker 2009: 66). Langacker gives the example of size-noun constructions such as *a lot of* X, where the original meaning of *lot* 'part, portion' recedes in the background, and the profile shifts to the meaning of size unit that was already pragmatically present. The concept of profile shift seems to imply that deprofiling one aspect automatically means profiling another, similar to Sweetser's (1988) idea of semantic enrichment accompanying bleaching. However, their simultaneity is not a logical necessity, and the respective timing of deprofiling and enrichment is an empirical question.

In the case of "BE *going to* INF", three types of deprofiling are at play. The source assembly "BE *going to* INF" conveys an instance of "ongoing controlled motion with a purpose". An agent, (i) by CONTROLLING his legs (or sometimes, metonymically, some other means of motion, such as a ship or a horse), (ii) IS MOVING to some location, (iii) WITH THE INTENTION of doing something there. It will be argued that the increased use of topicalization primarily deprofiles motion (semantic component (ii)); the increase in present-tense assertions deprofile first ongoingness and then intentionality (iii); and, finally, the development of assemblies with the passive shows an increased deprofiling of control (i).

3.3 The corpus

The focus of the present contribution is on the constructionalization of [BE *going to* INF], which can be seen as constituting the first episode of a longer grammaticalization process. Most of the literature on this stage has been qualitative in nature, for two obvious reasons. First, a novel construction is expected to be rare on its first appearance. Second, until recently historical corpora of English have generally been too limited in size. Combined, the number of data available to historical linguists was simply too small to do any useful quantitative analysis of this earliest stage. To realize a somewhat robust quantitative analysis it was therefore necessary to mine large parts from the database *Early-Modern English Books Online* (http://eebo.chadwyck.com/). This database contains scans of all available published texts between 1473–1700. The *Text Creation Partnership* (TCP; http://www.textcreationpartnership.org/) has provided accurate transcriptions for the majority of the texts in this database. All instances of *going* were retrieved from this corpus, and filtered. Given their infrequency at this early stage, inclusivity was essential. Attention was paid to spelling variants such as *a-going, agoing, goeing, goeinge, going, goinge, gooing, goyng, goynge*, as well as transcription errors such as *goin* or *go- ing*. The query was also deliberately not limited to a context window within which *going* and *to* had to cooccur. This way instances were found where the *to*-infinitive was separated from *going* by as many as 12 words, where the *to* was lacking or not properly transcribed, where *to* was realized as *t'* (once), and so on. I first extracted all instances of *going* from EEBOCorp 1.0, a selection from EEBO (Petré 2013). EEBOCorp 1.0 contains about 525 million words. This resulted in 3,673 occurrences. However, of these only 234 are dated between 1600 and 1640, and a mere 120 between 1477–1600. To make fine-grained qualitative-quantitative analysis feasible for these crucial early periods I complemented EEBOCorp 1.0 for the years before 1620 with texts from the entire EEBO-TCP database, and also analysed additional data from 1620–1640, mining approximately another 250 million words. This resulted in 218 additional data points.

4 Analysis

4.1 Introduction

In the following sections I turn to each of the three assemblies introduced in section 3.2. I will describe the different stages they go through and how these stages may be explained as a direct correlate of their routinization and increase in frequency. Section 4.5, then, zooms in on the combined effect of these independent developments. What this means for the constructionalization of [BE *going to* INF] will be discussed in section 5.

4.2 Topicalization

The first assembly combines [BE V*ing*], [GO] and [*to* INF] with a topicalized element belonging to the embedded infinitival clause. This element appearing in front position potentially – though not necessarily – invites a monoclausal reading with *be going* functioning as an auxiliary. The most common syntactic construction triggering topicalization is the relative clause, followed by *wh*-questions, cleft-constructions,[5] or without any syntactic trigger. The topicalization assembly may be schematically represented as in figure 7.2:

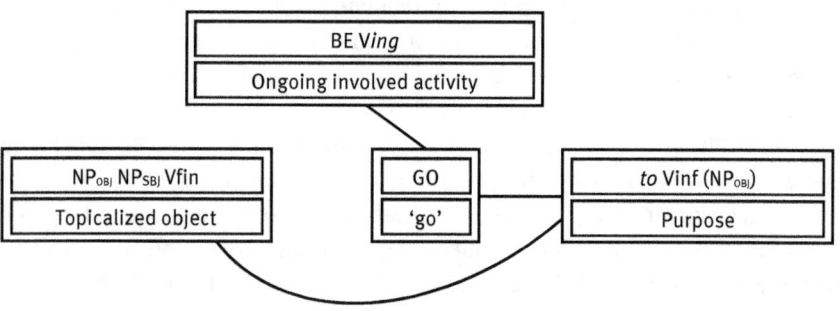

Fig. 7.2: Topicalization assembly

The lines between the different constructions in figure 7.2 represent their combination into a complex pattern, i.e. assembly.[6] The topicalized object construction (or

---

[5] While clefts increase significantly in Early Modern English (see Patten 2012), they seem unimportant in the development of [BE *going to* INF]. Only three out of 791 instances of topicalization in my data are clefts.

[6] The process of combining constructions is approximately equivalent to what has been called unification in certain types of construction grammar (for more details see, e.g. Friedman and Östman 2004: 58). It is a formalized form of combining constructions, stipulating that only compatible feature matrices can be unified. Cognitive construction grammar does not adhere to a strictly formalized notion of unification, as it acknowledges that a construction's meaning is too subtle to be captured by feature structures (e.g. Goldberg 2006: 213) – in fact, even practitioners

group of constructions) shares an element with the purpose adjunct construction, the *go*-construction shares an element (*going*) with the progressive construction.

The originally compositional nature of the assembly is suggested by instances that preserve the lexical semantics of its component parts, as in (9).

(9) *What an heavenly prayer! to give them both a taste and a pledge of that intercession* **which** *he* **was going** *to Heaven* **to make** *for them.* (1665)

However, preservation of a semantic component does not necessarily mean that it is fully profiled. In (9) the presence of a goal location *to Heaven* suggests that the motion-component of *going* is still profiled. This is, however, highly exceptional (there are only three clear instances in my data). An important function of a topicalization construction is precisely to profile one element more emphatically than others. In this case the topicalized element belongs to the embedded clause, which is about the agent's purpose or intended action, and not (anymore) about the motion towards a location. Motion is accordingly by default of secondary importance, and deprofiled. An early example is (10).

(10) Hort[ensio]. ... *I must pick it out of him by wit.*
Flo[rimell]. *As good say steale my Lord,* **what mary-bone** ['essential part'] **of witte** *is your iudgement* ['person capable of good judgment'] **going to pick** *now?*
Hort. *I must, like a wise Iustice of peace, picke treason out of this fellow.* (John Day, 1608)

In this fragment from John Day's play *Humour out of breath*, Hortensio is walking about with his assistant, searching for a "proper man without a beard". Hortensio then spots Aspero (the one they are looking for), and mentions to his assistant that he thinks this is the one, ending with "I must pick it [the truth] out of him by wit". Florimell, the woman that is accompanying Aspero, overhears Hortensio and reacts by asking what he *is going to* do. The context reveals that there is motion – the two parties meet each other while walking about in town – but at the same time it is clear that the emphasis is on the intended action of 'picking out treason'.[7]

---

of unification-based models acknowledge this (e.g. Friedman 2015: 990). However, in essence what the theories want to capture is the same, viz. how existing cognitive schemas are combined, and how such combinations are constrained by (lack of) compatibility.

7 Note that topicalization is particularly common with verbs of speech or communication, where motion is generally of little importance. About 33.5% (265/791) of all instances in the 17th century contain a speech or communication verb, as compared to only 7.5% in non-topicalized instances (233/3100). Not too much importance should be attached to the genre ("drama") of this

Pragmatically, then, most of these instances are primarily about an imminent future event (and as such are roughly equivalent to *be about to*) rather than motion with a purpose. An increased degree of entrenchment of this assembly, then, may lead to the loss of the idea of motion altogether. The earliest attestation is (11), from a guide to prayer. The speaker is on his knees and will not move, but, before praying, needs to tune in spiritually with the greatness of God's presence.

(11) *And with a hart thus deuout and recollected ... thou shalt thinke* **to what an excellent, and soueraigne maiesty** *thou* **art going to speak.** (1620)

The constructionalization approach of Traugott and Trousdale (2013) poses a problem here. The shift from (10) to (11) only involves semantic change (as an extreme form of backgrounding of motion, up to its loss), but no formal change. According to their analysis, this is not constructionalization, but only constructional change. But which construction, then, has changed? For we are dealing here with an assembly of four constructions. It cannot be GO that has changed, because outside this assembly GO still means 'move'. Alternatively, one may argue that the assembly already *was* a construction to start with, based on the wider interpretation by Goldberg (2006), which includes entrenched patterns. This would imply there might have been a micro-construction "[BE *going to* INF] + topicalization" prior to a more general [BE *going to* INF], which exists side by side with instantiations of [BE *going to* INF] that are *not* constructions. The evidence at least allows for the possibility that a compositional combination of constructions can develop some functional peculiarities. This may imply that the result is non-compositional anymore, but it seems reasonable to assume that, at least initially, topicalization merely coerced GO into a construction which is indeterminate as regards its motion meaning without this deprofiling being part of a new non-compositional construction.

Whereas constructional status of the topicalization assembly cannot be established qualitatively, more conclusive evidence is arguably found in the quantitative operationalization of the different effects of topicalization. Figure 7.3 outlines how the relative weight of topicalized versus non-topicalized instances of the string "BE *going to* INF" shifts throughout the 17th century. It also shows that,

---

early example. Eckhardt (2006: 100) has argued that drama was particularly conducive to loss of motion, because motion on the stage was associated with the performance rather than with actual real-life motion. However, early instances of indeterminate cases occur in all sorts of genres. Neither do the earliest instances where motion is lost show a special connection with drama (example (11) for instance is from a religious text).

while fully profiled motion is extremely exceptional, early instances remain consistently compatible with motion. The first attestation of topicalization dates from 1585. The first one where motion is no longer possible only appears in 1620 (example (15)). By the 1630s non-motion uses have become predominant.

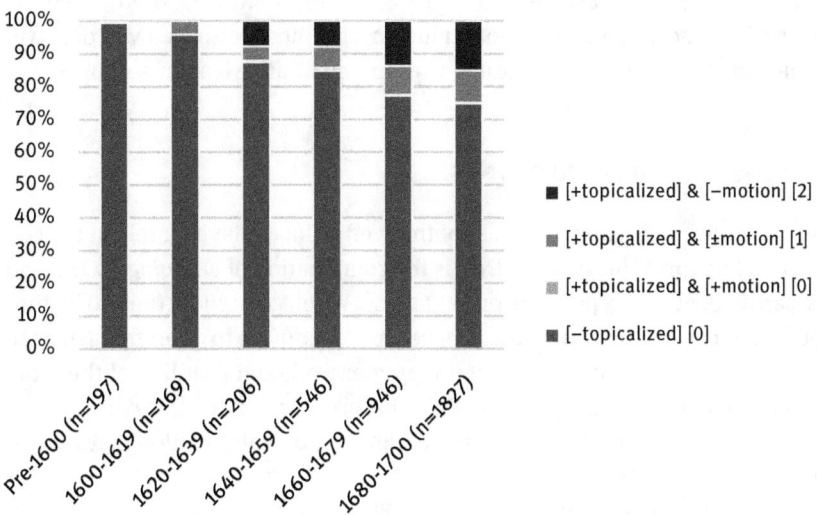

Fig. 7.3: Proportional frequency history of the topicalization assembly

Figure 7.3 provides a visualization of the development. To test for significance, I assigned scores from 0 to 2 to all instances of the string "*be going to* INF", where 0 includes all non-topicalized instances as well as the topicalized ones where motion is fully profiled (note that this last type – [+topicalized] and [+motion] [0] – only shows up as a very thin line in 1620–1639 and 1640–1659); 1 is assigned to those topicalized instances where motion is possible but deprofiled; 2 to those where motion is lost entirely. I then applied Kendall's correlation test. This test provides a p-value as well as an effect size (referred to as tau-b), which ranges between -1 and 1, where 0 means 'no trend whatsoever', and -1 and 1 represent a maximal (from 0 to 100%) upward or downward trend of a certain feature. The test tells that the increase in the relative share of topicalized instances where motion is lost constitutes a significant trend (effect size [tau-b] = 0.14, p < 0.001). It is remarkable that whereas up to 1620 there were no instances where motion was clearly lacking, topicalized instances without motion are already the predominant type in 1620–1639. Comparing Kendall's tau-b values for pairs of periods further reveals that the most significant change takes place precisely between periods 1600–1619 and 1620–1639 (effect size [tau-b] = 0.15, p < 0.01). This leap in the data is indicative of the qualitative leap associated with the conventionalization of a pattern, or, indeed, the emergence of a new construction. A second shift that reaches significance, though with a lower effect size, occurs between 1640–1659 and 1660–1679 (effect size [tau-b] = 0.10, p < 0.001). Between these periods the share of non-motion instances almost doubles. I will deal with the question whether this constitutes a second qualitative leap in section 5.

4.3 Present-tense assertions

A second type of assembly that is hypothesized to have played a role in the constructionalization of [BE *going to* INF] is the combination of BE, *going*, *to* INF, and an assertive sentence type in the present tense. When combined, the two features of present tense and assertiveness may become conducive to deprofiling of ongoingness (inherent in the function of the progressive), and profiling of the future action expressed in the purposive *to* INF. This may lead, in turn, to deprofiling of intention (inherent in the lexical verb *go*), and the overall function may shift towards that of prediction.

The combination of the [BE *going to* INF]-assembly with this set of sentence constructions is represented schematically in figure 7.4:

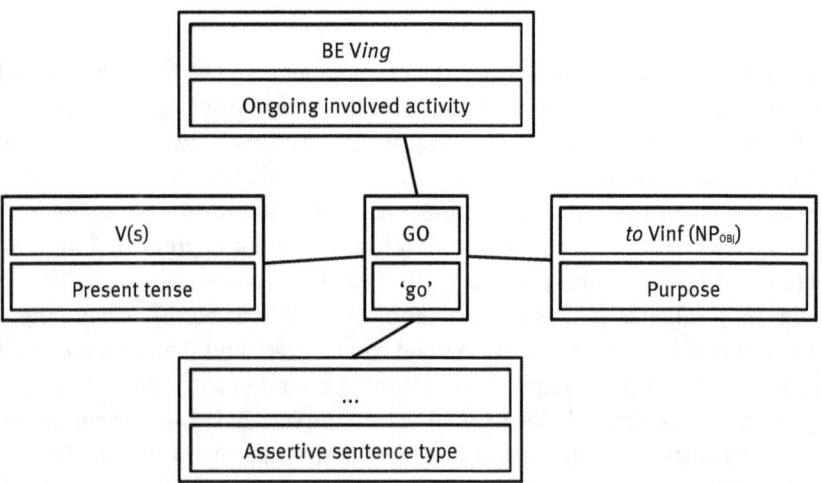

Fig. 7.4: Present-tense assertion assembly

Two distinctions, leading up to three categories, are relevant in order to understand how this shift unfolds. A first distinction is that between the egophoric and non-egophoric perspective. Egophoricity, in the sense of Dahl (2008), applies to expressions where no one is better equipped than the speaker/writer in making a particular statement about the future. Almost all early uses of "BE *going to* INF", before its grammatical constructionalization are egophoric. Within them, a further distinction needs to be made between (i) statements where the outcome is known or assumed, or where no commitment to the future is made; and (ii) those where a commitment is made to the realization of the future situation.

Category (i) contains past tense uses, generic statements, and non-assertive statements in the present tense. Predictions about the future in the past tense are generally about a future relative to the past, which is already known to the speaker/writer (see also Traugott 1989 on the development of *will* and *shall*) – past tense predictions about an absolute future do not occur at this stage. Generic statements are generalizations based on past situations with identical outcomes, and it has been generally inferred that identical future situations will yield identical outcomes. Every member of the community who subscribes to a generic statement will essentially agree on the outcome, making the statement a non-claim on the part of the current speaker. Non-assertive statements such as conditional subordinate clauses in the present tense do not imply any commitment to the realization of a future reality, and hence lack an independent testable outcome. In quantifying the effect of the present-tense assertion assembly, any instance falling within this range of uses receives a score of 0.

Category (ii) contains three types of sentence. The first is that of (mostly first-person) statements where the subject (and therefore the speaker/writer, either directly, or indirectly in the role of omniscient narrator) expresses its intended action.

(12) *I'me very sorry I can continue no longer ..., for **I am going to imploy my Eyes in the view of some French Clothes and Garnitures**.* (1674)

The subject in (12) expresses its intention. The emphasis on the intention deprofiles the ongoingness associated with the progressive construction. The speaker is not actually going right then, but rather announces that she is about to go. The unrealized nature of this intention may also activate the association with prediction. This profile shift is only a very slight one, since the progressive still preserves the function of signalling that the speaker/writer is already preparing the action. Deprofiling of ongoingness is more pronounced in the second sentence type that is included in category (ii). This type consists of statements where the speaker/writer reports the intentions of other agents, as in (13). The queen has informed the speaker that she is going forth to meet the prince, and he simply delivers her message. The statement is not a prediction, because neither the commitment of the subject nor its realization are questioned or guessed at. For that reason, reports are also egophoric. However, the degree of certainty about the actual situation is lowered because of the distance between subject and speaker/writer, which again paves the way to the establishment of a predictive function.

(13) *My Lord, the Queen hath sent for you,* **She is going forth to meet the Prince**, *and hath Commanded none be wanting to attend With all the State that may become her, to Congratulate the triumph now brought home.* (1652)

The third type, finally, is the one where the subject demands from someone else to do something (e.g. *tell them that you are going to Interpret the Indictment*, 1682). They are egophoric insofar as the speaker/writer is the source, while also not knowing what the eventual outcome will be. Any instance belonging to any of these sentence types has received a score of 1.

This leaves us with category (iii), which consists of statements where the egophoric perspective is completely abandoned, as in (14). Here the speaker/writer predicts what someone else is going to do based on circumstantial evidence.

(14) *He charged his Gun; whereat the Child Shrieked out,* **He's going to kill me!** (1699)

Unlike in the previous cases, the prediction made in (14) involves guesswork, and there is no longer direct access to the intentions of the agent. Instances of such predictions have received a score of 2.

Figure 7.5 below provides an overview of the distribution of the various categories. Category (i) is split up between [-present] (other tenses of BE than the simple present) and [+egophoric] and [+certainty] (generic and non-assertive statements in the present). Category (ii) is captured by [+egophoric] and [-certainty]. Category (iii), finally, by [-egophoric] and [-certainty]. A Kendall's correlation test indicates that there is an overall trend towards a higher score (so towards categories (ii) and (iii)) which is highly significant ($p<0.001$), but overall fairly weak (effect size [tau-b] = 0.06). Between specific periods there are no shifts that are significant at a level of $p<0.01$. It is nevertheless noticeable that the highest effect size (tau-b = 0.09) is once again found for the transition from 1600–1619 to 1620–1639, but it is only significant at a level of $p<0.1$ (exact p = 0.095). The transition from 1640–1659 to 1660–1679 is significant at a level of $p<0.05$, but the effect size is equal to the overall trend at 0.06. Interestingly, if we disregard category (ii) (first-person intentions and reported intentions), the transition to the last period turns out to be the most significant one (p = 0.017). This suggests that the relative importance of category (iii) increases towards the end of the 17th century. Recall that this is the category where the speaker/writer makes a guess about other people's intentions or future situations generally, implying the emergence of an epistemic layer of prediction (see also Budts and Petré 2016).

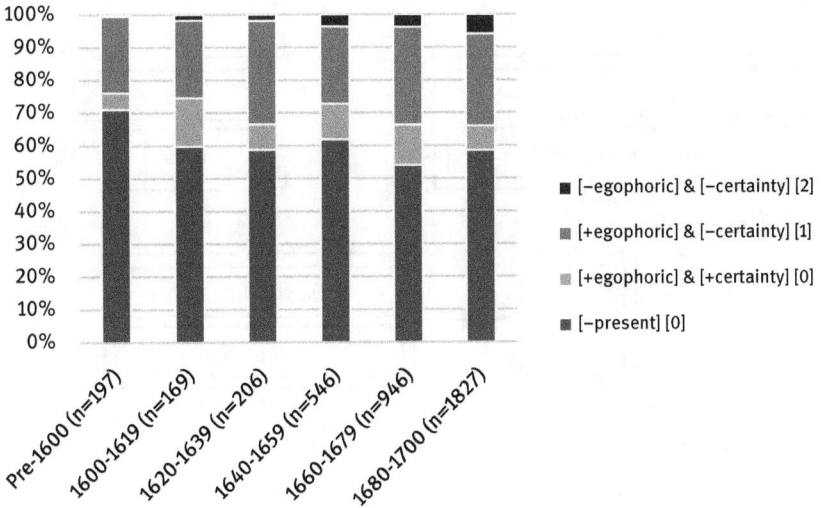

Fig. 7.5: Proportional frequency history of present-tense assertion assembly

4.4 Assembly with passive construction

The third assembly combines [BE V*ing*], [GO] and [*to* INF] with a passive construction, which can be schematically represented as in figure 7.6 below. The possible role of passive constructions in the constructionalization of [BE *going to* INF] has been pointed out early on by Hopper and Traugott (2003), who argue that "the passive demotes the inference that the subject of *go* is volitional or responsible with respect to the purposive clause" (Hopper and Traugott 2003: 89). A similar argumentation is repeated in Traugott and Trousdale (2013: 217–220). The immediate effect of a passive infinitive is limited to the demotion of agency with respect to the infinitive. Yet (some) hearers (at least) may infer that it also demotes the action of *going* more generally. Traugott and Trousdale (2013) give two very early examples (dated 1477 and 1483) where motion is still clearly present, but at the same time may be subsidiary to the idea of something happening at a later time. Their first example (*ther passed a theef byfore alexandre that **was goyng to** be hanged* [1477]) can serve as an illustration. The focus is clearly on the hanging, not on the going to the gallows. It should be noted, though, that this effect primarily resides on the perception side. On the production side, writers/speakers, at least initially, may well have combined the passive with "BE *going to* INF" precisely to *add* the idea of (controlled) motion to their message.

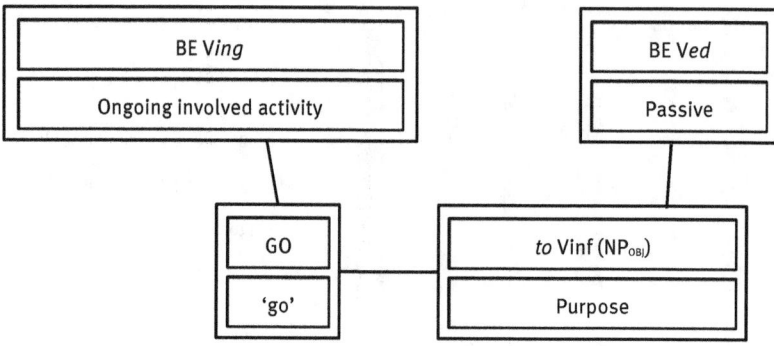

Fig. 7.6: Assembly with passive construction

Despite these two early attestations, the passive is by no means predominant at this earliest stage. Before 1600, only 10 out of a total of 197 instances is a passive (admittedly more than the single instance of topicalization predating 1600). Passives increase from 5% to 8% of all uses during the 17th century. This is only a slight rise (tau-b = 0.03), but it is significant at a level of $p<0.05$ (p = 0.02).

As such, a raw frequency increase does not provide much information on the question whether the passive contributed to the emergence of [BE *going to* INF], or merely followed suit. Petré and Van de Velde (2018) argue that a passive *to*-infinitive constitutes a formal feature that highly correlates with the semantic feature of lack of control over the composite action. The assumption is that the semantic extension to situations beyond the control of the subject is the more fundamental development. This semantics can be, and often is, realized by the use of a passive infinitive, but there is no one-on-one mapping between them. The more fundamental role of the semantic development is confirmed by a bi-directional stepwise variable selection procedure (see Levshina 2015: 149–151), which shows that the presence of a passive infinitive is only significant when certain semantic features are left out of the equation. When these semantic features (in the context of passives, animacy in particular) are taken into account, it is only those that turn out to be significant predictors of the overall development of [BE *going to* INF]. I would like to refine this argumentation here. The assembly with the passive construction may have played a more dedicated role in promoting the no-control uses of [BE *going to* INF], in line with the qualitative analysis by Traugott and Trousdale (2013). However, it *only* started to play this role in the course of the 17th century, after it had gone through an internal development towards higher correlation with no-control uses. Petré and Van de Velde (2018) consistently treat formal and semantic features separately, focussing on what each feature contributed on its own. If we want to know whether the assembly with the passive changed internally, we need to look more closely at the functions associated with this form across time. For this purpose, I have distinguished three main categories of passives in the data.

The first category comprises instances where the subject is both in control of its motion and in control of the planned activity at the destination. In such instances the formal realization of a passive does not at all affect the reading of *going*. A clear example where *going* preserves its semantics of controlled motion is (15).

(15) *The duke of Normandy* **is goynge** *to Reynes* **to be crowned**. (1523)

Instances belonging to this category received a deprofiling score of 0.

The second category is exemplified in (16). Instances of this category either clearly show motion (the 1477 sentence would be an example), or, as in (16), a motion reading is at least possible. In either case the subject is or would be in control of its (possible) motion. Yet in this case the subject is not in control of the composite action. The effect of this is that the semantic component of control (or agency) associated with *going* is deprofiled. Instances within this category therefore receive a deprofiling score of 1.

(16) *He is fumbling with his purse-strings, as a Schoole-boy with his points, when hee* **is going to bee Whipt**, *till the Master wearie with long Stay, forgiues him.* (1628)

It is examples such as (16) that pave the way for further extension to instances where the subject is no longer in control at all, and motion is automatically also (most likely) lacking. An instance of this third category is (17).

(17) *In all Appearance the same or worse Tragedies* **are going to be Played over** *again.* (1681)

In addition to these main categories, there is a small number of other cases (put between parentheses in the graph legend). These include (i) those where the subject cannot be in control of any motion (because motion is lacking entirely), but *is* in control of the composite action; (ii) cases where control over the target action is unclear. Both these minor categories receive a score of 1. (iii) cases where there is no control over the action, and control over motion is unclear – these receive a score of 2.

From figure 7.7, which shows only the passives in the data set, it appears that there is a shift towards passive assemblies where the subject lacks control entirely. These instances deprofile the lexical components of control and motion associated with GO the most.

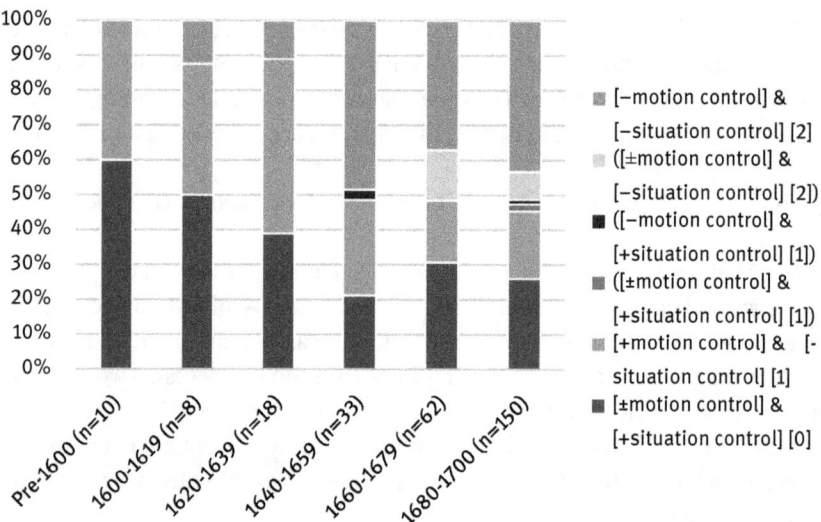

Fig. 7.7: Deprofiling of control and motion in assembly with passive construction

Kendall's correlation test reveals that the overall increase of categories other than the first (where all lexical components are preserved) constitutes a significant trend (effect size [tau-b] = 0.15, p = 0.003). Comparing Kendall's tau-b values for pairs of periods further reveals that the biggest effect occurs between 1620–1639 and 1640–1659. The effect size of the change between these periods is twice as strong as that of the overall trend (tau-b = 0.15), although only moderately significant (p = 0.016). What is most remarkable about the change between these two periods is that category 3, where motion and control are both deprofiled, suddenly becomes the predominant one. This leap is once again indicative of the qualitative leap associated with the conventionalization of a pattern, or, indeed, the emergence of a new construction. The fact that the leap is found a decade or two later than the one we observed for topicalization, might indicate that the development in the passive was accelerated by the topicalization development. Still, passives already seem to develop internally from the start, suggesting that what happened is a combination of internal entrenchment and strengthening by other assemblies such as topicalization. It seems reasonable to assume that the assembly with the passive helped [BE *going to* INF] in establishing a function of prediction beyond that based on activities controlled by the agent.

4.5 Deprofiling of assemblies combined

The initial hypothesis was that increasing entrenchment of assemblies might lead to the crossing of a threshold, impacting on the behaviour of the construction as a whole. In order to further inform the discussion of section 5, this section briefly looks at the aggregate deprofiling scores of the various assemblies combined. For example, a data point that combines a present-tense assertion score of 1 (egophoric intention) with a topicalization score of 2 (motion lost in topicalization context) has an aggregate score of 3. To test for significance, I carried out a loess regression. Loess calculates a polynomial function for each data point, based on a local subset of all data points. This local subset is defined by smoothing parameter α, which represents the fraction of all data points that is used for the calculation of each local function. Additionally, not all of the data points in each subset are equally weighted. Instead, data points that are closer to the data point for which the local polynomial is calculated get higher weights. The method effectively allows for looking for local developments along a more longitudinal development. Its locality means that the method does not try to fit all data into a single function (such as, for instance, a single s-curve), but remains agnostic as to how many significant sub-developments there are. A lower α will stick more closely to the actual data points, and therefore will generalize less (and overfit the data), whereas a higher α will result in a graph that approximates a global parametric function. Disadvantages to loess is that it is data-intensive and tends to wag at its tails (because it lacks symmetric data to calculate the local function for those areas). To reach a maximally unbiased picture, I averaged aggregate scores per year, and only ran the loess regression from 1560 onwards, when data becomes available on a yearly basis. I also ran the regression model with different smoothing parameters, to see how robust any sub-global trends are. Overall, the graph in figure 7.8 shows that the line gets steeper around 1620–1630. While the bumpiness of α = 0.30 (dashed line) might point to overfitting, this peak is still clearly visible when α is set at 0.50 (solid line), and weakly so with α = 0.70 (dotted line). The leap is therefore not likely to be the result of outliers, but may well signal a qualitative tipping point within a more global upward trend.

Besides the evidence of a qualitative leap around 1630, there is also evidence that the different assemblies are increasingly interconnected. As some constructs instantiate multiple assemblies simultaneously, the total score theoretically falls within the range of 0 to 6. This full range is attested in our data, but not right from the start. Scores of higher than 2 only appear from the 1620s onwards, and scores higher than 4 from the 1660s onwards. These findings are in line with those found for individual language users in Petré and Van de Velde (2018).

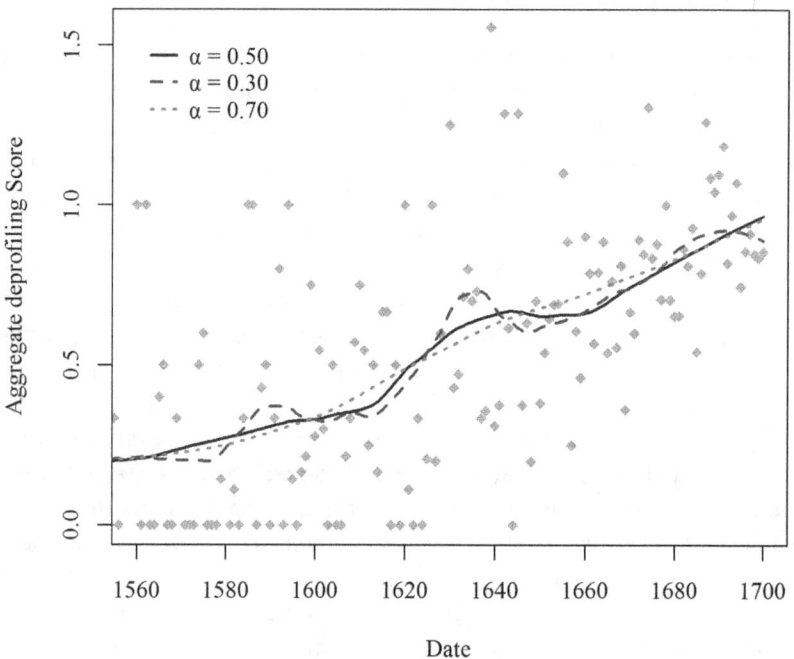

Fig. 7.8: Combined deprofiling scores

Qualitative evidence that the assemblies are shifting from local islands to realizations of a more global schema is also found in the introduction of inanimate subjects. Most inanimate subjects are not in control of what is occurring to them, have no intentions, and are incapable of motion. It is remarkable, then, that they occur almost simultaneously in all three assemblies. The first attestation in present-tense assertions and topicalization dates from 1629, while the first in a passive dates from 1630. This is about a decade after the deprofiling of lexical features had accelerated in topicalization and present-tense assertions, and coincides with such an accelaration in the passive.

5 Discussion

What do we learn from the history of these assemblies for the constructionalization of [BE *going to* INF]? In this discussion I would like to focus on two outcomes of the analysis: (i) assemblies have certain characteristics which may differentiate them from constructions traditionally conceived; (ii) the emergence of a new form–meaning pairing, i.e. construction is preceded by frequency shifts in assemblies, which gradually bring about semantic shifts.

A first outcome concerns the *sui generis* nature of assemblies. From the analysis of the frequency and functional histories of three assemblies featuring "BE *going to* INF", it appeared that over time each assembly increasingly deprofiled a particular semantic feature of the source composition "BE *going to* INF", thereby moving towards an entrenched linguistic entity of its own. The original meaning of the source composition was that of 'controlled motion with a purpose'. Instances of the topicalization assembly increasingly deprofiled motion in this semantic complex, present-tense assertions deprofiled intentionality (purpose), and passives deprofiled control. Of course, these deprofiled features are not exclusive to a single assembly. Passives also deprofile intentionality just as present-tense assertions deprofile motion, but their prototypical semantics correlate more with the loss of certain semantic features than with others.

The increase in deprofiling each time is assumed to correlate with the strengthening of the associations between the various constructions that constitute the assembly. From a connectionist perspective (e.g. Lamb 1999: chapter 4), one might argue that the change in associative strength (strength of the connection) is all there is, without implying any unique change to the assembly as a holistic unit. Yet it seems hard to reduce what is happening here to connectivity changes alone, precisely because the process involves multiple associations that change in sync, which suggests that a more holistic process is taking place. Indeed, the non-compositional part of an assembly is arguably not primarily about its meaning or form being holistic (as is the case with constructions traditionally defined), but instead about clustered frequency changes. The various associated constructions (or, in connectionist terminology, nodes) themselves preserve their compositionality, and may still happily occur with one construction less. The reason why they increasingly cooccur, then, is most likely related to pragmatic success rather than construction status in the narrow sense.

A second outcome relates to the timing of neoanalysis or the emergence of a new construction. The hypothesis is that the deprofiling effect of each assembly becomes so salient as to be associated across them. At some point speakers realize that the independent developments of these assemblies are underlyingly indices of a single phenomenon, which comes into being because of that realization. This point may differ between speakers – and it is still an open question whether it is possible beyond first-language acquisition – but as such signals the emergence of the new construction [BE *going to* INF]. It has been argued by Traugott and Trousdale that this is the point where [BE *going to* INF] is used to express deictic (or absolute) future (a prediction about an event in the future) rather than relative future (an imminent action that is expected to result from a controlled event that has already started). They associate the emergence of deictic future with the appearance of raised constructions and stative infinitives such as *be* (Traugott and Trousdale 2013: 118, 220–224), which first occurs towards the end of the 17th century. At the same time, instances where motion is absent, even if they are still about an imminent, hence relative future, already appear much earlier in the first few decades of the 17th century. Was [BE *going to* INF] a new construction already before the appearance of raising, then? Not if one sticks to the idea that a new construction involves a new form. Traugott and Trousdale (2013) account for the time gap between these early motionless instances and the later deictic futures by appealing to the notion of gradualness (referring to De Smet 2012). They also explicitly argue that in the early stages "BE *going to* INF" was not yet itself a construction, but rather a combination of constructions (Traugott and Trousdale 2013: 220). Their conclusion – even though this is not really made explicit – seems to be that constructionalization took place when the semantic shift towards deictic future was combined with the formal exponents of having become a full auxiliary (such as raising).

However, the precise ramifications of the notion of gradualness remain largely unaccounted for. Previous studies on gradualness such as De Smet (2012) have shown that actualization may proceed from one environment to the other on the basis of similarity relations between them. The environments discussed by De Smet (2012) are all "new" environments that are conquered in sequential fashion. An example is the extension of downtoner *all but* from predicative (*this is all but complete*) to attributive adjectives (*an all but complete story*). In the case of [BE *going to* INF] the reality seems more complex. Most of these early instances with inanimate subjects or lacking motion do not differ formally in any noticeable way from instances of the original combination of 'controlled motion with a purpose'. I believe the evidence provided in this paper enables us to pick up the explanation where De Smet (2012) stops. The gradual approximation of [BE *going to* INF] to an auxiliary is not the result of a sequence of extensions, but instead of the development of somewhat independent assemblies. The various types of evidence I presented suggest that these local developments meet up around 1630. Around this year we see that the various assemblies take a quantitative leap in visibility (significantly higher average deprofiling score). We also see the extension to inanimate subjects in motionless contexts at this point, which implies a more definitive break with the original lexical material. Finally, the metalinguistic evidence (conventionalization between 1620–1640) also points in this direction. The quantitative-qualitative leap, then, may indicate a first "point of no return", signaling that all these independent developments have been connected and have led to a new global cognitive schema for [BE *going to* INF]. In this view, constructionalization does not require a formal change in the sense of Traugott and Trousdale (2013). Its emergence can be detected on the basis of a combination of semantic change and frequency shift. But the development does not stop at this point. The various realizations of the new schema continue to strengthen and reinforce each other. This is for instance evidenced in the occurrence of ever more combinations of what before were more independent assemblies. The occurrence of raising in this scenario would be a final step in the establishment of the new construction, which has now become so entrenched and independently established that it is no longer constrained by the formal contours of the original construction. This formal innovation constitutes a second "point of no return", as the new construction is no longer merely a matter of semantic redistribution, but is now also formally distinct.

Theoretically, the evidence suggests that cognitive schemas show different behaviour at different levels of abstraction. In this respect, complex constructions-to-be may be viewed as clusters of even smaller schemas (assemblies, or perhaps also constructions, depending on one's definition), with their own properties emerging out of this quality of being clustered. More evidence for their independence comes from the pace and timing of the shifts in the different assemblies. The topicalization assembly is the last one to occur, but is the fastest one to lead to loss of lexical material (motion). Passives occurred from the very beginning, gradually shedding the component of control, but took a real leap only in the period 1640–1659, possibly triggered by what had happened to topicalization two decades before. Present-tense assertions show a more gradual development towards predictive uses, which seems largely unaffected by the leaps in the other assemblies. And yet together these local changes lead to what eventually will become the deictic future construction [BE *going to* INF].

The semantic shifts in the assemblies essentially imply new connectivity between the form [BE *going to* INF] and new meanings (the semantic outcome of deprofiling is also meaning extension). These shifts increase the similarity of [BE *going to* INF] to existing auxiliaries of the future such as *will* or *shall*. This growing similarity may have facilitated the emergence of deictic futures and raising structures (analogy). Non-parametric statistical tests such as loess regression are a good exploratory tool to detect the shift from local compositional assemblies (where mismatches between form and meaning are due to coercion) to more global non-compositional constructions (where the new semantics is an inherent part of the cognitive schema). An important question is how far this line of argumentation should be taken. A more radical approach to similarity may want to measure similarity in terms of frequency of occurrence in similar environments itself. The shift towards auxiliarihood of [BE *going to* INF], in such a view, would be truly gradual, with evermore auxiliary-like uses similar to those of, for instance, *will* and *shall*, appearing, and the semantics of futurity gradually becoming more and more entrenched. Even in an individual mind no abrupt neoanalysis needs to have taken place. Instead, every instance would be weighted for a number of similarity relations, and the more similar an instance is to an auxiliary use, the easier it will become to produce auxiliary-like uses in the future. At no point would there be a dichotomy between compositional and non-compositional (because forms may be associated with meanings, but not categorically linked to them), lexical and grammatical. In this type of reductionist connectionism constructions would disappear altogether, and only connections would remain. Scholars such as McClelland (2015) have argued that such a view is capable of capturing generalizations and higher-level schemas. Neurologically, however, much remains unknown. A more productive approach is perhaps to treat schemas (rules, constructions) and associations (connections, similarity strengths, analogy) as different dimensions of a single complex system (cf. Pothos 2005, who sees them as extremes on a cline). In this view, constructions would be special generalizations, that cognitively stand out, and where only a (smallish) subset of a construct's properties are involved (some meaning and some form). While they may be more flexible than exceptionless rules in that they can be argued to be radial categories around a prototype, they are still at a higher level of abstraction than similarity connections, which are pervasive and multidimensional in all the properties of a construct. Both may play an active role, but the rules may be less susceptible to frequency shifts than the similarities (though they may emerge out of such shifts). I believe the main contribution from corpus linguistic historical studies is to get at as accurate a picture as possible of how complex developments proceed along these lines. The notion of construction, in the present study realized as a global schema pairing [BE *going to* INF] to imminent future, with certain formal consequences, is meaningful in such a view, but not exclusive. The evidence shows signs of a pre-construction-stage with its own dynamics, leading up to a new schema only after pre-construction deprofiling has reached a certain threshold. Formal actualization of the change follows still later, again, after entrenchment of the new schema has reached a certain threshold. The local patterns responsible for the run-up in this development do not show compelling evidence for constructional status, and may therefore be better captured under the heading of assemblies.

References

Agresti, Alan. 2010. *Analysis of ordinal categorical data*. 2nd edn. New York: John Wiley & Sons.

Andersen, Henning. 2001. Actualization and the (uni)directionality. In Henning Andersen (ed.), *Actualization: Linguistic change in progress*, 225–248. Amsterdam: John Benjamins.

Bates, Elizabeth, & Jeffrey L. Elman. 1993. Connectionism and the study of change. In Mark H. Johnson, Yuko Munakata & Rick O. Gilmore (eds.), *Brain development and cognition: A reader*, 623–642. Oxford: John Wiley & Sons.

Heine, Bernd, Ulrike Claudi & Friederike Hünnemeyer. 1991. *Grammaticalization: A conceptual framework*. Chicago: University of Chicago Press.

Budts, Sara & Peter Petré. 2016. Reading the intentions of *be going to*. On the subjectification of future markers. *Folia Linguistica Historica* 37. 11–32.

Clark, Lynn, & Graeme Trousdale. 2009. The role of frequency in phonological change: Evidence from TH-Fronting in east central Scotland. *English Language and Linguistics* 13. 33–55.

Cleveland, William S., Eric Grosse 7 William M. Shyu. 1992. Local Regression Models in S. In John M. Chambers & Trevor J. Hastie. *Statistical models in S*, 309–376. Danvers, MA: CRC Press, Inc.

Cleveland, William S. & Clive Loader. 1996. Smoothing by local regression: Principles and methods. In Wolfgang Härdle & Michael G. Schimek (eds.), *Statistical theory and computational aspects of smoothing. Proceedings of the COMPSTAT '94 Satellite Meeting held in Semmering, Austria, 27–28 August 1994*, 10–49. Heidelberg: Physica-Verlag.

Croft, William. 2000. *Explaining language change: An evolutionary approach*. London: Longman.

Dahl, Östen. 2008. Animacy and egophoricity: Grammar, ontology and phylogeny. *Lingua* 118. 141–150.

De Smet, Hendrik, Lobke Ghesquière & Freek Van de Velde (eds.). 2015. *On multiple source constructions in language change*. Amsterdam: John Benjamins.

De Smet, Hendrik. 2012. The course of actualization. *Language* 88 (3). 601–633.

De Smet, Hendrik. 2016. How gradual change progresses: The interaction between convention and innovation. *Language Variation and Change* 28. 83–102.

Detges, Ulrich & Richard Waltereit. 2002. Grammaticalization vs. reanalysis: A semantic-pragmatic account of functional change in grammar. *Zeitschrift für Sprachwissenschaft* 21. 151–195.

Disney, Steve. 2009a. A domain matrix view of the uses and development of BE 'going to' + infinitive. *Linguistics & Language Teaching* 3. 25–44.

Disney, Steve. 2009b. The grammaticalisation of 'be going to'. *Newcastle Working Papers in Linguistics* 15. 63–82.

Eckhardt, Regine. 2006. *Meaning change in grammaticalization. An enquiry into semantic reanalysis.* Oxford: Oxford University Press.

Erman, Britt, & Beatrice Warren. 2000. The idiom principle and the open choice principle. *Text* 20. 29–62.

Fischer, Olga. 2007. *Morphosyntactic change: Functional and formal perspectives.* Oxford: Oxford University Press.

Fonteyn, Lauren. 2017. The aggregate and the individual: Thoughts on what non-alternating authors reveal about linguistic alternations – a response to Petré. *English Language and Linguistics* 21 (2). 251–262.

Fried, Mirjam & Jan-Ola Östman. 2004. Construction grammar: A thumbnail sketch. In Mirjam Fried & Jan-Ola Östman (eds.), *Construction grammar in a cross-language perspective*, 11–86. Amsterdam: John Benjamins.

Fried, Mirjam. 2015. Construction grammar. In Tibor Kiss & Artemis Alexiadou (eds.), *Syntax – theory and analysis: An international handbook*, 974–1003. Berlin: De Gruyter Mouton.

Garrett, Andrew. 2012. The historical syntax problem: Reanalysis and directionality. In Dianne Jonas, John Whitman & Andrew Garrett (eds.), *Grammatical change: Origins, nature, outcomes*, 52–72. Oxford: Oxford University Press.

Goldberg, Adele 2006. *Constructions at work: The nature of generalization in language.* Oxford: Oxford University Press.

Goldberg, Adele. 1995. *Constructions: A construction grammar approach to argument structure.* Chicago: University of Chicago Press.

Haspelmath, Martin. 1999. Why is grammaticalization irreversible? *Linguistics* 37. 1043–1068.

Hilpert, Martin. 2008. *Germanic future constructions: A usage-based approach to language change.* Amsterdam: John Benjamins.

Hilpert, Martin. 2018. Three open questions in Diachronic Construction Grammar. In Evie Coussé, Peter Andersson & Joel Olofsson (eds.), *Grammaticalization meets construction grammar*, 21–39. Amsterdam: John Benjamins.

Hopper, Paul J. & Elizabeth C. Traugott. 2003. *Grammaticalization.* 2nd edn. Cambridge: Cambridge University Press.

Israel, Michael. 2002. Consistency and creativity in first language acquisition. *Proceedings of the Annual Meeting of the Berkeley Linguistics Society* 28 (1). 123–135.

Lamb, Sydney M. 1999. *Pathways of the brain: The neurocognitive basis of language.* Amsterdam: John Benjamins.

Langacker, Ronald W. 1987. *Foundations of Cognitive Grammar.* Vol. I: Theoretical perspectives. Stanford: Stanford University Press.

Langacker, Ronald W. 2009. *Investigations in Cognitive Grammar.* Berlin: Walter de Gruyter.

Levshina, Natalia. 2015. *How to do linguistics with R. Data exploration and statistical analysis.* Amsterdam: John Benjamins.

Manning, Christopher D. 2015. Computational linguistics and deep learning. *Computational Linguistics* 41 (4). 701–707.

McClelland, James L. 2015. Gradience, continuous change, and quasi-regularity in sound, word, phrase, and meaning. In Brian MacWhinney & William O'Grady (eds.), *The handbook of language emergence*, 53–80. Chichester: Wiley-Balckwell.
Nesselhauf, Nadja. 2010. The development of future time expressions in Late Modern English: redistribution of forms or change in discourse? *English Language and Linguistics* 14 (2). 163–186.
Patten, Amanda. 2012. *The English it-cleft. A constructional account and a diachronic investigation*. Berlin: de Gruyter.
Petré, Peter. 2012. General productivity: How become waxed and wax became a copula. *Cognitive Linguistics* 23 (1). 28–65.
Petré, Peter. 2013. *EEBOCorp, Version 1.0*. Leuven: University of Leuven Linguistics Department.
Petré, Peter. 2016a. Grammaticalization by changing co-text frequencies, or why [BE Ving] became the 'progressive'. *English Language and Linguistics* 20 (1). 31–54.
Petré, Peter. 2016b. Unidirectionality as a cycle of convention and innovation. Micro-changes in the grammaticalization of [BE going to INF]. *Belgian Journal of Linguistics* 30. 115–146.
Petré, Peter. 2017. The extravagant progressive. An experimental corpus study on the history of emphatic [BE Ving]. In Alexander Bergs & Thomas Hoffmann (eds.), *Cognitive approaches to the history of English*. Special issue *English Language and Linguistics* 21 (2). 227–250.
Petré, Peter & Freek Van de Velde. 2018. The real-time dynamics of individual and community in grammaticalization. *Language* 94 (4). 867–901.
Petré, Peter & Sara Budts, 2020. Putting connections centre stage in diachronic construction grammar. In Lotte Sommerer & Elena Smirnova (eds.), *Nodes networks in diachronic construction grammar*. Amsterdam: John Benjamins.
Pothos, Emmanuel M. 2005. The rules versus similarity distinction. *Behavioral and Brain Sciences* 28 (1). 1–14.
R Core Team. 2013. *R: A language and environment for statistical computing*. Vienna: R Foundation for Statistical Computing (http://www.R-project.org).
Schmid, Hans-Jörg. 2016. A framework for understanding linguistic entrenchment and its psychological foundations. In Hans-Jörg Schmid, (ed.), *Entrenchment and the psychology of language learning: How we reorganize and adapt linguistic knowledge*, 9–38. Berlin: Walter de Gruyter.
Sweetser, Eve. 1988. Grammaticalization and semantic bleaching. In Shelley Axmaker, Annie Jaisser & Helen Singmaster (eds.), *Berkeley Linguistics Society 14: General session and parasession on grammaticalization*, 389–405. Berkeley: Berkeley Linguistics Society.
Tabor, Whitney. 1994. *Syntactic innovation: A connectionist model*. Stanford, CA: Stanford University Ph.D. dissertation.
Thompson, Sandra A. 2002. 'Object complements' and conversation. *Studies in Language* 26. 125–164.
Tomasello, Michael. 1992. *First verbs: A case study of early grammatical development*. Cambridge: Cambridge University Press.
Tomasello, Michael. 2000. The item-based nature of children's early syntactic development. *Trends in Cognitive Sciences* 4 (4). 156–163.
Torres Cacoullos, Rena, & James A. Walker. 2009. The present of the English future: Grammatical variation and collocations in discourse. *Language* 85 (2). 321–354.
Traugott, Elizabeth C. 1989. On the rise of epistemic meanings in English: An example of subjectification in semantic change. *Language* 65. 31–53.

Traugott, Elizabeth C. 2012. On the persistence of ambiguous linguistic context over time: Implications for corpus research on micro-changes. In Joybrato Mukherjee & Magnus Huber (eds.), *Corpus linguistics and variation in English: Theory and description*, 231–246. Amsterdam: Rodopi.

Traugott, Elizabeth Closs & Graeme Trousdale. 2013. *Constructionalization and constructional changes*. Oxford: Oxford University Press.

Traugott, Elizabeth Closs. 2015. Toward a coherent account of grammatical constructionalization. In Jóhanna Barðdal, Elena Smirnova, Lotte Sommerer & Spike Gildea (eds.), *Diachronic Construction Grammar*, 51–80. Amsterdam: John Benjamins.

Laura A. Michaelis
Constructions are patterns and so are fixed expressions

"Look closely at the most embarrassing details and amplify them."
Brian Eno and Peter Schmidt, *Oblique Strategies*

Abstract: In Construction Grammar, grammar is conceived as an inventory of form–function–meaning complexes of varying degrees of internal complexity and lexical fixity. These complexes range from single lexemes like the verb *demur* to multiword expressions like the VP *sweep x under the rug* to syntactic templates lacking any lexical content, like that used to form polar interrogative questions. Whether we are describing a lexeme, a class of lexemes, a word with highly constrained selection properties (e.g. the adjective *blithering*) or a way to create a headed phrase of a particular type, we are describing patterns, because in each case we are describing the combinatoric properties of words. But if we take a pattern to mean a recurrent configuration containing some fixed and some variable components, only a phrasal template would seem to qualify. A verb by itself does not constitute a configuration, and a fixed expression like *call it a day*, while arguably phrasal, does not contain any open slots – it is inflexible. So, can a word or a word class or a fixed formula really be a pattern? This puzzle is resolved in Sign-Based Construction Grammar (SBCG; Sag 2012; Michaelis 2012; Kay and Sag 2012): all linguistic expressions are modelled as feature structures, whether these are signs or sign configurations (constructs). The question of what forms the grammar licenses comes down to the question of whether a given feature structure of the type *sign* is well formed. SBCG analyses lexical signs and constructs in much the same way: each kind of model object is deemed well formed (or not) according to its conformity to a feature-structure description of the type *sign*. The well formedness of a construct is determined indirectly, according to whether the construct's mother sign conforms to a phrasal sign of the grammar. Because lexical signs and constructs are licensed in the same way, SBCG offers a uniform approach to all of the expressions – both lexemic and templatic – that populate the idiomaticity continuum and the meanings to be discovered at each point along this continuum.

Laura A. Michaelis, University of Colorado, Department of Linguistics, Boulder, CO 80309, USA, laura.michaelis@colorado.edu

1 Introduction

In traditional theories of syntax, there are words, rules of syntactic combination that combine words and multiword expressions (like *fill the bill* and *with flying colours*) that sit uncomfortably in between, having less internal cohesion than words and far fewer potential permutations than syntactic rules.[1] Construction Grammar replaces these categorical distinctions with a continuum. In Construction Grammar, the grammar is conceived as an inventory of form–function–meaning complexes of varying degrees of internal complexity and lexical fixity (Fillmore et al. 1988; Kay 1992; Kay and Michaelis 2012; Michaelis 2017). We will refer to this continuum as the *continuum of idiomaticity*. The complexes range from single lexemes like the verb *deign* to multiword expressions like the verb phrase *sweep x under the rug* to syntactic templates lacking any lexical content, like that used to form polar interrogative questions. But despite what has been implied in some constructionist works (Boas 2010; Dabrowska 2009), words and constructions are two different things. A construction is a description of a class of language objects (*constructs* or, equivalently mother–daughter configurations), while a word is a language object, a type of sign (Sag 2012).[2] Even if we

---

[1] This paper draws on research collaborations with Josef Ruppenhofer (Ruppenhofer and Michaelis 2016) and Paul Kay (Kay and Michaelis 2012, 2019). I gratefully acknowledge the contributions that each of these collaborators have made to my understanding of linguistic patterns. Special thanks are owed to Paul Kay for his keen insights about the data discussed here, and for all of the many ways in which he furthers my understanding of constructionist syntactic theory. I am additionally thankful to an anonymous reviewer for helpful feedback on this chapter. Finally, I owe a debt of gratitude to my fellow constructionists and *Patterns* authors Elizabeth Traugott and Peter Petré for discussion and constructive criticism that have enriched and improved the exposition here.

[2] Peter Petré (p.c.) points out that this passage might be construed as claiming that "lexical items are objects, not classes of objects". The passage, however, pertains to *words* rather than to lexical items (*qua* lexical signs) in general. In the Sign-Based Construction Grammar (SBCG) type hierarchy, the type *lexical sign* has two immediate subtypes: *word* and *lexeme*. Signs of the type *word* share with phrases the ability to be daughters in phrasal constructs – an ability that lexemes lack (Sag 2012: 90). To participate in phrasal syntax, a lexeme must give rise to a corresponding word. This is accomplished through an inflectional construction (Sag 2012: 101). Rather than participating in syntax, signs of the type *lexeme* represent the syntactic and semantic constraints common to the various inflectional and derivational instances of that lexeme. For example, the lexeme *love* "enforces the basic form-meaning correspondence that permeates nominal and verbal words based on this lexeme" (Sag 2012: 97). In sum, while a word is indeed a single object (a sign), a lexeme might be viewed as a class of objects, or, more accurately, as capturing what is common to a range of words based on that lexeme.

were to understand *construction* as *construct* when interpreting the dictum "A word is a construction", the equivalence would not be valid: a construct is a phrase, a combination of words.³ There is a reason, however, that Construction Grammar proponents have tended to see words and phrasal patterns as the same thing: both words and phrases are signs, and as such have specifications for phonological structure, morphological form, syntactic category, semantics and use conditions.⁴ The phrasal patterns range from those that are very constrained (partially lexically filled patterns of the "snow clone" variety, e.g. *I x therefore I am*) to those that are very open (like the construction that pairs a lexical head with its complements). What this means is that while the term *construction* has typically been used to refer to patterns with restrictive conditions both on form and use, canonical phrase-structure rules are constructions too:

> The [Construction Grammar] approach supposes a grammar to consist of a repertory of conventional associations of lexical, syntactic, and pragmatic information called constructions. Familiar grammar rules are simply constructions that are deficient in not containing any lexical information except for specification of rather gross syntactic categories – and, in some cases, lacking any pragmatic values as well. Every such conventional association that must be learned or recognized separately by the speaker of a language is a construction. This includes all idioms and partially productive lexico-grammatical patterns. (Kay 1992: 310)

Whether we are describing a lexeme with highly constrained selection properties (e.g. the adjective *blithering*), a class of lexemes (e.g. the class of ditransitive

---

3 In assuming this definition of construct, I depart from the practice of Traugott (this volume, page 129, fn. 8), who describes her use of the term as follows: "The term 'construct' ... [h]ere ... refers to an attested use. It is not necessarily licensed by a construction (... historically, the use of constructs precedes the development of a construction)".

4 Peter Petré (p.c.) interprets the claim that words are signs to entail that words are not classes of language objects, and that they lack "open slots": He says: "While I agree that there have to be units in language without open slots (the atomic elements of grammar, one might say), I'm not convinced 'word' is actually such an atomic unit. In the intuitive interpretation of what a word is, a word is a paradigmatic class of objects, including a singular and a plural form". I offer two responses here. First, the question of whether an expression has "open slots" is a distinct question from whether or not it represents a paradigmatic class of objects. A main point of this chapter is that words, like lexemes, most certainly can have open slots, represented by their VALENCE and ARG-ST sets. In fact, we distinguish lexical classes according to their combinatoric properties, and these combinatoric properties are inherited by words. For example, while the proper-noun word *Kim* has no valence, the transitive-verb word *eat* has two valence elements. Second, SBCG recognizes a word-lexeme distinction, as discussed in footnote 2. This means that while a word is not a "paradigmatic class of objects" a lexeme is. Words in SBCG are members of such paradigmatic classes rather than representing classes themselves.

verbs), an inflected word (e.g. the plural noun *copies*) or a way to create a headed phrase of a particular type, we are describing patterns, because in each case we are describing the combinatoric properties of words. But if we take *pattern* to mean a recurrent configuration with variable components (which is presumably the standard sense of the term) only a phrasal template would seem to qualify. A verb by itself does not constitute a configuration, and a fixed expression like *call it a day*, while arguably phrasal, does not contain any open slots – it is inflexible. So, can a word or a word class or a fixed formula really be a pattern?

This puzzle is resolved in Sign-Based Construction Grammar (SBCG; Sag 2012; Michaelis 2012; Kay and Sag 2012): all linguistic expressions are modeled as (functional) feature structures, whether these are signs or sign configurations; sign configurations are referred to as *constructs*. A functional feature structure maps each feature in its domain to an appropriate value (Sag 2012: 63). While feature structures are widely used in linguistic representation (as in Generative Phonology), the feature structures used to model signs in SBCG contain the particular array of features needed to represent the pairing of form with meaning. These features include those required to represent the expression's phonology (PHON), its morphological form (FORM), its syntactic category (CAT), its combinatoric potential or valence (VAL), its frame-semantic meaning (FRAMES), its semantic index (IND), and its contextual indices (CNTXT). The VAL feature is of particular importance, as it is the basis of lexicalist representation: we represent lexical classes (e.g. verb classes), lexically headed constructions (like the English *be V-ing* progressive construction) and idiomatically combining forms (like *take x to task*) by reference to the combinatoric properties of their head words. Constructs are sign configurations rather than signs, but they are represented as feature structures as well. The representation of constructs requires two additional features: MOTHER (MTR), whose value is a single sign and DAUGHTERS (DTRS), whose value is a non-empty list of signs. These features represent the hierarchical structure that tree-structure representation captures: constructs are in essence local trees with signs "at the nodes".

SBCG maintains a strict separation between descriptions and the linguistic objects that instantiate them: constructs and signs, as feature structures, contain determinate values for every feature, while combinatory constructions (descriptions of classes of constructs), listemes (lexical entries) and lexical-class constructions are partial descriptions, which characterize large classes of feature structures.[5]

---

[5] It is important to note that in SBCG, not all constructions license phrases. Another way of saying this is that not all constructions have phrasal signs as mothers. Some constructions, which we can call *lexical constructions*, describe unary-branching constructs, in which both mother

The question of what form–meaning pairs the grammar licenses comes down to the question of whether a given feature structure of the type *sign* is well formed. SBCG analyses lexical signs and constructs in much the same way: each kind of model object is deemed well formed (or not) according to its conformity to a feature-structure description of the type *sign*. The repertoire of signs includes lexemes with idiosyncratic valence requirements, e.g. the idiomatic verb *spill* that heads the idiomatic expression *spill the beans*. The well-formedness of a construct is determined indirectly, according to whether the construct's mother sign conforms to a phrasal sign of the grammar. Because lexical signs and constructs are licensed in the same way, SBCG offers a uniform approach to all of the expressions – both lexemic and templatic – that populate the idiomaticity continuum, and the meanings to be discovered at each point along this continuum. In SBCG, every linguistic pattern is a feature-structure description. Thus, to the question *what makes a construction a pattern?* we reply: the same thing that makes a lexical entry a pattern. Both constructions and lexical entries describe combinatory possibilities in a language and both do so by means of feature-structure descriptions.

The remainder of this paper will elaborate on this point, and the lexicalist perspective that it entails. Using illustrations from the idiomaticity continuum laid out in prior works (Kay and Michaelis 2012; Michaelis 2017), this paper will attempt to make the case for a lexicalist view of grammar in which, paradoxically, phrasal patterns are lexical and lexical patterns are phrasal. In the following section, section 2, I will describe the idiomaticity continuum as a scale of lexical fixity, using linguistic exemplars to describe each point on the scale. I will then choose two patterns, representing antipodal points on the continuum, to subject to formal analysis. The first, to be discussed in section 3, is a fixed expression: a noun phrase that functions as a negative-polarity item, *a red cent* (Ruppenhofer and Michaelis 2016). The second, to be discussed in section 4, is an abstract phrasal configuration that represents properties common to a family of "auxiliary inversion" patterns, the Auxiliary-Initial construction (Sag 2012; Sag et al. 2019). The upshot of both analyses will be that apparent phrasal patterns, whether lexically fixed or open, can and should be described in a manner that (a) highlights

---

and daughter are single signs. There are two kinds of lexical constructions: (1) derivational constructions, which describe lexeme–lexeme relationships and are used to represent valence-augmenting constructions like the English ditransitive construction (e.g. *We sent them a bill*), and (2) inflectional constructions, which describe word–lexeme relationships like that between a verbal lexeme and its past-tense form (Sag 2012). In addition to lexical-rule constructions, SBCG recognizes *lexical-class constructions*. These do not describe constructs but rather basic (non-derived) sign types. Lexical-class constructions describe both broad classes, like the class of strict transitive verbs, and narrow ones, like the class of auxiliary verbs.

the dependency relations that define particular words and word classes and (b) leaves the work of phrase formation to the general-purpose phrasal constructions that license such configurations. In section 5, I will summarize the purpose of the analytic enterprise: to capture what unites lexical entries and constructions by leveraging the selectional requirements of lexemes and lexeme classes. In this lexicalist framework, both syntactic patterns and lexical patterns are seen to arise from the combinatoric properties of words, including idiom words.

2 The continuum of idiomaticity

Meanings are assembled in various ways in a construction-based grammar, and this array can be represented as a continuum of idiomaticity. As depicted in figure 8.1, this continuum is a gradient of lexical fixity; it is based on Michaelis *in press* and Kay and Michaelis (2012):

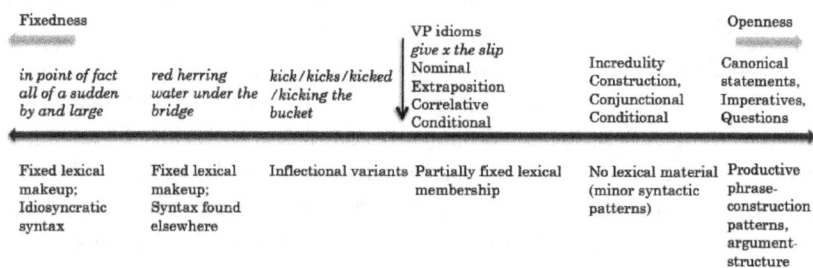

Fig. 8.1: The idiomaticity continuum

This continuum distinguishes types of complex expressions according to their relative degrees of productivity, and in particular the range of lexical, inflectional or syntactic variants attested for each type. The least lexically fixed types are canonical phrase-structure rules like the Noun Phrase (NP) construction, which constrain the grammatical category of each daughter but do not invoke specific lexemes. What is crucial here is that every pattern of the language, from the fixed formulas to the fully productive phrase-structure rules, falls at some point along the idiomaticity continuum.

At the leftmost, or "fixed", extreme of this continuum are frozen idioms, like *the salt of the earth* and *in the know*. As indicated, the set of frozen idioms includes those with idiosyncratic syntactic properties. For example, the fixed expression *by and large* (originally a nautical term referring to two different sailing conditions) represents an exceptional pattern of coordination, in which a preposition and adjective are conjoined. The expression *all of a sudden* is syntactically odd in a similar way: the complement of the quantifier head all is a prepositional phrase whose complement is an adjective (*sudden*) rather than a noun phrase. Other frozen idioms, like the modified noun *red herring*, feature syntax found elsewhere.

Next we encounter lexically fixed idiomatic expressions, verb-headed and otherwise, that are inflected in the same way they would be if their meanings were not idiomatic. One such expression is the verb phrase (VP) idiom *chew/chews/chewed the fat*, meaning 'engage in conversation'. It is important to note, however, that the direct objects of verb phrase idioms like *kick the bucket* and *chew the fat* are syntactically inert. We do not encounter variants like **Buckets were kicked*, **She kicked an unfortunate bucket* or **the bucket that was kicked* – or at least such variants do not preserve the idiomatic meaning. A class of expressions that features greater flexibility is that of patterns that have only partially fixed lexical membership. This class includes phrasal idioms like *spill the beans*, whose component words map in a one-to-one fashion to their literal paraphrases (e.g. 'tell the secret(s)' in the case of *spill the beans* and 'exercise influence' in the case of *pull strings*). In this respect, such verb phrase idioms differ from those like *kick the bucket*, in which the literal paraphrase ('die') assigns no role to the direct object, *the bucket*. Crucially, such idioms behave just like non-idiomatic verb phrases with regard to the allowable syntactic instantiations of their arguments; this is shown in (1)–(4):

(1) Quantification: *The Washington Post* **spilled lots of beans** *on this Bush brother.*
(2) Adjectival modification: *The pop icon's estranged sibling … **spilled some dirty beans**.*
(3) *Wh*-extraction: **the beans that were spilled** *under the effects of the drug …*
(4) Passive: **Beans will be spilled** *if they need to be.*

The syntactic flexibility exhibited by such verb-phrase idioms sets them apart from verb-phrase idioms like *kick the bucket*, which lack all but inflectional variants, as observed above. The permutability of verb-phrase idioms like *spill the beans*, which Nunberg et al. (1994) refer to as *idiomatically combining forms*, has led several theorists to analyse them as products of lexical selection (an idiomatic head verb selects for one or more idiomatic arguments), with phrasal properties determined by independently motivated phrasal constructions of the grammar (Kay and Michaelis 2019). The strategy used to prevent idiom words – like *beans* in *spill the beans* – from appearing without the appropriate idiom predicator is to constrain the valence set of the idiomatic predicator, such that an idiomatic *spill* verb (which carries semantic features that represent its 'reveal' meaning) seeks to combine with a definitely determined, plural nominal whose lexical identifier is *beans*, and which carries semantic features that represent its literal meaning ('secrets').[6] A similar "lexical hardwiring" strategy will be employed in the analysis of *a red cent* in section 3 below. Somewhat more open than idiomatically combining forms are those multiword expressions (MWEs) that contain variables in place of lexically filled arguments; an example is the verb phrase idiom *give x the slip* ('abandon x') and the noun phrase idiom *thorn in x's side* ('persistent problem for x'). SBCG represents idioms with variables by constraining the lexical identities of the fixed members of the head word's valence set but not the variable ones.

In addition to flexible and partially open MWEs, the "partially fixed lexical membership" class includes clausal constructions that resemble MWEs in evoking particular words (rather than word classes more broadly). The downward arrow in the figure indicates a decreasing amount of pre-specified lexical content among the expressions in this class. One such clausal construction is Nominal Extraposition (Michaelis and Lambrecht 1996), exemplified in (5)–(6):

(5) *It's amazing, the difference.*
(6) *It's remarkable, the people you see here.*

Nominal Extraposition is an exclamatory pattern in which an epistemic adjective (e.g. *amazing, remarkable, unbelievable*) takes expletive *it* as its subject and a definite noun phrase as its complement. The complement noun phrase metony-

---

[6] Peter Petré (p.c.) comments: "*Spill the beans* is a word with spaces because there is no lexical choice. As for verbal inflection of *spill*, that's easy to account for, because it's a normal verb (heading an idiom). There are, in that sense, no idiomatic restrictions on it. As for the *beans*, while one may modify *beans* (*the bad-tasting beans* or whatever), I wonder whether such an operation does not, *de facto*, destroy the idiom, turns it into a normal phrase, albeit with idiomatic function: this being some kind of word play that is precisely the effect that one's after: to put more emphasis on the idiom by 'de-idiomatizing' it."

I offer two responses. First, *spill* cannot be a "normal verb" heading an idiom, because it has abnormal selectional restrictions. One cannot preserve the idiomatic ('tell') sense of *spill* if one does not combine it with a noun phrase headed by the idiomatically interpreted noun *beans*. Second, if the option of converting an idiom to a non-idiom for the purpose of passive, modification, *wh*-extraction, etc. is always open to a verb phrase idiom why is it demonstrably not open to verb phrase idioms like *kick the bucket*? I maintain that the solution to this question is to distinguish two kinds of verb phrase idioms, one of which is headed by a verb that assigns a meaning to the direct object on its valence list, and the other of which is headed by a verb that does not.

mically denotes a scalar degree (amount, number, magnitude, etc.). Accordingly, sentence (6) means not 'People seen here are remarkable' but rather 'The number/variety/unusualness of the people seen here is remarkable'.

The set of partially lexically fixed constructions also includes the Correlative Conditional construction (Fillmore 1986; Michaelis 1994; Culicover and Jackendoff 1999; Capelle 2011), as illustrated by the proverbial expressions in (7–9):

(7) *The more, the merrier.*
(8) *The bigger they come the harder they fall.*
(9) *The more you have, the more you want.*

This biclausal construction (which has elliptical variants, as in [20]) is formally characterized by the presence of two clause-initial comparative phrases, each of which is introduced by the word *the* – a reflex not of the definite article but of Old English instrumental-case demonstrative pronoun *þy* 'by that much'. In this construction, the word *the* serves as a degree marker. Predications built from this construction express a causal relationship between the values of two variables, with the first clause expressing the independent variable and the second the dependent (Fillmore 1986; Michaelis 1994). In the case of (9), for example, the independent variable is the number of possessions, while the dependent variable is the degree of desire for possessions.

As we move toward fully open patterns, we encounter specialized syntactic patterns without lexical fillers, including the Incredulity Response (10), analysed by Lambrecht (1990) as an unlinked topic construction, and the Conjunctive Conditional, illustrated in (11):

(11) **What, me go to the gym? Never!** *I do ride my bike round Richmond Park, though, and I play a bit of golf, but that's all.*
One more remark like that and you're out of here.

While containing no lexical fillers, these minor patterns are not fully open: an Incredulity Response must contain a non-finite (or non-verbal) predicate and the Conjunctive Conditional must contain the conjunction *and*. At the rightmost, or "open" end of this continuum are fully productive patterns without lexically fixed portions (although they do contain lexical-class constraints of varying grains). This group of patterns includes argument-structure constructions like the Caused Motion construction (e.g. *The kids swam the logs upstream*), the Resultative construction (e.g. *You hurt my eyes open*) and the Ditransitive construction (e.g. *We recently adopted her a sister*). These correspond to both derivational constructions and lexical-class constructions in SBCG (see Sag 2012 for discussion). As described by Goldberg, these constructions express kinds of actions (e.g. transfer, caused motion, directed motion). Frame-semantic representations are used to represent these meanings. Each of these representations includes the array of participant roles appropriate to the denoted event type (agent, theme and recipient in the case of the Ditransitive construction). When "constructional" participant roles are distinct from those of the verb lexeme with which the construction combines, the construction alters the combinatoric potential of the verb lexeme. As an illustration of this effect, consider (12):

(12) *A patient at the Samsung Medical Center became a "superspreader" of Middle East respiratory syndrome after a misdiagnosis, leaving him to **wheeze and cough around the hospital**.* (NY *Times* 6/17/15)

In (12) the verbs *wheeze* and *cough*, which are otherwise single-argument verbs of sound emission, are combined with a prepositional phrase describing direction of motion (*around the hospital*). The interpreter's challenge in such contexts is to combine verb meaning and construction meaning in a coherent way. This exercise involves identifying the agent of motion with the emitter of the sound: wheezing and coughing are construed in this context as manner-of-motion verbs.

As is widely acknowledged (Pinker 1989, Goldberg 1995, 2006), argument-structure constructions have restricted or "partial" productivity owing to lexeme-class restrictions (e.g. certain classes of transfer verbs, including most Latinate verbs, do not generally combine with the Ditransitive construction). By contrast, phrase-building patterns exhibit few lexical-class restrictions; these are the patterns that correspond to the local trees built by phrase-structure rules. Among these rules (constructions) are those that license canonical *wh-* and polar-interrogative questions, imperatives and declarative sentences like *Kim blinked*, known as the Subject-Predicate construction. Constructional meanings are the meanings to be discovered at every point along the idiomaticity continuum. Constructional meanings are as rich and varied as the frames evoked by lexical items: they include metaphorical figures like that associated with the verb phrase idiom *spill the beans* (Kay and Michaelis 2019), event-structure frames like those associated with the Ditransitive construction (Goldberg 1995), temporal schemas like those associated with the progressive and perfect constructions (Michaelis 2011), scalar and conditional meanings like that associated with the Correlative Conditional (Fillmore 1986; Michaelis 1994; Sag 2010), exclamatory meanings like that associated with Nominal Extraposition (Michaelis and Lambrecht 1996) and information-packaging functions like those associated with various cleft constructions (Lambrecht 2001). Constructional meanings include those traditionally analysed as conventional implicatures, as well as less commonly recognized illocutionary forces like the "allusive pretense" function of the Split Interrogative, e.g. *What am I, chopped liver?* (Michaelis and Feng 2015).

While it might seem reasonable to assume that open patterns are licensed in SBCG by combinatory constructions and fixed expressions (like *water under the bridge*) by lexical entries, the picture is not that simple. Some patterns that are intuitively describable as clause types, like Nominal Extraposition (5–6), are modeled instead as lexical-class or lexical-rule constructions (see fn. 1). In the case of Nominal Extraposition, the class described is a class of exclamatory predicators with a shared valence value: <*it*, NP> (Michaelis 2015). The epistemic adjectives *amazing*, *remarkable* and *astonishing* belong to this class, among others. And, as mentioned in section 1, most MWEs, e.g. *spill the beans*, are not represented in SBCG as "words with spaces" but rather through combinatoric restrictions on individual idiom words, e.g. idiomatic *spill* (Kay and Michaelis 2019). The following section, section 3, will illustrate this "bag of words" approach to MWEs by focusing on a polarity-sensitive nominal expression, *a red cent*; it relies on the analysis of Ruppenhofer and Michaelis (2016). Section 4 will focus the lexicalist lens on a clausal construction, the Auxiliary-Initial construction (e.g. *Have you no decency?*, *Long may you reign*, *Was I shocked!*). As described by Sag (2012; Sag et al. 2019), this construction is an abstract construct type from which several more specific patterns inherit constraints. Key to this approach is the set of feature values that define the class of auxiliary verbs in English and the manner in which these features interact with those assigned to the head daughter of the Auxiliary-Initial construction. By comparing the treatment of the MWE *a red cent* to that of the Auxiliary-Initial construct type, we will eventually see (in section 5) that SBCG highlights the properties shared by these two very different kinds of patterns: both representations take the form of feature-structure descriptions and both feature lexical constraints, although of very different kinds.

3 The fixed expression *a red cent*

The expression *a red cent* (meaning 'a piddling amount of currency') is, like *water under the bridge* or *red herring*, a fixed lexical expression featuring syntax found elsewhere. Its syntax is that of an ordinary indefinite noun phrase. This expression belongs to the general class of polarity-sensitive items (PSIs) and in particular the class of negative-polarity items (NPIs). PSIs like *lift a finger* and *all the time in the world* play a crucial role in discourse routines like understatement and emphasis. Some PSIs, known as positive polarity items (PPIs), are confined to reports of actual or anticipated situations, e.g. *It's (gonna be) hot **as hell***. By contrast, NPIs occur only in utterances that evoke multiple potential outcomes, typically an array of things that failed to happen (e.g. *She didn't **ever** say a word*), but also multiple standards of comparison (e.g. *It's better than **ever***) and various contingencies, as in conditional sentences (e.g. *If you **ever** need anything…*).

Following Israel (1996), we view NPIs as triggering certain patterns of scalar inference, as part of their conventionalized meanings. Israel (1996) assumes four types of PSIs. These are shown in table 8.1,[7] taken from table 1 in Ruppenhofer and Michaelis (2016).[8]

Tab. 8.1: PSI types

Features	Polarity	Quantity, informativeness values	Example
emphatic, minimizing	NPI	-q, +i	*a red cent, sleep a wink, the first thing*
emphatic, maximizing	PPI	+q, +i	*tons, utterly, awfully*
attenuating, minimizing	PPI	-q, -i	*sort of, somewhat, a little bit*
attenuating, maximizing	NPI	+q, -i	*all that, much, long*

The binary features *emphatic/attenuating* and *minimizing/maximizing* are used in combination to represent two types of NPIs and two types of PPIs, as shown in the first column of table 8.1. The feature ±q refers to the scalar degree denoted by the particular polarity-sensitive expression, i.e. the quantity referred to by that expression. A value of +q reflects an extreme point on some contextually evoked scale; for example, both the PPI *tons* and the NPI *much* have the feature value +q. The feature ±i refers to the information value of the resulting predication – whether it entails upward relative to a scale in negative contexts (e.g. someone who does not have a penny lacks a dime, etc.) and downward in affirmative contexts (e.g. someone who is utterly exhausted is also somewhat exhausted, etc.).

---

7 This table was first published in Josef Ruppenhofer and Laura A. Michaelis. 2016. Frames, Polarity and Causation. *Corpora* 11: 259–290. (http://spot.colorado.edu/~michaeli/documents/Ruppenhofer_Michaelis_PSI.pdf). Reprinted by kind permission of Edinburgh University Press.
8 Ruppenhofer and Michaelis (2016) is a corpus study of the Fillmorean frames evoked by a range of PSIs, with a focus on those that denote monetary units (e.g. *a king's ransom, a small fortune, a red cent*). This section relies heavily on that work.

An attenuating sentence, by contrast, contextually implicates that what is meant is more specific than what is said. An attenuating sentence is a form of understatement; as patent violations of the Gricean lower bound on informativeness, such sentences generate particularized conversational implicatures. For example, someone who denies being "made of money" may be avoiding the admission that she has no money at all, just as someone who claims to be somewhat disappointed may intend to imply that she is very disappointed.

The focus of our attention here is the emphatic, minimizing NPI *a red cent*. As an expression referring to a small amount of currency (a copper penny), the noun phrase *a red cent* (henceforth ARC) is typically used in predications describing commercial activities like valuation of goods, as in (13), payment, as in (14), and collection, as in (15):[9]

(13) *In the old days, apartments belonged to the government, which assigned them to the people. They weren't worth **a red cent**. You couldn't buy an apartment and you couldn't sell one.*

(14) *She pointed to our record player. "I'll give you one dollar for it, and not **a red cent** more."*

(15) *I had this customer, a builder, who said to the Potawatomi band in Wisconsin[:] "I will build you a bingo hall, for free. You don't have to pay me **a red cent**. You just pay me out of cash flow when you get it up and running..."*

The use of ARC to denote a unit of currency typically "evokes a scenario in which a potential buyer is unwilling to expend even minimal resources for a potential reward", which is "thereby implied to be unattractive or worthless" (Ruppenhofer and Michaelis 2016: 274). Unlike other polarity-sensitive monetary-unit expressions investigated by Ruppenhofer and Michaelis, including *a king's ransom*, *a song*, *a small fortune* and *a pittance*, ARC has an alternate, emphatic form (the predominant one in COCA, in fact) in which it is determined by cardinal *one* rather than the indefinite article. In this respect, ARC has the syntactic behaviour of other indefinite, singular noun phrases denoting units of currency, e.g. *a dollar/one dollar*. Examples of *one red cent* are given in (16)–(18):

---

9 All numbered examples are from the *Corpus of Contemporary English* (COCA; Davies 2008) except as otherwise noted.

(16) Very few of those who are loudest in support of the Democrats have contributed **one red cent** to the great national wealth of which Clinton and Gore so love to boast.
(17) Now would you think a jury in America would give this guy **one red cent**?
(18) The bottom line is that Simpson has thumbed his nose at the courts, the criminal justice system. He has dared them to collect **one red cent**.

ARC has both lexical fixity and flexibility: while it necessarily contains the adjective *red* and the noun *cent*, and it is necessarily singular,[10] the determiner may be either the indefinite article or cardinal *one*. The main point here is that two idiom words – *red* and *cent* – are combined with a non-idiomatic determiner to compose the expression. I will postulate below that while the modifier *red* is an idiomatic word, *cent* is the ordinary noun denoting a one-penny monetary unit. But when we look at ARC's determination behaviour, we find that the article (or cardinal) makes the semantic contribution it makes elsewhere: it flags the nominal expression with which it combines as one that refers to a type-identifiable entity.

We assume here the Gundel et al. (1993) Givenness Hierarchy, according to which the morphosyntactic type of a referring form encodes the user's assumptions about the amount of information required to construe that particular act of reference. Gundel et al. (1993) identify six cognitive states, each of which represents necessary conditions on the appropriate use of a particular referring form. Use of an indefinite noun phrase (identified with the lowest status, *type identifiable*) is indicated when the speaker assumes that the hearer knows the category expressed by the nominal but need not recover a specific exemplar of that category. As fungible resources, units of currency are typically denoted by indefinite noun phrases in commercial-event predications. If I were to say *She bought it with a dollar*, you would have no need to ask "Which dollar?" because every instance of that monetary unit is equivalent in value to every other one. In sum, ARC acts like any other count noun that expresses a monetary unit.

---

10 We overlook apparent attested plural exceptions found on the web:
   a. *Many tramps refuse nothing that they can sell for* **two red cents**.
   b. *Poor Boger Oxenhope hasn't* **two red cents** *to knock together*.
Example (a) appears to be a literal reference to cost and (b) exemplifies an idiomatic relative-clause construction (albeit a NPI): *two [monetary units] to knock/rub together* ('sufficient financial resources'). In addition, we overlook a minor usage of *red cent* in which it functions as PSI:
   c. *Would I, like that faithful widow of old, give* **my last red cent**?
In cases like (c), Ruppenhofer and Michaelis (2016: 276) argue that "'red cent' occurs as a part of a larger phrase, 'every last + N', that is listed as a PPI by Israel".

While ARC, as regularly formed noun phrase, is interpreted by the same compositional mechanism that yields the interpretations of other indefinite singular noun phrases – as a function of the meaning of the article and the manner in which it is combined with its nominal sister – the *adjective* red and the noun *cent* mean something together that neither means individually. The expression *a/one red cent* does not mean 'a penny' or even, more generally, 'a unit of currency', but rather 'an insufficient monetary resource'. When filling the role of Theme in predications describing acts of payment, collection or giving, ARC creates highly informative propositions in negative and other non-veridical contexts. This is so because such predications entail upward relative to a numerical scale. For example, (17) is a strong critique of the merits of the plaintiff's case because it suggests that an American jury would not award a *tiny* settlement to this plaintiff, and thereby implies that this plaintiff could never receive an *adequate* settlement. Here now is a summary of the properties of ARC as we understand them:

- ARC has an idiomatic interpretation: 'piddling/inadequate monetary unit'.
- ARC is an emphatic NPI, and for this reason transfer predications in which it serves as theme argument entail upward relative to a numerical scale. For example, if I question your willingness to pay one red cent for a particular film, I am also questioning your willingness to pay $10 for it.
- Both the head noun *cent* and the adjective *red* are obligatory parts of ARC.
- The determiner in ARC is an indefinite article or cardinal.
- ARC is, so far as syntactic and semantic properties are concerned, an ordinary indefinite NP.

The final fact makes a lexicalist approach like that offered by SBCG particularly appealing, as it allows us to use rich lexical descriptions to capture the mutual dependence that exists between the two idiom words *red* and *cent* while turning over the job of noun-phrase assembly to major combinatory constructions of the grammar – that which pairs a head noun with a pre-nominal adjectival modifier and that which pairs a determiner with a nominal expression (N'). In SBCG, both determination and modification are products of the Head-Functor construction (Sag 2012: 150–152). In order to describe the Head-Functor construction and the dependency between the two fixed words in ARC, we must introduce three SBCG features beyond those discussed in section 1: LEXICAL IDENTIFIER, SELECT and MARKING:

- LEXICAL IDENTIFIER (LID) is used to distinguish lexical items according to their frame-semantic meanings: "the value of LID is a list of semantic frames that canonically specify the (fine-grained) meaning of a lexeme" (Sag 2012: 76). Idiomatic lexemes have idiomatic frames that enable headwords of multiword expressions to select their idiomatic dependents. Sag uses the English MWE *pull strings* to illustrate idiomatic frame values:

> We might treat the MWE pull strings via two listemes: an idiomatic pull whose meaning is 'manipulate' and an idiomatic string whose meaning is 'connections'. The frames required for such an analysis, presumably grounded in a metaphorical relation between situation types, will be indicated as pulling^{manipulating}-fr and i-strings^{connections}-fr, respectively. (Sag 2012: 122)

We will follow the practice of Kay and Michaelis (2019) and use square brackets to indicate the literal meanings of listemes with idiomatic LID values. Thus, the LID of idiomatic adjective *red* will be shown as *i-red [tiny-monetary-unit]-fr*. The LID value of a head noun is shared with that of its phrasal projections, and thus the (non-idiomatic) LID value of *cent* will percolate up to the noun phrase *a/one red cent*, but not the idiomatic LID value of the modifier *red*. This is the result we want, because *red cent* is not an idiomatically combining expression; in other words, it behaves just like unmodified, transparently interpreted *cent*.

– SELECT (SEL) allows a word to constrain what it can modify or combine with as a 'marker'. An expression whose SELECT value is a nominal sign is either a modifier or a determiner. What is selected is the LID value of the expression that is modified or determined. I will assume here that the adjective *red*, the selector of the nominal lexeme *cent*, is the bearer of idiomatic meaning in ARC.
– MARKING (MRKG) is primarily used to distinguish between a nominal that is "ready to go" as a complement within a head-complement configuration and one that is not. MRKG is a feature both of noun lexemes and the functors (adjectives and determiners) with which they combine via the Head-Functor construction. All nominal and adjective lexemes carry the MRKG value *unmk*. All determiners bear a determinate MRKG value; for example, the MRKG value of the definite article is *def* while that of the indefinite article is *indef*. The marking value of the nominal mother of a Head-Functor construct (e.g. *the issue, real issue*) will be the same as that of its functor daughter. What this means, for example, is that while the MRKG value of the listeme *cent* is *unmk*, and the MRKG value of the Head-Functor construct *red cent* is *unmk*, the MRKG value of the Head-Functor construct *a red cent* will be *indef*. This will be seen in the derivation of *a red cent* in figure 8.4 below.

Figure 8.2 shows the listeme *cent*. This listeme describes a typed feature structure. The type is that of *noun-lexeme*. What is noteworthy about this listeme is its semantic transparency: the same listeme covers both the head word of ARC and the vanilla noun *cent* that means "the 100th part of a US dollar". The commercial-event frame is included in the FRAMES set of *cent* to indicate that projections of the word play the role of the 'currency' participant in commercial-event predications like those in (13)–(18). Using the lexeme's semantic index (*x*), we identify it with (a) the sole argument of the *cent-frame* (its LID value) and (b) the currency argument of the commercial-event frame.

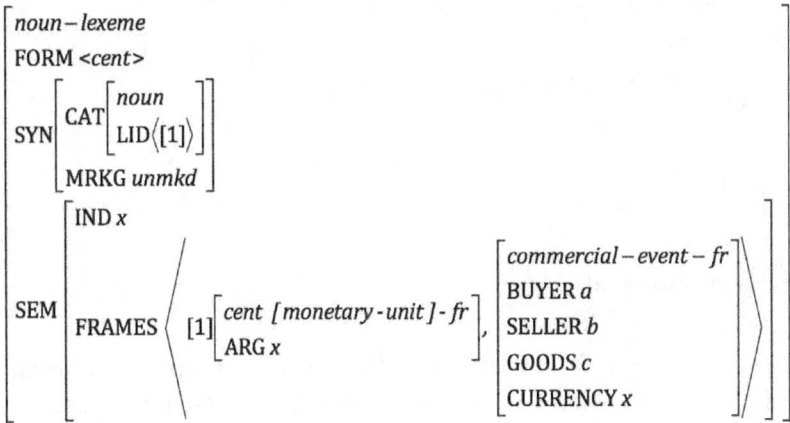

Fig. 8.2: The listeme *cent*

Figure 8.3 below shows the listeme (lexeme description) for the idiomatic adjective *red* that appears as the modifier of the idiomatic head noun *cent* in ARC. By making the selector of *cent* an idiomatic adjectival lexeme, we are in essence pushing the burden of idiomatic signification onto the adjectival selector. This move ensures that *red cent* does not have an idiomatic LID, which would prevent it from having a non-idiomatic "governour" (in this case a determiner functor). It also requires us to assume that the adjective is the bearer of polarity-sensitivity. Thus, the CNTXT value of this listeme contains a feature POL(ARITY), whose values are the two binary features used to classify PSIs in table 8.1. This combination of features (low-quantity, high-information-value) predicts that head-functor constructs in which this lexeme plays the role of functor are confined to non-veridical contexts of the kind that characterize NPIs in general.

$$\begin{bmatrix} \text{idiomatic-adjective-lexeme} \\ \text{FORM } \langle red \rangle \\ \text{SYN} \begin{bmatrix} \text{CAT} \begin{bmatrix} \text{adjective} \\ \text{LID} \langle [2] \rangle \\ \text{SEL}[\text{LID} \langle [1] \rangle] \end{bmatrix} \\ \text{MRKG } unmkd \end{bmatrix} \\ \text{SEM} \begin{bmatrix} \text{IND } y \\ \text{FRAMES } \langle [2] \begin{bmatrix} i-red[\,tiny-monetary-unit\,]\text{-}fr \\ \text{ARG } y \end{bmatrix} \rangle \end{bmatrix} \\ \text{CNTXT} \begin{bmatrix} \text{POL } [3] \begin{bmatrix} Q\text{-} \\ I\text{+} \end{bmatrix} \end{bmatrix} \end{bmatrix}$$

Fig. 8.3: Idiomatic listeme *red*

Figure 8.4 below shows the derivation of an ARC token, *a red cent*, through recursive application of the Head-Functor construction. The Head-Functor construction licenses both the determiner-noun construct *a red cent* and the modifier-noun construct that is its head daughter, *red cent*. The representation of the indefinite article *a*, which we see here for the first time, includes a CNTXT feature, GIVENNESS (GVNS), that is intended to represent the discourse-pragmatic status signaled by indefinite determination, type-identifiable status (*ti*). The value of this feature, like the values of the POLARITY feature, percolate to the noun phrase mother, as does the MRKG value of the indefinite article (*indef*). In addition, the idiomatic FRAMES values of both the modifier *red* and the modified noun *cent* are passed up to the phrasal mother.

The foregoing exposition has shown that the idiomatic nature of ARC, like that of many other MWEs, is lexical: it consists of two words with idiosyncratic combinatory requirements, as represented by the value of the SELECT feature in the idiomatic adjective *red*, the carrier of ARC's idiomatic content. As Kay and Michaelis (to appear) observe, the syntactic assembly of MWEs is indifferent to the special meanings and idiosyncratic combinatory properties of the individual idiom words.

> For most idioms, the phrase-structural configurations in which their words can appear derive exclusively from the syntactic potentials of the words themselves, which often mirror the syntactic properties of canonical words with similar meanings, subject of course to idiosyncratic limitations. The syntactic privileges of occurrence of the beans of *spill the beans* is a subset of the syntactic privileges of occurrence of the word secrets. The meanings of the

phrases and sentences in which most idioms occur are composed by the same processes as compose the meanings of phrases and sentences that contain no idiom words, and most phrasal idioms, properly analyzed, contain no phrasal information. (Kay and Michaelis to appear: 33).

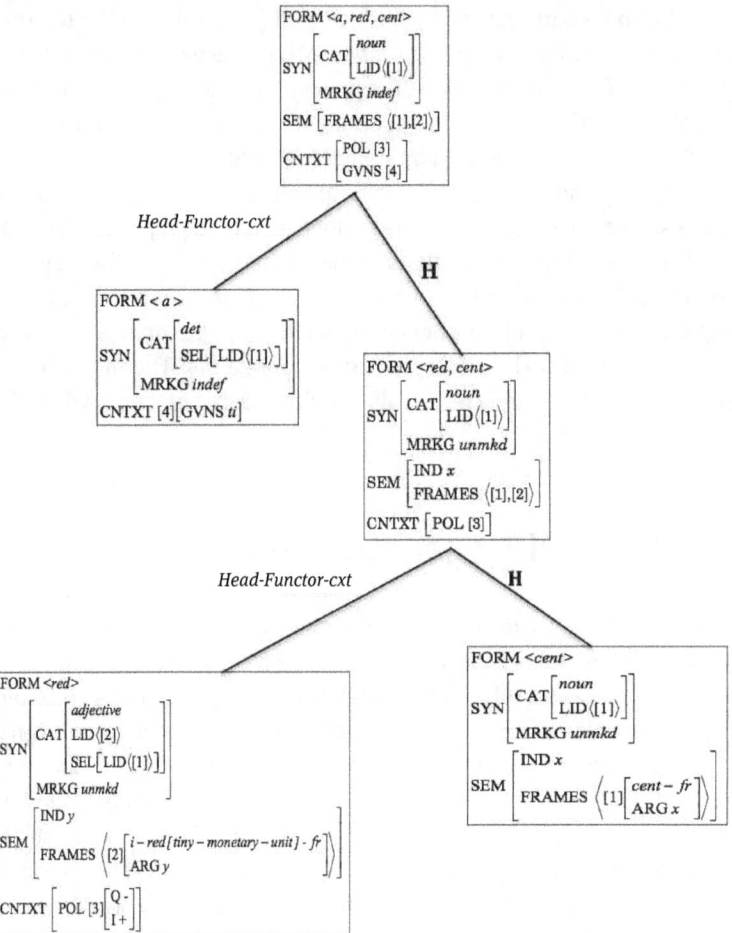

Fig. 8.4: An ARC derivation

What matters then are the dependencies that exist among idiom words, and we need only lexical entries to state these – as long as these entries capture the combinatory constraints of those idiom words, whether through use of the SELECT feature, the VALENCE feature or something else. With these points in mind, let us revisit the question posed at the outset of this paper: if, as we generally assume, a pattern must contain at least one open slot, how can a fixed expression like ARC qualify as a pattern? The answer is that fixed expressions are resolvable into the dependencies among idiom words, and in particular that there is an idiom head word calling for each of its idiomatic dependents via the lexical identifiers of these dependents. These patterns of dependency, which are captured by feature-structure descriptions, define each sign within an MWE. The pattern comes about because the presence of one thing entails the presence of another. In essence, an MWE is a bag of signs that becomes a sign configuration only when those signs are at the nodes of a local tree licensed by some construction.

In section 4, we will move from the combinatoric behaviour of lexemes to that of lexeme classes. We will apply the lexicalist model to a phrasal pattern with far greater flexibility than ARC: the Auxiliary-Initial pattern, as described by Sag (2012; Sag et al. 2019). Although the Auxiliary-Initial pattern is a construct (a mother-daughter configuration) and hence "syntactic" in a manner that ARC is not, we will see that it, like ARC, features lexical constraints. The moral of the story offered here is that we can rarely avoid evoking classes of words when describing syntactic patterns.

4 The auxiliary-initial construction

Having examined a pattern with fixed lexical structure, we will move to the opposite end of the idiomaticity continuum: the point occupied by productive phrase-construction patterns. Although such patterns are constructs (mother-daughter configurations with signs "at the nodes") rather than individual signs, they too are represented in SBCG as feature structures. An important property of feature structures is that they have types, indicated by italic labels, e.g. *noun lexeme, transitive verb, phrasal construct*.[11] A construction describes a feature structure of a particular type: one that contains an MTR feature whose value is a sign and a DTRS feature whose value is a list of signs. Any such feature structure is a construct. The construction that we will focus on in this section, the Auxiliary-Initial (AI) construction, is a *combinatoric construction*. This means that it describes a construct whose mother is a phrasal sign (i.e. a construct whose type of

---

11 Following SBCG convention, *construct* will be abbreviated in type labels as *cxt*.

phrasal-cxt).[12] The AI construction is a *non-maximal construction*. Non-maximal constructions express cross-constructional generalizations and have subtypes, while maximal constructions license the types that occupy terminal nodes in an inheritance hierarchy of typed feature structures.

English features a wide variety of auxiliary-initial clause patterns, illustrated by the following Google hits:[13]

(19) Polar-interrogative cxt: *Have you left yet?*
(20) Inverted-exclamative cxt: *Boy, was that disappointing.*
(21) Adverbial-inversion cxt: *Rarely have I felt so ridiculous.*
(22) Inverted-wish cxt: *May it never come to that.*
(23) Counterfactual-protasis cxt: [*Had I needed it for anything other than a very short distance*], *I would have needed the windows cleaned.*

The AI construction, described by Sag (2012; Sag et al. 2019), is used to represent properties that these patterns have in common. By exploring how this works we will gain insight into the means by which SBCG represents "constructional inheritance": the type hierarchy. SBCG allows a construction to define the characteristic properties of a construct type A, and another construction to define the properties of a type B. The type hierarchy tells us that B is a subtype of A and therefore that all feature structures of type B also obey the constraints that the grammar places on type A. What this means is that constructions describing the maximal construct types exemplified in (19)–(23) need only specify the properties that are particular to that subtype. These subtypes can add constraints to those of the dominating type but they cannot cancel any of the "inherited" constraints. The

---

12 It is important to bear in mind that not all constructs have mothers that are phrasal signs, because derivational and inflectional relationships are modeled in SBCG as constructs, i.e. *lexical constructs*. Inflectional constructs describe lexical constructs in which the MTR sign is of the type *word*, while derivational constructs describe lexical constructs in which the MTR sign is of the type *lexeme*.

13 An alert reader will have noticed that this list of auxiliary-initial patterns contains no example of the non-subject *wh*-question, e.g. *What do you have to lose?* The omission is warranted because the auxiliary-initial pattern within the *wh*-question pattern is not licensed by the AI construction in SBCG. SBCG constructions can describe only local trees (mother-daughter combinations), and for this reason a construction cannot describe a construct embedded in another construct, e.g. the AI construct embedded as the head daughter in the non-subject *wh*-question construct. In observing this locality constraint, SBCG is not different from other grammars based on phrase-structure rules. We would not, for example, find a phrase-structure like VP→V (PP→P NP).

additional constraints that characterize the maximal constructions involve syntactic, semantic, and discourse-pragmatic properties. Syntactic properties include the fact that the Counterfactual Protasis subtype is a subordinate clause. Semantic properties include the fact that the Inverted Exclamative subtype presupposes a property scale and asserts of some topical entity that it occupies an extreme position on that scale. Discourse-pragmatic properties include the fact that the Polar Interrogative subtype directs the addressee to confirm or deny the validity of a proposition.

Figure 8.5 depicts the AI construction, following Sag (2012: 183). It describes a feature structure of the type *headed-cxt*. This means that the AI construction is itself an "heir" to dominating types within the type hierarchy: as a type of headed construct – one that is in fact almost identical to the construct type described by the Head-Complement construction (see Sag (2012), (114)) – it is also a type of *phrasal construct*. A phrasal construct in turn belongs to the type *construct*, along with the type *lexical construct*.

$$\begin{bmatrix} headed-cxt \\ \text{MTR} \begin{bmatrix} S \\ \text{VAL} <> \end{bmatrix} \\ \text{DTRS} \left\langle \begin{bmatrix} V \\ \text{AUX+} \\ \text{INV+} \\ \text{VAL } L \end{bmatrix}, L \right\rangle \end{bmatrix}$$

Fig. 8.5: The Auxiliary-Initial construction

The AI construction describes a valence-saturated clause that consists of a lexical head verb specified as [AUX+] and [INV+], followed by all of the valence members of that verb. The order in which valence members appear is determined by an obliqueness hierarchy, according to which the subject immediately follows the verb and the XP complement of the auxiliary appears follows the subject, as in the inverted exclamative in (20), *Was that disappointing*! (We presume the verb *be* to have the valence <NP, XP>.)

Key to the mechanics of the construction are the binary features [AUX±] and [INV±], which capture lexical constraints of the AI construction. According to the featural analysis of auxiliaries proposed by Sag et al. (2019), auxiliary verbs are lexically unspecified for both AUX and INV, while non-auxiliary verbs have negative values for both AUX and INV. A clause that is verb-initial is specified as

[INV+], ensuring that no non-auxiliary verbs can appear as initial verbs.[14] In English, unlike, say, French and German, only auxiliary verbs can be [INV+]). The feature AUX is not used to distinguish auxiliary verbs from main verbs, but rather distinguishes those syntactic patterns that allow only an auxiliary verb as a head daughter from those, like the Subject-Predicate construction, that allow any class of verb. Because the head daughter of a Subject-Predicate construct can be either an auxiliary verb or a lexical verb, the AUX value of the head daughter is [AUX-], a feature specification to which any verb in the (AUX-unspecified) auxiliary class can accommodate. A syntactic environment restricted to auxiliary verbs is specified as [AUX+]. The critical syntactic environments, illustrated in (24)–(28) below, are sometimes known by the acronym NICER (Sag 2012, (122)):

(24) Negation: *We will not stumble.* / **We stumble not.*
(25) Inversion: *Have you eaten?* / **Eat you?*
(26) Contraction of *not*: *didn't, can't* / **laughn't*
(27) Ellipsis (of VP): *They aren't cooperating but I am* / **I don't like scallops, but she likes_.*
(28) Rebuttal (with prosodic peak on verb): *I DO like kids.*

Because all of these constructions require AUX+ head daughters, they accommodate all auxiliaries, since these are AUX-unspecified verbs. None of these constructions, however, can accommodate lexical verbs, which are [AUX-].

This feature-based system of representation for the auxiliary class, and the unification-based model of verb-construction interactions that it serves, offers a tidy way of representing lexical exceptions that have dogged transformational approaches based on head-to-head-movement. One such exception involves *aren't*. Ordinarily, *aren't* cannot have a first-person-singular subject argument, as shown in (30). In question contexts, however, it can, as shown in (29):

(29) *Aren't I the right choice?*
(30) **I aren't the right choice.*

This behaviour is hard to explain if *aren't* in (29) is presumed to have moved from the syntactic position it would occupy in a declarative clause to the head of a

---

[14] We exclude patterns like Locative Inversion and Deictic Inversion, in which subject properties are split across the pre-verbal "setting" constituent and a post-verbal constituent.

functional projection dominating that clausal unit. How would the requisite input structure have been generated in the first place and what would guarantee movement of the auxiliary? This conundrum disappears in the unification-based approach. By stipulating an *aren't* auxiliary listeme that differs from other auxiliary listemes in having the value [INV+], we ensure that words licensed by that listeme appear only in AI contexts. Another problematic exception is the semi-auxiliary *better*.

(31) *They better do that.*

(32) **Better they do that?*

Finally, the constructional analysis provides an account of the syntactic behaviour of auxiliary verb *do*, which, as Sag (2012) observes, "has required considerable machinery within previous transformational analyses" (Sag 2012: 155). If *do* is "moved" from the position it would occupy in a declarative clause, we must presume not only that it is generated in a syntactic position where it would not otherwise occur (see [33] below), but also that a *do* auxiliary so positioned must be earmarked in some way for movement. The unification-based analysis provides a simpler, more plausible account of the facts: auxiliary *do* is lexically specified as [AUX+]. While this allows it to appear in all of the NICER environments, it cannot appear in any syntactic context requiring it to take on the value [AUX-]. This means, for example, that it cannot appear as the head of a verb phrase in a Subject-Predicate construct, as in (33):

(33) **Kim did eat apples.*

The SBCG approach thus explains why auxiliary *do* "carries tense" where it does: it serves as the auxiliary daughter in construct types that require an auxiliary but where no perfect, progressive, passive or modal construction supplies one. It also explains why auxiliary *do* appears *only* in such contexts: its markedness prevents it from being used as the head of an ordinary verb phrase.

The lesson of the SBCG analysis is that there can be no auxiliary verbs without auxiliary constructions (the NICER environments). NICER is not a set of properties but rather a set of construct types. Just as in the case of ARC, we find that syntax serves the combinatoric needs of words and word classes – whether these combinatoric needs are idiosyncratic (as when the idiomatic adjective *red* selects the monetary-unit noun *cent*) or characteristic of a class (as when modal verbs select bare verb phrases headed by base-form verbs as their complements).

Patterns, whether they are MWEs or construct types, arise from the selectional requirements of words.

5 Conclusion

Grammar and lexicon are intimately interlinked. You can't have one without the other, as scholars of linguistic cognition have long observed (see e.g. Marchman and Bates 1994). SBCG uses a uniform format to represent both words (signs) and constructs (hierarchically organized sign combinations). Both kinds of linguistic objects are modeled as feature structures that contain specifications for syntactic, semantic and contextual features: a listeme describes a feature structure that is a sign, while a construction describes a feature structure that contains an MTR feature (whose value is a sign) and a DTRS feature (whose value is a list of signs). Words and constructs draw from one another: constructs realize word dependents, and words and word classes determine what daughter signs cooccur in constructs. Constructs and words are also licensed in the same way: via the Sign Principle (Sag 2012: 97): a sign is listemically licensed if it corresponds to some listeme of the grammar, and a sign is constructionally licensed if it is the mother of a construct described by a construction in the grammar. The licensing construction may describe a lexical construct (one whose mother sign is a word or lexeme) or a phrasal one (one whose mother sign is a phrase).

Feature structures have types and therefore both constructs and words/lexemes participate in the type hierarchy. Rather than seeing syntax, semantics and the lexicon as separate modules, and the lexicon as a jumble of idiosyncratic particulars, SBCG presumes a lexicon structured by hierarchically organized lexical classes and extends this model to relations among types of phrases.

Not every expression on the continuum of idiomaticity is a phrasal pattern, but all expressions, however fixed or flexible, are modeled as a feature structure. Perhaps the most important step toward making idiomatic MWEs part of syntax is to acknowledge that they contain no syntactic information, only dependencies. Idiomatic phrases are licensed by the same constructions used to compile the meanings of phrases that lack idiomatic headwords. Thus, to the question "What makes a construction a pattern?" we reply: the same thing that makes a lexical entry a pattern. Both constructions and listemes describe combinatory possibilities in a language and they do so by means of feature-structure descriptions.

Because it promotes a lexicalist version of Construction Grammar in which apparent phrasal patterns are resolved into cascades of lexical dependencies, this chapter might be seen to reject a consensus among constructionist works (see e.g. the chapters by Petré and Traugott in this volume) concerning the importance of "going big". All constructionist works "go big" in the sense that they allow units bigger than words as the building blocks of syntax. But as Sag et al. (2012) observe, there is more than one way to go big. Some multi-word expressions, like *add fuel to the fire*, are syntactically inert and are thus more or less like listemes. Others, like *pull strings*, act much like semantically compositional verb phrases with regard to quantification, modification and passive: *Strings were pulled, I pulled many strings, She pulled the right strings*. In sum, the lexicalist approach gives us analytic flexibility – the flexibility to see a multi-word expression as both a phrasal unit and a "bag of words" lacking any phrasal information. This flexibility is required by a usage-based approach to grammar, in which such multiple encodings are the norm. In such a grammar, the string *drive x crazy* is a multi-word expression, an instance of the resultative construction and an instance of the Head-Complement construction (Goldberg 1995). In such a grammar, the string *Shall we?* is both an entrenched formula and an instance of the Auxiliary-Initial construction. The lexicalist approach gives us multiple routes to an analysis of any given linguistic object. It is therefore a potentially powerful descriptive tool for the study of grammar as a dynamic system – how linguistic generalizations vary across users, how they evolve over historic time and how they change in the course of a learner's development.

References

Boas, Hans. 2010. The syntax–lexicon continuum in Construction Grammar: A case study of English communication verbs. *Belgian Journal of Linguistics* 24. 54–83.
Cappelle, Bert. 2011. The *the... the...* construction: Meaning and readings. *Journal of Pragmatics* 43. 99–117.
Culicover, Peter & Ray Jackendoff. 1999. The view from the periphery: The English comparative correlative. *Linguistic Inquiry* 30. 543–571.
Bresnan, Joan. 1994. Locative inversion and the architecture of Universal Grammar. *Language* 70. 72–131.
Dabrowska, Ewa. 2009. Words as constructions. In Vyvyan Evans & Stéphanie Pourcel (eds.), *New directions in Cognitive Linguistics,* 201–224. Amsterdam: John Benjamins.
Davies, Mark. 2008. The *Corpus of Contemporary American English*: 450 million words, 1990-present. (Available online at http://corpus.byu.edu/coca/).
Fillmore, Charles J. 1986. Varieties of conditional sentences. In Ann Miller & Zheng-Sheng Zhang (eds.), *Proceedings of the Third Eastern States Conference on Linguistics*, 163–182. Columbus, Ohio: Ohio State University Department of Linguistics.
Fillmore, Charles J., Paul Kay & Mary Catherine O'Connor. 1988. Regularity and idiomaticity in grammatical constructions: The case of *let alone*. *Language* 64. 501–538.

Goldberg, Adele. 1995. *Constructions: A construction grammar approach to argument structure.* Chicago: University of Chicago Press.
Goldberg, Adele. 2006. *Constructions at work.* Oxford: Oxford University Press.
Gundel, Jeanette K., Nancy Hedberg & Ron Zacharski. 1993. Cognitive status and the form of referring expressions in discourse. *Language* 69. 274–307.
Israel, Michael. 1996. Polarity sensitivity as lexical semantics. *Linguistics and Philosophy* 19. 619–666.
Kay, Paul. 1992. At least. In Adrienne Lehrer & Eva Feder Kittay (eds.), *Frames, fields, and contrasts*, 309–331. Hillsdale, N.J.: Lawrence Erlbaum.
Kay, Paul & Laura A. Michaelis. 2012. Constructional meaning and compositionality. In Claudia Maienborn, Klaus von Heusinger & Paul Portner (eds.), *Semantics: An international handbook of natural language meaning.* Vol. 3: 2271–2296. Berlin: de Gruyter.
Kay, Paul & Laura A. Michaelis. 2019. A few words to do with multiword expressions. In Cleo Condoravdi & Tracy Holloway King (eds.), *Tokens of meaning: Papers in honor of Lauri Karttunen*, 87–118. Stanford: CSLI Publications.
Kay, Paul & Ivan A. Sag. 2012. Discontinuous dependencies and complex determiners. In Hans Boas and Ivan A. Sag (eds.), *Sign-Based Construction Grammar*, 211–238. Stanford: CSLI Publications.
Lambrecht, Knud. 1990. 'What, me worry?': 'Mad Magazine Sentences' revisited. *Berkeley Linguistics Society* 16. 215–228.
Lambrecht, Knud. 2001. A framework for the analysis of cleft constructions. *Linguistics* 39. 463–516.
Marchman, Virginia & Elizabeth Bates. 1994. Continuity in lexical and morphological development: A test of the Critical Mass Hypothesis. *Journal of Child Language* 21. 339–366.
Michaelis, Laura. 2017. Meaning of constructions. In Mark Aronoff (ed.), *Oxford research encyclopedia of linguistics*. Oxford/New York: Oxford University Press. (DOI: http://dx.doi.org/10.1093/acrefore/9780199384655.013.309)
Michaelis, Laura A. 2015. Constructions license verb frames. In Juhani Rudanko, Jukka Havu, Mikko Höglund & Paul Rickman (eds.), *Perspectives on complementation*, 7–33. London: Palgrave-Macmillan.
Michaelis, Laura A. 2011. Stative by construction. *Linguistics* 49. 1359–1399.
Michaelis, Laura A. 2012. Making the case for construction grammar. In Hans Boas & Ivan A. Sag (eds.), *Sign-Based Construction Grammar*, 31–69. Stanford: CSLI Publications.
Michaelis, Laura A. 1994. A case of constructional polysemy in Latin. *Studies in Language* 18. 45–70.
Michaelis, Laura A. & Hanbing Feng. 2015. What is this, sarcastic syntax? *Constructions and Frames* 7. 148–180.
Michaelis, Laura A. & Knud Lambrecht. 1996. Toward a construction-based theory of language function: The case of nominal extraposition. *Language* 72. 215–247.
Nunberg, Geoffrey, Ivan A. Sag & Thomas Wasow. 1994. Idioms. *Language* 70. 491–538.
Pinker, Steven. 2013. *Learnability and cognition: The acquisition of argument structure.* Cambridge, MA: MIT Press.
Ruppenhofer, Josef & Laura A. Michaelis. 2016. Frames, polarity and causation. *Corpora* 11. 259–290.
Sag, Ivan A. 2010. English filler-gap constructions. *Language* 86. 486–545.

Sag, Ivan A. 2012. Sign-Based Construction Grammar: An informal synopsis. In Hans Boas & Ivan A. Sag (eds.), *Sign-Based Construction Grammar*, 69–202. Stanford: CSLI Publications.
Sag, Ivan A., Hans Boas & Paul Kay. 2012. Introducing Sign-Based Construction Grammar. In Hans Boas & Ivan A. Sag (eds.), *Sign-Based Construction Grammar*, 1–30. Stanford: CSLI Publications.
Sag, Ivan A., Rui P. Chaves, Anne Abeillé, Bruno Estigarribia, Dan Flickinger, Paul Kay, Laura A. Michaelis, Stefan Müller & Geoffrey K. Pullum. 2019. Lessons from the English auxiliary system. *Journal of Linguistics*. 1–69. (doi:10.1017/S002222671800052X).

Barış Kabak
A dynamic equational approach to sound patterns in language change and second-language acquisition: The (un)stability of English dental fricatives illustrated

Abstract: This paper argues for a dynamic approach towards sound patterns, where both phonetically and cognitively grounded developmental and processing principles are assumed to be the impetus behind variability in all facets and shapes of sound evolution, all arguably driven by similar principles. A sound pattern is by nature an epistemological entity (i.e. the answer to how we know what we know), which emerges from the entire sum of interacting variables (e.g. language-internal and language-external factors) that act upon ordinary sound structures (e.g. segments). Accordingly, sound structures (i) are discerned as sound patterns (dynamic images with a certain amount of frequency, probability, etc.) insofar as they modulate speech processing and consequently trigger phonological change within and across life-spans, and thus (ii) should be viewed as unfixed ontological entities, which cannot be considered a priori as "stable" or "unstable". It is consequently argued that the dichotomy between natural and unnatural patterns as advocated in evolutionary approaches to sound patterns (e.g. Blevins 2006) falls short in capturing (i) the fact that the so-called natural causes can lead to both the loss and the preservation of a certain "unstable" feature, as well as (ii) the unity in the way sound patterns manifest themselves in different synchronic and diachronic spheres of language use. These arguments are supported by various observations on the fate of English dental fricatives throughout its history, how they have generated unique sound patterns under a complex interaction of endogenous and exogenous forces, and how they get transmitted to speakers of other languages in second-language learning. The latter situation mimics language change through language contact, albeit within an individual's life span and arguably with the reincarnation of the same network of external and internal variables that operate in diachrony, yielding to the conclusion that there is no "organic" realm for the study of sound patterns.

Barış Kabak, Würzburg University, English Linguistics, 97074 Würzburg, Germany, baris.kabak@uni-wuerzburg.de

https://doi.org/10.1515/9783110596656-009

1 Introduction

All spoken languages have a unique phonological system, a set of interacting principles, rules and constraints forming the knowledge of sound structure. This knowledge underlies the mechanisms that encode meanings into speech, and conversely decode speech signals into linguistic units to retrieve those meanings. The remit of phonology as a scientific discipline is to investigate the mental representations of speech sounds and their realization and distribution in speech, searching for a set of principles that characterize the backbone of sound systems across the languages of the world. Needless to say, phonology is the voice of the grammar and the lexicon, significantly interacting with other sub-components of grammar, such as morphology, syntax and pragmatics, in complex ways, which consequently makes the task of phonologists more than a mere description of an inventory of sounds and their combinations in particular languages. Theoretically, phonological patterns are epistemological regularities that are observable, measurable and quantifiable, the culmination of which is expected to give each language its unique phonological signature. To illustrate, in some languages, stressed/full vowels are canonically followed by unstressed/weak vowels (a pattern commonly known as the "trochaic rhythm") while in others this alternating order is reversed (the "iambic rhythm"). Some languages only permit a restricted number and type of coda consonants (e.g. Japanese and Korean) while others have the cooccurrence of several consonants in a row (e.g. English and Russian), yielding patterns of recurrent segmental sequences known as phonotactic regularities. Some may prefer accentual prominence on fixed positions within a word, others may be relatively free in placing their accents on any position thus creating the potential to yield lexical contrasts with accent. Once acquired, these properties are known to influence the way speech (native or non-native) is processed, arguably leaving permanent traces in the mind, forming what Trubetzkoy (1969 [1939]) calls a "phonological sieve".

My main theoretical objective in this paper is to offer a *dynamic* approach towards patterns that appear when sound systems[1] evolve across generations or co-evolve when more than one system comes together. In this approach, *sound structure* and *sound patterns* are not necessarily the same entities. While the first is an ordinary variable of ontological nature such as phonemes, suprasegmentals and syllables, the latter is a characteristic emerging from the entire sum of inter-

---

[1] Here the term *sound system* is used analogous to a phonological grammar, which comprises of sound structures and sound patterns.

acting variables such as language-internal and language-external factors as well as associations, and thus is more of an epistemological matter (simply, how we know what we know). In particular, sound structures are discerned as *sound patterns* – be they regular (hence predictable, recurrent) or irregular (hence unpredictable, deviant, and static) insofar as these modulate speech processing and consequently trigger phonological change within and across life-spans. Since language processing and change are interrelated and both are characterized by an aura of dynamism, so are phonological patterns. The dynamic approach here is complemented by a methodological utility: Sound patterns are observable at any *point* and *type* of language evolution, such as in first- and second-language acquisition, language attrition, diachronic and synchronic variation, in the emergence of varieties, etc., all of which are hypothesized to be governed by similar laws. This may be taken to resonate with the *uniformitarian* approaches towards sound change (e.g. Labov 1974) insofar as the mirroring of principles in the past on synchronic phenomena is concerned. In the dynamic view that I propose in this article, patterns are emergent abstract regularities that become discernable not just when new systems emerge or when they shift, but also when they coincide with other systems – for instance, when language users encounter a different grammar – or even when phonological systems interact with systems external to language such as music.

The variables that create sound patterns are first and foremost "internal" to the language user (i.e. factors that are related to the speaker, the listener and their mind). In particular, these internal factors originate from an interaction between (i) acoustic and articulatory principles (which are governed by physical and biological laws) and (ii) memory (that is responsible for the encoding, storage, and retrieval of linguistic signals, as well as for the formation of their associations to other linguistic elements), all of which form a part of our linguistic knowledge. In simple terms, phonology is a by-product of phonetic regularities that are stored in memory, thus being first and foremost subject to the extents and limitations of the human brain. Sound patterns can emerge from regularly occurring phonological units (e.g. regular appearance of voiceless coda consonants in German, regular absence of postvocalic /r/ in some varieties of English, preponderance of trochaic foot in English and German, etc.), from static generalizations (e.g. three-member onset consonant clusters start with /s/ in English), or combinations and extensions of these two (e.g. preponderance of word-initial accentual prominence in English – see Cutler 2015a for a quantitative analysis and consequences for language processing). What makes them "real" is their manifestation in different spheres of language behaviour, such as in speakers' intuitions, speech learning and processing, as well as in sound evolution within an individual's life span (e.g. acquiring and adapting novel sounds by a second-language learner, the attrition of sound features of one's native language due to exposure to other languages), or across life spans (phonological change across generations). What is inherent to both the recurrent and the static sound patterns is their variable and gradient character, which is commensurate with the language user's experience with the language, society as well as the cultural context that the language is embodied in, all of which are what linguists typically refer to as "language-external" factors such as quality and quantity of linguistic input and various social and affective variables (e.g. literacy, social class, age, attitude, motivation, etc.). In sum, sound patterns are not only dynamic mental images that may modulate the way sound structures are learned, processed and changed, but they are also the product of a complex interaction of internal and external factors that determine their optimal realization in a given situation.

2 Focus and objectives

To demonstrate the complexity and dynamics of phonological patterns, I will use the category of dental fricatives as the object of inquiry in this paper. In which ways has this sound feature formed patterns throughout the history of English and how does it manifest itself as patterns in second-language acquisition? How similar are the patterns that emerge in diachrony and those that emerge in synchrony? In approaching these questions, I will additionally offer a critical analysis of a recent approach by Blevins (2006) towards a set of patterns that have emerged in segmental and phonotactic change in the history of English. According to Blevins (2006), dental fricatives are "unstable" features of English as opposed to, for instance, consonant clusters in the onset and coda position, which are characterized to be "stable" features of English. In particular, I will examine the realization of the dental fricative category from both synchronic and diachronic perspectives, and then focus on their variable realization in second-language (L2) speech perception and production. The claim in my critical analysis will be that the variable realization patterns observed in dental fricatives in varieties of English are due to both the so-called "natural" and "unnatural" causes of sound change, which are crucially interdependent. The dental fricatives have been around for centuries, and the voiced dental fricative indeed managed to show phonemic behavior even under phonetically highly sub-optimal circumstances (see section 4.1). We see a reincarnation of the same network of external and internal variables that operates in diachrony also in second-language phonology. Based on diachronic and psycholinguistic evidence, I will offer a dynamic equational approach towards sound patterns. The central tenets of my arguments will be that sound patterns are characterized by a certain degree of gradience and variability unless they are extremely fossilized, and that they arise by an interaction of both language-internal and language-external factors with sound structures in all facets and shapes of language evolution and change, which are arguably driven by similar principles.

3 (Un)natural sound patterns?

Given the unifying ambition of my claim that all sound patterns are a product of similar principles, the question arises as to whether there are "unnatural" sound patterns. To that end, in an attempt to postulate new perspectives on sound patterns in English on the basis of the research program of Evolutionary Phonology (Blevins 2004), Blevins (2006) proposes a distinction in recurrent sound patterns that have natural histories as opposed to those that are unnatural. She specifically defines sound patterns with a natural history, natural sound patterns, as those "that transparently reflect language-internal phonetically motivated sound change, whether these sound changes have sources in misperception, ambiguous feature localization, or articulatory variation" (Blevins 2006: 7). In other words, when phonetic features with such language-internal causes are phonologized, "the resulting sound pattern is natural and has a natural history" (Blevins 2006: 7). The motivation that underlies the distinction between natural and unnatural stems from an empirical necessity to investigate "organic phonetic origins of a particular sound change" and the diachronic stages of language-internal factors therein, stripped away from contact-induced change, "where outputs of a completed sound change are assimilated" (Blevins 2006: 9).

According to Blevins (2006: 15), the features given in (1) below – with illustrative lexical examples from Old English (OE) and Modern English (ModE) – have been intact for over 1,500 years since natural phonetically based sound change has *not* influenced them. However, in the presence of external factors (i.e. unnatural histories), as in the case of close contact with languages with different syllable structure and phonotactic properties, the same (stable) features may have become vulnerable. For example, Blevins provides examples from Fiji English, where complex onsets in words such as "cream", which is a stable feature – see (1c) below, are altered by way of epenthetic vowels (*kirimu*) due to the lack of such onset clusters in Fijian, the substrate language involved in the emergence of Fijian English.

(1) Stable features of English word/syllable structure (taken and adapted from Blevins 2006: 14)
   a. Words may begin phonologically with Vowel (V) or Consonant (C):
      OE: *æppel, fūl*   ModE: *apple, foul*
   b. Nuclei may be simple or complex:
      OE: *fūl, full*   ModE: *foul, full*
   c. Onsets may be simple or complex:
      OE: *gān, grōwan*   ModE: *go, grow*
   d. Words may end in V or C:
      OE: *cū, camb*   ModE: *cow, comb*
   e. Codas may be simple or complex:
      OE: *bed, east, fox*   ModE: *bed, east, fox*
   f. C-Liquid onsets are possible:
      OE: *bread, dream, grene*   ModE: *bread, dream, green*
   g. sC onsets are possible:
      OE: *stingan, springan, skill*   ModE: *sting, spring, skill*

As an instance of sound change with a natural history with a clear phonetic grounding in the history of English, Blevins (2006) provides the elimination of dental fricatives, /θ/ and /ð/, from the inventories of a number of English varieties, mostly relying on various contributions on English varieties in Schneider et al. (2004) (e.g. West Ireland English, Maori English, Fiji English, New Zealand English). Some of these varieties have been argued to exhibit a complete loss of the two phonemes (e.g. West Ireland English), while others show variability (e.g. New Zealand English). According to Blevins (2006), one of the mechanisms that initiates the change in question here is the resolution of an ambiguous signal: "The phonetic signal is misperceived by the listener due to acoustic similarities between the utterance and the perceived utterance and biases of the human perceptual system" (Blevins 2006: 7). Different strategies may be taken to resolve the ambiguity. Despite the fact that numerous varieties merged dental fricatives with coronal stops or fricatives, the reason why the so-called "standard" varieties of English, such as British and American English, have preserved interdental fricatives, according to Blevins (2006), is due to literacy. In particular, she claims that, unlike many other instances of grapheme-phoneme mismatches in written English, dental fricatives are written in English as <th>, which she argues to be consistently associated with a dental articulation.

The question arises here as to what makes the properties given in (1) above "stable"? According to Blevins, there is no phonetic motivation to change them.

In the course of language transmission, they will be acquired under reasonably robust replication. "Only when this transmission is filtered through an entirely different grammatical system, as happens in contact situations, can radical transformations ... take place" (Blevins 2006: 20). As such, unnatural external factors can not only *inhibit* instances of natural phonetically motivated sound change (as happened in the preservation of dental fricatives in "standard" varieties of English due to literacy) but also *give rise to* novel sound patterns in modern varieties of English (e.g. the simplification of onset consonant clusters, deletion of coda consonants, etc.). Since it controls for factors such as prescriptivism, literacy and standardization, the evolutionary approach may be taken as a rather hygienic way towards understanding sound change. However, it falls short on several grounds. First, it fails to capture the intricate links between phonetic, language-internal and language-external factors, all of which can co-vary, sometimes even in opposite directions. Specifically concerning language-contact, it also ignores the reality of multidialectalism and multilingualism throughout human history. Furthermore, it lacks empirical coverage for the repeatedly demonstrated findings in laboratory phonology that the very same language-internal principles that we observe to govern sound patterns in diachronic and synchronic varieties of English (which may have phonetic origins) are also observed in sound patterns that emerge under language contact, i.e. in the emergence of second-language phonological systems (e.g. Brown 2000; Major 2001; Altmann and Kabak 2011 for reviews), as well as in first-language phonological attrition under bilingualism (e.g. Himmel 2019). As we will see below, cross-linguistic interference does not always explain the nature and dynamics of contact-induced systems. Different strands of linguistic research on such systems have repeatedly suggested that they should instead be characterized as "interlanguage phonological systems" (e.g. Ioup and Weinberger 1987), which are better understood if the acquisition of an additional sound system is investigated in conjunction with natural laws of phonetics (perception and articulation) as well as a range of cognitive, psychological and social phenomena.

The following section will provide a number of facts and observations that shed light onto the fate of English dental fricatives throughout its history and discuss ways in which they generated unique sound patterns under a complex interaction of endogenous and exogenous forces and how these get transmitted to speakers of other languages in second-language learning situations.

4 English dental fricatives: Diachronic and synchronic patterns and variation

English dental fricatives (/θ, ð/) are known to form one of the most notoriously difficult sound patterns that second-language (L2) learners of English encounter. They come not only with a basket of articulatory challenges but also with lexical peculiarities, all of which reveal abstract "patterns" at least insofar as the description of these facts is concerned. In the following, I will list some of those that linguists may not help but notice if they investigate English dental fricatives from different perspectives.

Let us first characterize the sounds in question on the basis of their well-known phonetic properties. From an articulatory point of view, dental fricatives are produced with the tip of the tongue placed against (behind or below) the maxillary central incisors (the two upper central teeth), or sometimes between the maxillary and the mandibular central incisors (i.e. the upper and lower central teeth), which is the reason why these sounds are also referred to as "interdental". As dental consonants, they constitute one of the several sounds that belong to the large family of coronal sounds, which are characterized by an occlusion or narrowing of the airflow with the tip or the blade of the tongue in articulation. As fricatives, they are produced with a turbulent, continuous air flow. Although once allophonic, /θ/, the voiceless dental fricative (e.g. *throw*) and /ð/, the voiced dental fricative (e.g. *though*) are now two phonemes in the Modern English consonantal inventory, both of which are however indicated by the same letter combination in orthography. As we will discuss in more detail below, both /θ/ and /ð/ are non-sibilant fricatives such that they are produced at lower frequencies than truly sibilant fricatives like /s/ or /z/. Note that in comparison to sibilants, the non-sibilant feature in dental fricatives is known to trigger a different allomorph in plural inflection (e.g. *path*s vs. *bush*es, *dress*es).

From a distributional perspective, there is no doubt that dental fricatives form a separate phonemic category in present-day English: By surfacing in overlapping environments with other similar phonetic categories, they create minimal pairs in different word positions (*think* vs. *sink*, *loath* vs. *loaf*). Although it is difficult to find minimal pairs where the voiceless dental fricative contrasts with the voiced one (e.g. *wreath* vs. *wreathe*), the phonemic status of the dental fricative category as a whole is indisputable especially since the voiceless dental fricative makes the only sound of the regular exponent of the ordinal morpheme (e.g. *four-th*, *hundred-th*), which forms a morphemic contrast with, for instance, the plural -s (e.g. *four-s*, *hundred-s*).

Dental fricatives are rare consonants across the languages of the world. According to Maddieson (2013), they can be found in only 43 languages out of the 567 languages sampled, present in all continents of the world. As such rare sounds, they also pose a challenge even to children who learn English as their first language since they are two of the consonants that are known to be acquired very late in their language development. For instance, Ingram (1978) finds that the two dental fricatives are still to be acquired at stage four of his five-stage developmental trajectory that he proposed for the acquisition of English fricatives and affricates by children between 2 and 6 years old. Ingram et al. (1980) showed that in the same stage, a considerable number of children had problems with /θ/ while other fricatives and affricates were quite stable. The most salient substitution of this consonant by these children was [f]. This pattern seems to be phonetically grounded since perceptual confusion with labiodental fricatives has also been shown for both infant (Eilers and Minifie 1975) as well as for adult native speakers of English in different speech styles for different populations (e.g. Maniwa, Jongman and Wade 2008).[2]

Despite their inherent sub-optimal psychoacoustic properties and variable realization in many varieties of English, dental fricatives make up the first segment in some of the high-frequency words in the English lexicon (*this*, *they*, etc.). Indeed, the most frequent word in English, *the*, begins with /ð/, which should signal, presumably to both L1 or L2 learners of English, that dental place of articulation is one of the most salient articulatory patterns of English. The maxillary central incisors are the most visible of all teeth and the apical tongue movement against these should easily be observable by a language learner.

From a distributional point of view, the voiced dental fricative is known to exhibit interesting asymmetries: Concerning the word-initial position, there are no content words that begin with this sound. Instead, it is restricted to function words (e.g. *the, this, thus*), and at the end of word, to both verbs as well as function words (e.g. *bathe, with*). We also observe instances of the voiced dental fricative in the word-medial position in lexical items with the etymological <-*der*> sequence (Minkova 2014: 124), some of which are spelled with <*th*> in present-

---

2 Maniwa, Jongman and Wade (2008), in their experimental study with normal-hearing and simulated hearing-impaired listeners, showed that sibilant fricatives were easier to identify than non-sibilants for normal-hearing listeners overall, with clear speech providing greater intelligibility benefits for sibilants than non-sibilants. When the same stimuli were adapted to simulate hearing loss, however, a clear speech effect was seen only for sibilants. Furthermore, they take their results to suggest that clear speech may have even hurt intelligibility for voiceless non-sibilants, which were identified most unsuccessfully by the listeners. Altogether, these results clearly demonstrate the vulnerability of dental fricatives as non-sibilant segments in speech perception.

day English (e.g. *mother, father, weather, whither*, etc.). Interestingly, these forms were subject to variation between the 16th and 18th centuries in that Minkova (2014: 125), citing Britton (2007), shows that forms such as *chylthereyn* "children" were attested in written records dating back to the sixteenth century (see section 4.1 for details).

Now, all of the above-mentioned observations do not constitute patterns as long as they do not emerge to explain a particular linguistic and psycholinguistic phenomenon – how a sound pattern emerges within and across life-spans, how it is processed in real time, or how it changes over time. In the context of patterns, the case of dental fricatives raises several empirical questions. From a diachronic perspective, one may ask: How did they emerge and become phonemic despite the fact that they constitute "unstable" contrasts from typological and phonetic points of view (e.g. Blevins 2006)? Why was the voiced dental fricative phonemicized in spite of the fact that voiced fricatives are typologically more marked and phonetically sub-optimal, and that this happened most remarkably in prosodically weak positions? (See section 4.1 below.) Why did alveolar stops turn into dental fricatives, yielding words such as *father* in Modern English, despite those natural causes that presumably spell doom for dental fricatives? From a language processing perspective, one may ask: How can we explain the unity and variability in the substitution patterns for the same category among adult second-language learners of English?

Below, I turn to patterns in sound change and focus on the evolution of dental fricatives, followed by an excursion to the patterns that emerge when they have to be processed as a learner encounters them. The essence of both of these excursions will be that, throughout history, dental fricatives were tailored and tuned by both internal factors and external factors, which are delicately interconnected, and that one should not consider unidirectional natural causes of sound change stripped away from realities exogenous to the hearer. In sound histories involving dental fricatives, language-external phenomena were the tailwinds for the extension and preservation of the so-called "unstable" patterns to this date, despite the headwinds of natural forces working against them. Furthermore, we will see that natural laws of sound change did not necessarily dictate the loss of dental fricatives, but to the contrary preserved them or gave way to them.

4.1 Patterns in sound change: How natural and unnatural histories got intricately fused to create the dental fricatives

The story of the dental fricative sound category in English goes back to a period approximately between 750–250 BC, when the Germanic branch was splitting further away from Proto-Indo-European (Minkova 2014: 62). The voiceless dental fricative emerged as a result of the First Germanic Consonantal Shift, also known as *Grimm's Law*, where the Proto-Indo-European voiceless stops */p, t, k/ turned into /f, θ, h/. Let us first see how various patterns in contemporary English emerged with respect to the distribution of /θ/ and /ð/. As most handbooks and grammars of English would argue, the distribution of the voiced and voiceless fricatives in Old English was allophonic, the voiced ones predictably occurring between voiced segments such as two vowels, within a unit that we may roughly refer to as the Prosodic Word (voicing did not take place after prefixes or between the members of a compound). The phonemic split in Middle English essentially yielded /f, v, θ, ð, s, z/ as separate phonemes, creating some minimal pairs such as *ferry-very* and *thistle-this*.

In her article where she critically evaluates Laker's (2009) alternative account for the emergence of voiced fricatives in English,[3] Minkova (2011) provides convincing arguments to endorse the traditional position that the phonemic split of the Old English fricative allophones took place after 1100. Furthermore, she cautions the reader about the problematic nature of providing a one-size-fits-all solution to all fricatives in all positions, and that we should treat the developments in the three fricative sets (labiodental, dental and alveolar categories) separately and identify different triggers for each. In general, we see the prevalence of four factors that gave way to the phonemic split of the predictable variants of fricatives in Middle English (see Minkova 2014: 90–98). We will focus on three of them below.[4]

---

[3] Laker (2009) hypothesizes that the voiced fricative had already been phonemicized through language contact between Brittonic and Old English as early as the middle of the 5th century, leading to a subsequent language shift. To put simply, since Late Brittonic had both voiceless and voiced fricatives, including /ð/, as phonemes, Brittonic speakers interpreted Old English allophonic voiced fricatives as phonemes in their own varieties. See Minkova (2011), however, for arguments against this view on the basis of, most notably among others, empirical evidence from patterns of alliteration in Old and Middle English.
[4] Minkova (2014) also highlights some dialectal developments accounting for the occurrence of voiced fricatives in word-initial position in Kentish, late West Saxon in Old English, and the south and south-west Midlands in Middle English. She claims that although initial fricative

The first factor is the influence of a massive amount of borrowings from Old French that are /v/-initial (e.g. *vile, vain*). Likewise, loans with word-medial /f/ provided input against the active voicing rule in the same position (e.g. *sacrifice*). Old French devoiced voiced fricatives word finally, so word-final voiced fricatives in present-day English cannot be due to loans from Old French. The contribution of loans to the phonemization of /z/ is less significant since there were not many /z/-initial loans. Furthermore, Old French had the same type of intervocalic voicing rule for /s/, predictably yielding [z], and the final-devoicing rule gave way to no word-final-/z/. As such, word-medial and word-final /z/ cannot be due to loans (see also Minkova 2011).

The contribution of loans is wholly excluded from the establishment of the phonemic opposition between /θ/ and /ð/ since the latter consonant did not appear in borrowings. Instead, Minkova (2014: 93) brings up "system-internal phonological changes", which obscured the evidence for the earlier complementary distribution of voiced and voiceless fricatives, as an additional factor that seemed to have played a major role. The phonological changes in question are (i) the gradual degemination of fricatives, and (ii) the loss of final unstressed vowels, which yielded many minimal pairs. Briefly, geminate fricatives, which were not subject to the by now familiar allophonic voicing process in Old English, gradually turned into singletons in original -VGə sequences (where G stands for a geminate consonant) as the final schwa was losing ground (e.g. *blisse* "bliss" ended up being pronounced as *bli*[s]). However, singleton voiceless fricatives in the same sequence, which were subject to the allophonic voicing rule, became the lexical property of the word after the final schwa was apocopated (e.g. *wise* "wise" ended up being pronounced as *wi*[z] with no schwa following the fricative). Since dental fricative geminates (i.e. /-θθ-/) were rare, we owe /θ/-/ð/ contrasts in word-final position primarily to the above-mentioned schwa-loss, yielding, for example, *breathe, loathe, and cloathe.*

Prosody was yet another factor, according to Minkova (2011, 2014), which is specifically proposed to explain why at the beginning of function words, the dental fricative must feature as voiced (e.g. *the, this, that, those, thus,* etc.) in contemporary English. Before turning to Minkova's specific claims, a number of facts on the phonetics of voicing are in order since several contradictory forces may interact and preserve voicing in fricatives.

---

voicing in southern dialects lent dialectal forms such as *vane, vat, vixen* to the standard, "it did not contribute independently to the establishment of phonemically contrastive fricatives in the standard language" (Minkova 2014: 95).

First of all, on top of the marked place of articulation, voicing is known to add further aerodynamic "challenges" to fricatives. Fricatives, by definition, require continuous airflow. Voicing, to the contrary, requires the oscillation of the vocal folds, i.e. a periodic opening and closing of the folds. To do that, the folds need to be brought close enough to build up air pressure below the larynx, causing the fold tissues to vibrate in a wave-like motion. Furthermore, to keep the pressure below the larynx as high as possible, the pressure inside the mouth needs to be lowered. However, air pressure needs to be higher in the mouth in order to produce friction so that a fricative, instead of a stop, is created. Smith (2009) suggests that balancing the two contradictory requirements can be problematic since narrowing the closure in the mouth to increase oral pressure for frication can easily result in a stop production. The flip side of this, that is relaxing the vocal tract to lower the pressure, would however result in an approximant. These phonetic scenarios suggest that the production of voicing in fricatives arguably involves sub-optimal configurations. Indeed, voiced fricatives are known to be less loud and crucially shorter in frication noise than their voiceless counterparts, perhaps as a result of the optimization of these contradictory forces. They are approximately 40 percent shorter than their voiceless counterparts, according to Lavoie's (2009) own measurements. We also have to bear in mind another phonetic property associated to voicing and frication, which will be crucial to understanding the distribution of voiced dental fricatives: Cole and Cooper (1975) find that listeners make use of temporal information to process voicing distinctions in fricatives such that *shortening* frication duration suffices to establish a change in percept from voiceless to *voiced* (cf. Jongman 1989, who also finds a significant correlation between frication duration and the identification of voicing, but suggests that short frication does not necessarily lead to more voiced percepts; see Maniwa, Jongman and Wade 2008 for a review of various phonetic cues to English fricative identity in different listener populations).

What do these acoustic-phonetic facts and features imply for the emergence of certain dental fricative patterns? The link between the aerodynamic complexities in voicing and fricative articulation and the subsequent shortening of frication find an optimal place to survive: function words. Function words are known to be subject to reduction and subsequently more variability not just because they are characteristically prosodically weak morphemes (Selkirk 1995), but also due to their frequency (e.g. Bybee 2000; Pierrehumbert 2001). The well-known effects of this reduction are the cliticization and subsequent morphologization of function words as affixes across the languages of the world. As a possible factor contributing to the voicing of word-initial dental fricatives in function words, Smith (2009) hypothesizes that their high frequency may have allowed a larger amount of variation, which became generalized as a voicing contrast, compounded by the paradigm levelling that reduced the number of forms (e.g. the definite article, *the*, became the sole form from approximately twelve different exponents that marked case, gender, and number in Old English).[5] From Smith's variationist account, it is however not clear why such a level of instability did not lead to sound change. The argument that the extent of variation has been stable throughout history is nothing more than a speculation. As such, there is no obvious empirical reason as to why the dental fricative category alone should constitute a show-case for variability within the phonemic inventory of English. In fact, a considerable amount of phonetic variation can also be observed for other voiced phonemes, especially when they occur in unfavourable contexts. For instance, despite the full support from orthography, English word-final voiced obstruents (e.g. *cab, page*, etc.) are known to exhibit a great deal of devoicing, surrendering themselves to the universal effect of coda-neutralization. Nevertheless, just as we cannot dismiss the fact that voiced phonemes were lexicalized in word-final position, we should also agree on the fact that function words such as *the, this, these*, etc. all begin with a voiced dental fricative although this may be less "categorical". As correctly pointed out by Minkova (2011: 56), the issue lies in the fact that categorization continues to be a gradient notion, and that a completed stage of lexicalized fricative voicing has not yet been reached in the history of English.

Let us go back to Minkova's instructive idea that the prosody of function words (Minkova 2014: 94–95), in particular the phonetic reflexes of (lack of) stress, contributed to the phonemization of the voiced dental fricative. To that end, she presents additional pieces of evidence that other fricatives including the dental one show final voicing in some function words (e.g. *has, was, is, of, with*) as well as in the inflection <-es>, all of which are also arguably prosodically weak morphemes. The phonetic argument that is linked to prosodic weakness is as follows: lack of stress correlates with no stretching of the vocal folds. Stretching the cartilages at the bottom of the vocal folds is however linked to *voicelessness*. Since function words are stressless, no stretching leads to *voicing*.

The phonetic support for the correlation between stretching and voicing is rather sketchy. Here an alternative account can be proposed based on the temporal dynamics of voicing in fricatives. It could be suggested that the pattern of voicing in function words was the outcome of the most optimal solution to the

---

[5] Smith (2009) reports results from an unpublished study of hers with Ohio residents that showed that the voiced dental fricative showed greater variation in both *manner* (e.g. as a stop or an approximant) and *voicing* than did the voiceless, which she takes to suggest that /θ/ may be more stable.

conflicting aerodynamic properties of frication and voicing. In particular, (i) consonants and vowels are known to be shorter in weaker positions than in stronger positions, and (ii) voiced consonants are shorter than voiceless consonants in general (see Lavoie 2009 and the references therein). Besides, Cole and Cooper (1975) showed that shortened frication noise in [fa] and [sa] created the perceptual shift from voiceless to voiced. Short frication duration in function words must have enabled listeners to extract a pattern of correlation between morphological position and voicing. Hence, function words must have become the most consummate hosts for voiced dentals, where they could be salient unless other factors intervened in this process (note that there are function words with voiceless fricatives such as *for, from*, etc.).

In summary, the weakest of the unstable, i.e. the voiced dental fricative, was preserved in the prosodically weakest context of all. Evolutionary Phonology fails to make any prediction as to which factors prevail in such sub-optimal circumstances. Note that this was in spite of the absence of a consistent orthographic distinction between the voiced and voiceless dental fricative throughout history (the letters <Þ> and <ð> were not consistently used to mark voicing; see Hogg 1992: 76–77; Minkova 2014: 90–91). As such, the dental fricative category cannot be upheld as the bellwether for instability throughout the segmental history of English.

So, only "natural stories" can be narrated to tell the tale of how voiced dental fricatives were *phonemicized* in defiance of the again "natural" acoustic and articulatory factors that should have worked for the demise of the dental fricative category. Leaving voiced dental fricatives aside, the establishment of a voicing opposition among fricatives in general could not have been possible without an interaction between language-internal and language-external forces, as has been convincingly argued for by Minkova (2011). Essentially, phonetic experience with voicing distinction among the fricative series paved the way for the acceptance of voiced fricatives as lexically contrastive in massively filtrating loan words into English in the Middle English period. The lexicalization of the opposition between the voicing feature among fricatives in loan words and voiceless fricatives in native words and elsewhere was extended to the dental fricative category. We see instructive parallelisms between such diachronic developments and the acquisition of novel contrasts in the second-language acquisition of phonology, to which we turn below (see section 4.2).

Before closing the diachronic story, however, it should be noted that it is not only the First Consonantal Shift in the history of English that is responsible for the emergence of the dental fricative category by turning /t/ into /θ/. Indeed, centuries later, the English sound system created new additions to the lexical items with dental fricatives by way of phonetically motivated sound change. In particular, there was a coarticulatory, assimilatory sound change that was initiated by the variable realization of /d/ as [ð] intervocalically, before schwa-/r/ and occasionally schwa-/l/ sequences (Minkova 2014: 124–125). The first attestation of this variation seems to go back to the 15th century, when words in etymological <-der> started to appear as <-ther> in orthography, essentially in the shapes that they are in today. Examples for such words are *father, mother, gather, weather*, etc., which showed extensive variation in the 16th to 18th centuries. The phonetic grounding here, according to Minkova (2014), lies in the assimilation of the /d/ to an apical trill, thereby acquiring frication from it. Furthermore, she notes that the acoustic similarity between [dr̥] and [ðr̥] must have facilitated this process. Interestingly, the reverse development (i.e. as a result of a dissimilatory process), was also attested, whereby Old English forms such as *byrðen, morðor, geforðian, fiðele* turned to *burden, murder, afford, and fiddle*, respectively.[6] Such developments independently suggest that phonetically-grounded sound change did not always work against dental fricatives in the history of English. Natural causes either led way to these so-called unstable sounds or conversely replaced them with other, perhaps less marked, consonants.

4.2 Acquiring second-language sounds mirrors (un)natural histories in diachronic phonology: Phonetic universals and the perception–production mismatch

A significant amount of research has so far shown that non-native phonemic contrasts do not always yield difficulties in speech perception, although there is no doubt that non-native phonemic categories broadly pose more challenges than native ones (e.g. Werker et al. 1981; Werker and Tees 1984; Polka 1991, 1992). Generally, non-native contrasts are known to yield a significant amount of variability in perceptual behaviour, crucially modulated by the type of contrast in question and the native language of the listener in question. The level of success at perceiving non-native sounds can hence range from chance-level to native-like performance (e.g. Best et al. 1988; Burnham 1986; Polka 1991, 1992; Pruitt 1995). Therefore, it is not always the native-language sound inventory, i.e. the *phonemic* status of the target language contrast in question in the native language of the learner, that can predict the outcome of second-language sound learning. Accordingly, theoretical models have emerged that prioritize the role of acoustic and perceptual factors in determining the outcome of non-native speech percep-

---

6 Examples are taken from Minkova (2014: 125).

tion, making explicit predictions about the relative perceptual and production difficulty commensurate with the phonetic *nature* of non-native segments. For instance, perceptual similarity is the centrepiece of a range of well-known theories such as the Perceptual Assimilation Model (Best 1995), the Speech Learning Model (Flege 1995), the Native Language Magnet Model (e.g. Iverson and Kuhl 1995, 1996) that attribute the degree of perceptual difficulty to how well the members of the non-native segments in contrast are perceived as instances of existing native sound categories. These models roughly differ from one another in the way "phonetic similarity" is characterized and (if at all) quantified, which is beyond the scope of the present paper.[7] Research in this trend has so far generated a substantial amount of psycholinguistic studies in non-native speech perception that suggests that the perception of non-native sounds and phonemic contrasts is not solely driven by the specific phonological properties of the languages in question, but also explained by acoustic and articulatory properties of the sounds involved in the contrast. Here, listeners' experience with non-native categories as free variants or allophones of native sounds has been proposed as a factor (e.g. Burnham 1986; Ingram and Park 1998; Harnsberger 2000, 2001; Kabak and Maniwa 2007).

A classic example comes from the perception of English liquids by Japanese and Korean listeners, neither of which has the /r/–/l/ contrast. Ingram and Park (1998), for example, predicted the relative difficulty of the American English /l/–/r/ contrast for Korean and Japanese listeners in different positions of a word, based on the distribution of liquids in these positions in the listeners' native languages. The Korean singleton liquid is phonetically realized as an alveolar flap ([ɾ]) and it geminates as an alveolar lateral (i.e. [ll]) between vowels. Therefore, Korean listeners were assumed to have a *phonetic model* available to them that they can use to approximate to the English /r/–/l/ contrasts in this position based on the phonetic experience they have in their native language. Accordingly, they are expected to treat English /r/ as their singleton liquid, and the English /l/ as geminate liquid. Indeed, in Park and Ingram's study, the phonetic approximation of [ɾ]–[ll] for the English /r/–/l/ contrast was suggested to enable the Korean listeners to perceive the English contrast significantly better than the Japanese listeners, who treat both sounds as variants of the same category in their native

---

7 Relevant to dental fricatives and their differential substitution in second-language acquisition, see for example the Auditory Distance Model of Brannen (2011), who provides an algorithm that assesses the auditory distance between the target and first-language representations in the processing of L2 phonetic input by employing feature salience through enhancement (see also section 4.2.2).

language (see An 2015 for a review of previous studies on non-native perception of English liquids).

Turning to dental fricatives, there has been relatively little research on the second-language acquisition of these sounds. My aim here is not to present a comprehensive summary of previous studies on this matter. The reader is referred to Brannen (2011) for a detailed review of most relevant studies. Instead, I will dwell on how the second-language speech perception and production of dental fricatives (and the voicing contrast therein) shows variability depending on phonetic experience with similar categories in the native language. Crucially, this variability will be shown to be commensurate upon universal psychoacoustic aspects of the sounds in question, mirroring the kind of diachronic developments highlighted above.

4.2.1 Perception

Kabak and Maniwa (2007) highlighted the interaction of language-particular *phonetic* and *phonemic* experience with psychoacoustic factors in the perception of English fricatives. Concerning psychoacoustic factors, they employed Burnham's (1986) binary distinction between "robust" and "fragile" contrasts that is used to account for the variability observed in cross-language speech perception. Briefly, "fragile" contrasts are known to have a weaker psychoacoustic basis while "robust" contrasts are associated with more distinctive acoustic cues. Furthermore, robust contrasts are argued to be typologically more common and more likely to be acquired earlier and more easily in both first- and second-language acquisition. In their perception study with two different non-native listener groups (Standard German and Swabian German learners of English),[8] a two-alternative forced-choice segment identification task was administered using the eight English fricative phonemes (f, θ, s, ʃ, v, ð, z, ʒ). The fricatives were contained in VCV stimuli (e.g. [asa] vs. [afa]), yielding eight minimal pairs based on place of articulation (/f/-/θ/, /v/-/ð/, /s/-/ʃ/, /z/-/ʒ/) and voicing (/f/-/v/, /θ/-/ð/, /s/-/z/, and /ʃ/-/ʒ/) distinctions. These VCV pairs were taken from a previous study on clear fricatives by Maniwa (2007), who used an interactive computer program to elicit these stimuli in clear and conversational speech styles from native American

---

8 Swabian German refers to an Alemannic dialect of German spoken primarily in Southwestern Germany, especially in the state of Baden-Württemberg and Southwestern Bavaria. Each non-native group had 14 normal-hearing participants who studied English for a minimum of 7 years (Average=10.36 for the Standard German; Average=9.35 for the Swabian German dialect group).

English speakers. The perception study used an adaptive procedure, and for each speech style it measured the signal to multi-talker babble noise ratio thresholds at which the non-native listeners identified the fricative categories in the CVC stimuli with 75% accuracy. As a control, the perception data from the two non-native listener groups were compared to those from 14 native speakers of American English originally reported in Maniwa (2007) (see also Maniwa, Jongman and Wade 2008).

A closer inspection of the fricative inventories of the respective native languages shows instructive differences that will be relevant for us to revisit the diachronic stories discussed above. First, the voicing distinction for sibilant fricatives ("robust" contrast *a la* Burnham 1986) is highly restricted in Standard German, which contains only a few minimal pairs (e.g. *reißen* [s] vs. *rei_s_en* [z]). Generally, [s] and [z] are in complementary distribution, with [z] occurring syllable-initially before a vowel and [s] appearing syllable-finally (due to coda devoicing in German). The voiced palato-alveolar [ʒ] is found only in loan words and considered to be a "peripheral" phoneme since it occurs neither in contrastive distribution nor in free variation with [ʃ]. Second, Swabian German lacks voiced sibilants altogether (they do not even occur allophonically). These observations allowed Kabak and Maniwa to test the influence of phonetic exposure in the native language of the speaker on speech perception, i.e. allophonic experience as well as experience with "peripheral" sounds coming from loans. Essentially, since the Standard German listeners have more experience with sibilant voicing distinctions, better discrimination ability was expected on the part of these listeners than the Swabian German listeners.

It should be noted that none of the German varieties in question has the dental fricative category, which constitutes a "fragile" contrast, especially when they are presented in opposition with other "fragile" sounds (in particular with labial fricatives, /f/ and /v/). Thus, both acoustic salience and phonological accounts predicted worse performance for the German listeners than the native English controls.

In all speech styles, the voiceless contrast /s/–/ʃ/, followed by their voiced counterparts /z/–/ʒ/, were the easiest to identify for all groups, corroborating their salient psychoacoustic properties ("robust contrasts"). To the contrary, "fragile" non-sibilant pairs /f/–/θ/ and /v/–/ð/ were the most challenging across speech styles and for all listener groups, including native speakers of American English. The results from non-native listeners not only support previous studies with native English listeners (e.g. Miller and Nicely 1955; Wang and Bilger 1973; Jongman, Waylane and Wong 2000), but are also in line with the most common substitution patterns discussed in child language acquisition of English (see section 4.1 above). This indicates that, irrespective of the language-particular phonemic system in language contact, universal acoustic factors corroborate the ambiguous properties of dental fricatives. Furthermore, phonetic/allophonic experience seemed to be a significant predictor, which was evidenced by a comparison of the two German groups for the voicing distinctions in sibilants. As predicted, Standard German speakers, who had allophonic experience with the respective sounds in their native language, outperformed Swabian German speakers, who lacked voiced sibilant fricatives in their native language altogether. So, both types of exposure to the sounds, i.e. when they occur in complementary distribution (as in the case of /s/–/z/), or as "peripheral" phonemes (as in the case of /ʃ/–/ʒ/ contrast), offered similar perceptual benefits. The contribution of acoustic factors is more saliently represented in the Swabian German group with their better performance for /z/–/ʒ/ (robust contrast) than /θ/–/ð/ (fragile contrast) although all four sounds are absent from Swabian German.

4.2.2 Production

From the perspective of production, my pilot study with four German young learners of English as a foreign language (ages 11–13) with minimum 2 years of exposure to school English shows a similar pattern to the kind of difficulty that Swabian German listeners experienced with voicing in the English sibilant series in Kabak and Maniwa (2007). In particular, the children in the pilot experiment came from an area near Nuremberg, Germany, and spoke Middle Frankish,[9] which, just as in the case of Swabian German and unlike Standard German, is known to lack voicing contrasts in sibilants altogether. They were asked to hear clearly pronounced English words (with the target sounds /θ, ð, v, z/ in different word positions) twice in a sequence and repeat them in a carrier phrase "I can say...".[10] Table 9.1 summarizes the results of the experiment.

---

9 This terminological choice follows from the political name given to the region in which Nuremberg is located, and it reflects the term the local community would commonly use to refer to their variety, in contrast to what is meant by "Franconian".
10 The production experiment included 92 test words that were produced by a near-native speaker in clear speech. The test items contained 30 words with /z/ and 30 /v/, equally distributed to each of the three word positions (initial, medial, and final). There were also 32 words with dental fricatives (10 in the initial, 12 medial, 10 final position). The voiced dental fricative could only be tested in the word-medial position. Therefore, half of the 12 medial dental fricatives were /ð/. Since the focus of the experiment was purely on the accurate repetition of the heard items, the participants' familiarity with the words was not checked although several words were arguably known to them since they appeared in their textbook.

Tab. 9.1: Percent accuracy rates in target-like productions of English fricatives in different word positions

	Initial	Medial	Final	Total
/θ/	57.5	79.5	75	70.6
/ð/	N/A	66.8	N/A	66.8
/v/	82.5	92.5	27.5	67.5
/z/	5	20	5	10

A striking generalization that arises from these results is that the voiced alveolar fricative /z/ is the fricative with the worst production accuracy in all positions of the word, with an overall accuracy rate of 10%. Remarkably poor performance in the voiced fricatives in the word-final position can be straightforwardly explained by robust coda-neutralization in German. In the word-medial position, where all four of the fricatives in question could be tested without the confound of coda-devoicing, we again see that both the dental and the labiodental fricatives were produced significantly better than /z/.

These results show that voicing contrast could be more accurately produced in the newly acquired place of articulation in the fricative series, i.e. dental fricative, than the voicing contrast in the already existing alveolar fricative category (/s/ exists in Middle Frankish). We can thus suggest that the already available place of articulation feature, i.e. alveolar articulation, in the fricative category strongly resisted the redeployment of the voicing feature. Combined with the perceptual findings, these results show, on the one hand, that phonetic experience with the sound in question contributes positively to non-native perception (English fricatives with which participants had phonetic experience were better perceived). On the other hand, they point to the fact that the availability of a phonetic feature in the native language does not always lead to success. Here, acoustic salience as well as language-specific restrictions on feature combinations matter.

An analysis of the non-target like productions revealed instructive patterns concerning sound substitutions. Although the most likely sound to confuse /θ/ with is /f/, as shown for the non-native listeners of English (Kabak and Maniwa 2007), the most likely substitution in production was not this sound. Indeed, /f/ accounted for less than 5% of all the sound substitutions for the two dental fricatives. Although a more systematic study with acoustic analyses and more participants is called for, a robust discrepancy between the most common substitutions for dental fricatives can be seen: /s/ for /θ/ but /d/ for /ð/ (see figure 9.1).

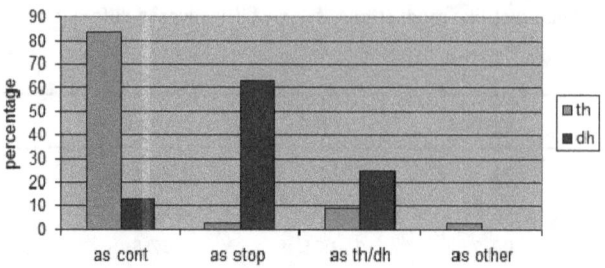

Fig. 9.1: Rates for differential substitution of dental fricatives in the pilot production study

Interestingly, a number of substitutions emerged with the target place of articulation albeit mismatching the target in voicing (25% of the substitutions for /ð/ were /θ/ while 9% of the substitutions for /θ/ were /ð/). The discrepancy between the most common substitutions for /θ/ and /ð/ can be accounted for, again, by the fact that this dialect group lacks voiced sibilants, so /z/ was not an alternative, which is in alignment with the difficulties the children showed with target /z/ productions (which were substituted with /s/ 87% of the cases) in the same study. So, the second-language productions in these young learners remained faithful to the voicing feature, which is reminiscent of the assimilatory process that changed the medial <-der> sequences into <-ther>, and conversely the <-ther> sequences back to <-der>, where the voicing feature was kept constant (see section 4.1 above). The stop substitution (i.e. /d/) for /ð/, and not a continuant substitution with /s/ or /z/, mirrors this latter diachronic development.

Similar discrepancies between perception and production were observed in Brannen (2011), where English as a second language (ESL) learners with Japanese, Quebec French, European French, and Russian native language backgrounds were tested on their discrimination of dental fricatives from other places of articulation, as well as on their production of dental fricatives. The major prediction of Brannen's Auditory Distance Model is that languages with a less or non-strident /s/ should tend to replace the target /θ/ with their native /s/. In particular, since [s] in Quebec French is phonetically farther from the dental fricative than is the /s/ of European French, Japanese, and Russian, the latter groups were expected to confuse /θ/ with /s/ more often. Brannen's (2011) results largely confirmed her predictions. There was a correlation between contrasts that caused problems in her discrimination experiments and the errors that occurred in her production study. Roughly, those non-native speaker groups who most often confused [θ] with /s/ in perception were also those who most often produced /s/ for the dental fricative. These were European French, Japanese and Russian ESL learners. Quebec French speakers, however, confused /θ/ with /t/, and also showed more substitution errors with /t/.

However, for the /f/–/θ/ (and also /ʃ/–/θ/) contrasts, in line with the production study with the Middle Frankish young learners of English, Brannen (2011) observed more errors in *perception* than in *production*. Furthermore, although the Russian, European French and Japanese groups produced more variants as substitutes for the dental fricative, the Quebec French ESL learners were categorical in their production, always substituting /t/, and never /f/, /s/, or /ʃ/. Brannen (2011: chapter 6) offers various explanations for this disparity such as the role of orthography, the detailed discussion of which would however exceed the limits of this paper.

On a final note, similar substitution patterns are given in the list of English varieties that Blevins (2006) lists to show the loss of the English dental fricatives due to natural causes, albeit never mentioning the role of language-contact in this matter (most of the varieties she lists are straightforwardly contact varieties). Although I would not exclude the role of native languages or other exogenous forces as factors in the second-language findings I have presented so far, the sound substitutions are largely phonetically motivated (note that, albeit significantly less, /θ/ emerged as the second most likely substitution for /z/ in my production data, which is arguably due to hypercorrection). This suggests that sound evolution involving language-contact is not immune to the shaping of phonetic forces that mirror diachronic patterns.

5 Discussion

Both strands of inquiry into sound patterns, one from a diachronic and the other from a synchronic or psycholinguistic perspective, converge on the following observation: Cognitively and phonetically grounded developmental and processing principles are the impetus behind variability in *all* types of sound evolution, including contact-induced scenarios.[11] Both also show a complex interaction between language-internal and language-external variables. In particular, voicing gradually slipped into the fricative series as a contrastive feature and appeared in different parts of the word due to a combination of grammar-internal (e.g. prosodic

---

11 The reader is referred to Hayes, Kirschner and Steriade (2004) for some exemplary work that explains phonological phenomena, including diachronic change, on the basis of phonetic principles, mostly couched in Optimality Theoretic (Prince and Smolensky 2004) constraints.

factors, final-schwa deletion, phonetic experience with voicing, etc.) and grammar-external factors (e.g. the type of new sounds involved in the loans and the differential rate at which these were brought into English). Crucially, allophonic experience with voicing would not yield a phonemic split in the absence of a massive influx of words with /v/. We observed similar patterns in second-language learners, where their phonetic experience (e.g. allophonic *or* peripheral) with novel sounds in the native language improved language learners' perception of these sounds. Conversely, lack of phonetic experience made the same process challenging. Here, it should be noted that experience does not need to be direct. Instead, already existing (similar) features within and across different levels of linguistic organization can be redeployed and extended to learn second-language contrasts. For instance, the nature of native language utterance-level prosody has been shown to predict success in lexicalizing tonal contrasts in a second language (e.g. Braun, Galts and Kabak 2014).[12]

Naturally, variability in the rate of success in second-language acquisition of sound structure depends on the complex interaction of phonetic factors with psychoacoustic and other language-internal (e.g. phonemic experience) and language-external factors (e.g. orthography).[13] Although I did not go into the role of social and affective factors in the acquisition of second-language sounds, there is a growing amount of literature on the way foreign accent is modulated by factors such as attitudes, motivation and age (see Moyer 2013 for a comprehensive review). Recently, there has also been a growing interest in how language-external factors interact with and predict the variable realization of phonological features and how that interaction can be accounted for by theoretical models couched in constrained-based phonological theories, such as Noisy Harmonic Grammar (e.g. Coetzee 2016; Himmel 2018).

---

12 Braun, Galts, and Kabak (2014) show that limited pitch-inventory at the utterance level (e.g. as in Japanese and French) exerts a negative effect on the ability to store second-language lexical tones while speakers with native languages with a rich intonational system show better performance. That is, linguistic experience with different pitch patterns at the post-lexical level helps the learner in storing tonal patterns at the *lexical* level. Therefore, along with concrete strategies to map novel contrasts to already existing native categories, learners' overall experience with similar variables across different levels of linguistic organization needs to be taken into account. Structural analogy can operate across different domains.
13 See Cutler (2015b) for a review of the contribution of orthography to the lexical representations of non-native sounds.

6 All sound patterns are dynamic, gradient and natural

While dichotomies such as "stable" vs. "unstable" are better construed as descriptive tools to discuss the relative susceptibility to variability in diachronic terms, we cannot ignore the fact that gradience and variation are at the heart of *every* phonological feature, including the so-called stable features of Blevins (2006) given in (1) above. Most remarkably, several studies with speakers of a range of vernacular varieties of American English convincingly demonstrated that language-internal factors such as segmental context (phonetic environment) and morphosyntactic complexity as well as grammar-external factors such as level of formality, social class and language-contact interact to yield variable realizations of coda consonant clusters (e.g. *east*), which are assumed by Blevins (2006: 14) to be stable features of English that could only be manipulated by language-external factors. In many varieties of American and British English, however, when and how a consonant cluster is reduced crucially depend on *language-internal forces*, such as the phonetic context in which the consonant cluster finds itself. For instance, less sonorous environments show resistance to cluster reduction while more sonorous ones are more prone to this (see Schreier 2005 for a review).

Therefore, the variable realization of any feature in different varieties of English (many of which are arguably contact varieties) cannot be used as an argument to make a distinction between natural vs. unnatural patterns of sound change because the argumentation needs to make a priori distinction between a stable and an unstable feature in the history of a particular language.

Furthermore, "unnatural" factors such as literacy, standardization and globalization do not offer a unified explanation as to why an unstable feature (in our case, the dental fricative category) *has been* preserved because this also applies to our "stable" feature, coda consonant clusters, which also have robust, highly stable, orthographic cues in English, and which nevertheless show a great deal of variation across English varieties. Therefore, it is unclear why the unnatural factor appears to preserve the first but not the latter. Instead, the so-called "loss of" dental fricatives is claimed to be due to an interplay of the "marked" nature of dental fricatives and language contact. The latter is what Blevins considers as yet another unnatural factor although, as argued above, the consequences of language contact on linguistic systems are characteristically principled, given the interplay of crosslinguistic interference and structural factors such as markedness, one of the most well-entrenched foundations of the field of second-language acquisition as a scientific discipline. It should be noted that Blevins additionally uses language contact to explain why *stable* patterns (e.g. consonant clusters in English) may not be completely immune to change. Here, it should be added that the fact that speech perception, a natural phonetic factor, is inevitably shaped by language users' experience with their native language phonological system would actually render several instances of sound change neither natural nor unnatural, perhaps an undesired result for an approach that attempts to distinguish regular sound changes that have unequivocal phonetic bases from those that are unnatural.[14] As such, the distinction between natural and unnatural becomes superfluous since the so-called "unnatural" forces (e.g. language contact) are in an undeniably intricate relationship with "natural" forces, influencing *both* the so-called "stable" and "unstable" patterns.

We have seen that it is difficult to tease apart "natural" factors from factors involved in language evolution under contact, most remarkably in the case of second-language acquisition of sound structure. Given the reality that no variety of English stands completely apart from contact with other dialects and that, as Wolfram (2004: 97) puts it, "[i]n all cases of English, there is always some type of interaction with other groups, though there are, of course, vast differences in the regularity and intensity of contacts (e.g. Schreier 2003)", seeking for the "organic phonetic origins of a particular sound change" (Blevins 2006: 9) by comparing different varieties of English is nothing more than a romantic idea.

The consequences of the facts, observations and studies presented above can be summarized in the following:

(i) simple cause-and-effect approaches to sound patterns that individuate sound phenomena as fixed, organic properties, cannot capture the complex network of patterns that emerge in sound evolution within and across life spans,

(ii) there is no end-state to sound patterns (i.e. languages will not converge in the simplest, most natural or unmarked states such that non-directionality is tolerated),

(iii) the human brain is not isolated from society and culture so that the variables therein crucially interact with sound phenomena to yield patterns.

---

14 Indeed, in her recent work, Blevins (2017) offers an example for such an in-between type of change from vowel epenthesis into "stable" onset consonant clusters such as initial #TR sequences, which, for her, is a type of sound change that is not due to a purely language-internal development. Arguably, epenthesis in this case has a language-specific perceptual basis (e.g. Dupoux et al. 1999; Kabak and Idsardi 2007).

In conclusion, the distinction between natural and unnatural patterns falls short in capturing the *unity* in the way sound patterns manifest themselves in different synchronic and diachronic spheres of language use. In the remainder of this paper, I will propose a theoretical approach towards sound patterns that unifies the observations and claims that emerged in the discussion above.

7 A dynamic equational approach to sound patterns

How can we approach the dynamic nature of sound patterns within and across life spans? What is their utility in understanding language and linguistic behaviour? Just like internal and external variables, I propose that a given sound structure (e.g. a segment, a syllable, or a foot) should also be viewed as a variable (i.e. in the sense of a determinant or a factor), which is expected to be gradient and to co-vary with other variables. To explicate this better, I will build an analogy to an algebraic (polynomial)[15] equation that I believe to capture dynamism in sound patterns more vividly. Let us assume that a sound pattern is a *dynamic image* (as opposed to a static image) of a sound structure with a certain amount of frequency, probability, strength, and directionality, etc. that emerges as the sum of all other interacting factors. In this sense, a particular sound structure as a variable is essentially just an ordinary term in a mathematical equation, where multiple other variables interact with a group of coefficients, constants and exponents to yield a "solution" – a pattern in a given context with a certain probability and strength. The methodological utility of considering sound patterns as equations can become visible if we consider patterns as compact representations of implied directions, strengths, frequencies and associations pertaining to sound structures that determine, for example, their salience or the directionality of their influence in a given context. To illustrate hypothetically, a sound structure such as the vowel phoneme /i/ is perhaps uninteresting without observing what becomes of the segment in a particular context or at a given time, or without knowing the circumstances that give way to its particular realization. The vowel /i/ may be inserted with a certain frequency to break up illicit onset consonant clusters in a certain language because it could be that high vowels are the most

---

15 An anonymous reviewer points out that polynomial functions can be considered as an attractive illustration here due to their potential non-linearity and the fact that they provide a more straightforward means to demonstrate how different variables can be combined.

unmarked segments and that /i/ is the optimal phonetic solution to the specific phonotactic problem at hand. But it could also be that such an insertion may be stigmatized in the speech community, or that prosodic factors such as word stress or focus may work against that epenthetic vowel, which may consequently suppress its realization with a certain probability. Although, from the perspective of theory building, it is difficult to construe such a dynamic image to be part of the underlying representation of the structure in question, it is arguably part of the phonological knowledge of the speaker, which should be represented and accounted for. To take another example, the fact that stress regularly appears on the final syllable of words in a language yields a dynamic image, a pattern, again with a certain probability and associations (e.g. the right edge of the word), which obviously has consequences for phonological processing (see Kabak, Maniwa and Kazanina 2010). As such, the complex interactions of the potential factors that lead to the emergence of a given structure in a particular context, i.e. the *pattern* that outgrows from the structure, constitute the dynamic mental representations of that sound structure.

Furthermore, in its most neutral sense, an equation is a statement of an equality containing one or more variables although there is significant amount of variation in the way equations are interpreted in different languages and settings, such as its common metaphorical use to refer to complex situations.[16] The solution to an equation involves finding out which values of the variables make the equality true. The values assigned to each variable that satisfy the equality are referred to as solutions to the equation. My metaphoric rendering of the term *equation* in the present context stems from a necessity not only to reflect the complex relations among the many variables involved in the generation of a sound pattern, but also to promote the idea that sound patterns are best explored when all other variables that co-determine the shape, direction, magnitude and associations of a sound structure are treated as equally unknown. Essentially, the values we assign to these variables and their specific relations to each other will lead to an ultimate understanding of how and why patterns emerge, and what their implications are for language learning, processing and change.

The immediate consequence of this approach is that a sound pattern turns into a dynamic notion, which is unfixed and is only meaningful when it is viewed in association with other language-related (internal or external) variables. To illustrate, postvocalic /r/ is one of the most defining characteristics of English varieties, which however only yields a pattern in conjunction with the way it is

---

[16] The reader is referred to Marcus and Watt (2012) for a discussion of the historical origins of the term "equation" and its variable usage in different settings and languages.

modulated by linguistic (e.g. stress position, vowel quality) as well as non-linguistic factors such as age and task (see Himmel 2019 for a review).

Yet another meaning that I attach to equations is that we should treat all facets of language behaviour *equally* real and systematic. This resonates with the Dynamic Systems Theory (DST) approach to multilingualism and second-language acquisition (SLA), where languages (including second or additional languages) are viewed as complex and dynamic systems (Herdina and Jessen 2002; de Bot, Lowie and Verspoor 2007). An important property of dynamic systems is that they are in a constant flux. Language as a complex system therefore exhibits transience.

> Through iterations of simple procedures that are applied over and over again with the output of the preceding iteration as the input of the next, complexity in language emerges. (De Bot, Lowie and Verspoor 2007: 19)

The linguistic system as a whole and the various sub-systems that it generates is thus hypothesized to show a significant amount of variation. Undoubtedly, DST provides a useful framework to merge cognitive, social, and environmental factors in an attempt to discover how their interaction can lead to linguistic development in the case of second-language acquisition. Along similar lines, I extend the dynamism in patterns to *all* spheres and facets of language behaviour as being uniformly governed by the same set of phonetic, cognitive, and social constraints, although their weights and magnitude of influence may differ.[17] Just as predictable sound alternations – be they conditioned by structural or social factors – have indisputably been objects of inquiry in the field of Phonology (Labov 1972), sound variation and change due to language contact and multilingualism in whichever form this may be realized, e.g. loan-word phonology, first-language attrition, emergence of interlanguage grammars, creoles, and third-language acquisition, etc. also constitute sound patterns that are down to earth natural. Essentially, these different forms of contact are different reincarnations of a dynamic interaction of linguistic systems that are forced to interact with one another, each being subject to the same set of laws.

---

17 It should be noted that the weighting of constraints is a commonly established heuristic in stochastic grammars such as Maximum Entropy Grammar (e.g., Hayes and Wilson 2008) or Noisy Harmonic Grammar (NHG, Coetzee and Pater 2011). NHG allows, for instance, the weights of faithfulness constraints to be scaled by language external factors, thus is a promising way to capture the interaction between different types of factors in one and the same model to account for variation (e.g. Coetzee 2016; for an extension of NHG to second-language acquisition and first-language attrition of phonology, see Himmel 2019).

8 Conclusion

To conclude, the take-home message is that there is no "organic" realm for the study of sound patterns. That is, *all* sound systems, be they part of a developing grammar as in infant language acquisition, a form of interlanguage system as in second-language acquisition, or attrited or incomplete as it may be the case in bilingual language contact situations, are a logical consequence of laws that are natural to our existence. Unless they are fully static (e.g. highly grammaticalized or lexicalized), sound regularities are expected to be *gradient* and *variable* proportional to the degree of interaction between the variables that modulate them. Novel patterns emerging therein are thus expected to be not random, but require a joint effort of typologists and psycholinguists that may indeed ask very similar questions as to what linguistic patterns are, and how and why they come about. Dental fricatives, which I explored in this paper, are ordinary sound structures. They turn into instructive patterns for linguistic inquiry only in relation to their co-variance with various factors.

Discovering the unity and variation across linguistic patterns that stem from different domains and spheres of language behaviour remains to be one of the most instructive remits in linguistics. To that end, second-language acquisition and bilingualism provide us with methodological utilities to inspect sound patterns because patterns that emerge when sound systems meet are not only familiar to us from the native language of the speaker or listener, but are also reflective of the universal laws of phonetics and human cognition. At the crossroads of unity and variation across the languages of the world, studying second-language sound patterns therefore gives us a unique window of opportunity to understand the nature of linguistic processes and representations as well as the extent of human grammars. All of these shape "patterns" that linguists are fond of because, after all, patterns are manifestations of how we get to know what we know. For one thing, second-language acquisition is expected to mimic linguistic change through language contact, albeit – and perhaps luckily – observable within an individual's life span.

References

Altmann, Heidi & Barış Kabak. 2011. Second language phonology. In Nancy Kula, Bert Botma & Kuniya Nasukawa (eds.), *The Continuum companion to phonology*, 298–319. London: Continuum.

An, Lee Jung. 2015. Effects of native language on perception and neurophysiologic processing of English /r/ and /l/ by Native American, Korean, and Japanese Listeners. New York: City

University of New York, doctoral dissertation. (Available from CUNY Academic Works, http://academicworks.cuny.edu/gc_etds/838)

Best, Catherine T., Gerald McRoberts & N.M. Sithole. 1988. Examination of perceptual reorganization for non-native speech contrasts: Zulu click discrimination by English-speaking adults and infants. *Journal of Experimental Psychology* 14. 345–360.

Best, Catherine T. 1995. A direct realist view of cross-language speech perception: New directions in research and theory. In Winifred Strange (ed.), *Speech perception and linguistic experience: Issues in cross-language research*, 171–204. Baltimore, MD: York Press.

Blevins, Juliette. 2004. *Evolutionary phonology: The emergence of sound patterns*. Cambridge: Cambridge University Press.

Blevins, Juliette. 2006. New perspectives on English sound patterns: 'Natural' and 'unnatural' in evolutionary phonology. *Journal of English Linguistics* 34. 6–25.

Blevins, Juliette. 2017. Between natural and unnatural phonology: The case of cluster-splitting epenthesis. In Claire Bowern, Laurence Horn & Raffaella Zanuttini (eds.), *On looking into words (and beyond)*, 3–16. Berlin: Language Science Press.

Brown, Cynthia. 2000. The interrelation between speech perception and phonological acquisition from infant to adult. In John Archibald (ed.), *Second language acquisition and linguistic theory*, 4–63. Malden, MA: Blackwell.

Braun, Bettina, Tobias Galts & Barış Kabak. 2014. Lexical encoding of L2 tones: The role of L1 stress, pitch accent and intonation. *Second Language Research* 30 (3). 323–350.

Brannen, Kathleen J. 2011. *The perception and production of interdental fricatives in second language acquisition*. Montreal: McGill University, doctoral dissertation. (Available from http://digitool.library.mcgill.ca/webclient/StreamGate? folder_id=0&dvs= 1490795098907~157)

Britton, Derek. 2007. The dialectal origins of the language of Henry Machyn. In Christopher M. Cain & Geoffrey Russom (eds.), *Studies in the history of the English language III: Managing chaos: Strategies for identifying change in English*, 251–267. Berlin: Mouton de Gruyter.

Burnham, Denis K. 1986. Developmental loss of speech perception: Exposure to and experience with a first language. *Applied Psycholinguistics* 7. 207–239.

Bybee, Joan. 2000. The phonology of the lexicon; evidence from lexical diffusion. In Michael Barlow & Suzanne Kemmer (eds.), *Usage-based models of language*, 65–85. Stanford: CSLI.

Coetzee, Andries W. & Joe Pater. 2011. The place of variation in phonological theory. In John Goldsmith, Jason Riggle & Alan C.L. Yu (eds.), *The handbook of phonological theory*, 401–434. 2nd edn. Malden, MA: Wiley-Blackwell.

Coetzee, Andries W. 2016. A comprehensive model of phonological variation: Grammatical and nongrammatical factors in variable nasal place assimilation. *Phonology* 33. 211–246.

Cole, Ronald A. & William E. Cooper. 1975. Perception of voicing in English affricates and fricatives. *Journal of the Acoustical Society of America* 58. 1280–1287.

Cutler, Anne. 2015a. Lexical stress in English pronunciation. In Marnie Reed & John M. Levis (eds.), *The handbook of English pronunciation*, 106–124. Chichester: Wiley.

Cutler, Anne. 2015b. Representation of second language phonology. *Applied Psycholinguistics* 36 (1). 115–128.

De Bot, Kees, Wander Lowie & Marjolijn Verspoor. 2007. A Dynamic Systems Theory approach to second language acquisition. *Bilingualism: Language and Cognition* 10 (1). 7–21.

Dupoux, Emmanuel, Kazuhiko Kakehi, Yuki Hirose, Christophe Pallier & Jacques Mehler. 1999. Epenthetic vowels in Japanese: A perceptual illusion? *Journal of Experimental Psychology: Human Perception and Performance* 25. 1568–1578.

Eilers, Rebecca E. & Fred D. Minifie. 1975. Fricative discrimination in early infancy. *Journal of Speech and Hearing Research* 18. 158–167.

Flege, Jim E. 1995. Second language speech learning: Theory, findings, and problems. In Winifred Strange (ed.), *Speech perception and linguistic experience: Issues in cross-language research*, 233–273. Baltimore, MD: York Press.

Herdina, Philip & Ulrike Jessner. 2002. *A dynamic model of multilingualism. Perspectives of change in psycholinguistics*. Clevedon: Multilingual Matters.

Himmel, Marie-Christin. 2019. *Phonetic and phonological variability in the L1 and L2 of late bilinguals: The case of /r/ and /l/*. Würzburg: University of Würzburg, doctoral dissertation.

Harnsberger, James D. 2000. A cross-language study of the identification of non-native nasal consonants varying in place of articulation. *The Journal of the Acoustical Society of America* 108. 764–783.

Harnsberger, James D. 2001. On the relationship between identification and discrimination of non-native nasal contrasts. *The Journal of the Acoustical Society of America* 110. 489–503.

Hayes, Bruce, Robert Kirchner & Donka Steriade (eds.). 2004. *Phonetically based phonology*. Cambridge: Cambridge University Press.

Hayes, Bruce & Colin Wilson. 2008. A maximum entropy model of phonotactics and phonotactic learning. *Linguistic Inquiry* 39. 379–440.

Hogg, Richard. 1992. Phonology and morphology. In Richard Hogg (ed.), *The Cambridge history of the English language*. Vol I: *The beginnings to 1066*, 67–167. Cambridge: Cambridge University Press.

Ingram, David. 1978. The acquisition of fricatives and affricates in normal and linguistically deviant children. In Alfonos Caramazza & Edgar B. Zurif (eds.), *The acquisition and breakdown of language*, 63–85. Baltimore, MD: Johns Hopkins University Press.

Ingram, David, Lynda Christensen, Sharon Veach & Brandon Webster. 1980. The acquisition of word-initial fricatives and affricates in English by children between 2 and 6 years. In Grace H. Yeni-Komshian, James F. Kavanagh & Charles A. Ferguson (eds.), *Child phonology*. Vol. 1: 169–192. New York: Academic Press.

Ingram, John C. L. & See-Gyoon Park. 1998. Language, context, and speaker effects in the identification and discrimination of English /r/ and /l/ by Japanese and Korean listeners. *Journal of the Acoustical Society of America* 103. 1161–1174.

Ioup, Georgette & Steven H. Weinberger (eds.). 1987. *Interlanguage phonology: The acquisition of a second language sound system*. Cambridge, MA: Newbury House.

Iverson, Paul & Patricia K. Kuhl. 1995. Mapping the perceptual magnet effect for speech using signal detection theory and multidimensional scaling. *Journal of the Acoustical Society of America* 97. 553–562.

Iverson, Paul & Patricia K. Kuhl. 1996. Influences of phonetic identification and category goodness on American listeners' perception of /r/ and /l/. *Journal of the Acoustical Society of America* 99. 1130–1140.

Jongman, Allard. 1989. Duration of frication noise required for identification of English fricatives. *Journal of the Acoustical Society of America* 85. 1718–1725.

Jongman, Allard, Ratree Wayland & Serena Wong. 2000. Acoustic characteristics of English fricatives. *Journal of the Acoustical Society of America* 108. 1252–1263

Kabak, Barış & William J. Idsardi. 2007. Perceptual distortions in the adaptation of English consonant clusters: Syllable structure or consonantal contact constraints? *Language and Speech* 50 (1). 23–52.

Kabak, Barış & Kazumi Maniwa. 2007. L2 perception of English fricatives in clear and conversational speech: The role of phonetic similarity and L1 interference. *The Proceedings of the International Congress of Phonetic Sciences 2007*. 781–784.

Kabak, Barış, Kazumi Maniwa & Nina Kazanina. 2010. Listeners use vowel harmony and word-final stress to spot nonsense words: A study of Turkish and French. *Journal of Laboratory Phonology* 1. 207–224.

Labov, William. 1972. *Sociolinguistic patterns*. Philadelphia: University of Pennsylvania Press.

Labov, William. 1974. On the use of the present to explain the past. In Luigi Heilmann (ed.), *Proceedings of the eleventh International Conference of Linguists*. Vol. 2: 825–851. Bologna: Società editrice il Mulino.

Laker, Stephen. 2009. An explanation for the early phonemicisation of a voice contrast in English fricatives. *English Language and Linguistics* 13. 213–226.

Lavoie, Lisa. 2009. Testing consonant weakness phonetically. In Donka Minkova (ed.), *Phonological weakness in English: From Old to Present-Day English*, 29–44. Basingstoke: Palgrave Macmillan.

Maddieson, Ian. 2013. Presence of uncommon consonants. In Matthew S. Dryer & Martin Haspelmath (eds.), *The world atlas of language structures online*, chapter 19. Leipzig: Max Planck Institute for Evolutionary Anthropology. (https://wals.info/chapter 19)

Major, Roy C. 2001. *Foreign accent: The ontogeny and phylogeny of second language phonology*. Mahwah, NJ: Lawrence Erlbaum Associates.

Maniwa, Kazumi, Allard Jongman & Travis Wade. 2008. Perception of clear fricatives by normal-hearing and simulated hearing-impaired listeners. *Journal of the Acoustical Society of America* 123. 1114–1125.

Maniwa, Kazumi. 2007. *Acoustics and perception of clear fricatives*. Lawrence, KS: University of Kansas, Ph.D. dissertation.

Marcus, Solomon & Stephen M. Watt. 2012. What is an equation? In Andrei Voronkov (ed.), *Proceedings of the 2012 14th International Symposium on Symbolic and Numeric Algorithms for Scientific Computing, (SYNASC 2012)*, Sept 26–29 2012, 23–29. Timișoara: IEEE Computer Society.

Miller, George A. & Patricia A. Nicely. 1955. An analysis of perceptual confusions among some English consonants. *Journal of the Acoustical Society of America* 27. 338–352.

Minkova, Donka. 2011. Phonemically contrastive fricatives in Old English? *English Language and Linguistics* 15. 31–59.

Minkova, Donka. 2014. *A historical phonology of English*. Edinburgh: Edinburgh University Press.

Moyer, Alene. 2013. *Foreign accent: The phenomenon of non-native speech*. Cambridge: Cambridge University Press.

Pierrehumbert, Janet B. 2001. Exemplar dynamics: Word frequency, lenition, and contrast. In Joan Bybee & Paul Hopper (eds.), *Frequency and the emergence of linguistic structure*, 137–158. Amsterdam: John Benjamins.

Polka, Linda. 1991. Cross-language speech perception in adults: Phonemic, phonetic, and acoustic contributions. *Journal of the Acoustical Society of America* 89. 2961–2977.

Polka, Linda. 1992. Characterizing the influence of native experience on adult speech perception. *Perception & Psychophysics* 52. 37–52.

Prince, Alan & Paul Smolensky. 2004. *Optimality Theory: Constraint interaction in Generative Grammar*. Malden, MA: Blackwell.

Pruitt, John S. 1995. *The perception of Hindi dental and retroflex stop consonants by native speakers of Japanese and American English*. Tampa: University of South Florida, doctoral dissertation.

Schneider, Edgar W., Kate Burridge, Bernd Kortmann, Rajend Mesthrie & Clive Upton (eds.), 2004. *A handbook of varieties of English*. Vol. 1: *Phonology*. Berlin: Mouton de Gruyter.

Schreier, Daniel. 2003. *Isolation and language change: Contemporary and sociohistorical evidence from Tristan da Cunha English*. Basingstoke: Palgrave Macmillan.

Schreier, Daniel. 2005. *Consonant change in English worldwide: Synchrony meets diachrony*. Basingstoke: Palgrave McMillan.

Selkirk, Elisabeth. 1995. The prosodic structure of function words. In Jill Beckman, Laura Walsh Dickey & Suzanne Urbanczyk (eds.), *Papers in Optimality Theory*. (University of Massachusetts Occasional Papers 18), 439–469. Amherst, MA: GLSA.

Smith, Bridget. 2009. Dental fricatives and stops in Germanic: Deriving diachronic processes from synchronic variation. In Monique Dufresne, Fernand Dupuis & Etleva Vocaj (eds.), *Historical linguistics 2007. Selected Papers from the 18th International Conference on Historical Linguistics, Montreal, 6–11 August 2007*. (CILT 308), 19–36. Amsterdam: John Benjamins.

Trubetzkoy, Nikolai. 1969 [1939]. *Principles of Phonology*. [Translated by Christiane A. M. Baltaxe]. Berkeley, CA: University of California Press.

Wang, Marilyn D. & Robert C. Bilger. 1973. Consonant confusions in noise: A study of perceptual features. *Journal of the Acoustical Society of America* 54. 1248–1266.

Werker, Janet F., John H. Gilbert, Keith Humphrey & Richard C. Tees. 1981. Developmental aspects of cross-language speech perception. *Child Development* 52. 349–355.

Werker, Janet F. & Richard C. Tees. 1984. Phonemic and phonetic factors in adult cross-language speech perception. *Journal of the Acoustical Society of America* 75. 1866–1878.

Wolfram, Walt. 2004. The sociolinguistic construction of remnant dialects. In Carmen Fought (ed.), *Sociolinguistic variation: Critical reflections*, 84–106. Oxford: Oxford University Press.

Martin Zettersten
Learning by predicting: How predictive processing informs language development

Abstract: An increasingly influential attempt to provide a unified theory of the mind is grounded in the notion of prediction. On this account, our minds are prediction engines, continuously matching incoming input to top-down expectations. Higher-level predictions or expectations are generated by internal cognitive models at multiple hierarchical levels that jointly serve to minimize prediction error at lower levels in the information processing hierarchy. In language research, prediction has become an increasingly influential approach to understanding how language comprehension unfolds in real time. But how can predictive processing inform our understanding of how we come to learn language in the first place? In this review, I consider how prediction-based theories of the mind can aid in explaining how language development unfolds. First, I review research in perception and language on predictive processes and assess the degree to which they are found in infancy. Next, I consider how prediction-based mechanisms contribute to our understanding of learning, as well as the kinds of patterns that models grounded in prediction can learn. I review research on infants' prodigious ability to track novel patterns and relate these statistical learning abilities to prediction-based explanations. Finally, I sketch how prediction-based accounts fit within current theoretical positions and debates in the field of language development and suggest directions for future research into how predictive processes support language learning.

1 Introduction

At the heart of cognitive development lie two fundamental mysteries:[1] What is the nature of the infant mind, and how does an infant mind develop into an adult mind? The answers to these questions have historically diverged radically, with

---

1 This work was supported by NSF-GRFP DGE-1256259 to MZ. I am grateful to Jenny Saffran, Gary Lupyan, Viridiana Benitez, and the participants in the 2017 Kavli Summer Institute in Cognitive Neuroscience for helpful discussion.

Martin Zettersten, University of Wisconsin-Madison, Department of Psychology, Madison, WI 53706, USA, zettersten@wisc.edu

https://doi.org/10.1515/9783110596656-010

some suggesting the infant mind initially encounters the world as a "blooming, buzzing confusion" (James 1890: 488), while others suggest that the infant mind is from the beginning endowed with rich, adult-like cognitive structure and knowledge (Chomsky 1959, 1980). Modern approaches to cognitive development in general and language development in particular explore different solutions that lie somewhere between these two extremes, either by positing strong continuities in knowledge and ability between the infant and the adult mind (Spelke and Kinzler 2007; Baillargeon and Carey 2012; Dehaene-Lambertz and Spelke 2015) or by exploring how adult-like cognitive structure and knowledge can emerge despite apparently humble cognitive beginnings (Elman et al. 1996; McClelland et al. 2010; Smith and Thelen 2003). Yet the underlying questions are still fundamentally unresolved.

What makes the mystery of early cognition and development so difficult is that the most basic question in psychology itself remains elusive: how does the mind work? What are the general organizing principles underlying how we learn about and engage with the world? One increasingly influential proposal is grounded in the notion of prediction (Clark 2013; Hohwy 2014; Friston 2010; Bar 2009). In these accounts, the brain is conceptualized as "proactive", in that it "continuously generates predictions that anticipate the relevant future" (Bar 2009: 1235). On this view, our minds are essentially prediction engines, continuously deploying top-down expectations to anticipate what will occur next and reduce errors that occur when these expectations do not match incoming input.

The view of the mind as a prediction engine has particularly gained traction in the study of language processing (Kuperberg and Jaeger 2016; Huettig 2015; Pickering and Garrod 2007; Pickering and Clark 2014; Kutas, Federmaier and Urbach 2014). Prediction-based accounts of cognitive processing are intuitively appealing in the domain of language, because they make sense of what otherwise appears to be an almost impossible task: as each sentence unfolds, a language comprehender must parse a continuous stream of incoming fluctuations in sound into a coherent collection of phonemes, syllables, words, and sentences while decoding their meaning within mere fractions of a second. The only hope for the hearer would seem to involve bringing to bear a strong set of expectations about incoming linguistic elements in order to arrive at the speaker's intended message quickly.

Given its merit as key explanatory principle in the functioning of the mind, can prediction theory help us solve the fundamental questions in language development? In the following article, I explore what prediction can tell us about how infants develop and learn language. In the first part, I review evidence from sensory and language processing for prediction both in adults and in infants. Next, I investigate the relationship between prediction and learning, particularly how they relate to infants' powerful pattern-learning abilities. In the final section, I consider where prediction-based approaches fit within classic theoretical debates in language development.

2 Minds as the products of predicting brains: The (abridged) case for prediction

2.1 What is prediction?

Predictive processing accounts seek to explain the key mechanisms governing how the brain works. There are many different families of predictive processing accounts (Friston 2010; Rao and Ballard 1999; Hawkins and Blakeslee 2004; O'Reilly, Wyatte and Rohrlich 2014; Clark 2013; Hohwy 2014; Bar 2009; Kuperberg and Jaeger 2016), but they all share the basic idea that prediction is the key principle to how the brain – as well as the mind – functions. The goal of the brain is to predict incoming input – what will occur in the very next moment. In order to make these predictions, the brain develops a hierarchical model, with each level attempting to predict the input it receives from the level below. The overarching goal of the system is to reduce prediction error as best as possible. Operating under these constraints, the brain builds ever richer and more precise models of its environment, all in service of making efficient and accurate predictions.

Prediction-based accounts come in many flavors. One particularly influential account introduces the principle of predictive coding (Rao and Ballard 1999; Friston 2010; Clark 2013). What gives this account its name is how it reconceptualizes the nature of neural signals. Rather than representing information about the currently processed stimulus, neural signals encode prediction errors: discrepancies between predicted and actual input. These prediction errors then feed forward, becoming the input to the next level of cortical hierarchy. This level in turn attempts to predict incoming signals and passes error signals to the next level of the hierarchy, and so on. In this sense, neural responses are "signaling the news" (Clark 2015: 18), passing along unexplained or unpredicted information in the incoming signal.

In this paper, I will not seek to weigh different prediction accounts against one another, but instead use basic ideas shared among all of them to illuminate language development. I will focus in particular on how prediction-based accounts have begun to be applied to language processing and learning. There are two major ways in which language researchers have used the term prediction, in a broad sense and a narrower sense. In the broad sense, prediction refers to the idea that the mind is constantly engaged in a process of probabilistic inference. As Kuperberg and Jaeger (2016) put it in an influential review:

> ... prediction implies that, at any given time, we use high-level information within our representation of context to probabilistically infer upcoming information at this same higher-level representation. (Kuperberg and Jaeger 2016: 47)

On this view, the mind is continuously engaged in a cycle of updating its beliefs and expectations at multiple levels of its hierarchical representation of incoming language input.

A related, but somewhat more narrow sense focuses on the timing of activations in cognitive processing. Kutas, Federmaier and Urbach (2014) define prediction as encompassing any form of cognitive processing "involv[ing] the activation of or information about likely upcoming stimuli, prior to their receipt, that plays a causal role in stimulus processing" (Kutas, Federmaier and Urbach 2014: 649). Note that predictions, on this definition, can take many forms: they can be consciously or unconsciously generated, they may be explicit or implicit, they can be more fine-grained or more coarse-grained, and they can be generated at multiple levels. For instance, when processing a sentence such as *I love ...*, prediction may involve an expectation[2] for the specific word that will come next (*babies*, for instance), for a particular meaning to be expressed ('something cute or lovable'), for a particular grammatical structure (e.g. a noun phrase), for a particular phonetic feature (e.g. that the next word will begin with a voiced consonant), and so on.

One of the recurring difficulties in interpreting the psychological literature is determining what "counts" as evidence for prediction, in particular disentangling prediction effects from effects of integration or facilitation (Kutas, Federmaier and Urbach 2014; Kuperberg and Jaeger 2016). In language processing, for instance, if participants respond faster in a serial reading task to a more predictable word as compared to a less predictable word, this finding can often be explained in two ways: it could be that the previous linguistic context is allowing participants to begin activating information relevant to the word before encountering it (pre-activation) or it could be that the word, once encountered, is more easily integrated with the previous linguistic context (integration). In the broad

---

[2] While it may not always be practical to distinguish between predictive behaviour and the cognitive construct of prediction, I will generally use the terms "expectation" or "expectancy" to refer to the cognitive processing that generates a prediction, and "anticipation" to refer to behavioural responses that reflect these predictions (Haith, Hazan and Goodman 1988; Canfield et al. 1997).

sense of prediction in terms of probabilistic inference, this distinction collapses somewhat, since probabilistic expectations should lead to both pre-activating and integrating cognitive processes further down the hierarchical processing stream. In the following sections, I will review evidence that supports an explanation in terms of predictive processing, both in the broad sense of probabilistic inference and in the narrow sense of pre-activation, but this evidence will also be interwoven with a broader psychological literature, some of which could be interpreted as effects of pre-activation or as effects of integration. In all cases, I hope to show that adopting the lens of prediction leads to a fruitful interpretation of a wide variety of experimental evidence.

What makes predictive processing accounts of the brain so powerful is their ability to unify a vast amount of what we know about behaviour across a variety of domains, including classically perceptual processes such as vision and the higher-level cognitive processes involved in language comprehension. Why does the brain respond to the *absence* of expected stimuli? Why are we subject to "garden-path" effects in language processing? Why are infants drawn to regularities, and why do they seem to automatically detect patterns in their environment? In the following sections, I briefly review how prediction unifies these disparate phenomena, to provide an intuition as to why prediction is a useful unifying framework for understanding cognition. While by no means a comprehensive treatment of predictive processing accounts, the goal is to offer a glimpse of the explanatory breadth and depth of this family of accounts and to motivate why prediction is an attractive lens through which to consider the development of the mind.

2.2 Processing expected and unexpected sensory input

Some of the most compelling evidence that the brain is consistently developing expectations about what it will encounter in the world comes from studying what happens when predictions go wrong. A vast number of studies have studied cortical responses to unexpected events (e.g. den Ouden et al. 2009; Bendixen et al. 2014; Chennu et al. 2013; Wacongne et al. 2011). Of particular interest are cases in which an expected stimulus does not appear. A purely bottom-up account of cortical processing predicts that early sensory areas should show little or no activation when an expected stimulus is absent, since the sensory system is not receiving any bottom-up input from the world. Instead, studies that investigate neural response patterns in sensory cortex to withheld stimuli find very different results: early sensory areas show strong activation in the absence of bottom-up input when a sensory stimulus is expected. For instance, when processing temporal auditory sequences, sensory cortices show strong activation when expected items in the sequence are omitted, i.e. even in the absence of a stimulus (Wacongne et al. 2011; Wacongne, Changeux and Dehaene 2012). This has led researchers to reinterpret early cortical responses associated with unexpected events as signatures of prediction. For instance, Wacongne et al. (2012) offer a model of the mismatch negativity (MMN) – an event-related potential that registers roughly 100–200 ms after an infrequent unexpected auditory event[3] – as indexing a prediction violation, which explains why this characteristic signature is found in response to the omission of expected input.

A converse result is that cortical activity can disappear even in the presence of a stimulus, provided that the stimulus is highly predictable. For instance, in functional magnetic resonance imaging (fMRI) studies, cortical activity elicited by a stimulus is increasingly reduced each time that stimulus is repeated, a phenomenon known as repetition suppression (Grill-Spector, Henson and Martin 2006). Recent studies suggest that the reduction in cortical activity results from the stimulus becoming progressively more precisely predicted (Todorovic and de Lange 2012; Todorovic et al. 2011; Andics et al. 2013; Summerfield et al. 2011; Summerfield et al. 2008). The key finding is that repetition suppression is modulated by how predictable the repetition is: when a repetition is more frequent or predictable, cortical activity is suppressed more strongly, presumably reflecting more accurate and precise predictions (e.g. Summerfield et al. 2008).

Further evidence that the cortex is generating active predictions about incoming perceptual input comes from studies that show that participants' expectations bias early visual representations (Kok et al. 2013; Kok, Failing and de Lange 2014; Kok, Jehee and de Lange 2012). For instance, in one study (Kok et al. 2013), participants' expectations about the orientation of an upcoming visual stimulus was manipulated with an auditory cue played shortly before the visual input – different auditory cues systematically predicted specific orientations. The central result was that information about the orientation of the stimulus could be reconstructed from early visual areas prior to the actual onset of the visual stimulus, demonstrating that predictions about the upcoming visual input reshaped early visual representations. The picture emerging from these studies is that the

---

[3] Event-related potentials (ERPs) are changes in electrical brain activity time-locked to a specific sensory or cognitive event that are measured through electroencephalography (EEG) – an electrophysiological method used in cognitive neuroscience to detect electrical activity in the brain using electrodes placed on the scalp. ERPs can be described and analysed as waveforms with peaks and troughs that are thought to index different cognitive processes. The MMN is a particular ERP component that is typically found 100–200 ms after the onset of an infrequent or surprising ("oddball") element in a sequence of stimuli (usually a visual or an auditory sequence).

perceptual system rapidly generates predictions – in the sense of pre-activation – about upcoming sensory input.

2.3 A garden of forking paths in language processing

Contextual effects pervade language (Kuperberg and Jaeger 2016). For instance, a classic finding in language comprehension is the so-called "garden-path" phenomenon. If an ambiguous phrase such as (1) is resolved into a less frequent syntactic parse such as (2), as opposed to a more salient syntactic interpretation such as (3), this leads to processing difficulty that manifests as slower reading times or worse comprehension (MacDonald, Just and Carpenter 1992; Ferreira and Clifton Jr. 1986; Ferreira and Patson 2007).

(1) *The researcher expected to finish the paper ...*
(2) *... fell asleep.*
(3) *... by the end of the day.*

Another example is that people react faster to and spend less time processing predictable than unpredictable words across a number of paradigms (Stanovich and West 1979, McClelland and O'Regan 1981; Staub 2015).

A longstanding controversy in the field is whether these contextual effects are best understood as effects of prediction or as effects of integration (Kuperberg and Jaeger 2016; Kutas, Federmaier and Urbach 2014). Responses to garden-path sentences might be slower because the system must explain prediction error, or because the system must engage more cognitive resources to integrate the end of the sentence with the preceding linguistic context. However, recent studies have provided strong evidence that the language comprehension is consistently engaged in prediction.

First, relatively abstract linguistic expectations can modulate sensory processing in its earliest stages. For instance, expectations about the form of words belonging to different syntactic categories can affect visual processing at early stages when reading sentences (Dikker et al. 2010). Second, recent research has provided compelling evidence that words become pre-activated prior to their occurrence during language comprehension. A classic finding from electroencephalography (EEG) studies is that semantically unexpected words generate a characteristic neural response about 200–500 ms post word onset, the N400 (Kutas and Hillyard 1980).[4] Interestingly, the amplitude of the N400 correlates strongly with how expected a word is based on the preceding context (Kutas and Hillyard 1984; Kutas and Federmaier 2011). In one of the strongest demonstrations that the N400 reflects prediction, rather than integration, DeLong et al. (2005) presented participants with sentences which generated expectations for specific nouns (e.g. *The day was breezy so the boy went outside to fly* ...). Crucially, the form of the indefinite article preceding the noun (*a* or *an*) could be consistent or inconsistent with the expected noun (in this example *kite*), but both articles were equally easy to integrate with the preceding context. DeLong et al. found an N400 effect in response to the inconsistent articles (*an*), before encountering an unexpected noun (*airplane*), an effect that could only be found if participants were pre-activating the corresponding noun.[5] This study, along with many others using a similar design, show that – at least in some contexts – language comprehenders are generating expectations about upcoming words (Wicha et al. 2003; Wicha, Moreno and Kutas 2004; Van Berkum et al. 2005; Brothers, Swaab and Traxler 2015; Wicha, Moreno and Kutas 2003) and word classes (Szewczyk and Schriefers 2013). These results are key highlights within a converging literature suggesting that prediction – in the sense of generating expectations about upcoming language input – is integral to language processing (Kuperberg and Jaeger 2016).

3 Infants as predictors

There is a substantial amount of evidence that has accrued for the predictive processing account in adults. But how well does this account mesh with existing evidence in developmental research? Are babies' brains fruitfully construed as prediction engines? None other than Jean Piaget noted that "anticipatory function ... is to be found over and over again, at every level of the cognitive mechanisms and

---

[4] The N400 is a component of an event-related potential (ERP) – see also fn. 3 – first observed in response to semantically unexpected words. The name is derived from the fact that the component is associated with a negative deflection in the ERP waveform around 400 ms after the onset of an unexpected word/stimulus.

[5] There is currently some controversy surrounding the specific anticipatory results from Delong et al. (2005) following recent failures to replicate this result (Ito, Martin, and Nieuwland 2017; Nieuwland et al. 2018) and subsequent rebuttals from the original authors (DeLong, Urbach, and Kutas 2017a, 2017b). Regardless of the final determination regarding this particular result about pre-activation on the phonological level of words, there is a broad literature supporting evidence for the pre-activation of words more generally across different contexts and languages (see the studies cited in the text and Kuperberg and Jaeger 2016 for a review).

at the very heart of the most elementary habits, even of perception" (Piaget 1971: 19). In the following section, I invite the reader to see the developmental literature through the lens of prediction. Prediction casts new light on a vast number of phenomena spanning all domains of cognitive developmental research, including perception and language, and even the very methods cognitive development researchers employ to understand the infant mind.

3.1 Looking to predict: Infant looking behaviour

Some of the most important and influential insights in the field of infant development stem from measurements of infants' gaze and looking preferences (Hespos and Spelke 2004; Wynn 1992; Baillargeon, Spelke and Wasserman 1985; Baillargeon and Carey 2012; Gergely et al. 1995; Fantz 1961; 1963). Yet there is still substantial debate in the field as to what various behavioural measurements reflect in terms of infants' processing, leaving open the question of "what's in a look" (Aslin 2007). A particularly vexing question is why infants sometimes show novelty preferences, looking longer to events that are more surprising or less consistent with previous experience, but on other occasions show familiarity preferences, looking longer to events that are more expected or consistent with previous experience

The traditional view of infant looking times is that they are reactions to visual or auditory experience, that may be driven by exogenous factors (e.g. how salient a stimulus is) or endogenous factors (e.g. how robustly a stimulus is encoded in memory; Aslin 2014). More recently, infant looking behaviour has begun to be reconceptualized as a more active process (Kidd, Piantadosi and Aslin 2012; Kidd and Hayden 2015). On this model, infants' looking behaviour may reflect an active attempt to sample information from the environment. This perspective is consistent with a predictive processing account, whereby infants' looking behaviour should reflect a continuous process of collecting information about the visual environment to reduce uncertainty (Itti and Baldi 2009; Henderson 2017).

A key result in understanding infants' gaze behaviour as a more active process is the so-called *Goldilocks effect* (Kidd, Piantadosi and Aslin 2012, 2014). Both in the visual and in the auditory domain infants appear to prefer events that are "just right" in terms of their predictability: neither perfectly predictable nor completely predictable. For instance, in Kidd et al. (2012), infants viewed objects disappearing and reappearing behind a screen. By varying how predictable the pattern of reappearance of an object was from behind a particular screen, Kidd et al. obtained a measure of a given event's predictability or complexity. For example, if an object can appear from behind one of two screens, an extremely predictable event is one in which an object appears from behind screen 1 after having appeared repeatedly from screen 1 on previous events (e.g. creating the sequence 1–1–1–**1**). On the other end of the continuum, if an object suddenly appears from behind screen 2 after having only appeared from behind screen 1 (i.e. the sequence 1–1–1–**2**), then the event is much more surprising. An event can also lie in between these two extremes, creating a pattern that has some variability, but is also somewhat predictable (e.g. 1–2–1–**2**). Crucially, the predictability or complexity of a particular event within a pattern influenced how long infants would continue to watch the event sequence. Infants showed a U-curve preference, with infants looking longest to patterns that were neither too predictable nor too unpredictable (i.e. events such as 1–2–1–2 in the example above). This U-shaped curve held for every individual infant, not just for the group of participants overall (Piantadosi, Kidd and Aslin 2014).

These results lend themselves to an account of infant looking behaviour based on prediction: if infants organize their gaze behaviour around minimizing prediction error, their looking behaviour will depend on how successfully they can reduce prediction error for a given visual event. If an event is highly predictable, the visual system will rapidly learn to predict upcoming events and will move on from the current event sequence to make predictions about other aspects of the environment. If, on the other hand, the event is too unpredictable, the system will quickly plateau in its ability to reduce prediction error and therefore seek out other events where prediction error can be reduced more efficiently. When stimuli lie between these two extremes, they will hold infant gaze longer to the extent to which longer looking continues to reduce prediction error. Sequential patterns that will hold gaze the longest are those that lie at the "sweet-spot" of informativeness, where continuing to look improves infants' predictions regarding the task currently in focus (e.g. in the case of the Kidd et al. task, predicting where an object will appear next in a sequence).

This view of infant looking behaviour offers a principled way to predict when infants will show novelty or familiarity preferences. Looking preferences will ultimately depend on the relative effectiveness with which prediction error can be reduced for novel and familiar stimuli. This is consistent with the fact that infants often show novelty preferences in studies with lengthy habituation phases, e.g. in statistical learning studies (Saffran, Aslin and Newport 1996; Aslin 2014): infants in these studies have minimized prediction error to the familiar stimulus and thus spend more time looking at the novel stimulus to reduce prediction error. It also explains why infants often show familiarity preferences in studies in which infants listen to their native language without an extended habituation phase (Jusczyk and Aslin 1995). Fluent speech provides ample opportunity for an infant's processing system to attempt to reduce prediction error. Similarly, this explains why infants show a preference for speech rather than a variety of non-speech stimuli (Vouloumanos et al. 2010; Vouloumanos and Werker 2004) and for their native language rather than a non-native language (Moon, Cooper and Fifer 1993). Infants' predictive models of their auditory environment in these cases are more effective in reducing prediction error for speech, and particularly for their native tongue, which even in the absence of a habituation phase is a rich source of prediction error that can be productively reduced.

On a predictive processing account, looking times are more than simply measures of a learning outcome or an infant's ability to discriminate two different stimuli. Longer looking times reflect an active process of predicting upcoming stimuli and integrating information about the outcome of these predictions into a dynamically updated model of the world. This view of looking times brings into focus that these looking events are themselves learning events.

3.2 Vision and multimodal sensory processing

From a young age, infants rapidly build expectations and anticipate what will occur in their environment. When viewing a video in which engaging stimuli occur in one of two possible locations (either on the left or the right side of a screen), infants as young as 2–3 months of age begin to anticipate the onset of an upcoming visual stimulus, as measured by fixation shifts to the likely location of the stimulus that begin before an eye movement could be programmed in reaction to the onset of the stimulus (Canfield and Haith 1991; Haith, Hazan and Goodman 1988; Canfield et al. 1997). The extent to which infants show anticipatory shifts depends on the predictability of the sequence: by 3 months, infants will show more anticipatory shifts when a sequence is regular (e.g. when the visual stimulus alternates between two locations) than when it is irregular (e.g. when the next stimulus location cannot be predicted from the previous two or three events in the sequence; Canfield and Haith 1991). By 12 months of age, infants show regular anticipatory looks even to more probabilistic event sequences, and their anticipatory fixations become increasingly accurate (Romberg and Saffran 2013).

The fact that infants will reliably attempt to predict upcoming visual events is exploited by various research paradigms that measure infants' learning and knowledge in terms of anticipatory behaviour. In anticipatory eye movement paradigms, researchers expose infants to associations between a cue (e.g. an auditory cue such as a word) and a reinforcing event occurring in a particular location (e.g. a circle appearing on the left or on the right side of the screen). By 6 months, infants will regularly anticipate the reinforcing event's location on perceiving the cue. Researchers can then infer that infants distinguish two cues (e.g. the different words) if they differentially predict where the reinforcing stimulus will appear on the screen based on the specific cue presented. This paradigm has used infants' anticipatory behaviour to demonstrate the types of auditory categories 6-month-olds form (McMurray and Aslin 2004) or to investigate how 7-month-olds rapidly and flexibly learn to distinguish speech patterns (Kovács and Mehler 2009a, 2009b). Though not always considered in the context of predictive processing accounts of the mind, these studies reveal that infants form expectations about where visually interesting events will occur after only brief exposure to predictive cues, and actively orient their attention in anticipation of visual events.

While these studies show that infants anticipate *where* perceptual events will occur, it leaves open the question of whether infants predict *what* they will see, i.e. the perceptual content of the events themselves. Recent work investigating the neural processing in cross-modal priming events provides compelling evidence that by 6 months of age, infants' perceptual processing reflects sensory expectations (Emberson, Richards and Aslin 2015; Kouider et al. 2015). In one study, Emberson and colleagues (2015) measured changes in blood oxygenation using functional near-infrared spectroscopy (fNIRS) while 6-month-old infants watched movies in which novel sounds and visual stimuli were paired. After establishing the mutual predictability of sound and visual stimuli, infants saw a series of trials either consistent with the induced sensory expectation (i.e. in which both auditory and visual stimuli appeared; about 80% of the trials) or inconsistent, such that the expected visual stimulus was omitted (about 20% of trials). The striking finding was that infants' occipital cortex responded not only when a visual stimulus appeared, but also when an expected visual stimulus was omitted. Importantly, infants' occipital cortex did not show similar levels of activation in a control condition in which infants did not learn an association between visual and auditory stimuli. Infants' cortical responses in this condition reflected the type of incoming input: when an auditory stimulus was presented without a visual stimulus, temporal cortex, but not occipital cortex, showed changes in blood oxygenation level. Infants who had formed associations between auditory and visual stimuli, on the other hand, showed a strong occipital response to the exact same auditory stimulus. Infants' cortical responses do not simply reflect bottom-up visual input; instead, early cortical responses reflect in part what infants expect to see.

Infants also rapidly form expectations about patterns in upcoming auditory input. For instance, in studies measuring event-related potentials in infants, 3-month-old infants exposed to sequences of repeated auditory stimuli (such as the syllable *i*, i.e. *i–i–i–i*) will show an early cortical mismatch response analogous to the adult MMN when a novel auditory oddball (such as the syllable *a*) breaks this repetition (Dehaene-Lambertz and Dehaene 1994). Moreover, infants show a later cortical response (the late negative slow wave, NSW) depending on whether the sequence as a whole (regardless of local deviations) is expected (Basirat, Dehaene and Dehaene-Lambertz 2014). In light of predictive coding explanations of early mismatch responses in adults (Wacongne, Changeux and Dehaene 2012; Wacongne et al. 2011), these patterns of cortical responses suggest that infants form both local (about the next syllable in a sequence) and global (about the frequency of a sequence as a whole) predictions about auditory sequences (Basirat, Dehaene and Dehaene-Lambertz 2014).

Together, these results provide diverse evidence that infants' early visual and auditory processing is future-oriented: from an early age and across a variety of tasks, infants generate predictions about upcoming perceptual input and organize their behaviour in anticipation of expected perceptual events.

3.3 Language

By the latter half of their first year, infants have begun to form expectations about the words they commonly hear in their environment and their meanings (Bergelson and Swingley 2012). Forming word-like representations appears to change how infants process auditory sequences such as those used in the oddball paradigm (Dehaene-lambertz and Dehaene 1994), allowing infants to more rapidly process auditory information when new syllables are consistent with their linguistic knowledge. In one study, 12 and 24-month-old Finnish-speaking infants recognized an unexpected auditory syllable such as [kɑ] more quickly (as indexed by an earlier differential electrophysiological brain response) when it was in the context of the familiar word *kukka* (flower in Finnish) than as an isolated syllable (Ylinen et al. 2017), suggesting that infants use linguistic context to form expectations about upcoming syllables based on their knowledge about word forms.

Infants also begin to develop the ability to use their word knowledge to make predictions about their visual environment over the course of their second year of life. While there is little direct evidence that infants are able to make visual predictions based on the words they are hearing before around two years of age, there is intriguing evidence that infants' cortical processing shows early distinct ERP signatures in response to unexpected word-object pairings, similar to the N400 response to semantic violations found in adults. By 12 months of age, infants show an early negative event-related potential when viewing images of known objects and listening to familiar words (Friedrich and Friederici 2004, 2005). Differences between familiar words that match versus familiar words that do not match an image emerge between 100–250 ms post auditory stimulus onset. Given how rapidly these responses to mismatching words unfold, and the evidence from adults that ERP signatures of this kind may stem from errors in prediction, these ERP signatures may reflect violations of infants' expectations about the words they will hear in the context of a known object. Similar ERP effects emerge when exposing infants as young as 3–6 months to violations of newly learned word-object associations (Friedrich and Friederici 2011, 2017), suggesting that infants are rapidly forming expectations about how a novel word relates to the visual world.

Infants and children form linguistic expectations that they can use to recognize not only words presented in isolation, but also when processing sentences. Many key results come from the looking-while-listening paradigm, in which infants view a set of images (usually two, e.g. an image of a ball and an image of a shoe), one of which is subsequently labeled (*Where is the ball?*). The speed and accuracy with which children fixate the target image is a measure of children's language processing, particularly their ability to recognize the target noun. Using this paradigm, researchers have shown that, around the ages of 2 and 3 children can use verb semantics (Mani and Huettig 2012), grammatical gender (Lew-Williams and Fernald 2007), and even coarticulatory cues (Mahr et al. 2015) to recognize word meanings more quickly. Lew Williams and Fernald (2007) find that 3-year-old Spanish children shift looking towards the target image faster when the grammatical gender of the name of the target image and of the distractor image differ (i.e. the gender of the article disambiguates the two images). Mahr et al. (2015) showed that infants can use coarticulatory information present in the vowel of the word *the* to more efficiently process a subsequent noun. Including coarticulatory information about the upcoming noun leads to faster looking towards the target image as compared to a condition that does not include coarticulatory information.

These contextual effects in language processing are subject to the question raised earlier about whether facilitating effects are due to prediction or to more rapid integration of upcoming information. For some types of linguistic cues, however, in particular semantic cues, the results are more clear-cut that children can predict upcoming language input (Gambi, Pickering and Rabagliati 2016; Gambi et al. 2018; Mani and Huettig 2012). Mani and Huettig (2012) show that 2-year-olds use the meaning of verbs to anticipate which noun they will encounter. When hearing a verb such as *eat* (but not a neutral verb such as *see*), children begin looking toward a picture of a cake (rather than an image of an inedible object) even before the noun *cake* occurs. These predictions do not appear to rely merely on associations: Gambi et al. (2016) find that when hearing the verb *ride* in a sentence such as *Pingu will ride the horse*, 3–5-year-olds look predictively to an image of a probable patient such as horse. However, children do not look toward a picture of a cowboy, which is also strongly associated with the word *ride*, but unlikely to take the patient role in the sentence. Interestingly, the ability to predict upcoming nouns from verb semantics relates strongly to vocabulary knowledge in 3–10-year-old children (Borovsky, Elman and Fernald 2012; see also Mani and Huettig 2012).[6] Though most studies in language processing in infants show facilitative, rather than truly anticipatory effects of visual and linguistic cues, the general picture that emerges is that infants use an array of cues to form expectations about incoming linguistic input.

4 Prediction and learning

4.1 Learning in "bootstrap heaven"

Infants are actively predicting what will occur in the world around them, in particular how linguistic signals will unfold over time. But what are these predictions for? Is predicting simply a processing strategy adopted "for the moment", with errors in prediction hastily discarded to anticipate the next input? Or is prediction a processing principle that is more deeply connected to how a cognitive system develops? One of the most intriguing possibilities is that generating predictions is integrally connected to learning (Huettig 2015; Rabagliati, Gambi and Pickering 2016; O'Reilly, Wyatte and Rohrlich 2014).

On predictive processing accounts, learning is a natural consequence of the mechanisms by which we perceive the world (Clark 2015). When we experience an unexpected event, the discrepancies between top-down predictions and bottom-up input are fed forward through the processing system, essentially becoming error signals that catalyse learning. Prediction-generating models are revised and adjusted in response to these error signals, which changes the kinds of predictions we will make for future events. In other words, every perceptual event is simultaneously a learning event.

---

[6] Since these data are correlational, there is an interesting question as to the direction of the causal effect here (see also Reuter et al. 2018 for additional evidence with children between 12 and 24 months of age). Are children with larger vocabularies better able to predict upcoming input? Or are children who are better predictors more effective word learners? Or is there some third variable (e.g. some construct such as "general intelligence") that is the source of the relationship?

Viewing prediction error as a learning signal is particularly attractive for developmental theories because it reframes the developmental question of how infants are able to learn so much over the first years of life. Infants, on this view, are "learning in bootstrap heaven" (Clark 2015: 17). This picture of early cognitive development stands in clear contrast to a traditional view of infants as passive organisms faced with James's "blooming, buzzing confusion". Instead, by actively attempting to predict what will happen next, infants can exploit the dense information in their world as a rich source of error signal, which in turn catalyses learning. This point is made eloquently by O'Reilly and colleagues (2014):

> [P]redictive forms of learning are particularly compelling because they provide a ubiquitous source of learning signals: if you attempt to predict everything that happens next, then every single moment is a learning opportunity. This kind of pervasive learning can for example explain how an infant seems to magically acquire such a sophisticated understanding of the world, despite their seemingly inert overt behavior ... – they are becoming increasingly expert predictors of what they will see next, and as a result, developing increasingly sophisticated internal models of the world. (O'Reilly, Wyatte, and Rohrlich 2014: 3)

In the following sections, I explore the idea that prediction – in particular responding to prediction errors – is crucially involved in the learning process.

4.2 Prediction error and learning

The idea that prediction error is intimately connected with learning has enjoyed broad application in psychology. The key insight that many models grounded in prediction share is that prediction error is not only a *signal* to update expectations, it is also a *guide* as to how to update expectations. Prediction error communicates information about which expectations to adjust: for instance, by tracing an error backwards through a generative model, a model can adjust the specific expectations that contributed to the error. This is a key idea behind the training of neural networks, discussed below (Rumelhart, Hinton and Williams 1986). Prediction error also contains information about how strongly to adjust expectations, a key idea behind the Rescorla-Wagner model of association learning.

The Rescorla-Wagner model is one of the most productive applications in psychology of the idea that prediction error drives learning. In its basic form, the Rescorla-Wagner model provides a rule according to which a learner should adjust an association between two stimuli. Crucially, the model updates associations according to the difference between actual and expected outcomes, the prediction error. Originally proposed as a descriptive model of conditioning in animals, the model has seen broad application across psychology (Miller, Barnet and Grahame 1995), and has been successfully applied in explaining diverse phenomena in language development, such as how infants learn word meanings (Baayen et al. 2016) and inflectional morphology (Ramscar, Dye and McCauley 2013). Modern reinforcement learning models built on this basic prediction-based learning mechanism have been expanded to learning complex structured representations, that allow a system to e.g. map a spatial environment or make context-sensitive decisions in a multidimensional task (Niv et al. 2015; Gershman 2017; Daw 2012).

In a different modeling tradition, the notion of prediction error as a driver of learning has been extensively mined in research on neural networks (McClelland et al. 2010; Rumelhart and Todd 1993; McClelland and Rumelhart 1981; Rumelhart and McClelland 1986), particularly in models implementing backpropagation of error (Rumelhart et al. 1986). In the backpropagation algorithm, errors between model output and target are fed backward through the neural network model, with the weights between individual nodes in the network continuously adjusted (or "penalized") according to how much they contributed to the error (Hinton 2014; Rumelhart et al. 1986). Greater error means greater adjustment of the weights responsible for error, in the service of reducing future error. In other words, greater prediction error leads to larger revisions of the underlying model governing the system's predictions. Error in a model's output is both the signal to learn and the guide as to how to update the system.

While these modeling traditions show the power of prediction-error driven learning, to what extent is there support that our brains function in this manner? A long line of evidence has documented that prediction errors are encoded in the brain (e.g. Schultz and Dickinson 2000; Schultz, Dayan and Montague 1997; O'Doherty et al. 2004) and influence reward-seeking behavior (e.g. Pessiglione et al. 2006). Recent evidence suggests that prediction error plays a more general role in the neural implementation of learning. In one study, participants performed a visual-detection task in the presence of auditory distractors (den Ouden et al. 2009). Unbeknownst to the subjects, some auditory distractors were predictive of the presence or absence of the visual stimulus. Across the course of the experiment, the visual primary cortex (V1) showed progressively greater activation to unpredicted and progressively less activation to predicted visual stimuli, demonstrating learning of the dependency between predictive auditory distractors and visual targets. Moreover, participants showed greater response in V1 for unexpected stimuli even in the absence of a visual stimulus, indicating that the activations being measured were truly prediction error responses and not simply (more or less attenuated) bottom-up visual inputs. Most interestingly, the magnitude of prediction error predicted changes in visual-auditory connectivity. This indicates that prediction error not only encodes violations of expectation (i.e. surprise), but also plays a functional role in learning, reshaping connections to adapt to ongoing tasks.

4.3 Patterns from predictions: What recurrent neural networks can learn

An early illustration of the power of learning driven by prediction is Elman's (1990, 1991) recurrent neural network model of sentence processing. Elman set out to adapt neural network models to predict outcomes as they unfold over time. Elman constructed a simple three-layer neural network model with a deceptively simple tweak: he introduced a context layer that copies hidden unit activations from the previous learning event. The context layer subsequently provides inputs to the hidden units in the next learning event (see figure 10.1). This creates a recurrent processing loop that allows previous representations to influence current activations. The model was given a very simple task: given the current word, predict what word will come next. For this task, the model was fed the model a corpus of two- and three-word sentences with simple subject-verb and subject-verb-object structure. Although the model was not tasked with discovering syntactic structure or semantic relationships between words, the model's hidden units developed latent structure that represented complex grammatical and semantic relationships between words – since these prove helpful to the task of predicting what word will come next. For instance, the hidden units represented nouns differently from verbs, even though words were not tagged with this information. The model also represented semantically similar words as more similar to each other: for example, inanimate nouns were represented as more similar to each other than animate nouns. This latent structure in the hidden units of the model emerged simply as a consequence of the model attempting to minimize prediction error on the next word it encountered. The lesson from Elman's model is that relatively complex representations of the kind needed in language processing can emerge from a simple mechanism – predicting what word will come next (Elman 1990, 1991, 2004, 2009).

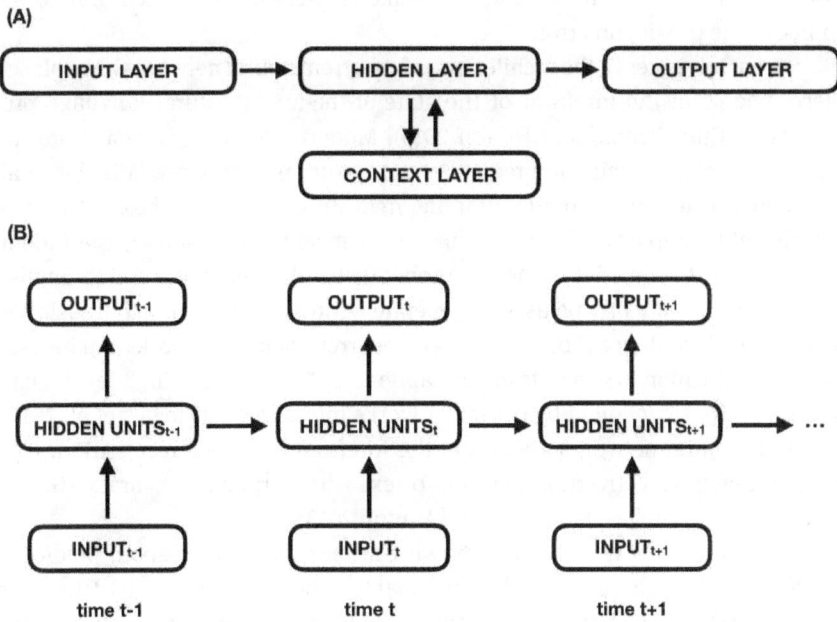

Fig. 10.1: Schematic representation of a simple recurrent network
(A) A simple representation of a three-layer recurrent neural network (Elman 1990). (B) The same recurrent network "unfolded" in time to illustrate its recurrent structure. At time t, the hidden layer receives input both from the input layer at time t and crucially from the hidden layer of the previous time step t-1.

The same logic has been fruitfully extended to show that recurrent neural networks can learn non-adjacent dependencies (Cleeremans and McClelland 1991; Willits 2013), sequence and event structure (Botvinick and Plaut 2004, 2006), abstract rule-like structure (Willits 2013), semantic categories from child-directed speech corpora (Huebner and Willits 2018), as well as perform more complex language comprehension and production tasks (Chang, Dell and Bock 2006; Chang 2002). For instance, Chang and colleagues (2006) developed a model of language processing that learned from a far greater set of training sentences than Elman's original model and was subsequently tested on both comprehension and production. The model succeeded at developing relatively complex abstract syntactic representations. While the architectural constraints underlying the model were far more complex than Elman's original model, the fundamental task of the model and the mechanism by which the model learned remained the same. The model incrementally predicted upcoming words, and when a prediction deviated from the target word, the weights of the model were updated according to the source of the prediction error.

Recent advances in the architecture of recurrent neural networks have placed these models at the forefront of the state-of-the-art in natural language processing (LeCun, Bengio and Hinton 2015). Modern recurrent networks are not only excellent at learning to predict the next word in a sequence (Mikolov et al. 2013), but the underlying representations yield structure that can be used to solve surprisingly complex tasks. For instance, in machine translation, the hidden units learned by a model trained to probabilistically predict upcoming English words can subsequently be used to generate a (probabilistic) French translation of the English sentence (Cho et al. 2014). Recurrent neural networks can be used in a similar fashion to generate image captions by "translating" high-level image representations generated by neural networks into phrases (Vinyals et al. 2015). Recurrent neural networks are also at the forefront of speech recognition, with modern networks converting audio into text with surprising accuracy (Graves and Jaitly 2014; Graves, Mohamed and Hinton 2013).

Some caution is warranted in drawing strong conclusions about predictive mechanisms from these successes, since many of these breakthroughs depend on specific modeling techniques, e.g. adjustments to the memory structure of the model that allow it to learn otherwise difficult long-term dependencies.[7] While the key idea of predicting an upcoming word in a sequence is preserved, the architecture and training methods are much more complex than in Elman's (1990) original simple architecture, and it is still unclear how these architectures relate to the cognitive architecture of the mind. More generally, how recurrent neural networks actually succeed at diverse tasks once trained – the computations they perform – is still something of a black box. However, recent research is beginning to investigate the underlying computations performed in recurrent neural networks (Sussillo and Barak 2013) and to demonstrate analogs to neural dynamics, e.g. in the prefrontal cortex (Mante et al. 2013). Recurrent predictive processing is rapidly being recognized not just as a framework for creating surprisingly powerful models capable of discovering complex patterns in visual and linguistic data, but a promising framework for understanding the architecture of the mind (Hunt and Hayden 2017).

---

[7] See http://colah.github.io/posts/2015-08-Understanding-LSTMs/ (last accessed June 23, 2018) for an accessible explanation – along with excellent visualizations – of some of the key features of these architectures.

5 Predicting patterns: Prediction and statistical learning

One of the most fruitful discoveries of the past twenty years has been uncovering the powerful statistical learning mechanisms that support pattern-learning from early infancy (see Aslin 2017, and Saffran and Kirkham 2018 for two recent reviews; see Romberg and Saffran 2010 for a review focusing on the role of statistical learning in language development). A seminal finding in statistical learning is that infants can use transitional probabilities to learn word boundaries in a continuous sequence of spoken syllables (Saffran, Aslin and Newport 1996; Aslin, Saffran and Newport 1998). In Saffran et al. (1996), 8-month-old infants heard a spoken sequence constructed from four nonsense words presented in random order, resulting in a continuous auditory stream, e.g. *pabikugolatudaropipabikudaropi...* Crucially, the auditory stream contained no acoustic or prosodic cues to word boundaries such as pauses or differences in stress. The only cues to word boundaries were the transitional probabilities between syllables (see figure 10.2 below): syllables within a word (e.g. *pabi*) had higher transitional probabilities (1.0, i.e. *pa* was always followed by *bi*) than syllables between words (0.33, i.e. *ku* was equally likely to be followed by the three beginning syllables *go*, *ti* or *da*, the first syllables in the three other words). After a brief exposure to the auditory stream, infants discriminated "part-words" (constructed from syllables that crossed word boundaries, e.g. *kugola*) from words (e.g. *pabiku*), showing that infants had learned to identify words within the sequence.

This study opened the door to a host of other findings showing that statistical learning mechanisms operate across a variety of domains, including learning visual regularities (Fiser and Aslin 2002; Kirkham, Slemmer and Johnson 2002), predicting actions and events (Baldwin et al. 2008; Endress and Wood 2011; Stahl et al. 2014), and learning in social contexts (Tummeltshammer et al. 2014; Wu et al. 2011). Statistical learning has also often come to be construed in a broad sense to describe learners' prodigious ability to extract statistical patterns from the input (e.g. Romberg and Saffran 2010). In this more general sense of sensitivity to statistical structure in the environment, statistical learning has been proposed as a method by which infants can learn many aspects of their language environment, including phonological categories (Maye, Werker and Gerken 2002) and learning to map words to their referents (Smith and Yu 2008). Moreover, statistical learning has been argued to aid in uncovering more complex relations such as dependencies between non-adjacent linguistic elements (Gómez 2002; Newport and Aslin 2004) and learning more abstract rule-like patterns (Marcus et al. 1999).

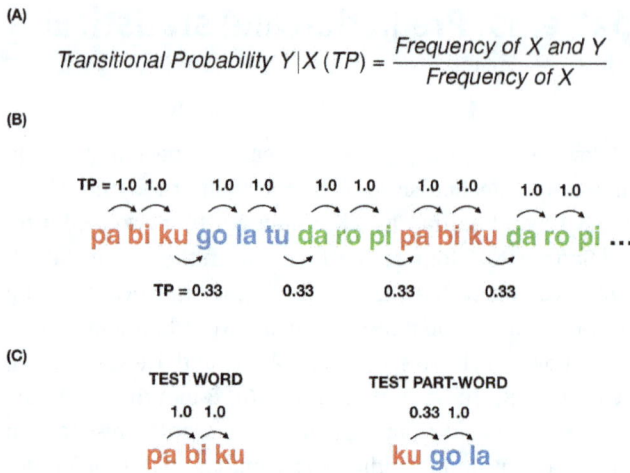

Fig. 10.2: Illustration of the design of Saffran et al. (1996)
(A) The formula for computing transitional probabilities. (B) An example of an auditory sequence of syllables from the experiment, including the transitional probability between syllables. The colours are used here only to illustrate the underlying structure of the auditory stimulus stream and do not reflect a difference in auditory cues. (C) Examples of the words and part-words used at test, along with their statistical structure.

One question that remains controversial is how statistical learning mechanisms operate. In the case of word segmentation, the initial proposal was that participants compute transitional probabilities between items in a sentence (Aslin 2017; Aslin, Saffran and Newport 1998; Saffran, Aslin and Newport 1996). This fits well with a prediction-based account of statistical learning, by which learners are developing probabilistic expectations about upcoming units. These expectations track the transitional evidence in the data over the course of exposure to a continuous stream of syllables. Parsimonious models of sequential pattern learning that are grounded in computing transitional probabilities can account for a diverse pattern of both behavioural and neuropsychological results (Meyniel, Maheu and Dehaene 2016). Other proposals suggest that learners instead extract larger chunks of syllables (French, Addyman and Mareschal 2011; Perruchet and Vinter 1998; see Frank, Goldwater, Griffiths and Tenenbaum 2010 for a comparison of different models) and focus on the role of memory structure in statistical learning (Thiessen 2017).

Regardless of the outcome of these specific debates, there is diverse evidence that statistical learning in general may be grounded in our ability to generate probabilistic expectations. For instance, adults use statistical learning to anticipate future events and elements in sequences (Misyak, Christiansen and Tomblin 2010; Dale, Duran and Morehead 2012). Moreover, recent evidence from intracranial recordings of neural assemblies suggests that adults generate forward-looking probabilistic predictions about likely upcoming syllables when processing known words (Leonard et al. 2015). Another intriguing line of evidence suggests that statistical learning helps to sharpen our predictions about expected inputs (see also Saffran and Kirkham 2018), with predictability helping to enhance the representation of items involved in a sequence (see e.g. Otsuka and Saiki 2016). For example, more predictable items in a visual sequence become easier to visually detect, suggesting that forming expectations about upcoming elements in a pattern has beneficial consequences for the representation of predictable elements (Barakat, Seitz and Shams 2013).

Amid these models, an important goal for future research will be to tease out the degree to which infants' statistical learning is grounded in developing probabilistic expectations – do infants anticipate upcoming units during statistical learning, and how does this relate to learning? One way to approach this question is to test predictions that follow from explanations grounded in prediction-based probability computation. One prediction of such models is that past transitional probabilities should be preserved such that they can influence later learning: for example, if the transitional probabilities between syllables at an early time point T1 change during a later learning experience at time point T2, the transitional probabilities from T1 should influence the degree to which infant learners adapt to the transitional probabilities at T2.[8]

A second prediction is that the global context within which a pattern is embedded can differentially constrain expectations about upcoming elements in a sequence. For instance, do infants develop higher-level expectations about the predictability of different contexts? In the statistical word segmentation task from Saffran et al. (1996), infants could encounter words with high within-word transitional probabilities in two different contexts: a context with little regularity based on transitional probabilities (i.e. a highly noisy syllable transition context) or a context with a more regular pattern for transitional probabilities (i.e. a more predictable syllable transition context). The degree to which infants make predictions that use transitional probabilities may depend on whether transitional probabilities yield useful predictions in the larger context, not just their

---

[8] One caveat here is that learners are exquisitely attuned to changes in context and are able to rapidly update their expectations to contextual changes (Qian, Jaeger, and Aslin 2016). Thus, care would need to be taken to maintain the continuity of the learning context from T1 to T2.

informativity within a particular word. This fits well with the notion that the particular information that enters into a learner's prediction is highly context-sensitive and may crucially depend on the expected utility of that information for making accurate predictions in the future (see Kuperberg and Jaeger 2016).

6 Language development theory in light of prediction

While prediction offers a unified perspective from which to view language development, it is important to recognize that it does not adjudicate many of the central theoretical debates in the field, in particular the classic dialogue between nativist and empiricist/constructivist theories regarding the origin of linguistic knowledge and the role of experience in language development (see e.g. Ambridge and Lieven 2011 for an overview over theoretical debates in different areas of language). Are the foundations of linguistic knowledge present from birth, or does linguistic knowledge emerge from language experience over the course of development? The prediction-based approaches sketched here appear to be largely agnostic about this question. Crucially, prediction-based theories may vary in how they explain the source of initial expectations that constrain prediction, the types of linguistic elements over which probabilistic expectations are computed and how expectations are updated, leaving room to interpret these mechanisms in terms of domain-general or domain-specific constraints. However, prediction offers a domain-general computational principle operating across language learning mechanisms.

The prediction-based framework may advance theoretical discussion by focusing on learning and inference over statistical patterns. Prediction-based approaches establish a deep continuity between language processing and learning (Chang, Dell and Bock 2006; Kuperberg and Jaeger 2016), helping to connect our understanding of how learners accumulate and exploit statistical knowledge about linguistic patterns (see e.g. MacWhinney and Bates 1987; Seidenberg and MacDonald 1999). A key aspect of prediction-based theories is their emphasis on the ubiquity of learning. Every moment of processing linguistic input is simultaneously providing information updating infants' probabilistic expectations about future language patterns they may encounter. One consequence of this view is that it reframes debates about the "impoverished" nature of leaners' language input (Laurence and Margolis 2001; Chomsky 1965) by demonstrating the vast amounts of probabilistic inferences that can be made from the language input a child experiences (e.g. Huebner and Willits 2018). The focus of the debate can thus be moved to the problem of constraining possible probabilistic inferences from the rich language data available to a prediction-driven learner (see also, e.g. Clark and Lappin 2011).

Prediction may also help to address specific problems in the language development literature, such as the *no-negative-evidence* problem (Bowerman 1988). Children sometimes overgeneralize in their use of lexical items, e.g. using an intransitive verb transitively in phrases such as *don't giggle me*. Children rarely – if ever – receive direct feedback that these usages are ungrammatical (negative evidence), presenting a puzzle as to how children successfully "unlearn" these ungrammatical forms. Prediction suggests that children might in some sense create negative evidence themselves during learning. If children are creating probabilistic expectations about linguistic structures (e.g. that *giggle* can be used transitively), but these expectations are violated (*giggle* is only used intransitively, and *tickle* is encountered in transitive situations), then children could update their expectations based on the internally generated prediction error (negative evidence). Chomsky himself recognized the potential importance of what he described as "indirect negative evidence" (see also Rabagliati et al. 2016 for discussion):

> [A] not unreasonable acquisition system can be devised with the operative principle that if certain structures or rules fail to be exemplified in relatively simple expressions, *where they would expect to be found*, then a (possibly marked) option is selected excluding them in the grammar, so that a kind of "negative evidence" can be available even without corrections, adverse reactions, etc. (Chomsky 1981: 9; emphasis mine)

Since we are constantly making predictions about upcoming input, we are generating, in some sense, our own evidence as we develop more refined linguistic expectations.

7 Conclusion

The task faced by young learners of language is daunting. Syllable after syllable unfolds at a rapid pace, with ambiguity at virtually all levels of processing. Prediction offers a framework for understanding how infants succeed at this task by exploiting patterns in their language environment to develop expectations about upcoming auditory signals and the meanings they communicate. There are many questions left unanswered in prediction-based theories in their current form – simply recognizing the predictive nature of infants' early language learning cannot explain language development in all of its complexity. However, the prediction framework offers a fruitful way of unifying many of the central insights in the field and opens up new avenues for exploring how infants come to uncover the patterns in language.

References

Ambridge, Ben & Elena V. M. Lieven. 2011. *Child language acquisition: Contrasting theoretical approaches*. Cambridge: Cambridge University Press.

Andics, Attila, Viktor Gal, Klara Vicsi, Gabor Rudas & Zoltan Vidnyanszky. 2013. FMRI repetition suppression for voices is modulated by stimulus expectations. *NeuroImage* 69. 277–283.

Aslin, Richard N. 2014. Infant learning: Historical, conceptual, and methodological challenges. *Infancy* 19 (1). 2–27.

Aslin, Richard N. 2017. Statistical learning: A powerful mechanism that operates by mere exposure. *Wiley Interdisciplinary Reviews: Cognitive Science* 8 (1–2). 1–7.

Aslin, Richard N., Jenny R. Saffran & Elissa L. Newport. 1998. Computation of conditional probability statistics by 8-month-old infants. *Psychological Science* 9 (4). 321–324.

Aslin, Richard N. 2007. What's in a look? *Developmental Science* 10 (1). 48–53.

Baayen, R. Harald, Cyrus Shaoul, Jon Willits & Michael Ramscar. 2016. Comprehension without segmentation: A proof of concept with naive discriminative learning. *Language, Cognition and Neuroscience* 31 (1). 106–128.

Baillargeon, Renée & Susan Carey. 2012. Core cognition and beyond: The acquisition of physical and numerical knowledge. In Sabina Pauen (ed.), *Early childhood development and later achievement*, 33–65. Cambridge: Cambridge University Press.

Baillargeon, Renée, Elizabeth S. Spelke & Stanley Wasserman. 1985. Object permanence in five-month-old infants. *Cognition* 20. 191–208.

Baldwin, Dare, Annika Andersson, Jenny Saffran & Meredith Meyer. 2008. Segmenting dynamic human action via statistical structure. *Cognition* 106 (3). 1382–1407.

Bar, Moshe. 2009. The proactive brain: Memory for predictions. *Philosophical Transactions of the Royal Society of London. Series B, Biological Sciences* 364 (1521). 1235–1243.

Barakat, Brandon K., Aaron R. Seitz & Ladan Shams. 2013. The effect of statistical learning on internal stimulus representations: Predictable items are enhanced even when not predicted. *Cognition* 129 (2). 205–211.

Basirat, Anahita, Stanislas Dehaene & Ghislaine Dehaene-Lambertz. 2014. A hierarchy of cortical responses to sequence violations in three-month-old infants. *Cognition* 132 (2). 137–150.

Bendixen, Alexandra, Mathias Scharinger, Antje Strauss & Jonas Obleser. 2014. Prediction in the service of comprehension: Modulated early brain responses to omitted speech segments. *Cortex* 53 (1). 9–26.

Bergelson, Elika & Daniel Swingley. 2012. At 6–9 months, human infants know the meanings of many common nouns. *Proceedings of the National Academy of Sciences of the United States of America* 109 (9). 3253–3258.

Berkum, Jos J. A. van, Colin M. Brown, Pienie Zwitserlood, Valesca Kooijman & Peter Hagoort. 2005. Anticipating upcoming words in discourse: Evidence from ERPs and reading times. *Journal of Experimental Psychology: Learning, Memory, and Cognition* 31 (3). 443–467.

Borovsky, Arielle, Jeffrey L. Elman & Anne Fernald. 2012. Knowing a lot for one's age: Vocabulary skill and not age is associated with anticipatory incremental sentence interpretation in children and adults. *Journal of Experimental Child Psychology* 112 (4). 417–436.

Botvinick, Matthew M & David C Plaut. 2004. Doing without schema hierarchies: A recurrent connectionist approach to normal and impaired routine sequential action. *Psychological Review* 111 (2). 395–429.

Botvinick, Matthew M & David C Plaut. 2006. Short-term memory for serial order: A recurrent neural network model. *Psychological Review* 113 (2). 201–33.

Bowerman, M. 1988. The "no negative evidence" problem: How do children avoid constructing an overly general grammar? In John A. Hawkins (ed.), *Explaining language universals*, 73–101. Oxford: Blackwell.

Brothers, Trevor, Tamara Y. Swaab & Matthew J. Traxler. 2015. Effects of prediction and contextual support on lexical processing: Prediction takes precedence. *Cognition* 136. 135–149.

Canfield, Richard L & Marshall M Haith. 1991. Young infants' visual expectations for symmetric and asymmetric stimulus sequences. *Developmental Psychology* 27 (2). 198–208.

Canfield, Richard L, Elliott G Smith, Michael P Brezsnyak, Kyle L Snow, Richard N Aslin, Marshall M Haith, Tara S Wass & Scott A Adler. 1997. Information processing through the first year of life: A longitudinal study using the visual expectation paradigm. *Monographs of the Society for Research in Child Development* 62 (2). 1–160.

Chang, Franklin. 2002. Symbolically speaking: A connectionist model of sentence production. *Cognitive Science* 26 (5). 609–651.

Chang, Franklin, Gary S Dell & Kathryn Bock. 2006. Becoming syntactic. *Psychological Review* 113 (2). 234–272.

Chennu, Srivas, Valdas Noreika, David Gueorguiev, Alejandro Blenkmann, Silvia Kochen, Agustín Ibáñez, Adrian M Owen & Tristan A Bekinschtein. 2013. Expectation and attention in hierarchical auditory prediction. *The Journal of Neuroscience* 33 (27). 11194–11205.

Cho, Kyunghyun, Bart van Merrienboer, Caglar Gulcehre, Dzmitry Bahdanau, Fethi Bougares, Holger Schwenk & Yoshua Bengio. 2014. Learning phrase representations using RNN encoder-decoder for statistical machine translation. In Alessandro Moschitti, Bo Pang & Walter Daelemans (eds.), *Proceedings of the 2014 Conference on Empirical Methods in Natural Language Processing*, 1724–1734. Stroudsburg, PA: Association for Computational Linguistics.

Chomsky, Noam. 1959. A review of B.F. Skinner's Verbal Behavior. *Language* 35 (1). 26–58.

Chomsky, Noam. 1965. *Aspects of a theory of syntax*. Cambridge, MA: MIT Press.

Chomsky, Noam. 1980. On cognitive structures and their development: A reply to Piaget. In Massimo Piatelli-Palmarini (ed.), *Language and learnability: The debate between Jean Piaget and Noam Chomsky*, 35–52. Cambridge, MA: Harvard University Press.

Chomsky, Noam. 1981. *Lectures on government and binding*. Dordrecht: Foris.

Clark, Alexander & Shalom Lappin. 2011. *Linguistic nativism and the poverty of the stimulus*. Chichester: Wiley-Blackwell.

Clark, Andy. 2013. Whatever next? Predictive brains, situated agents, and the future of cognitive science. *The Behavioral and Brain Sciences* 36 (3). 181–204.

Clark, Andy. 2015. *Surfing uncertainty: Prediction, action, and the embodied mind*. Oxford: Oxford University Press.

Cleeremans, Axel & JL McClelland. 1991. Learning the structure of event sequences. *Journal of Experimental Psychology* 120 (3). 235–253.

Dale, Rick, Nicholas D Duran & J Ryan Morehead. 2012. Prediction during statistical learning, and implications for the implicit/explicit divide. *Advances in Cognitive Psychology* 8 (2). 196–209.

Daw, Nathaniel D. 2012. Model-based reinforcement learning as cognitive search: Neurocomputational theories. In Peter M. Todd, Thomas T. Hills & Trevor W. Robbins (eds.), *Cognitive search: Evolution, algorithms, and the brain*, 195–208. Cambridge, MA: MIT Press.

Dehaene-Lambertz, Ghislaine & Elizabeth S. Spelke. 2015. The infancy of the human brain. *Neuron* 88 (1). 93–109.

Dehaene-Lambertz, Ghislaine & Stanislas Dehaene. 1994. Speed and cerebral correlates of syllable discrimination in infants. *Nature* 370 (6487). 292–295.

DeLong, Katherine A., Thomas P. Urbach & Marta Kutas. 2005. Probabilistic word pre-activation during language comprehension inferred from electrical brain activity. *Nature Neuroscience* 8 (8). 1117–1121.

DeLong, Katherine A., Thomas P. Urbach & Marta Kutas. 2017a. Is there *a* replication crisis? Perhaps. Is this *an* example? No: a commentary on Ito, Martin, and Nieuwland (2016). *Language, Cognition and Neuroscience* 32 (8). 966–973.

DeLong, Katherine A., Thomas P. Urbach & Marta Kutas. 2017b. Concerns with Nieuwland et al. multi-lab replication attempt (2017). (http://kutaslab.ucsd.edu/pdfs/FinalDUK17 Comment9LabStudy.pdf; accessed 24 June 2018)

Dikker, Suzanne, Hugh Rabagliati, Thomas A. Farmer & Liina Pylkkänen. 2010. Early occipital sensitivity to syntactic category is based on form typicality. *Psychological Science* 21 (5). 629–634.

Elman, Jeffrey L. 1990. Finding structure in time. *Cognitive Science* 14 (2). 179–211.

Elman, Jeffrey L. 1991. Distributed representation, simple recurrent networks, and grammatical structure. *Machine Learning* 7. 195–225.

Elman, Jeffrey L. 2004. An alternative view of the mental lexicon. *Trends in Cognitive Sciences* 8 (7). 301–306.

Elman, Jeffrey L. 2009. On the meaning of words and dinosaur bones: Lexical knowledge without a lexicon. *Cognitive Science* 33. 547–582.

Elman, Jeffrey L., Elizabeth A Bates, Mark H Johnson, Annette Karmiloff-Smith, Domenico Parisi & Kim Plunkett. 1996. *Rethinking innateness: A connectionist perspective on development*. Cambridge, MA: MIT Press.

Emberson, Lauren L., John E. Richards & Richard N. Aslin. 2015. Top-down modulation in the infant brain: Learning-induced expectations rapidly affect the sensory cortex at 6 months. *Proceedings of the National Academy of Sciences* 112 (31). 9585–9590.

Endress, Ansgar D. & Justin N. Wood. 2011. From movements to actions: Two mechanisms for learning action sequences. *Cognitive Psychology* 63 (3). 141–171.

Fantz, Robert L. 1961. The origin of form perception. *Scientific American* 204 (5). 66–72.

Fantz, Robert L. 1963. Pattern vision in newborn infants. *Science* 140 (3564). 296–297.

Ferreira, Fernanda & Charles Clifton, Jr. 1986. The independence of syntactic processing. *Journal of Memory and Language* 25. 348–368.

Ferreira, Fernanda & Nikole D. Patson. 2007. The 'good enough' approach to language comprehension. *Language and Linguistics Compass* 1 (1–2). 71–83.

Fiser, József & Richard N. Aslin. 2002. Statistical learning of higher-order temporal structure from visual shape sequences. *Journal of Experimental Psychology: Learning, Memory, and Cognition* 28 (3). 458–467.
Frank, Michael C., Sharon Goldwater, Thomas L. Griffiths & Joshua B. Tenenbaum. 2010. Modeling human performance in statistical word segmentation. *Cognition* 117 (2). 107–125.
French, Robert M., Caspar Addyman & Denis Mareschal. 2011. TRACX: A recognition-based connectionist framework for sequence segmentation and chunk extraction. *Psychological Review* 118 (4). 614–636.
Friedrich, Manuela & Angela D. Friederici. 2017. The origins of word learning: Brain responses of 3-month-olds indicate their rapid association of objects and words. *Developmental Science* 20 (2). e12357.
Friedrich, Manuela & Angela D. Friederici. 2004. N400-like semantic incongruity effect in 19-month-olds: Processing known words in picture contexts. *Journal of Cognitive Neuroscience* 16 (8). 1465–1477.
Friedrich, Manuela & Angela D. Friederici. 2005. Phonotactic knowledge and lexical-semantic processing in one-year-olds: Brain responses to words and nonsense words in picture contexts. *Journal of Cognitive Neuroscience* 17 (11). 1785–1802.
Friedrich, Manuela & Angela D. Friederici. 2011. Word learning in 6-month-olds: Fast encoding-weak retention. *Journal of Cognitive Neuroscience* 23 (11). 3228–3240.
Friston, Karl. 2010. The free-energy principle: a unified brain theory? *Nature Reviews Neuroscience* 11 (2). 127–138.
Gambi, Chiara, Fiona Gorrie, Martin J. Pickering & Hugh Rabagliati. 2018. The development of linguistic prediction: Predictions of sound and meaning in 2-to-5 year olds. *Journal of Experimental Child Psychology* 173. 351–370.
Gambi, Chiara, Martin J. Pickering & Hugh Rabagliati. 2016. Beyond associations: Sensitivity to structure in pre-schoolers' linguistic predictions. *Cognition* 157. 340–351.
Gergely, György, Zoltán Nádasdy, Gergely Csibra & Szilvia Bíró. 1995. Taking the intentional stance at 12 months of age. *Cognition* 56 (2). 165–193.
Gershman, Samuel J. 2017. Predicting the past, remembering the future. *Current Opinion in Behavioral Sciences* 17. 7–13.
Gómez, Rebecca L. 2002. Variability and detection of invariant structure. *Psychological Science* 13 (5). 431–436.
Graves, Alex & Navdeep Jaitly. 2014. Towards end-to-end speech recognition with recurrent neural networks. *JMLR Workshop and Conference Proceedings* 32 (1). 1764–1772.
Graves, Alex, Abdel-rahman Mohamed & Geoffrey Hinton. 2013. Speech recognition with deep recurrent neural networks. *Proceedings of the International Conference on Acoustics, Speech and Signal Processing*, 6645–6649.
Grill-Spector, Kalanit, Richard Henson & Alex Martin. 2006. Repetition and the brain: Neural models of stimulus-specific effects. *Trends in Cognitive Sciences* 10 (1). 14–23.
Haith, MM, C Hazan & GS Goodman. 1988. Expectation and anticipation of dynamic visual events by 3.5-month-old babies. *Child Development* 59 (2). 467–479.
Hawkins, Jeff & Sandra Blakeslee. 2004. *On intelligence*. New York: Henry Holt.
Henderson, John M. 2017. Gaze control as prediction. *Trends in Cognitive Sciences* 21 (1). 15–23.
Hespos, Susan J. & Elizabeth S. Spelke. 2004. Conceptual precursors to language. *Nature* 430 (6998). 453–456.
Hinton, Geoffrey. 2014. Where do features come from? *Cognitive Science* 38 (6). 1078–1101.
Hohwy, Jakob. 2014. *The predictive mind*. Oxford: Oxford University Press.

Huebner, Philip A. & Jon A. Willits. 2018. Structured semantic knowledge can emerge automatically from predicting word sequences in child-directed speech. *Frontiers in Psychology* 9. 1–18.

Huettig, Falk. 2015. Four central questions about prediction in language processing. *Brain Research* 1626. 118–135.

Hunt, Laurence T. & Benjamin Y. Hayden. 2017. A distributed, hierarchical and recurrent framework for reward-based choice. *Nature Reviews Neuroscience* 18 (3). 172–182.

Ito, Aine, Andrea E. Martin & Mante S. Nieuwland. 2017. How robust are prediction effects in language comprehension? Failure to replicate article-elicited N400 effects. *Language, Cognition and Neuroscience* 32 (8). 954–965.

Itti, Laurent & Pierre Baldi. 2009. Bayesian surprise attracts human attention. *Vision Research* 49 (10). 1295–1306.

James, William. 1890. *The principles of psychology*. Vol. 1. New York: Holt, Rinehart, and Winston.

Jusczyk, Peter W. & Richard N. Aslin. 1995. Infants' detection of the sound patterns of words in fluent speech. *Cognitive Psychology* 29. 1–23.

Kidd, Celeste & Benjamin Y Hayden. 2015. The psychology and neuroscience of curiosity. *Neuron* 88. 449–460.

Kidd, Celeste, Steven T. Piantadosi & Richard N. Aslin. 2014. The Goldilocks effect in infant auditory attention. *Child Development* 85 (5). 1795–1804.

Kidd, Celeste, Steven T. Piantadosi & Richard N. Aslin. 2012. The Goldilocks effect: Human infants allocate attention to visual sequences that are neither too simple nor too complex. *PLoS One* 7 (5). e36399.

Kirkham, Natasha Z., Jonathan A. Slemmer & Scott P. Johnson. 2002. Visual statistical learning in infancy: Evidence for a domain general learning mechanism. *Cognition* 83 (2). B35–B42.

Kok, Peter, Gijs J. Brouwer, Marcel A. J. van Gerven & Floris P. de Lange. 2013. Prior expectations bias sensory representations in visual cortex. *Journal of Neuroscience* 33 (41). 16275–16284.

Kok, Peter, Michel Failing & Floris P. de Lange. 2014. Prior expectations evoke stimulus templates in the primary visual cortex. *Journal of Cognitive Neuroscience* 26 (7). 1546–1554.

Kok, Peter, Janneke F. M. Jehee & Floris P. de Lange. 2012. Less Is more: Expectation sharpens representations in the primary visual cortex. *Neuron* 75 (2). 265–270.

Kouider, Sid, Bria Long, Lorna Le Stanc, Sylvain Charron, Anne-Caroline Fievet, Leonardo S. Barbosa & Sofie V. Gelskov. 2015. Neural dynamics of prediction and surprise in infants. *Nature Communications* 6. 8537.

Kovács, Agnes Melinda & Jacques Mehler. 2009a. Cognitive gains in 7-month-old bilingual infants. *Proceedings of the National Academy of Sciences* 106 (16). 6556–6560.

Kovács, Agnes Melinda & Jacques Mehler. 2009b. Flexible learning of multiple speech structures in bilingual infants. *Science* 325v(5940). 611–612.

Kuperberg, Gina R. & T. Florian Jaeger. 2016. What do we mean by prediction in language comprehension? *Language Cognition & Neuroscience* 31 (1). 32–59.

Kutas, Marta, Kara D. Federmaier & Thomas P. Urbach. 2014. The "negatives" and "positives" of prediction in language. In Michael Saunders Gazzaniga (ed.), *The cognitive neurosciences*, 649–656. 5th edn. Cambridge: MIT Press.

Kutas, Marta & Kara D. Federmeier. 2011. Thirty years and counting: Finding meaning in the N400 component of the event-related brain potential (ERP). *Annual Review of Psychology* 62. 621–647.

Kutas, Marta & Steven Hillyard. 1980. Reading senseless sentences: Brain potentials reflect semantic incongruity. *Science* 207 (4427). 203–205.
Kutas, Marta & Steven Hillyard. 1984. Brain potentials during reading reflect word expectancy and semantic association. *Nature* 307 (5947). 161–163.
Laurence, Stephen & Eric Margolis. 2001. The poverty of the stimulus argument. *The British Journal for the Philosophy of Science* 52. 217–276.
LeCun, Yann, Yoshua Bengio & Geoffrey Hinton. 2015. Deep learning. *Nature* 521. 436–444.
Leonard, Matthew K., Kristofer E. Bouchard, Claire Tang & Edward F. Chang. 2015. Dynamic encoding of speech sequence probability in human temporal cortex. *Journal of Neuroscience* 35 (18). 7203–7214.
Lew-Williams, Casey & Anne Fernald. 2007. Young children learning Spanish make rapid use of grammatical gender in spoken word recognition. *Psychological Science* 18 (3). 193–198.
MacDonald, Maryellen C., Marcel Adam Just & Patricia A. Carpenter. 1992. Working memory constraints on the processing of syntactic ambiguity. *Cognitive Psychology* 24 (1). 56–98.
MacWhinney, Brian & Elizabeth A. Bates. 1987. Competition, variation, and language learning. In Brian MacWhinney (ed.), *Mechanisms of language acquisition*, 157–194. Hillsdale: Lawrence Erlbaum.
Mahr, Tristan, Brianna T.M. McMillan, Jenny R. Saffran, Susan Ellis Weismer & Jan Edwards. 2015. Anticipatory coarticulation facilitates word recognition in toddlers. *Cognition* 142. 345–350.
Mani, Nivedita & Falk Huettig. 2012. Prediction during language processing is a piece of cake – but only for skilled producers. *Journal of Experimental Psychology: Human Perception and Performance* 38 (4). 843–847.
Mante, Valerio, David Sussillo, Krishna V. Shenoy & William T. Newsome. 2013. Context-dependent computation by recurrent dynamics in prefrontal cortex. *Nature* 503 (7474). 78–84.
Marcus, Gary F., Subramanijan Vijayan, S. Bandi Rao & Peter M. Vishton. 1999. Rule learning by seven-month-old infants. *Science* 283 (5398). 77–80.
Maye, Jessica, Janet F. Werker & Lou Ann Gerken. 2002. Infant sensitivity to distributional information can affect phonetic discrimination. *Cognition* 82 (3). B101–111.
McClelland, James L. & J. Kevin O'Regan. 1981. Expectations increase the benefit derived from parafoveal visual information in reading words aloud. *Journal of Experimental Psychology: Human Perception and Performance* 7 (3). 634–644.
McClelland, James L. & David E. Rumelhart. 1981. An interactive activation model of context effects in letter perception: Part 1. An account of basic findings. *Psychological Review* 88 (5). 375–407.
McClelland, James L., Matthew M. Botvinick, David C. Noelle, David C. Plaut, Timothy T. Rogers, Mark S. Seidenberg & Linda B. Smith. 2010. Letting structure emerge: Connectionist and dynamical systems approaches to cognition. *Trends in Cognitive Sciences* 14 (8). 348–356.
McMurray, Bob & Richard N. Aslin. 2004. Anticipatory eye movements reveal infants' auditory and visual categories. *Infancy* 6 (2). 203–229.
Meyniel, Florent, Maxime Maheu & Stanislas Dehaene. 2016. Human inferences about sequences: A minimal transition probability model. *PLoS Computational Biology* 12 (12). 1–27.
Mikolov, Tomas, Ilya Sutskever, Kai Chen, Greg Corrado & Jeffrey Dean. 2013. Distributed representations of words and phrases and their compositionality. *Proceedings of Advances in Neural Information Processing Systems* 26. 3111–3119.
Miller, Ralph R., Robert C. Barnet & Nicholas J. Grahame. 1995. Assessment of the Rescorla-Wagner model. *Psychological Bulletin* 117 (3). 363–386.

Misyak, Jennifer B., Morten H. Christiansen & J. Bruce Tomblin. 2010. Sequential expectations: The role of prediction-based learning in language. *Topics in Cognitive Science* 2 (1). 138–153.

Moon, Christine, Robin Panneton Cooper & William P. Fifer. 1993. Two-day-olds prefer their native language. *Infant Behavior and Development* 16 (4). 495–500.

Newport, Elissa L. & Richard N. Aslin. 2004. Learning at a distance I. Statistical learning of non-adjacent dependencies. *Cognitive Psychology* 48 (2). 127–162.

Nieuwland, Mante S., Stephen Politzer-Ahles, Evelien Heyselaar, Katrien Segaert, Emily Darley, Nina Kazanina, Sarah von Grebmer zu Wolfsthurn et al. 2018. Large-scale replication study reveals a limit on probabilistic prediction in language comprehension. *eLife* 7. e33468.

Niv, Yael, Reka Daniel, Andra Geana, Samuel J. Gershman, Yuang Chang Leong, Angela Radulescu & Robert C. Wilson. 2015. Reinforcement learning in multidimensional environments relies on attention mechanisms. *Journal of Neuroscience* 35 (21). 8145–8157.

O'Doherty, John, Peter Dayan, Johannes Schutlz, Ralf Deichmann, Karl J. Friston & Raymond J. Dolan. 2004. Dissociable roles of ventral and dorsal striatum in instrumental conditioning. *Science* 304 (5669). 452–454.

O'Reilly, Randall C., Dean Wyatte & John Rohrlich. 2014. Learning through time in the thalamo-cortical loops. *arXiv* 1407.3432. (https://arxiv.org/abs/ 1407.3432; accessed 24 June 2018)

Otsuka, Sachio & Jun Saiki. 2016. Gift from statistical learning: Visual statistical learning enhances memory for sequence elements and impairs memory for items that disrupt regularities. *Cognition* 147. 113–126.

Ouden, Hanneke E. M. den, Karl Friston, Nathaniel D. Daw, Anthony R. McIntosh & Klaas E. Stephan. 2009. A dual role for prediction error in associative learning. *Cerebral Cortex* 19 (5). 1175–1185.

Perruchet, Pierre & Annie Vinter. 1998. PARSER: A model for word segmentation. *Journal of Memory and Language* 39 (2). 246–263.

Pessiglione, Mathias, Ben Seymour, Guillaume Flandin, Raymond J. Dolan & Chris D. Frith. 2006. Dopamine-dependent prediction errors underpin reward-seeking behaviour in humans. *Nature* 442 (7106). 1042–1045.

Piaget, Jean. 1971. *Biology and knowledge*. Chicago: Chicago University Press.

Piantadosi, Steven T., Celeste Kidd & Richard Aslin. 2014. Rich analysis and rational models: Inferring individual behavior from infant looking data. *Developmental Science* 17 (3). 321–337.

Pickering, Martin J. & Andy Clark. 2014. Getting ahead: Forward models and their place in cognitive architecture. *Trends in Cognitive Sciences* 18 (9). 451–456.

Pickering, Martin J. & Simon Garrod. 2007. Do people use language production to make predictions during comprehension? *Trends in Cognitive Sciences* 11 (3). 105–110.

Qian, Ting, T. Florian Jaeger & Richard N. Aslin. 2016. Incremental implicit learning of bundles of statistical patterns. *Cognition* 157. 156–173.

Rabagliati, Hugh, Chiara Gambi & Martin J. Pickering. 2016. Learning to predict or predicting to learn? *Language, Cognition and Neuroscience* 31 (1). 94–105.

Ramscar, Michael, Melody Dye & Stewart M. McCauley. 2013. Error and expectation in language learning: The curious absence of mouses in adult speech. *Language* 89 (4). 760–793.

Rao, Rajesh P. N. & Dana H. Ballard. 1999. Predictive coding in the visual cortex: A functional interpretation of some extra-classical receptive-field effects. *Nature Neuroscience* 2 (1). 79–87.

Reuter, Tracy, Lauren Emberson, Alexa R. Romberg & Casey Lew-Williams. 2018. Individual differences in nonverbal prediction and vocabulary size in infancy. *Cognition* 176. 215–219.

Romberg, Alexa R. & Jenny R. Saffran. 2010. Statistical learning and language acquisition. *Wiley Interdisciplinary Reviews: Cognitive Science* 1 (6). 906–914.

Romberg, Alexa R. & Jenny R. Saffran. 2013. Expectancy learning from probabilistic input by infants. *Frontiers in Psychology* 3. 610.

Rumelhart, David E., Geoffrey E. Hinton & Ronald J. Williams. 1986. Learning representations by back-propagating errors. *Nature* 323 (6088). 533–536.

Rumelhart, David E. & James L. McClelland. 1986. On learning the past tense of English verbs. In David E. Rumelhart & James L. McClelland (eds.), *Parallel distributed processing*. Vol. 2: *Psychological and biological models*, 216–271. Cambridge: MA: MIT Press.

Rumelhart, David E. & Peter M. Todd. 1993. Learning and connectionist representations. In David E. Meyer & Sylvan Kornblum (eds.), *Attention and performance XIV: Synergies in experimental psychology, artificial intelligence, and cognitive neuroscience* 2, 3–30. Cambridge, MA: MIT Press.

Rumelhart, David E., Geoffrey E. Hinton & Ronald J. Williams. 1986. Learning internal representations by error propagation. In David E. Rumelhart, James L. McClelland & PDP Research Group (eds.), *Parallel distributed processing*. Vol. 1: *Foundations: explorations in the microstructure of cognition*, 318–362. Cambrigde, MA: MIT Press.

Saffran, Jenny R., Richard N. Aslin & Elissa L. Newport. 1996. Statistical learning by 8-month-old infants. *Science* 274 (5294). 1926–1928.

Saffran, Jenny R. & Natasha Z. Kirkham. 2018. Infant statistical learning. *Annual Review of Psychology* 69 (2). 1–23.

Schultz, Wolfram, Peter Dayan & P. Read Montague. 1997. A neural substrate of prediction and reward. *Science* 275 (5306). 1593–1599.

Schultz, Wolfram & Anthony Dickinson. 2000. Neuronal coding of prediction errors. *Annual Review of Neuroscience* 23. 473–500.

Seidenberg, Mark S. & Maryellen C. MacDonald. 1999. A probabilistic constraints approach to language acquisition and processing. *Cognitive Science* 23 (4). 569–588.

Smith, Linda B. & Esther Thelen. 2003. Development as a dynamic system. *Trends in Cognitive Sciences* 7 (8). 343–348.

Smith, Linda B. & Chen Yu. 2008. Infants rapidly learn word-referent mappings via cross-situational statistics. *Cognition* 106 (3). 1558–1568.

Spelke, Elizabeth S. & Katherine D. Kinzler. 2007. Core knowledge. *Developmental Science* 10 (1). 89–96.

Stahl, Aimee E., Alexa R. Romberg, Sarah Roseberry, Roberta Michnick Golinkoff & Kathryn Hirsh-Pasek. 2014. Infants segment continuous events using transitional probabilities. *Child Development* 85 (5). 1821–1826.

Stanovich, Keith E. & Richard F. West. 1979. Mechanisms of sentence context effects in reading: Automatic activation and conscious attention. *Memory & Cognition* 7 (2). 77–85.

Staub, Adrian. 2015. The effect of lexical predictability on eye movements in reading: Critical review and theoretical interpretation. *Language and Linguistics Compass* 9 (8). 311–327.

Summerfield, Christopher, Emily H. Trittschuh, Jim M. Monti, M. Marsel Mesulam & Tobias Egner. 2008. Neural repetition suppression reflects fulfilled perceptual expectations. *Nature Neuroscience* 11 (9). 1004–1006.

Summerfield, Christopher, Valentin Wyart, Vanessa Mareike Johnen & Vincent de Gardelle. 2011. Human scalp electroencephalography reveals that repetition suppression varies with expectation. *Frontiers in Human Neuroscience* 5 (July). 67.

Sussillo, David & Omri Barak. 2013. Opening the black box: Low-dimensional dynamics in high-dimensional recurrent neural networks. *Neural Computation* 25 (3). 626–649.

Szewczyk, Jakub M. & Herbert Schriefers. 2013. Prediction in language comprehension beyond specific words: An ERP study on sentence comprehension in Polish. *Journal of Memory and Language* 68 (4). 297–314.

Thiessen, Erik D. 2017. What's statistical about learning? Insights from modeling statistical learning as a set of memory processes. *Philosophical Transactions of the Royal Society B: Biological Sciences* 372 (1711). 20160056.

Todorovic, Ana, Freek van Ede, Eric Maris & Floris P. de Lange. 2011. Prior expectation mediates neural adaptation to repeated sounds in the auditory cortex: an MEG study. *The Journal of Neuroscience* 31 (25). 9118–9123.

Todorovic, Ana & Floris P. de Lange. 2012. Repetition suppression and expectation suppression are dissociable in time in early auditory evoked fields. *The Journal of Neuroscience* 32 (39). 13389–13395.

Tummeltshammer, Kristen Swan, Rachel Wu, David M. Sobel & Natasha Z. Kirkham. 2014. Infants track the reliability of potential informants. *Psychological Science* 25 (9). 1730–1738.

Vinyals, Oriol, Alexander Toshev, Samy Bengio & Dumitru Erhan. 2015. Show and tell: A neural image caption generator. *Proceedings of the IEEE Computer Society Conference on Computer Vision and Pattern Recognition*, 3156–3164.

Vouloumanos, Athena, Marc D. Hauser, Janet F. Werker & Alia Martin. 2010. The tuning of human neonates' preference for speech. *Child Development* 81 (2). 517–527.

Vouloumanos, Athena & Janet F. Werker. 2004. Tuned to the signal: the privileged status of speech for young infants. *Developmental Science* 7 (3). 270–276.

Wacongne, Catherine, Jean-Pierre Changeux & Stanislas Dehaene. 2012. A neuronal model of predictive coding accounting for the mismatch negativity. *Journal of Neuroscience* 32 (11). 3665–3678.

Wacongne, Catherine, Etienne Labyt, Virginie van Wassenhove, Tristan Bekinschtein, Lionel Naccache & Stanislas Dehaene. 2011. Evidence for a hierarchy of predictions and prediction errors in human cortex. *Proceedings of the National Academy of Sciences* 108 (51). 20754–20759.

Wicha, Nicole Y. Y., Elizabeth A. Bates, Eva M. Moreno & Marta Kutas. 2003. Potato not Pope: Human brain potentials to gender expectation and agreement in Spanish spoken sentences. *Neuroscience Letters* 346 (3). 165–168.

Wicha, Nicole Y. Y., Eva M. Moreno & Marta Kutas. 2003. Expecting gender: An event-related brain potential study on the role of grammatical gender in comprehending a line drawing within a written sentence in spanish. *Cortex* 39 (3). 483–508.

Wicha, Nicole Y. Y., Eva M. Moreno & Marta Kutas. 2004. Anticipating words and their gender: An event-related brain potential study of semantic integration, gender expectancy, and gender agreement in Spanish sentence reading. *Cognitive Neuroscience* 16 (7). 1272–1288.

Willits, Jon A. 2013. Learning nonadjacent dependencies in thought, language, and action: Not so hard after all ... *Proceedings of the 31st Annual Conference of the Cognitive Science Society*, 2570–2575. Austin, TX: Cognitive Science Society.

Wu, Rachel, Alison Gopnik, Daniel C Richardson & Natasha Z Kirkham. 2011. Infants learn about objects from statistics and people. *Developmental Psychology* 47 (5). 1220–1229.

Wynn, Karen. 1992. Addition and subtraction by human infants. *Nature* 358 (6389). 749–750.

Ylinen, Sari, Alexis Bosseler, Katja Junttila & Minna Huotilainen. 2017. Predictive coding accelerates word recognition and learning in the early stages of language development. *Developmental Science* 20 (6). e12472.

Index

abstraction 14ff., 30, 35ff.
accent 222, 244
actualization 135, 158, 168, 186, 189
addressee 63, 214
Akkadian 70
American English 101, 105, 107f., 115f., 118, 226, 237, 239, 245
analogization 131, 137, 149f., 161
analogy 21, 25, 37, 125, 128, 130f., 138, 158, 161, 188, 222, 244, 247, 266, 274
– analogical extension 131
– analogical reasoning 24f., 26, 130, 137, 149
– paradigmatic analogy 131
annotation 4, 99ff.
anthropological linguistics *see cultural linguistics*
architecture of the mind 274
argument structure 126, 201f.
assembly 5, 23, 128, 157, 159, 162ff., 169ff., 179, 181ff., 207, 210
attrition
– of language 223, 249f.
– of phonology 224, 227, 249
Auden, W. H. (Wystan Hugh) 58
auxiliary inversion 128, 197
auxiliary verbs 128, 158, 167ff., 172, 186ff., 197, 203, 212ff.

backpropagation 271
Bailey, Nathan 71, 73, 80, 83, 91
Bakhtin, Mikhail 48
Baret, John 73, 75
Barlement, Noel 75
Barthes, Roland 48f.
BE *going to* 158ff., 163f., 166ff., 174ff., 179ff., 183, 185ff.
Beardsley, Monroe C. 51
Benveniste, Emile 16
Berkeley, Lord Thomas 83
Bible 51f., 54
Bickerton, Derek 19f., 31
Blankaart, Steven 90

Bloomfield, Leonard 15
Blount, Thomas 71, 80, 90
Bondanella, Peter E. 53f., 56
Borges, Jorge Luis 53ff.
British English 100, 105ff., 115f., 118ff., 226, 245
Bullokar, John 75f., 79f., 89
Burdet, Robert 83, 87

Calepino, Ambrogio 74
categorization 11, 21f., 24f., 27, 29, 31f., 98, 121, 131, 157, 177ff., 181f., 188, 194ff., 198, 206, 224, 228, 230f., 234ff., 241, 244f., 261, 266, 273, 275
Cawdrey, Robert 75f., 79, 83, 89
Caxton, William 74f., 83, 86
Chambers, Ephraim 71, 83
change
– constructional 127, 138, 150, 158f., 174, 181, 187
– contact-induced 225, 249f.
– contextual 128f., 137, 277
– definition of 128f.
– diachronic 99, 101, 109, 126, 130f., 158, 160, 164, 176, 182, 185, 189, 221, 225, 230, 243, 248
– gradual 131, 135, 149, 161f., 188, 218
– phonological 221, 223ff., 230, 232, 234ff., 242, 245f.
– post-constructionalization constructional 164
– semantic 164, 174, 187
Chomsky, Noam 14, 18ff., 30f., 56, 256, 278f.
chunking 22, 85, 132, 149, 162
Cockeram, Henry 75f., 79f.
cognition 11, 20, 22
cognitive control network 85
cognitive development 256, 263, 270
cognitive linguistics 11, 13f., 20f., 23ff., 28f., 31f., 36ff., 59, 129, 136, 161, 164, 206, 227, 243, 249
cognitive model 255
cognitive neuroscience 260

cognitive processing 256, 258ff.
cognitive system 257, 259, 261, 264f., 269, 271, 279
Coles, Elisha 83, 90
colligation 4, 17, 27, 29, 35, 97ff., 103, 118ff.
collocates 61, 98, 103ff.
– first-order collocates 103f.
– second-order collocates 103f., 106ff.
collocation 3ff., 27, 29, 35, 60, 76, 80, 83ff., 127, 135ff., 164
collocation network 97, 99, 102ff., 118, 121
collostruction 27, 126
combinatory properties 12f., 15ff., 21, 23, 25f., 28, 32ff., 37
communication 14, 21, 27, 30ff., 39
communicative function 21, 32, 36
competence
– linguistic competence 14, 21f.
– literary competence 56
compositionality 5, 126, 148, 157, 160ff., 166, 173f., 185f., 188, 207, 218
conceptualization 11, 22, 25ff., 31
concordance data 47, 59f., 104, 108, 118
connectionism 164, 185, 188
connectivity 157, 185, 188, 271
construct 6, 129, 135, 149f., 193ff., 203, 208ff., 212ff.
construction 1f., 5f., 14, 17, 22ff., 37f., 101, 115, 126ff., 130f., 138, 147ff., 154, 157ff., 165f., 170, 172ff., 176, 179, 185ff., 194ff., 207, 213ff.
construction grammar (see also Sign-Based Construction Grammar) 1, 5f., 14, 24, 125f., 129, 148, 150, 157, 159, 162, 166, 172, 193ff., 217
constructionalization 5, 127, 129f., 135f., 141, 143, 149f., 154, 157ff., 163, 165, 171f., 174, 176f., 179, 185ff.
constructivism 1f., 11, 278
constructivist linguistics 21, 23, 36
context 13, 20, 22, 25, 27, 29, 31, 33, 37, 127ff., 134ff., 141f., 148ff., 159, 162, 164, 171, 173, 181, 183, 196, 202, 204f., 216f., 230, 234f., 245, 247f., 258, 261f., 266ff., 271f., 277
– critical 5, 130, 134, 136
– cultural 129, 224

– local 54, 61, 130
– situational 59
– systemic 127, 130, 144
– textual 61
conventionalization 6, 126ff., 135, 143, 145, 149f., 157f., 160, 167, 169, 176, 183, 187, 204
conversation analysis 32
conversational implicature 205
Cooper, Thomas 75f., 83, 88
Coote, Edmund 76, 79
corpus linguistics 11, 14, 17, 27ff., 38, 47, 49, 60, 99f., 188
– corpus-based approach 28, 36, 106
– corpus-driven approach 28f.
co-text 159, 162, 164
Cotgrave, Randle 75f., 78f., 82f., 89
Cowell, John 76
crossword puzzles 69f.
Culler, Jonathan D. 55
cultural linguistics 14, 32
culture 49, 63, 246

De Beaugrande, Robert 49
default mode network 84
Defoe, Benjamin Norton 82f., 91
degree modifier 132, 136ff., 144, 149, 201
deixis 186, 188, 215
Delta P 103f., 106, 109, 115, 117
dental fricatives 6, 221, 224, 226ff., 237ff., 245
deprofiling (see also profiling) 159, 164f., 169f., 173ff., 181ff.
Desainliens, Claude 77, 85
dialect 231f., 238, 242, 246
dialogicity 139, 143
dictionary 69, 71ff., 79ff., 83, 85, 93, 95, 147
– definitions 62
– view of meaning 63
– vs. encyclopaedia 60, 61
Diewald, Gabriele 127, 129
discourse 13f., 19f., 25f., 28, 30f., 36f., 49, 62f., 65, 98, 127, 139f., 142f., 203
discourse linguistics (see also pragmatics, text linguistics) 14, 32
discourse marker 125, 128, 139ff., 143f.
discourse-pragmatics 210, 214

discourse topic 49, 51, 55, 63, 65
domain-general 278
domain-specific 278
Doyle, Arthur Conan 55, 57
Dynamic Systems Theory 249
dynamicity 38f.

Early Modern English 70, 72f., 78, 133, 172
Eco, Umberto 47ff., 52ff., 57f., 60
egophoricity 177f., 183
Elman, Jeffrey 256, 269, 272ff.
Elyot, Sir Thomas 74ff., 83f., 87
emergence 127f., 131, 138, 149, 158f., 161f., 164f., 167, 169, 176, 179f., 183, 185ff., 221, 223f., 227, 230f., 236, 242f., 246ff., 256, 268f., 272, 278
Emergent Grammar 21, 131
empirical methods 48f., 65, 161, 170, 225, 227, 230f., 234
empiricism 2, 11, 278
encyclopaedia 60f., 71, 73
entrenchment (see also frequency) 6, 36f., 129, 142f., 149, 160f., 163, 174, 183, 185, 187ff., 218, 245
epistemic modality 140, 179, 200
epistemology 58, 221ff.
equation 247ff.
error signal 257, 269f.
event-related potential 260, 262, 267
Everett, Daniel 31, 39
exemplar 149f., 162f., 197, 206
existentialism 1f.
expectation 7
eye movement, anticipatory 265

Fairclough, Norman 49
falsifiability 48, 65
feature combination 12f., 15ff., 23ff., 32ff., 38
Fillmore, Charles J. 11, 14, 20, 22
fixed expression 85, 133f., 193, 196ff., 203, 207, 212, 217
Florio, John 72, 75, 83, 89
form–meaning pairings 24
Foucault, Michel 48, 64
frame semantics 22, 196, 207ff.
frames of reference 11, 38, 59

frequency 2, 4, 6, 27ff., 36f., 61, 63f., 108f., 115, 118, 126, 130, 132, 157, 159ff., 163ff., 170, 172, 175, 179f., 185, 187f., 221, 229, 233, 247, 267
Fried, Mirjam 126f., 130, 138, 149
Frye, Northrop 56
functional linguistics 20, 32
future tense 158, 164, 166f., 176f., 179, 186, 188
– absolute 177, 186
– imminent 158, 167, 174, 186, 189
– relative 167, 186

garden-path phenomenon 259, 261
generative linguistics 14, 18ff., 26, 28, 30
Genette, Gérard 48
genre conventions 56
Goldberg, Adele E. 14, 23f., 38, 126ff., 148f., 159ff., 169, 172, 174, 202, 218
Goldilocks effect 263
Googe, Barnabe 79
Google 69f., 84
Gouldman, Francis 90
gradualness 135f., 145, 158ff., 164, 185, 187f., 232, 243
grammatical replication 127, 129f., 135, 143, 149f., 227
grammaticalization 25, 127, 129f., 158, 161, 163f., 171, 250
grammaticalization episode 158, 171

Halle, Morris 16
Halliday, Michael A.K. 98f.
Hanks, Patrick 62
hard words (see also headword, lemma, lexical definition, word-entry) 74, 79f., 82, 84
Harris, John 71
headword (see also hard words, lemma, lexical definition, word-entry) 69ff., 73ff., 80ff., 84ff., 207, 217
Heine, Bernd 129, 164
Henry VIII 74f., 77
Herder, Johann Gottfried 13
hierarchical processing 255, 257ff.
hierarchy 12, 17f., 32, 194, 196, 213f., 217
Higden, Randulf 83, 86

historical corpora 100, 171, 188
historical data 125, 128, 131
historical linguistics 100f., 128, 131, 164
Hjelmslev, Louis 16
Hockett, Charles F. 17f., 20, 39
Hoey, Michael 97
Hollyband, Claude 77f., 80
Holmes, Sherlock 53, 55ff.
Holyoake, Francis 76
Holyoake, Thomas 75
Hornby, Albert S. 16f.
Howlet, Richard 75f., 78f.
Hüllen, Werner 49
Humboldt, Wilhelm von 13

idiolect 18
idiom 22, 24, 35, 76f., 80, 82, 85, 129, 162, 195ff., 202f., 206ff., 216f.
– extragrammatical 130
idiom principle 17, 22
idiomaticity continuum 6, 193, 197f., 202, 212
innateness hypothesis *(see also nativism)* 19ff., 30f., 129
innovation 128f., 145, 148f., 169, 187
intentional fallacy 51
intentionality 47, 51, 167, 170, 185
interactional linguistics 32
International Corpus of English 100, 139, 141
intertextuality 3f., 47ff., 52ff., 60, 62, 65
intonation 85, 244

Jackendoff, Ray 20
Jakobson, Roman 16
Johnson, Samuel 72f., 81ff., 91

Kersey, John the younger 82f., 90
key semantic field 51, 61
knowledge 70, 72, 74, 130f., 140, 144, 148, 157, 160, 169, 222f., 248, 256, 265, 267, 269, 278
– literary and cultural 50, 53, 55f., 58, 60, 63, 65
– of language 13, 23, 27
Kristeva, Julia 48

Labov, William 128, 131, 223, 249

labyrinth 51, 54, 60, 69, 82ff., 90f.
#LancsBox 97, 99, 102f., 105, 107f., 115, 118, 121
Langacker, Ronald W. 14, 20, 23ff., 160, 162, 164, 169f.
language acquisition 17, 21ff., 28f., 38
– first-language acquisition 150, 162f., 186, 223, 279
– second-language acquisition 223f., 235, 237f., 244, 246, 249f.
language as a tool 21, 31
language change 5, 25, 29, 34f., 37, 39
language comprehension 255, 259, 261, 273
language contact 25, 221, 225, 227, 231, 240, 243, 245f., 249f.
language evolution 32
language learning 1, 7, 15, 17, 126, 161, 195, 221, 223f., 227, 229, 236, 244, 248, 255ff., 264ff., 269ff.
language norm 34, 38
language processing 30
language system *(see also langue)* 121, 127, 129f., 149, 163, 218, 222f., 226f., 232, 235, 240, 244ff., 249f.
language use 13f., 19, 23, 27, 38f., 127, 129, 132, 195, 221, 247
language, world, and mind 47ff., 52, 58, 64f., 69, 73, 169, 223, 255ff., 263, 266, 274, 281
language-external factors 221, 223ff., 227, 230, 235, 243ff., 247ff.
language-internal factors 221, 223ff., 227, 230, 232, 235, 243ff.
langue (see also language system) 14ff., 23f.
Late Modern English 133, 225, 228, 230
lemma *(see also hard words, headword, lexical definition, word-entry)* 50, 59, 63f., 69f., 76, 79f.
lexical definition *(see also hard words, headword, lemma, word-entry)* 71ff., 76ff., 83ff.
lexical family 73
lexicalist approach 163, 196ff., 203, 207, 212, 217f.
lexicalization 250
lexicogrammar 4, 97ff., 102ff., 108ff., 118, 121

lexicographer 63, 69, 71, 74, 77, 84
lexicons of Early Modern English 70f., 73
Lily, William 70
linguistic relativity 31
linguistic sign 15
listeme 6
looking time measure 263, 265
looking-while-listening paradigm 268

machine translation 274
magic number 85
Martin, Benjamin 81f.
meaning
– constructional 125f., 128ff., 132f., 135ff., 141ff., 150, 157f., 160f., 164ff., 170, 172, 174, 185, 188
– pattern meaning 127, 149
– sentence meaning 126
meaning (unit of) 69f., 72f., 97f., 222, 256, 258, 267f., 271, 279
memory 78, 85, 160, 223, 263, 274, 276
mental grammar *(see also Universal Grammar)* 13f., 18ff., 30
mental representation 128, 222, 224, 248
metonymization 25f.
metonymy 12, 26
Michaelis, Laura A. 125ff., 132, 144, 148, 150, 157, 163
Middle English 72, 133, 135, 140, 145, 150, 231, 235
Minsheu, John 75, 79f.
model of the mismatch negativity (MMN) 260, 267
Mulcaster, Richard 76
multimodality 33ff.
multi-word expression 218

N400 261f., 267
names 69f., 77, 87f.
nativism *(see also innateness hypothesis)* 20f.
neoanalysis *(see also reanalysis)* 5, 135ff., 144, 158, 161f., 168, 186, 188
neural assemblies 277
neural network 164, 270f., 274
– recurrent 272ff.
neural signal 257

neuroscience *(see also cognitive neuroscience)* 69, 85
no-negative-evidence problem 279

objectivity 48, 58, 64f.
Occam's Razor 53
Old English 72, 77, 133ff., 145, 201, 225, 231f., 234, 236
ontology 57f., 221f.
order 14, 16, 19, 26f., 29, 31, 38, 48, 52, 63ff.
over-interpretation 54
Oxford English Dictionary Online 69, 84

Palsgrave, John 74, 77
paradigm 86, 98f., 135, 150, 195, 234, 261, 265, 267f.
paradigmatization 125, 130
parody 50f., 55, 58
parole (see also utterance, level of) 14, 16ff., 23f.
passive construction 137, 169f., 179ff., 185, 200, 216, 218
pattern
– as concept 1ff., 5, 7, 11ff., 15f., 21, 25f., 29, 38, 128, 149, 162, 193, 199, 212, 250, 255, 264
– as term 11, 13, 15ff., 23f., 26f., 38, 125ff., 150, 196
– combinatoric 196
– communicative 1
– configurational 144
– connectivity pattern 157
– dynamic 249
– false 64f.
– grammatical 127
– intertextual 47, 49, 51, 57
– lexical 69f., 75f., 79ff., 159, 197f.
– lexicogrammatical 47, 60, 99, 102f., 105, 109f., 119, 172, 195, 201
– lexicographical meta-pattern 75
– linguistic 1, 22, 34f. 85, 125f., 129, 143, 160, 194, 197f., 250, 278, 280
– linguistically relevant 1, 34f.
– local 189
– morphosyntactic 147
– neural response pattern 259
– novel 255

- of communicative behaviour 30ff., 38
- of usage 4
- on the mind 4, 6, 14, 23f., 26ff., 28f., 36, 39, 78
- pattern detection 264, 274
- pattern development 131, 135f., 148f., 151
- pattern-finding skills 21, 23f., 36, 39, 259, 279
- pattern-learning 257, 275f.
- pattern matching 161
- pattern recognition 2ff., 48
- pattern storage 160
- phrasal 126, 150, 163, 195, 197, 212, 217
- predictability of 263, 266, 272, 277
- schematic 157
- semantic 48f., 54, 63f.
- sentence pattern 126, 150, 198, 201, 212, 215
- sound pattern 6, 13, 15, 18, 36, 221ff., 227f., 230, 243ff.
- speech pattern 266
- statistical 275, 278
- transitional 130, 149f.
- vs. construction 150, 159, 176, 183, 197, 217
- vs. rule 275
- word-formation pattern 125, 128, 145, 148
Pattern Grammar 28, 128
pattern-based morphology 145
Peirce, Charles Sanders 49, 51, 55, 60
perception 20f., 26f., 36, 255, 259ff., 263, 266f., 269
performance 14, 18, 20, 22, 24, 26, 28, 32, 35, 236, 239ff., 244
Petré, Peter 125, 127f., 135, 142, 146, 194f., 200, 218
Phillips, Edward 90
phonemization 232, 234
phonetic experience 235, 237ff., 241, 244
phonology, second-language 224, 227, 235f., 238, 244
phraseologism 27, 29
Piaget, Jean 31f., 262f.
Pidgin and Creole Studies 20
pidgin language 20
Poe, Edgar Allan 56
polarity items 98, 134, 197, 203ff., 209

pragmatic implicature 135
pragmatic marker 139f., 143f.
pragmatics *(see also discourse linguistics, stylistics, text linguistics)* 14, 20, 25, 30, 32f., 62, 102, 110, 145, 163, 170, 186, 195, 222
prediction 255ff., 276ff.
prediction error 255, 257, 261, 264, 270ff., 274, 279
predictive coding 257, 267
predictive processing 7
preferential looking 264
- familiarity preferences 263f.
- novelty preferences 263f.
priming 22, 266
productivity 37, 144f., 147f., 158, 195, 198, 201f., 212
profile shift 169f., 177
profiling *(see also deprofiling)* 169f., 173, 175f.
prosody 232
psycholinguistics 29, 32, 39, 99, 160, 224, 230, 237, 243, 250

quantification 27, 177, 218, 222, 237
quantifier 135, 144, 199
quotation 47, 50, 52ff., 74, 81ff., 85

Rastell, John 77
Rastell, John and William 76
reanalysis *(see also neoanalysis)* 135
recurrence 127, 144, 148, 150, 159, 162f., 165, 193, 196, 222ff., 272ff.
recursion 19
recursivity 210
register 25, 29f., 35
register variation 100
repetition 12, 13, 15, 17f., 21, 23ff., 33ff., 37f., 47ff., 69, 79, 108, 240, 260, 267
repetition suppression 260
Rescorla-Wagner model 270
Rider, John 75f., 80, 89
Riffaterre, Michel 48
ritual 33
routinization 60, 166, 171
rule 14, 19f., 26f., 37f.
- grammatical 130, 188, 194f.

– phonological 222, 232
– phrase-structure 195, 198, 202, 213

– rule-learning 270, 273, 275

Saffran, Jenny 255, 264f., 275ff.
saliency 37
Sapir, Edward 31
Saussure, Ferdinand de 11, 14f., 19, 47, 49, 59
schema 5, 13, 21ff., 26f., 32, 35ff.
– cognitive 59, 69, 125, 127, 130f., 133, 135f., 138f., 143ff., 147ff., 166, 173, 184, 187ff., 202
– constructional 145, 147
– macro-schema 128, 138
– micro-schema 127f., 132f., 135, 137f., 143ff.
schematicity 158
Scott, Joseph Nicol 71ff., 81f.
Searle, John R. 58
Sebeok, Thomas A. 49
semantic prosody 137
semiosis, unlimited/infinite 49, 55, 60
semiotics 49, 52, 57, 65
sensory processing 256, 259ff., 265f.
sequence, linear 12, 15ff., 21, 25f., 28f., 34f., 38, 60, 62, 105, 127f., 135, 138f., 144, 149f., 163, 186f., 222, 229, 232, 236, 240, 242, 246, 259f., 264ff., 273ff.
Sherry, Richard 72f.
Sievers, Eduard 13
sign 51
– iconic 32f.
– indexical 32ff.
– linguistic 73f., 167, 193ff., 208, 212f., 217
– symbolic 23f., 32f., 51, 57
Sign-Based Construction Grammar 6, 127, 193ff., 200, 202f., 207, 212f., 216f.
signified 70ff., 77
signifier 73
Sinclair, John M. 14, 17, 22, 27ff., 63
slot-and-filler model 19
Smirnova, Elena 127, 129f.
sociolinguistics 14, 32, 34, 39
sound change 7
sound perception 7
sound production 7

speaker–hearer interaction 14, 32ff.
speech act (theory) 30, 33, 61, 63
speech perception 224ff., 229, 233, 235ff., 246
speech processing 6
speech production 20, 26, 30, 36, 224, 233, 236ff., 240ff.
speech signal 222f., 226, 229, 239
speech verbs 173
standard language use 226f., 232
standardization 101, 227, 245
statistical learning abilities 7
stimulus 257ff., 262ff., 268, 271, 276
Structuralist Linguistics 14ff., 18, 24, 26, 63
structure 14ff., 24ff., 35, 37f., 69, 76, 78, 84f., 99, 101, 118, 121, 128, 130f., 135, 158, 161ff., 172, 188, 193, 195ff., 203, 208, 212ff., 216f., 256, 258, 271ff., 279
– sound structure 221ff., 244, 246ff., 250
Stubbs, Michael 137
style 108
stylistics *(see also pragmatics, text linguistics)* 32, 34
Sumerian 70
Sweet, Henry 13
syllogism 64
syntax 136f., 142, 194, 199, 203, 216ff., 222
system level *(see also langue)* 26
system of thought 73

Teubert, Wolfgang 49, 60, 63, 65
text linguistics *(see also discourse linguistics, pragmatics, stylistics)* 32
theory of meaning 65
theory of reference 57, 65
Thomas, Thomas 75f., 78ff., 83f., 88
Thomas, William 80
Tomasello, Michael 11, 14, 20ff., 24, 32f., 36
top-down expectations 255f.
topic *(see discourse topic)*
topicalization 169f., 172ff., 180, 183, 185, 187, 201, 214
Traheron, Bartholomew 79
transitional probabilities 275ff.
translation 47f., 50, 53, 64, 69, 74ff., 78, 81, 83, 274

Traugott, Elizabeth C. 130, 132, 157ff., 166ff., 174, 177, 179, 181, 186f., 194f., 218
Trevisa, John 83, 86
Trousdale, Graeme 125, 130, 147, 157ff., 163, 166f., 174, 179, 181, 186f.
Trubetzkoy, Nikolai 16, 222
typology 230, 238, 250

unit of meaning 49, 65
Universal Grammar *(see also mental grammar)* 19f., 86
universality 160, 234, 236, 238, 240, 250
universals
– narrative 56
usage-based linguistics 11, 14, 17, 20ff., 29, 38, 129ff., 148, 159, 218
utterance, level of *(see also parole)* 61, 159, 226, 244

variability 35, 38
variation 15, 18, 26, 30, 35, 39, 76, 80, 82f., 101, 129, 131, 161, 171, 193, 196, 198ff., 221, 223ff., 228ff., 233f., 236, 238f., 243ff., 248ff., 264

variational linguistics 14, 30, 32, 35
variationist perspective 161
Vegetius, Flavius 83, 86
Véron, Jean 75f.
Verstegan, Richard 75
visual system 260f., 263ff., 271, 274f., 277
visualization 97, 99f., 102f., 115f., 118ff., 175
Voltaire [François-Marie Arouet] 56

Webster, Noah 83, 91
Whorf, Benjamin Lee 31f.
Wilkins, John 73, 90
Williams, Raymond 64
Wilson, Edward O. 56
Wimsatt, William K. 51
Withals, John 75, 78f.
Wittgenstein, Ludwig 52f., 56
word formation 125, 128, 145ff., 150
word recognition 268
word-entry 69ff., 76ff., 83ff.
working-memory capacity 85
Wynkyn de Worde 75, 87

www.ingramcontent.com/pod-product-compliance
Lightning Source LLC
Chambersburg PA
CBHW061933220426
43662CB00012B/1897